MEANING, USE AND TRUTH

MEANING, USE AND TRUTH
Introducing the Philosophy of Language
© 2010 Finn Collin, Finn Guldmann, Automatic Press / VIP
Photo: Vincent F. Hendricks
Cover design: Vincent F. Hendricks
Printed in Great Britain and the United States of America 2010
ISBN-13 978-87-92130-28-0

For more titles with Automatic Press / VIP, visit
http://www.vince-inc.com/automatic.html

MEANING, USE AND TRUTH
Introducing the Philosophy of Language

FINN COLLIN
University of Copenhagen
Denmark

FINN GULDMANN
University of Copenhagen
and Roskilde University
Denmark

AUTOMATIC PRESS / VIP

Contents

Preface	vii
Introduction	1
1. Some classical theories of meaning	7
2. The phenomenology of language	21
3. The semantics of singular terms	41
4. Predication	65
5. Theories of truth	89
6. Davidson's programme	117
7. Intensional semantics	139
8. Speech acts	175
9. On the borderline between linguistics and philosophy: recent developments in the theory of meaning	205
10. Theory of interpretation	227
11. Two critics: Quine and Dummett	243
12. Wider philosophical perspectives	269
References and suggestions for further reading	285
Bibliography	291
Index	297

Preface

The aim of this book is to offer an accessible introduction to the philosophy of language as it has evolved in analytical (Anglo-American) philosophy during the twentieth century, focusing on the theory of meaning. This book is meant to surpass existing introductory texts mainly by telling a more smoothly flowing, more tightly integrated story about language from a philosophical point of view. It also gives more equal attention to the two main divisions within the theory of meaning, viz. truth-conditional semantics and speech act theory, of which existing presentations tend to privilege one or the other.

This book is built around the idea, taken to be quite uncontroversial, that the notion of *use* is the core concept in a theoretical account of language, and constitutive of the notion of meaning. This idea, which became dominant in Anglo-American philosophy from around the mid-twentieth century, thanks to the genius of Ludwig Wittgenstein, was adopted and adapted in the work of such figures as John Austin, Paul Grice and John Searle in a more systematic form that has come to be known as 'speech act theory'. Reflection on human language as a system of actions points towards the notion of the success conditions of such actions as being crucial for an understanding of the nature of language, and it turns out that in this theoretical enterprise, the notion of truth conditions is pivotal. This has occasioned a split in the theory of meaning, with the topic of meaning as a function of truth conditions being pursued by a school of formally-minded theoreticians, the formal semanticists and model theoreticians, while the idea of language as a mode of human action has been explored by the speech acts theorist in a rather non-formal manner. In this book, we make a point of devoting equal attention to language understood as a concrete human activity, and as an abstract system of signs conjoined with a formal interpretation. In traditional texts, speech act theory is often demoted to the status of an adjunct or appendix to the truth-based account. Not so here; on the contrary, we show how the truth-based approach emerges from and can only be understood on the background of a broader use-based approach.

In dealing with the way that the components of sentences contribute to fixing the latter's truth conditions, this book expounds the standard theories of reference of singular expressions, but goes beyond current introductory texts in the attention devoted to the other main "part of speech", namely predication. A concise account is given of the most important candidate for a truth-conditional semantics, viz. Davidson's theory, as well as of the way that this model-theoretical approach has been extended into the realm of "possible worlds" within intensional semantics. A hearing is also given to philosophers and linguists who in one way or another have been critical of the orthodox truth-based account, such as Dan Sperber, Deirdre Wilson, George Lakoff, Mark Johnson, Willard Van Orman Quine and Michael Dummett. Furthermore, this book offers an introduction to the theory of linguistic interpretation (hermeneutics), a topic that is largely bypassed in contemporary introductions to philosophy of language.

Throughout this book, much attention is given to the extensionality of the preferred model of semantic meaning, to the rationale for this preference, and to the familiar obstacles to the development of a purely extensional semantics for natural languages. It turns out that these obstacles are merely the symptoms of deep and fundamental metaphysical problems of very long standing in Western philosophy. In the final chapter, we give an overview of these problems and the way they have interacted with technical issues in the philosophy of language.

In the interest of uncluttered presentation, we have avoided crowding the text with references and footnotes. Such information is placed at the end of the book in sections corresponding to each chapter, where the works cited in the chapter are listed together with suggestions for further reading. There is a modest deviation from this strategy in chapters 7 and 9 where we address recent developments in formal semantics and speech act theory, respectively, and where more precise reference would appear useful.

We wish to thank Gyldendal Publishers, Copenhagen for permission to reuse material from our Danish introductory text on the philosophy of language, *Sprogfilosofi* from 1998. A big thank you is owed to Susan Dew, who translated the largest part of the original book and revised our supplementary English chapters. She showed patience far beyond the call of duty in putting up with our interminable contentual revisions of chapters which she had already put in perfect literary form. Ingrid Egerod and Jack Fishstrom rendered us a great service in checking supplementary parts of the text.

The Danish text upon which this book is based has been used in teaching at Danish universities. We want to thank our colleagues who have offered suggestions for improvements to the English text. The book has profited greatly from their comments and criticisms. Pernille Sys Hansen provided invaluable assistance in putting our manuscript into camera-ready form.

Thanks are due to Gads Fond and to Lillian og Dan Finks Fond for helping to make this project possible. We are also indebted to the Department of Education, Philosophy and Rhetoric of the University of Copenhagen and to the Faculty of Arts of the same institution for providing additional funding. Finally, we wish to record our gratitude to Aslaug and Bent Collin for their unfailing support of the project.

Finn Collin and Finn Guldmann
Copenhagen
September 2004

Introduction

1. Language is such an intrinsic part of the texture of our lives that it gets taken for granted and fails to prompt the wonderment for which it truly calls. It is indeed remarkable that there is such a thing as language at all. We need almost to be "alienated" from it if we are to be capable of appreciating what makes it so extraordinary, and one way of achieving that detachment is to undertake an objective investigation of its distinctive features. Once we do that, perplexing questions soon start to proliferate.

On one perspective, language is a straightforward physical phenomenon – jottings on paper, intricate marks on the page of a book, or the sounds people produce through the complex interplay of vocal chords, tongue, palate and teeth. But these physical phenomena are also the bearers of the remarkable properties which we group under the terms 'meaning' or 'sense'. It is in virtue of its meaning that language somehow enables us to connect with items in the world, including those infinitely distant from us in time or space. If Jack says to Jill, 'Sirius was unusually bright last night', he has, in some mysterious fashion, drawn the star Sirius into what he is saying: some connection has been set up between Jack, earthbound as he is, and a heavenly body many light years away. And if Jack should come across a science feature in the paper and calls out to Jill: 'It says here that dinosaurs became extinct as the result of a gigantic meteor crashing to earth', he would be talking about an astronomical event that occurred 65 million years ago.

Further, language allows the transfer of a thought complex from one mind – or one brain, if you like – to another. What Jack recounts to Jill about the crashing meteor puts her in touch with a highly complex scientific hypothesis. So too, the reader of this book will absorb key elements of a body of thought that it has taken philosophers several centuries, indeed, more than two millennia, to evolve.

These brief remarks, albeit preliminaries, point to essential structural features of language that will remain cornerstones in our account. One such feature is the fact that language involves a "sender" and a "receiver" of messages: we shall refer to these collectively as language users. Second, that there exists a *reality* that speech is about. And third, that language possesses a property which enables language users to communicate with one another, viz.

meaning. Any theory of language must do justice to that banal but important fact.

This triadic structure is depicted in the figure below.

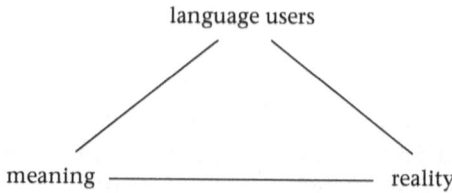

Fig. 1.1 *Triadic structure of language*

In saying that language relates to reality, we are naturally not claiming that linguistic utterances are always about real existents. Utterances may of course be false and so fail to reflect any reality; more interestingly, they may figure in fictional contexts of language use such as novels or plays. The fictional use of language must be regarded as secondary, however, for it is dependent on the existence of a serious use in which language relates to reality. The fictional use of language is thus once removed from reality; the utterer play-acts, as it were, merely pretending to be making utterances, just as one might play at being a shopkeeper or a policeman. Such uses are only possible if bona fide exemplars exist in the form of genuine agency or speech. Language used in earnest is thus prior to its ludic counterpart; consequently, the latter use can only be understood once the former has been grasped. It follows, then, that it is language in its serious use that will be the object of analysis in this book.

2. The puzzles surrounding the concept of meaning referred to above, along with the other problems that language presents, make up the subject matter within philosophy that we call the philosophy of language. The philosophy of language, as we shall understand the term here, concerns precisely the philosophical investigation of language. It focuses on those features that are specific to language – sense, meaning, truth, reference, names, understanding, interpretation, generative capacity, and so on.

But why precisely a *philosophy* of language? Why are these questions not topics for the scientific study of language, for linguistics? Well, some of them clearly are. One such topic is the generative power of languages: what is the mechanism underlying the capacity of natural languages to generate an infinite multiplicity of distinct, well-formed sentences on the basis of a finite vocabulary? However, other questions are not in the same way effective targets for empirical investigation: for many issues in linguistics, scientific methods have not yet been devised. Moreover, it is not always clear how the issues should even be defined. In such situations, the remit is more appropriately one for philosophy than for linguistics.

Typically, philosophy operates in areas where empirical science has not yet established a foothold. The situation in respect of the theory of meaning might be compared to that of the understanding of the physical universe in the Middle Ages before the advent of the scientific revolution. There was indeed a sense in which a host of 'observations' of empirical reality had been amassed: the mundane control of natural phenomena on the part of artisans, architects and engineers was based on a vast amount of practical experience. The problem was that of hitting upon the right theory and, by implication, the right conceptual system, by which such observations might properly be described and explained.

Prior to the scientific revolution theorizing about everyday human experience of the physical world proceeded on the basis of a fundamentally erroneous conceptual system. Descriptions of physical events invoked the idea of entities and processes seeking their final ends; there was no recognition of their dependence on efficient causes. The fall to earth of a stone was explained by Aristotle (and countless subsequent theorists) in terms of its seeking its 'natural place', allegedly the centre of the earth. The advent of science in the sixteenth and seventeenth centuries did away with such descriptive modes, arguing instead that the earth exercised a force – gravity – that pulled things towards its centre. Falling objects do not home in on the centre of the earth and no intentionality whatever informs their descent.

If we turn to language, it may well be the case that linguistics is in the same situation as was natural science (physics) in the Middle Ages: it is highly conceivable that we are currently using entirely the wrong theoretical concepts to describe the meaning-aspects of language. At any rate, we do not know for sure which, if any, of the many alternative conceptual systems currently on offer is correct.

The comparison with physics enables us to formulate a more precise goal for the philosophy of language. We can say that it is the task of the philosophy of language to assist linguistics in clarifying the nature of language and so pave the way for an adequate theory of meaning. This is a more ambitious remit for the philosophy of language than that suggested above, the aim of which was limited to the clarification of certain core concepts such as 'meaning', 'reference', 'name', and so on. This alternative aim presupposes the possibility of outlining a feasible conception of the proper remit of linguistics.

Since no consensus is available among linguists on this issue, it would seem that this issue recommends itself to philosophical resolution. Still, it would be a mistake to imagine that it might be resolved independently of the scientific study of languages. The two approaches are intimately connected.

One characterization of the proper task of linguistics might run as follows. Linguistics should be capable of framing a theory for every natural language – languages such as English or French – that tells us, in the first place, which linguistic expressions are well formed. This particular task falls to *grammar*, the discipline comprising morphology (the study of the form and structure of words) and syntax (the study of how words are grammatically arranged in sentences). Generically, then, grammar is about words and the rules for their concatenation. Next, the theory must specify the meanings of these words; this is the job of *semantics*, whose focus is the relation of words and sentences to reality. Third, the theory must tell us what people are up to when they use language in communication; this topic belongs to *pragmatics*, which is about the relation between language and human subjects. (This is a very rough and approximate taxonomy of the subject matter of linguistics, dating back to Charles Morris's classical account (Morris 1938). In particular, the distinction between semantics and pragmatics is both crucial and controversial from a philosophical point of view, and will require redrawing as our analysis unfolds in the following chapters.)

The optimal way of solving the first task is to formulate a theory which generates all well-formed linguistic expressions and only such expressions. The second task would be solved by a complementary theory that, for each of the expressions so generated, specifies its meaning. These theories are fruitfully conceived of on analogy with computer programs. The task is, then, to set up a program that will write out all (and only) well-formed sentences in a given language and further, one capable of specifying, for each sentence, what it means. The third task, that of pragmatics, will be solved by the delivery of an account of the various communicative ends to which the use of language is put.

Pivotal to pragmatics is the issue of how language users grasp communicated contents. What does a person's understanding of a verbal expression consist of? In one sense the answer is given once we have answered the previous question concerning the nature of linguistic meaning. For then we can simply say that to understand a linguistic expression is to know its meaning. The difficulty with that answer is that it would seem to suggest that we might specify what meaning is independently of specifying what constitutes understanding, and then turn to the implications for the latter. But this option is not open to us; we have to answer the two questions at once, both that concerning meaning and that concerning understanding. For example, it would be futile to formulate a theory of linguistic meaning one of whose implications was that language was neither understandable nor learnable. That both understanding and acquisition need to be accounted for imposes constraints on any theory of meaning. One such constraint is that a theory of meaning be *generative*, which is to say, capable of showing how the meanings of sentences are delivered through the (in principle, unlimited) application of particular mechanisms. In the absence of such an account, we would have no explanation of how it is that language users are capable of understanding sentences they have not heard or read before. The reader of this book will not previously have come across precisely the sentences printed on this page, and yet he or she is able to understand them. This shows that the sentences of a language are not learned one at a time, on analogy with, say, road signs, but that their meaning is construed by the application of general principles to familiar sentential constituents in that most of the words met with in the text are common English words. The meanings of these new sentences can thus be construed on the basis of familiar words and through the use of certain known principles.

3. There is another field of endeavour in philosophy which is sometimes referred to as 'the philosophy of language'. However, its proper denomination is 'linguistic philosophy' and it is primarily pursued within Anglo-American philosophy. It is a 'philosophy of language' in the sense that it represents an attempt to build a general philosophy with the investigation of language as its ground plan. Indeed, there are philosophers, such as Michael Dummett, who conceive of it as a 'first philosophy', the philosophical discipline on which other philosophical disciplines are founded. In our final chapter we shall touch very briefly upon the 'philosophy of language' in this broader sense inasmuch as we shall consider the question of what may be learned about the constitution of reality from reflection on the nature and workings of language. But that chapter aside, this book will deal only with the philosophy of language in the sense of 'philosophical reflection on language'.

Chapter 1
Some classical theories of meaning

1. Statements are distinguished by their possession of semantic content or meaning. But how is this to be understood? What is it that invests signs on paper and vocal sounds with meaning?

Offhand, we might reply that linguistic meaning consists in the thoughts and ideas that pass through people's minds when they speak. The following situation is a familiar one. You arrive in a foreign country suddenly to find yourself surrounded by people who speak a language of which you have no grasp. Bombarded with a torrent of words that you have no chance of understanding straightaway, you try to guess your way to what they might be saying. What is it, then, that you are trying to get a grip on when struggling to fathom the meaning of what you hear? It would seem that you are trying to discover what is going on in the speakers' heads – the thoughts and ideas that accompany their flow of words.

This answer draws support from another consideration. Parrots, mynah birds and certain other bird species learn to articulate particular sounds in ways closely resembling human speech. But if you teach your parrot to utter the sound sequence which runs 'Hey! Is there anyone at home?', these words as uttered by the parrot mean nothing. For the parrot has not really asked whether there is anyone at home. It does not understand a word of what it says: no appropriate mental conceptions accompany the uttered sounds.

2. A first answer to the question of what linguistic meaning is, then, is that it consists in those thoughts and conceptions in the mind of the speaker which accompany or precede his utterance. This explanation has a long lineage in the history of philosophy. Its classic formulation is owed to John Locke who in Book 3, Chapter 2 of *An Essay Concerning Human Understanding* writes:

> 'The use then of words, is to be sensible marks of *ideas*; and the *ideas* they stand for, are their proper and immediate signification […] *words, in their primary or immediate signification, stand for nothing, but the ideas in the mind of him that uses them* …' (Locke 1690 (1961), p. 12)

Locke amplifies this claim with a general reflection on the role and utility of language in human life:

> 'Man, though he have great variety of thoughts, and such from which others, as well as himself, might receive profit and delight, yet they are all within his own breast, invisible, and hidden from others, nor can of themselves be made to appear. The comfort and advantage of society not being to be had without communication of thoughts, it was necessary that man should find out some external sensible signs, whereby those invisible *ideas*, which his thoughts are made up of, might be made known to others.' (*ibid*, p. 11)

Language, then, serves as a tool that affords individuals access to the hidden contents of each other's minds and so enables mental contents to be passed from one person to another. The delivery of lexical meaning is precisely effected by the mental items accompanying the utterance of sentences.

On Locke's conception of them, these mental items assume a distinctly concrete and graphic form. Locke was a protagonist of the philosophical school of *empiricism*, which dominated British philosophy in the seventeenth and eighteenth centuries. The empiricists argued that the immediate content of the mind is 'ideas' comprising concrete sensory ideas and images. These ideas were conceived of as copies of impressions that the individual has previously received through the senses (or through introspection as, for example, with the sensation of pain). The mind contains nothing that had not first been apprehended by the senses. Every species of thinking about an item consists in the mind's manipulation of an image of that item. When we think of a pear, this activity consists in our bringing to mind the distinctive shape of a pear and its yellowish-green colour – something we have previously encountered in experience but which is now before our minds in a "faded" version. We recall too the characteristic fragrance and delicate flavour that pears have. When, then, in speech, we use the word 'pear', we are referring to the mental images that are constitutive of the semantic content of the word.

3. How should we set about assessing a theory of meaning predicated on the notion of ideas? A preliminary step would be to divide words up into classes and see how the 'ideational' semantics functions for each class.

We can start with proper names. Proper names are the particular names of persons, animals, geographical localities and other individual items. To know the meaning of a name is, according to the idea theory, to be able to form a mental image of the person or whatever individual item it might be that is the bearer of the name – to be able to conjure up the appropriate mental image. And this does indeed seem to capture an important aspect of what it is to know the meaning of a name. We are all familiar with the conversational situation where someone mentions a name, say, 'Sally Field', but which finds you at that precise moment incapable of homing in on its bearer. To jog your memory your interlocutor begins to enumerate a string of films that Sally Field has appeared in, but you still cannot call to mind the individual to whom the name refers. Then suddenly the image of a face flashes before your inner eye and you say, 'Ah! Now I know who she is!' You have succeeded in retrieving a mental image of the bearer of the name. For proper names, then, the idea theory would seem to function satisfactorily.

Even more persuasive evidence for this idea-based semantics may be drawn from the way simple adjectives are used. For it is plausible to say that to know the meaning of a word such as 'red' one must be able to present this colour to one's inner gaze. By the same token, an individual's inability to conjure up a particular quality in the mind – *sepia* for instance – indicates that he does not know what the term denoting it stands for: he does not know what 'sepia' means.

4. It soon becomes apparent, however, that serious problems attach to this theory of language. One fundamental divide in language runs between names and other so-called singular terms on the one side and general terms on the other. The former stand for individual things, whereas the latter stand for "things in general" or for *kinds* of things. In his philosophy of language, Locke stresses the importance of these general terms and of common nouns in particular: since, he argues, it is not possible for us to have particular names for all the individual things in the world, we need general concepts capable of comprising, say, all the dogs in the world, under one linguistic label.

What, according to Locke, marks out the semantics of common nouns and adjectives from that of proper names is their standing for *general* ideas in the mind. When a speaker uses the word 'dog' and in so doing summons up the image of a dog before his inner gaze, he engages with a general idea. Its generality results from all the specific characteristics attaching to any particular dog having been abstracted away. Ultimately, the idea a person attaches to a general name may well trace back to an individual observation of a particular exemplar at a particular time and in a particular place. This is perhaps unlikely in the case of 'dog' but it might be the case with names of more exotic species such as 'rhinoceros'. An individual might have derived his idea of it from a single observation of a particular rhinoceros in the zoo. In the mental conception of a rhino that this individual subsequently possesses, however, the particulars of context have been abstracted away. Any features of the image that might trace it back to this concrete example have been airbrushed out: the image has been anonymized. It figures as a general image, representative of all the specimens belonging to the genus rhinoceros and bearing no special relation to the particular exemplar in the zoo.

That this doctrine is not without its problems was first pointed out by one of Locke's empiricist successors, George Berkeley. Take a general idea like that of a triangle. According to Locke, this idea should be understood in terms of a mental image of a triangle. However, it would have to be a rather peculiar triangle since it is neither an isosceles nor a non-isosceles exemplar, neither rectangular nor non-rectangular. For were it one or the other, rectangular say, then the idea in question would automatically apply to rectangular triangles and not to triangles in general, and with obtuse-angled exemplars excluded in consequence. But this results in incoherence since it is impossible to envisage a triangle that is neither rectangular nor non-rectangular; between them, these two types exhaust the field. The same reasoning applies *mutatis mutandis* to other features of triangles such as the length of their sides: they admit no determinate length. We end up, then, with the idea of the triangle as generally incapable of having any particular properties. This result constitutes a refutation of the notion of general ideas, and *ipso facto* of the thesis that general ideas constitute the semantic contents of general terms.

These difficulties would seem to be severely compounded when we turn to abstract and non-imageable terms such as 'not', 'or', 'provided that', 'the square root of 7', and so on. For what mental image attaches to the term 'not'? What mental image attaches to the sentence 'There is no food on the table'? The image of a bare table? But that image would also illustrate the sentence 'There is no bust of Beethoven on the table'. And what about 'on condition that'? What mental image must be elicited as a check on one's grasp of this concept? No satisfactory answer to these questions appears to be forthcoming.

The example of the bare table shows that images are typically many-ways ambiguous in a way that sentences are not. And this equivocalness is irremediable. One might be able to avoid the Beethoven-interpretation of the imaged table by envisaging a bust of Beethoven placed upon it. But no such image uniquely picks out 'There is no food on the table' as the correct interpretation; for it might with equal cogency be contended that the image illustrates the sentence 'There is no bust of Schubert on the table' – or, more obviously, 'There is a bust of Beethoven on the table'. No matter what graces this imagined table, infinitely many interpretations of what the image is of will be admissible. (Consider the freedom enjoyed by the artist in fixing on a title for his picture.)

5. We have seen that serious problems for Locke's theory of language are presented by general ideas and words such as 'not', 'or', 'provided that', and so on. If we now return to the type of word considered at the outset, and which seemed to support the idea theory, viz. proper names, we shall see that this success was in fact only apparent. For Berkeley's argument is also an attack on the application of the theory to this word class. It may well be the case that a speaker sometimes associates a concrete image with a proper name. But acquaintance with the meaning of the name cannot consist in the possession of a relevant image. For every particular image of a person depicts the person in a particular way – as perceived from a particular angle, in a particular perspective, and so on. So if we took the idea theory at face value, a name such as 'Leo Jones' would accordingly not refer to a person but to Leo Jones-viewed-frontally-cum-obliquely or Leo Jones's-shoulders-head-and-chest regions. We have to conclude that the idea theory cannot begin to explain how proper names function.

Indeed, the same holds true of the example which above appeared to provide the idea theory with its most robust support, namely adjectives. If on hearing the word 'red' uttered a person calls to mind an image of red, this image cannot possibly be what constitutes the semantic content of the word. For the image will inevitably be of a quite specific shade of red. In consequence, it is unfit to supply the word 'red' with its semantic content but can at best serve as the semantic content of the name of some highly specific shade of red – a name which presumably is not to be found in the language. For we simply do not have words for all the many thousands of shades that the human eye is able to discriminate. This observation leads us, then, to one of the idea theory's somewhat paradoxical consequences – that ordinary colour names (and other adjectives) have no semantic content, that privilege being reserved to particular names for highly determinate shades. Such specific terms, however, are not to be found in natural languages, despite that the numerical codes on the colour cards at the DIY store might count as an approximation to them. This result is obviously fatal to the idea theory of meaning.

6. There is a further fundamental defect intrinsic to Locke's theory of meaning. As we have noted, Locke stresses that the chief purpose of language is to serve as a means of communication between humans. As Locke quaintly puts

it, language is needed because a person's thoughts 'are all within his own breast, invisible, and hidden from others'. It is therefore necessary that there exist something such as a language that can make what is hidden, public. But here Locke overlooks the fact that language cannot serve this end if its semantic content comprises these selfsame hidden entities. Locke's claim is that human thoughts are concealed and that language is needed to make them accessible to others. But for this to be possible it is required not just that the expressive aspect of language – the spoken word – be public, but that the semantic content of language be so too. But as we have seen, the semantic content is equally private inasmuch as this content comprises those very ideas that 'men ... have within their breasts', and so we are brought no further.

Compare this with the situation in which we use language to recount something that is "hidden" from others because it lies beyond the range of their sensory experience, as when we regale our friends with accounts of our holidays abroad. Availing ourselves of a common language with a common semantic content, we try to make our experiences vivid to them. Using expressions such as 'cliff face', 'fast-flowing river' in describing what we have seen, we draw on a familiar lexicon to talk about places unfamiliar to our listeners. But going by the theory Locke outlines for us, it would seem that it is the semantic content itself that is private, and so we are brought no nearer the thoughts that are "hidden" in individual minds.

Some philosophers have deemed the public nature of language so decisive a feature as to warrant the imposition on any putative theory of language the constraint that it respect a principle sometimes referred to as 'the publicity principle'. This principle specifies that those features of reality that determine the meaning of a linguistic expression must, in principle, be fully and equally accessible to all parties engaged in a conversational exchange. This principle is both plausible and important, as will emerge from the chapters to follow – as will, too, the contentiousness of its implications.

Still, the idea theory of meaning contains valuable insights which must not be overlooked. As we have noted, the notion of an 'idea' is linked to the empiricists' distinctive conception of how human cognition proceeds. Thus, the idea theory of linguistic meaning is the particular empiricist version of a more general theory to the effect that linguistic meaning is a question of the language user's mental processes when using words. Words are bearers of thoughts and knowledge; the meanings of words are determined by the conceptions, cognitive contents and beliefs that figure in the speaker's thought at the time of utterance. Linguistic meaning is ingredient in the mental contents of the human subject; language use is *thought*. This is an important insight to which we shall return later in this account. But we must repudiate the particular formulation that the empiricists give it, including the claim that meaning consists merely in the ideas present to the speaker's consciousness.

7. We have now seen how Locke's theory of language, in common with all other theories that identify linguistic meaning with certain private items, runs aground on the issue of human communication. For it is a constraint on any theory of language that it be capable of rendering an account of how language actually functions as a means of communication: how semantic content is in fact conveyed by one person to another. This is an essential strand in the publicity principle.

The next step, then, must surely be to try to attain to a better theory of meaning simply by asking how in fact we get the meanings of words across to others. How do we succeed in teaching foreigners the meanings of the words of our language? And how do young children learn to speak their native tongue?

Straight off, we would tend to reply that we point to things around us and say what they are called. If someone does not know what the word 'rhinoceros' means, the easiest way to rectify the situation is to take him to the zoo, position him in front of an appropriate specimen and tell him that this is what 'rhinoceros' means. For this is basically how young children acquire language: they listen to their parents talking, and come to associate the words they hear with items in the world. It constitutes a particularly effective procedure when the talk revolves around concrete items in the here-and-now, but becomes more difficult in the case of abstract, or in other respects unobservable, entities. The child picks up the meaning of such words as 'frying pan', 'carving knife' and 'tomato' by seeing its parents at work in the kitchen, and hearing their running commentary on what they are doing.

Indeed, a moment's thought will convince us that there are words in the language that could not be learned in any way other than through confrontation with what they stand for. How would one be able to convey to others what the terms 'red' or 'rancid' mean without enabling them to have first hand experience of samples? The alternative is to cite other words that they already understand and which, in combination, have the same meaning as the word one seeks to explain. This is a feasible option in the case of some words: one might explain 'car' by saying that a car is a motor vehicle designed primarily for the transport of people, typically fitted with four wheels and powered by its own engine. But how might 'red' be explained along the same lines? There are no words whose combined meanings give the meaning of the word 'red'. The only way of conveying the meaning of the word to another is to confront him with something that is red – a tomato, a pillar box, a well-done lobster – and inform him that what he currently has before him is the property red.

This provides us with a significant clue in the further search for a theory of meaning. If language is ultimately acquired through items being pointed out to us, ought we not to conclude that the meaning of language *is* the contents of the surrounding world so identified?

8. Let us examine this theory, which we shall call the *referential theory of meaning*, by focusing on the area where its application seems most promising, that of proper names. In the case of proper names it seems intuitively obvious that their meaning simply is the bearer of the name. This particular linkage is reinforced by the fact that in the case of proper names there is a particular baptismal ceremony in which the name is attached to the bearer; the bearer is subsequently known by this name, and the meaning of the word in the language is uniquely specified by its possession of a particular bearer.

If the meaning of a name is its bearer, a sentence becomes meaningless or at least semantically deviant if a name occurs in it that has no bearer. We should note in passing that the deviant character of such a sentence need not be obvious from the sentence itself; it is only by having independent knowledge of the absence of any bearer that we know that the sentence figures as deviant. But it is clear that we get an anomalous sentence, linguistically speaking, if a speaker uses a name while simultaneously acknowledging that the name is "empty".

Let us imagine that a club enjoying charitable status for tax purposes has, by the inclusion of empty names, artificially swelled the number of local people allegedly making donations to it and on which it can reclaim tax. Let us imagine further that these false entries come to the notice of the Inland Revenue in the course of a routine check. A tax official comes across the first fabricated name and in total bemusement exclaims 'Christopher Trickman has never existed!' Now, as it stands, this sentence has an odd ring to it, and its oddity becomes the more apparent if we imagine a colleague overhearing the retort and, since the name is new to him, asks, 'Who is Christopher Trickman?' This enquiry finds the first tax official stuck for an answer since it is obvious that he can only say 'No one', which is hardly going to satisfy his colleague. For the latter might well ask 'But then who are you talking about?' The exchange begins to border on farce. The first official might have avoided this if he had simply begun by saying, 'There's no one living round here called 'Christopher Trickman''.

The semantic theory just outlined explains why the first sentence sounds odd and the second formulation better. When you use the name 'Christopher Trickman' you plainly presuppose that the name has a meaning, that there is someone who is the bearer of the name; but the official in the example goes on to deny that any such bearer exists, thereby undermining one condition of the name's having meaning. The utterance would seem to be self-stultifying. The theory of meaning sketched above is obviously able to explain the special deviant status of the sentence and, by the same token, this apparent deviance would seem to lend support to the theory.

But while the referential theory of meaning seems to be supported by this illustration, the results are less favourable when we turn to other examples. Let us take a famous example featured by the philosopher and logician Gottlob Frege in the context of a principled criticism of the referential theory of meaning. If it is the case that the meaning of a name is the item to which it refers, all identity sentences must be trivial. Let us look at a particular identity sentence to examine this claim, viz. Frege's example: 'The Morning Star is identical with the Evening Star' (the stars are identical with the planet Venus). If it is correct that the meaning of a name is its bearer then this sentence has the same meaning as, and, by implication, no more informational content than that contained in the sentence 'The Morning Star is identical with the Morning Star'. Both names have the same bearer and hence the same meaning. However, it is very clear that the first sentence is informative while the second is not. The first expresses a state of affairs that went unrecognized throughout long swathes of human history: that it obtained constituted an astronomical discovery. By contrast, the second can scarcely at any time have been concealed from thinking persons since it is true in virtue of the meanings of the words. There is no need for it to be established by a scientist exploring the skies with the aid of a telescope and sextant; knowledge of one's native language suffices.

9. Even worse problems arise when we turn to another important type of expression, viz. predicates (general names and adjectives). These comprise expressions such as 'green', 'car', 'zebra', 'heavy', and so on, each expressing something common to the items of which it is predicated. Accordingly, one classical conception has it that they refer to a 'universal', viz. an entity which is in some sense general, inasmuch as it embraces a plurality, as it were. Such a theory has obvious defects. It is doubtful that the postulation of entities such as 'greenness in itself', 'zebrahood in itself' are at all capable of explaining what they are purported to explain. It was Plato who first introduced these abstract entities which he called *Forms*; Plato's Forms were not,

however, subjective, mental entities as were the ideas of Locke and the empiricists but objective entities that exist independently of human subjects. The notion of a universal 'Form' purported to make it intelligible how a manifold such as a herd of animals can all be of one and the same kind – all zebras, for instance. The answer ushered in by that notion is that they all participate in one and the same entity, 'zebrahood in itself' or the Form of the zebra. But this means that the Form of the zebra is at once both general and a particular. It has to be general since all zebras are alleged to participate in it, and so it is distributed across the entire zebra population. But it must at the same time be one single "thing" because without that unity no explanation will have been given of what all zebras have *in common*.

The obvious way to avoid these difficulties would simply be to drop the mysterious Platonic entities altogether and define a predicate by reference to the things to which it applies. The concept 'giraffe' is thus defined by reference to the set of (individual) giraffes, and the concept 'red' by reference to the class of all red things in the universe. This solution avoids the postulation of a mysterious independent entity, the Form of the giraffe, over and above the sum of individual giraffes. And similarly for redness.

One problem with this proposal is that it assigns the same meaning to all those predicates that apply to the same class of entities. To the term 'blue whale' is assigned the same meaning as that accorded 'the largest animal that has ever existed'. For the two predicates are associated with the same class of things: the class of blue whales is identical to the set of the largest animals (belonging to the same species) that have ever existed. Nevertheless, the two terms do not *mean* the same.

This difficulty sounds a theme to which we shall be returning more than once in the chapters that follow, so it is apposite to introduce the relevant terminology at this point. The technical term for the class to which a predicate applies is that predicate's *extension*. More precisely put, its extension comprises the items to which the predicate has application in the past, present and future, and not simply the relevant entities that exist at any given moment. However, the extension does not encompass those things to which the predicate would apply to in hypothetical situations. If someone says, 'Just think if Rex were a rhinoceros – we would be the only family in the road to keep a pet rhinoceros', this hypothetical rhinoceros, Rex, would not belong to the extension of the term 'rhinoceros'. Only properly existent (in past, present and future) rhinoceroses belong there. The difficulty noted above indicates that the meaning of a term is not equivalent to its extension. Again, this problem is one we shall be returning to a number of times in the following chapters.

A purely terminological comment is in place here. There is an element of linguistic legislation in play when we declare that meaning is not the same as extension. For 'meaning' is a word somewhat loosely applied in everyday contexts, and sometimes we do indeed use the word in a way that makes it synonymous with 'stand for'; this equates meaning with extension. The above account reveals, however, that the role of a predicate exhibits two aspects, viz. its extension and a further component, namely that which distinguishes 'blue whale' from 'the largest animals that have ever existed'. This second aspect too might have been presented by means of a technical term, for philosophers have introduced the term 'intension' to that end. Still, for the time being we prefer to use as little terminological jargon as possible (even though the term 'intension' will be invoked later), and since the ordinary term 'meaning' roughly covers what the distinction between 'blue whale' and 'the largest animals that have ever existed' highlights, we have chosen to use that word here. But the reader should note that the word 'meaning' is thus being used in a narrower and more exact sense than is typical in everyday language.

Another problem facing the referential theory is the fact that there are words of which it plainly does not seem meaningful to ask what they refer to. These turn out to coincide with the words of which, as we saw above, it is impossible to specify any mental image that a language user might conceivably be thought to associate with them. Examples include words such as 'not', 'inasmuch', 'unless', and so on. It makes no sense to say that there exists an entity such as 'unlessness' and that 'unless' gets its meaning by reference to this thing. Such words are completely devoid of any reference or extension that could define their meaning.

10. The idea that every expression in the language refers to a concrete entity or a class of such entities has been a major influence on philosophical thinking throughout history. It has been the cause of certain crucial philosophical misconceptions.

The thought of the Austrian philosopher Alexius von Meinong is a case in point. Meinong's starting point was the linguistic model we have just been considering and which is founded on an analysis of the way proper names function. Take the word 'Kilimanjaro'. It stands as the name of a particular mountain in Tanzania; if we happened to be on the steppes of Tanzania, the name's referent could be pointed out to us.

But what about an expression like 'the golden mountain'? It is a meaningful linguistic expression and this poses a difficulty to anyone in thrall to the idea that language acquires meaning by referring to particular entities in the world. For there is no golden mountain, so what invests the expression with its meaning?

Meinong replied that the expression does indeed derive its meaning from its reference to an object, namely the golden mountain. Admittedly, this mountain does not actually exist, but it enjoys another and somewhat less substantial mode of being: it "subsists". Unfortunately, Meinong has nothing to tell us about this special mode of being. The subsistence of the golden mountain is a sheer postulate designed to rescue a fallacious theory of meaning.

But there is worse to come. There are expressions in language that refer not only to things that do not actually exist but to ones which could not possibly exist since their designations contain a contradiction. Meinong's example is the expression 'the round square'. Nonetheless, this expression (according to Meinong) is meaningful – at least in the sense that it is not a mere "letter salad" like 'pzxyygigiaks'. It must, then, on Meinong's view, refer to some object; but since the expression is self-contradictory, the putative object enjoys neither existence, nor subsistence (as did the golden mountain). It is a nonexistent and non-subsistent object.

It is clear that Meinong is in the grip of a particular picture of how language works, modelled on the relation between a proper name and its bearer. Wedded to this conception, he is forced to postulate a special domain for entities enjoying low-grade existence so as to be able to accommodate entities such as the golden mountain and to postulate a special class of objects that do not exist in any sense of that word, such as the round square.

Most other philosophers have taken the ultra-radical solution to which Meinong found himself driven as a clear indication that this theory of language is simply wrong. Brief reflection on the examples just given suggests a route that permits their avoidance. Consider the expression 'the round square'. It seems obvious that to account for the apparent meaningfulness of this expression we do not need to postulate a non-existent item, viz. the round square. Instead we can simply note the fact that the expression consists of words that are individually meaningful, and that the difficulty arises from their combination into a complex expression. 'Round' and 'square' are individually in order; difficulties arise only when they are compounded. (We shall return to this topic in chapter 4).

A related issue is the so-called problem of universals, which under a variety of names has engaged thinkers from Greek antiquity onwards. We concluded above that the referential theory must be rejected for general names such as 'human being', 'dog', 'rhinoceros', and for adjectives such as 'red', 'heavy', and 'unselfish': what these terms stand for (their extension) cannot constitute their meaning. But, historically, the conclusion drawn has been the converse, and not unrelated to Meinong's. The argument has been that since these linguistic expressions are meaningful and perform an essential function in language, there must be something they stand for, and that 'something' constitutes their meaning.

The most extreme version of this theory is undoubtedly to be found in Plato's theory of Forms. As we saw above, Plato declared that to each general expression of the type 'human being', 'animal', and so on, there corresponds an independently existing entity, the Form. When we say of a group of individuals – Peter, Paul and Harry – that they are all human beings, we are aligning them all with one and the same thing, the property 'humanity' or, as we might say, the property of being human. Since all the named individuals and all other human beings have an equal share in humanity the property 'humanity' must be a universal thing, which Plato calls a Form or an idea. As noted above, these Forms or ideas are not, in contradistinction to Locke's ideas, the content of any mind, but have independent existence. Indeed, they enjoy a more sublime mode of existence than the individual items we ordinarily encounter, and are the archetypes of the latter: mundane individual items have their being qua imitations of Forms. Ideas cannot be apprehended in sensory experience: the objects of sensory experience are always concrete individual things. Ideas are apprehended through a particular species of intellectual intuition.

Plato's theory of ideas was undoubtedly not exclusively motivated by an interest in the way language functions and the nature of the subject-predicate relation. It was also influenced by various metaphysical considerations, including the aspiration to identify an unchangeable reality underlying the mutability of the empirical world. For Plato, the world of ideas constituted just such a reality. Its articulation was in part driven by the urge to identify objective semantic contents for such words as 'justice' and 'goodness' and so substantiate the claim that ethical disagreements do indeed have objective answers. Finally, it was motivated by certain epistemic considerations, including the aspiration to evolve an epistemology for mathematics capable of doing justice to the circumstance that mathematical truths are eternal and immutable and not subject to the vicissitudes of empirical reality. In spite of this, there can be no doubt that reflection about the way language works, in particular, the analyses of what happens when a general property is predicated of a particular thing, played a significant role in the elaboration of the theory of ideas.

Chapter 2
The phenomenology of language

> If I had to say what is the main mistake made by philosophers of the present generation, including Moore, I would say that it is that when language is looked at, what is looked at is a form of words and not the use made of the form of words.
> (Wittgenstein 1966, p. 2)

1. In the preceding chapter, we looked at a number of classical philosophical theories of meaning and the equally classical difficulties with which they had to contend. In this chapter we shall make a fresh start and attack the problem of meaning from a different perspective – one that has dominated the philosophy of language during the second half of the twentieth century. Following in the footsteps of Ludwig Wittgenstein, quoted above, and John Austin, philosophers began to attend to language in its actual use. This approach to language involved seeing it in terms of linguistic acts, in speech or writing: a perspective seeming to offer a means of getting a fix on the problems language presents.

Wittgenstein encapsulates this insight in the slogan 'meaning is use': the meaning of linguistic expressions is best elucidated through a description of actual language use rather than by the postulation of obscure metaphysical meaning-conferring entities ("Forms", "ideas", "universals" and the like). A core notion in Wittgenstein's philosophy of language is that of the "language game", which combines both the unity of a language (a semiotic system) and the concrete context of use in which the semiotic system is embedded. Wittgenstein used the device to describe and analyse simple, made-up language games in order to shed light on those that figure in actual language use.

The following anecdote serves to illustrate the fruitfulness of a use-oriented approach. There was once a television contest which featured two teams, each comprising three actors, who vied at guessing the proper uses of the items with which they were presented. The teams took turns. An item was placed on the table and one of the three-member teams was given three descriptions of it, one to each member, who, in turn, proceeded to give a description-based demonstration of how the relevant item functioned in practice. The members of the opposing team had to guess which of the three demonstrated uses best fitted the item in question with the team chalking up most correct guesses winning. One of the teams is presented with something resembling a coat hanger – even though it seems somewhat broad for the purpose, and has neither a hook nor an aperture into which a hook might go. The first actor from the opposing team pretends to be using it as a hammer. This use is less than convincing. The edges are too sharp; they would soon break. The second actor pretends to be using it as a sickle, but, again, it fails to convince. The object is not sharp enough, being made of wood. The third actor proceeds to the far end of the studio, takes firm hold of the object and hurls it up into the air. Flying through the air, it traces an elliptic path before returning to the thrower, who promptly seizes it. It is a boomerang, then: a hunting implement, so fashioned that it returns to the hunter if he fails to strike his quarry.

Now both the participant actors and we, the viewers, understand better why the object has its singular shape, reminiscent of the wing of a plane; and we notice that it exhibits a slight twist, which we had not spotted at first. The shape of the boomerang is defined by its function: it has to be able to glide, strike its quarry, or return to the thrower. The taut twist in its construction is essential to this function.

Only when we know what a thing is used for do we know what features of its form are relevant, and why. So long as we were thinking that the thing might be a hanger we did not notice the curve; this property seemed quite incidental on the hanger hypothesis, possibly a manufacturing fault. But the feature is intrinsic to a boomerang. What this process shows us provides us with a handle on the understanding of language. To understand language we must first understand its function. Only an understanding of function can reveal to us which properties are part of the essential structure of language and which are contingent.

2. The theories of linguistic meaning that we looked at in chapter 1 were all misconceived in that they all offend against the above principle. They address the issue of linguistic meaning in abstraction from actual speech and other forms of interaction involving language. Granted, there was no blanket neglect of the fact that language is a tool – note, for instance, Locke's reflections on the function of language – but they failed to attend to the structure of language and the interaction of its elements in the light of this function in a systematic way. It is this failure that undermines the classical theories of

meaning, rendering them finally inadequate. The light shed by the tool-function parallel enables us, by analogy, to advance the hypothesis that the structure of language is a function of the use we make of it: the proper constraint on a theory of meaning is that it should give an account of language and its elements in terms of the uses to which they are put. What precisely is the purpose of a linguistic assertion? And what contribution does each of the elements of language make to the fulfilment of that purpose? Such questions offer a clue to the solution of the problem of linguistic meaning. We shall be pursuing this line in what follows, by focusing on language qua speech and communication.

The importance of the role played by speech in human relationships can hardly be exaggerated. Strictly speaking, 'speech' means oral communication, but in a broader sense it also covers the use of gesture, symbols and writing. These are the vehicles for our communication with one another – whether it take the form of ordinary conversation, the sharing of information, questions, requests, commands, the forging of agreements, and so forth. Such verbal exchanges are, in innumerable ways, part of the warp and weft of our lives and endeavours. We quarrel, declare war, transact property and goods, tell stories, pass the time of day, tie the matrimonial knot and bury the dead – all of it by means of or to the accompaniment of language.

In this chapter, we will pursue a strategy akin to Wittgenstein's in the *Philosophical Investigations* in that we will devise a diversity of language games with the aim of exploring those aspects of language that are relevant to its semantic content. Weaving these language games into an evolutionary scenario, we shall elaborate a fable about how language might have developed – from the simple signal language of early human beings to fully developed generative languages. We call it a fable to indicate that there is probably only a loose connection between the narrative we recount and the actual historical process, but there is to date no well-supported going theory of how language emerged. What is of interest, however, is the heuristic value of the exercise: conjectures about the progression of language from simple to more complex language games allow us to arrive at an understanding of the structure of language as we find it today. The structure of language is a function of its use or of the general purposes that it fulfils in the actual speech and communication of language users. What finds articulation in the fable in the form of distinct phases in the evolution of language is today bound into its implicit structure.

What we have in focus, then, is the elaboration of the theory of meaning for natural languages, building on the concepts and distinctions yielded by our reconstruction. The aim of this chapter is to arrive at a general characterization of the theory of meaning and its key concepts, a characterization subject to the constraint that it account for the use of language as a semiotic system enabling the performance of particular speech acts.

3. Naturally, language was not "invented" as the result of some deliberated process, and certainly not in an instant. It probably developed gradually from a system of signals, starting with simple sounds and cognate responses and moving on to something more complex which we today would recognize as a language. But our focus here will be on the invention of a distinctly primitive language – a so-called protolanguage, as contrived by our prehistoric ancestors. To add vividness to our narrative, let us attribute the invention of language to a particular prehistoric genius, Zork. Zork and his fellows forage in the woods, all the while keeping a sharp eye out for dangers. They grunt occasionally and possess a repertoire of signals to which their response is instinctive. Many higher animals command such a repertoire in which warning signals are prominent, sounded whenever a predator is spotted. But these warning signals are typically unspecific: they indicate that there is a danger but give no indication as to what the danger consists of. Granted, vervet monkeys have been observed to have a muster of different warning signals, correlated to different types of dangers. But even these signals are far from being as numerous and specific as the dangers that threaten.

Zork takes the first step towards the invention of language on a day when the tribe is out scavenging. Zork spots a bear approaching from a direction that obscures it from the others, and he is concerned for their safety. A sudden illumination prompts him to imitate the sound of a bear in order to draw the attention of the others to the proximity of one such specimen so that they can flee to safety. His fellows immediately register his strange grunt and from its resemblance to an authentic bear grunt conclude that, in emitting it, Zork is seeking to draw their attention to the presence of a bear so they can get out of harm's way. Zork, in other words, has succeeded in his communicative intent.

Let us take a closer look at the intentionality informing Zork's contrived grunt: Zork *wants* his tribal fellows to get out of the way of the bear. He seeks to achieve this by drawing their attention to the fact that there is a bear close at hand. And what suddenly strikes him as the most expedient means is the performance of an act – grunting – which will conduce to the realization in his fellows that it is his intention to get it across to them that there is a bear nearby. Note that it is not his intention to get the others to believe that the grunt comes from the bear itself – they are to understand that it is *Zork* who is grunting and that he does so in order to get them to realize that there is a bear in the vicinity. Insofar as they realize this, and insofar as they have no relish for a close encounter with a bear, they will rapidly make themselves scarce – precisely as Zork wished them to do.

What makes it possible for Zork to convey such complex intentions to his fellows? Zork is familiar with the grunts of the bear, a familiarity he knows to be shared by his tribal fellows. Zork persists in grunting until he has caught the attention of the others. Once that attention is secured, he is in a position to influence his audience's beliefs. To repeat, it is important to appreciate that Zork is not trying to get them to believe that a real bear is producing the grunts; the others are to realize that the sound comes from Zork and start wondering what he is up to. Zork's expression of alarm – spontaneous or contrived – suggests that he believes that danger is at hand. This enables the others to associate this expression of danger with the grunting, bear-like sound and so surmise that Zork wants them to understand that danger threatens. Knowing his sharp-sightedness, they have confidence in the reliability of his observation that a bear is close at hand; they conclude that there probably is a bear, and are swift to seek safety.

4. The analysis of Zork's simple speech act has uncovered a rather complicated structure of nested intentions, features of which speech acts share with other types of agency. Let us briefly digress from the analysis of speech acts to take a closer look at the structure of acts in general. Speech acts will prove to be a special case.

Acts possess a characteristic end-means structure: to achieve A we need to do something else, B, and in order to perform B we must do C, and so on. C is the means by which to achieve B, which is the means to accomplishing the ultimate end constituted by A. To hang a picture you need to knock a nail into the wall. To undertake that modest feat you need to get hold of a hammer. To procure a hammer, you might have to visit the DIY store. And perhaps getting the picture up on the wall is not even the ultimate goal, but only a means to some further goal such as, say, impressing the neighbours.

An alternative way of describing the matter is to see the entire process as the performance of a single act that comprises a primary aim and a series of secondary objectives. The primary aim is to impress the neighbours; the secondary objectives include getting the picture up on the wall, knocking a nail into the wall, and so on. Each of these objectives is defined in terms of a success condition specified by the state the world has to be in if we are to be able to say that the act was successfully executed. The primary aim of the act has a range of secondary aims embedded in it, and by implication a range of embedded success criteria. The primary success criterion is that the neighbours be impressed, the secondary criteria are that the picture be up on the wall, that a nail be knocked into the wall, that a hammer be procured, and so on. The realization of these aims and secondary objectives are, to some extent, independent of one another. You might be able to impress the neighbours in some other way than by having the picture up on the wall, and you may succeed in getting the picture on the wall even though you do not succeed in impressing the neighbours.

The same features are exhibited by Zork's speech act. Zork's primary aim is to secure the safety of his fellows; the means is the articulation of a grunt to get them to understand that there is a bear nearby. And that end, in turn, is achieved by getting them to grasp that Zork is grunting in order that they should recognize that this threat obtains. It is clear that, as in the case of other actions, these intentions feature serially nested objectives with correlated success criteria. The fulfilment of Zork's communicative aim spans an entire range of nested objectives and success criteria which may be met more or less independently of each other and in several different ways. We may expect to find similar structures in other speech acts.

5. Let us now imagine some later scenario where the tribe is out looking for prey. One of them spots a bear rearing on its hind legs not far off. This tribesman now utters a bear-grunt – just as Zork did on the first occasion, and does so precisely because he recalls that Zork achieved his aim by emitting that first imitative grunt. He too wants the others to realize that there is a bear close by and for them to become apprised of this through their recognizing that it is to this fact that he seeks to alert them. He wants his intervention to result in their seeking safety. Zork and the others do recognize his intention and act accordingly. The new form of communication can chalk up another success.

If past successes conduce to a gradual take-up of the practice, it will result in tribespeople responding more directly to the bear-style grunt. They will think: 'On all previous occasions when a tribal member grunted like a bear he did so to warn of the presence of a bear close by, so must not the same apply in this present situation? The betting is that there's a bear in the vicinity.' And those persons who articulate the grunts will expect those who hear them gradually to come to reason in precisely this way.

Time passes, and the tribespeople grunt every time they want to warn of the presence of a bear. As a result, their intentions undergo a further change. Now they no longer think, 'On every earlier occasion etc ...', since, for a start, the occasions are now so numerous that they can no longer be recalled individually. Instead the tribespeople think 'We normally make grunting noises whenever there is a bear nearby, or at least, whenever there is a threatening bear. So I too will use the grunting sound when I see a bear'. Or else they think, 'It's our custom to grunt on sighting a bear, so that the others will be aware of the danger'. Indeed, it may well be that the tribespeople punish a person who grunts when there is no bear at hand, just as they do an individual who omits to grunt when aware that there is. It thus becomes *the done thing* or common *practice* to grunt on sighting a threatening bear. At this stage of the evolutionary process we can say that this grunt *means* that there is a bear nearby, or rather, since the sound takes the form of a warning (it is only used of threatening bears): 'Watch out for the bear!' So we can say that a highly rudimentary species of language has now emerged – a protolanguage.

Now it might be objected here that it would hardly have been possible for our protolinguistic ancestors to be in possession of such highly developed thought processes as are here being attributed to them. How could primitive man have a sophisticated concept such as 'custom' at his disposal to describe a situation? The entire account is surely incoherent. To this we may reply that we do not need to attribute to these early humans any explicit reasoning of this kind; it is sufficient that they evince behaviour which described in terms of our more explicit concepts would run, 'It is customary to ...' It is not difficult to imagine these early humans conducting themselves in a way that might plausibly be so described. We have conjectured that they punish those who utter grunts when no bear is present. Similarly, that they punish a person who omits to grunt on sighting a bear, and a person who fails to repeat another person's grunt to a third party who missed the first grunt and is unaware that danger threatens. The mothers teach their children to use the grunting sound by uttering it while pointing to a bearskin with an expression of fear and horror.

All of this may be set alongside certain non-linguistic patterns of behaviour in the tribe that are best described as 'conventions' or 'customs'. It may, for example, be a tribal convention that its members bow to the tribal chief when they meet him, and for bear meat to be eaten only by the adult males. Members of the tribe punish those who flout these conventions and mothers teach their children to observe them. In consequence, we harbour no scruples about describing such (non-linguistic) practices as conventions even though the individuals concerned master no such concepts. In chapter 7 we shall return to the term 'convention' and give it a more precise content.

6. The emergence of a convention governing the use of a sound to execute an utterance marks a clear distinction between two different strata in the speech

act, each with its corresponding success conditions. There is the intention conventionally expressed by what the speaker says, and further, an underlying individual objective motivating his utterance. Put differently, there is both what the utterer says and what he seeks to achieve by saying it.

Let us assume that Zork catches sight of a bear near the settlement and utters a bear-warning. He does so in part to warn his fellows, but also to highlight the fact that this constitutes yet another bear sighting close to the settlement and it is high time to strike camp. On another occasion it is Zork's son, Argg, who articulates the imitative grunt to warn his father but also, and more importantly, with the intention of showing his father that he is now old enough to join the hunting party. Later, Argg, now a member of the hunting party, spots a bear while it is still a long way off, and utters appropriate grunts to warn the others; but he overdoes it a touch, rather pointedly signalling to them that he has the keenest eyesight of anyone in the tribe.

In these examples we find dual sets of intentions correlated with their respective success conditions. On the one hand there is the intention that has become conventionally associated with the articulation of bear-style grunts: their utterance now counts as a warning to the tribespeople that there is a bear at hand. The communication of this intention succeeds through the tribespeople, having now assimilated the convention, registering the signal and reaching safety. (In chapter 7 we shall modify this analysis.) On the other hand there is the individual intention of the grunter who, beyond the delivery of a warning, aims at achieving some further end. It might be a collective exhortation to find a better settlement, an advertisement of the fact that the grunter is eminently eagle-eyed, and so forth. These ends are not fulfilled through the tribespeople fleeing from the bear. Here the convention serves as a vehicle for the fulfilment of other, individual, aims.

What is being conventionalized is the intention common to all users of the grunt signal, viz. that their tribespeople should become cognizant of the fact that there is a bear nearby and seek safety. The incorporation into the convention of the utterer's secondary aims would hardly be expedient since such intentions are person-specific and occasion-sensitive. To accommodate such a range, a vast number of different warning signals for bear sightings would be needed, one for every discrete secondary intention. For instance, one might mean 'Watch out for the bear, and surely we all agree that it's high time we moved on to where there are fewer bears!' while another might mean, 'Watch out for the bear, and notice that I'm always the first to spot a bear', and suchlike. It is much more expedient merely to conventionalize the intention to issue a warning. Secondary intentions are better expressed in separate sentences, as is the case in our developed languages – a possibility that becomes available once the protolanguage has evolved into language proper.

Once a convention is established, it becomes vulnerable to abuse through the conventional sound being uttered in the absence of the intention that conventionally informs it. For example, Zork may hit upon the sly idea of emitting a grunt in a situation where he has spotted succulent berries that he is disinclined to share with the others. All flee from the putative threat whereupon Zork sneaks back to feast upon the delicacy. He has misused the grunting convention in the pursuit of personal advantage.

7. To this point, the protolanguage has comprised just one sentence. Let us now imagine that the grunting sound retains its currency but that its use undergoes differentiation so as sometimes to be associated with intentions other than that of warning of the bear threat.

Suppose that one day Zork's mate, Ygg, articulates the bear-style grunt in a situation in which it is clear both to her and to Zork that no bear is present. Here the sound no longer has the function of a warning but is intended to serve a different purpose. This is manifested by it not being emitted in the usual fashion but by being given a different, plaintive modulation. By introducing this variation, Zork's mate is seeking to get Zork to procure some bear meat for her to roast. She wants him to recognize that this is her intention. And she wants him to procure bear meat precisely because he has grasped that this is what she wants him to do. She seeks to convey this complex intention in part by her modified emission of the grunting sound, and in part by seizing Zork's spear and pointing to the empty hearth. Zork construes this complex intention correctly and acts accordingly. He leads a group of his tribespeople into the woods where they run down a bear and return with it to the settlement.

This language game then takes a further twist through its becoming a convention that a person who acknowledges a command repeats the very same sound through which it was expressed but gives it a slightly different, soothing tone and pitch. This counts as an avowal of the intention to do what was commanded. Zork's grunt means, 'OK, I'll hunt a bear for bear meat'. Soon that species of utterance too acquires a self-standing conventionalized status. It takes on the character of an undertaking (even in the absence of a command): 'I promise to bring down a bear before nightfall'.

These two types of communicative act contain both unifying and differentiating elements. Using her distinctive new-version grunt, Zork's mate urges him to bring the carcass of a bear to the hearth before sunset. With his gently articulated response Zork promises that he will see to it that before long a dead bear lies extended in front of the hearth. Here we see two different communicative acts: the utterance of a command and the expression of the intention to obey it, or, more generally, a promise – both articulated in respect of the same content. What Ygg commands him to do is precisely what Zork undertakes to do or promises to do. By virtue of their respective communicative acts, Zork and his mate relate in two separate modes to one and the same content.

In describing language it is necessary, then, to distinguish between types of communicative action and their contents. We can illustrate the distinction as follows:

a) A plaintive grunt at an empty hearth counts as command [to procure bear meat].
b) A soothing grunt at a hearth counts as a promise [to procure bear meat].

In (a) and (b) we see two different types of act: a command and a promise, and a common content which is respectively commanded as a state of affairs to be realized, and a state of affairs whose realization is promised. The common content is enclosed by square brackets. In line with standard terminology, we shall call the variable aspect of these speech acts *force*, and say that commands and promises are speech acts distinguished from each other by their respective forces.

These communicative modalities thus enable the tribespeople to do different things with one and the same content: they can command something's being brought about or promise to bring it about. These instruments become especially effective when conventionalized, as we saw in relation to warnings. To begin with, the other members of the protolinguistic community repeat the new grunting sound because they remember that Ygg succeeded in getting her mate to hunt a bear and want to be able to do the same. Soon they forget who first used the sound and instead frame the thought, 'The plaintive grunt has been successfully used by countless tribespeople when trying to get someone to kill a bear. So I too will use it now'. At a later point still in this evolutionary process the thinking may run 'This particular grunt is one we customarily employ whenever we want someone to kill a bear'. They have reached the stage, then, at which the plaintive grunt becomes a conventional expression and means something in order of 'Go kill a bear'.

8. Let us now look at how a particularly important type of speech act, *assertion*, might conceivably have arisen. We have witnessed how our prehistoric

people encounter bears in two contexts: one where they are out in force and well armed, set upon killing bears, and another where they are few in number or unarmed, and at risk of becoming prey themselves. Two utterances have emerged, appropriate for the one or the other situation: a powerful grunt that serves as a bear warning, and a softer grunt that has the force of 'I'll go kill a bear' or, 'Let's go hunt a bear'.

With these utterances in place, the need arises for yet another bear noise: one to be used, for instance, when one member of the tribe has observed bears near the settlement and conveys this information to his fellow tribespeople gathered around the camp fire. The new utterance type is not intended as a bare warning, since in all likelihood the men will now go out on a bear hunt; nor is it merely as an exhortation to hunt, since it also serves as a warning to women and children of the risk of bear attack. Instead, the utterance is seen as articulating what is common to warnings and exhortations, namely, the bare fact that there are bears close to the settlement. This is information that hunters and children can put to their respective uses: to go hunting or to keep away from the area in question. The new speech act is an *assertion*.

We see here the same mechanism in play as that whose relevance was manifest in the case of warnings: that it is practical to develop a separate linguistic form to express what figures as a common element in a large collection of individual speech acts which otherwise differ in purport. Those further discriminations are best expressed by additional linguistic material. Since there is a common factor in both bear warnings and exhortations to hunt bears – namely the assumption that bears are currently in the vicinity – it is expedient to have a speech act which expresses just this assumption. The assertion is a kind of "null case" of speech acts whose contentual kernel is implicitly present in many other kinds of speech acts, and there will inevitably be a pressure towards finding a separate linguistic form to express it. (This is not to say that every language must necessarily feature the assertive form of utterance. Wittgenstein may well be right in claiming in the *Philosophical Investigations* that we can conceive of a simple, primitive language consisting entirely of commands.)

9. Our next step is to establish what concepts we need in order to account for the success conditions of assertions and, by implication, in order to characterize the meanings of sentences in general. Here is a proposal:

a) The aim of the utterance of an assertion is to induce in the hearer the belief that things are in a certain way. If this objective is not achieved the utterer will deem his utterance to have failed. The bringing about of the relevant belief in others is a success condition of the act of assertion (but see the slightly modified analysis in chapter 7).

b) Further, it is a success condition that things actually are as the speaker seeks to have his hearers believe that they are. If this proves not to be the case the hearers can justifiably reproach the utterer. He is forced to withdraw his utterance. If a person grunts in a situation where no bear is present his tribe will punish him.

c) It is not sufficient, however, that there actually be a bear present when the bear-style grunt is uttered. If Zork mischievously emits a grunt in a situation in which he does not believe a bear to be present he will be punished even if it later turns out that there was in fact a bear present, unnoticed by Zork and the others. If the grunt is to have communicative purport, it is essential that it can be relied on, so that in the great preponderance of cases where it is uttered, the ursine threat will be real. Chance coincidences between signal and reality are not enough. So the tribe must insist that an individual only emit a bear-style grunt when he is sufficiently certain that there is a bear close by, i.e. when he has adequate grounds for believing that that actually is the case.

We can now arrange these success conditions in a more systematic way. This may be done by making the truth condition (condition (b)) pivotal – making it the condition by reference to which other success conditions are defined:

i) The key success condition for assertion is that the assertion be true.
ii) Second, it is a success condition that the hearer should believe that the utterance is true.
iii) Finally, it is a success condition that the utterer have good grounds for the belief that the utterance is true.

The concept of truth is absolutely central to the characterization of the content of assertions. But since the success conditions of other types of linguistic acts are also expressible by means of formulae in which are embedded the key success condition of the corresponding assertion, the centrality of truth extrapolates into these other speech acts – as is clear from the following schema in which 'p' stands for any arbitrary declarative sentence. The schema features some speech acts which we have not encountered previously, namely requests and questions:

- NN asserts that p is the case. The success condition is that it is the case that p.

- NN commands that it be the case that p. The success condition is that the person who receives the command make it the case that p.

- NN requests that it be the case that p. The success condition is that it be the case that p.

- NN promises to make it the case that p. He fulfils the promise by making it the case that p, i.e. the success condition is that he make it the case that p.

- NN asks whether it is the case that p. The success condition is that NN receive the relevant information, i.e. that NN is led to believe that p if it actually is the case that p, and not to believe that p if it is not the case that p.

Thus, the conventional success conditions of the various speech acts are specified through their being tied in with the success condition of a corresponding assertion. This does not mean, of course, that those other kinds of speech act comprise that assertion as part of their content, but merely that their success conditions are (in part) *characterizable* by reference to those of the corresponding assertion – more specifically, the truth condition.

10. We have seen how the tribe develops a language in which a bear-style grunt, according to modulation, counts as an assertion that there is a bear close by, as a command that a bear be run down and killed, or as a warning that a bear is present. We may safely assume that the tribe will go on devising utterances signalling the presence of other threats, as well as valuable discoveries such as prospective sources of food.

It is now but a short step to the conjecture that the various tribal language games will display a systematic interconnectedness, so that if a certain modulation is deployed in one language game – say, the bear language game – with a certain force (in the sense introduced above) as in the case of warnings, that same modulation will recur in other language games where it will carry the same force. The characteristic tone of urgency evinced by the grunt when used to warn of bears is transferable to other utterances where the discovery of poisonous snakes, wolves, stinging wasps and other nuisances cues a similar response. The same holds for the modulation used in bald assertions of the fact that such fauna are in the vicinity. The fact that this particular modulation has been used with a particular force in previous language games gives hearers grounds to believe that the same force is signalled when it is attached to a new warning sound. The utterer is thus motivated to use this modulation in fresh contexts since he has grounds to believe that his intention will be correctly identified if he does so.

Obviously, such a system affords a certain intellectual economy. If every language game were to have its own distinctive modulatory patterns, or if the same patterns represented a different type of force in each language game, there would be an enormous amount to learn and remember; getting acquainted with any language game would be the equivalent of learning a new language from scratch. It is far simpler to build on the elements already operative in the language.

11. The foregoing narrative, then, is conceived as a fable, not as a hypothesis about how language actually emerged. The point of the fable was to point up certain abstract features of linguistic meaning by presenting them as stages in the evolution of language. These features are present in the languages in use today in the guise of abstract features distinguishable in any analytic description. The fable made it easier to identify these features, which point to what a theory of language needs to account for if it is to reflect language adequately.

We offer, then, the following outline of a theory of meaning with application not only to prehistoric protolanguage but also to the fully evolved languages with which we are familiar today. The theory identifies the meaning of an utterance by specifying the uttered sentences' success conditions. There are two components. First, for every well-formed sentence S in the language, the theory specifies an assertion with the same success condition as S (the relevant success condition is the key one, i.e. the truth condition). Second, it provides a specification of the force with which the sentence S may be uttered.

Zork's warning grunt is thus analysed as follows. The grunt as uttered by a tribesman is successful if and only if there is a bear in his whereabouts or in the direction in which he points, i.e. it has the same success condition as the assertion, 'There's a bear'. Further, it is a condition of its success that the hearer registers that there is a bear nearby and responds by fleeing to safety. This feature, signalled by a warning tone, indicates that the utterance counts as a warning rather than the mere assertion of the presence of a bear or, indeed, the promise to kill a bear.

The concept of truth thus becomes not just the core concept governing assertion but also the core concept of the theory of meaning per se, since it is the concept that renders a dual-component theory capable of accounting for the specific contentual meaning of the sentence. Such a theory specifies, first, the success condition of the individual sentence by presenting an assertive sentence and its correlated truth condition. It then accounts for the particular force with which the sentence is uttered: it is able to say whether the sentence simply asserts that the truth condition is satisfied, is a command that it be satisfied, a promise that it will be satisfied, a question as to whether it is satisfied, and so on.

In according the concept of truth pivotal status, we are moving beyond the original Wittgensteinian doctrine that equates meaning with use; indeed, to some extent we are pursuing a line that runs counter to his thinking. This is entirely deliberate, since Wittgenstein's position has a tendency to stymy any attempt to formulate a theory of meaning. The uses to which language – by individual speakers on particular occasions of utterance – is put, are endlessly diverse and multifarious; they resist capture in any systematic theory. On the other hand, focus on the notion of truth allows us, for assertions, to distinguish between a narrower, privileged set of success conditions which directly defines their meaning, and further conditions which may reflect what was in the speaker's mind but which do not give the meaning of the sentence uttered (cf. the examples above). Moreover, this strategy equips us to spell out the meaning of other sentential moods. We shall return to this in chapter 7.

12. When we translated the utterances of the primitive primordial language into English above, they were always rendered as whole sentences, not as sentence parts such as names or predicates. The bear grunt of those early humans was translated into such sentences as 'Watch out for the bear!', 'This is a bear', 'I promise to kill a bear', in accordance with the force inherent in these utterances. But there was no constituent element which we simply rendered by the referential expression 'this bear' or predicates such as '... is a bear' or '... is dangerous'. Their utterances, then, constitute whole sentences. This calls for further comment.

The focus in the present chapter has been the study of linguistic meaning as related to acts performed by means of speech, and with sentences being highlighted in consequence. For, as Wittgenstein pointed out, sentences are the smallest linguistic units with which it is possible to make any move in a language game – that is to say, by means of which a speech act may be performed.

The following reflection validates Wittgenstein's claim. When Zork and his fellows invented language they performed speech acts which, translated into our language, corresponded to whole sentences. It is inconceivable that these early humans should have begun by inventing the various sentential components, joining them up to form sentences, and only then using them to perform complete speech acts.

It is scarcely plausible to imagine that Zork's first experiments with language consisted in going about giving things names. Had that been the case, Zork's grunt would merely have signified something like 'Let us use the bear-style grunt as a name for these animals'. The response of his nonplussed fellow tribespeople would have been: 'What on earth is a "name"?' 'What's the point of a "name"?' For names have a meaning only insofar as they feature in a linguistic context, a sentence, and are used to perform a complete speech act. Until whole sentences have become part of language it makes no sense to speak of 'names'.

There is a further consideration which points to the fact that sentences are prior relative to their components: there is no logical or semantic necessity to sentences having recognizable or re-usable elements at all. In principle we could manage with a signal language comprising signals all of which were simple with set functions and so without elements recurring in other signals. Each signal would express a complete utterance. Sentences such as 'Passage through this crossroads by vehicles approaching this light is presently permitted' and 'Passage through this crossroads by vehicles approaching this light is presently prohibited', which have a clear semantic structure, and which have many linguistic elements in common may, as we know, be replaced by signals devoid of either, namely green and red traffic lights, respectively. Clearly, a language comprised of such unstructured signals would be intellectually uneconomical and would, for us finite beings, result in a language of very limited expressive power. For there are upper bounds to the number of distinct signals we have the capacity to learn and commit to memory.

13. The last named consideration points to a circumstance which is as important for the understanding of the workings of natural language as is the fact that the sentence is the primary semantic unit: our range of expression is vastly extended if our language is *generative*, i.e. if we can form new sentences by re-using and re-ordering elements (words) that have appeared in sentences used previously. The creativity of language enables us, by using a finite list of words in conjunction with rules governing their concatenation, to form new sentences. If we then add words that conjoin sentences – so-called 'sentential connectives' – such as 'not', 'and', 'or', 'if ... then', as well as rules for their application in the creation of new compound sentences, we have the beginnings of a language which through the reiterated use of finite sets of

expressions and rules makes possible the construction of a potentially infinite set of sentences.

Through the re-use of linguistic elements in the formation of compound expressions, the inventory of linguistic symbols remains perspicuous to, and learnable by, human agents. There exists a finite number of linguistic elements – words – which enter into the complex wholes which are sentences. The basic elements have the same semantic content regardless of where they occur.

Let us take a brief look at some of the elementary components of natural languages and the way these reflect the jobs which language performs. It is thanks, notably, to Peter Strawson, that certain crucial links can be stated clearly, albeit roughly. The experience that we describe in language typically involves repeated encounters with the same items. In our progress through the world we are continually confronted with the same people, buildings, cats and dogs, roads, cars and trees. Often it is important to be able to register that our perceptions are of one and the same exemplar and not of different ones that look alike. For instance, our suppositious tribe might discover a bubbling spring at the foot of a particular slope. It is important to them to be able to distinguish this slope from others in the forest. They need, then, a linguistic symbol, a name, for it, so as to be able to refer to it in a clear and unambiguous way.

We ourselves form attachments to particular individuals even though there might be other 'specimens' that are barely distinguishable from them. One is attached to one's particular spouse but not to his or her identical twin; one is attached to a certain dog, but not to another from the same litter even though it is difficult to tell them apart.

Consequently, we need the linguistic means that enables us to pick out particular recurrent individual items. The linguistic categories that identify these items are names, demonstratives and so-called 'definite descriptions'. We use expressions such as 'Zork', 'Napoleon', 'my wife', 'Rover', 'my old coat', 'the house over there', 'this cup' and the like. In his work on "descriptive metaphysics", Strawson points out how the system of spatio-temporal relations forms an intersubjective framework which makes possible unique and unambiguous reference to individual things of every ontological category. In the final analysis, determinate reference to individual things is made possible by that fact that any item we might wish to refer to either has, itself, a position in this framework, or is linked to other items that do; this latter group includes mental states. Hence such items are identifiable by reference to a particular location, and may be picked out in a way that involves reference to that.

It is equally much a feature of our experience that the things we routinely encounter resemble one another in countless ways. We need linguistic expressions to signal these resemblances, and indeed predicates (adjectives and common nouns) do the job. Some things strike us as perceptually similar in a certain respect and so we introduce the predicate '... is/are red' to denote them; others taste alike and we introduce the predicate '... is/are sweet' for them. Others still resemble each other in more abstract respects and we call them 'mammals', 'fluids', 'vegetables', 'carbon compounds', and so on. Getting along in life at all requires the ability to pick out and name both readily noticeable similarities between things and those less obtrusive affinities and differences that can have momentous implications for humans: the subtle differences in observable properties that indicate whether a fungus is poisonous or edible, a fruit ripe or indigestible and a dog ready to attack or take flight.

In assembling one group of similar things under one linguistic label, and in assembling an analogously cohesive group under another, we mark a distinction between the two. Drawing distinctions between different species of item is the reverse of collating similar things; identities exist only in the face of differences. Noticing salient likenesses is as important in human life as noticing crucial differences. Taken together, collating the similar and distinguishing the dissimilar constitutes *classification*, an activity essential to any kind of human or animal existence. Hence, putting the point summarily we can say that predicates are instruments of classification.

14. We have now introduced two fundamental linguistic categories, namely so-called 'singular terms' (names, definite descriptions) and predicates (adjectives and common nouns). When co-occurring in utterances, they form *subject-predicate sentences*, which are the core components of most human languages. In the chapters that follow we shall be examining these categories to show how their semantic content is determined. The procedure will be to look at their respective meanings in terms of the contribution each makes to the determination of the meaning of the sentence in which they are constituent, i.e. their contribution to the success conditions (in particular truth conditions) of the sentence. The thrust of this approach draws on the gains yielded by the collapse of the old theories of meaning conjoined to the insight to the effect that the general concept in the description of speech acts is that of truth. We now see the meanings of expressions as the contribution they make to the fixing of truth conditions.

The traditional approach to meaning, exemplified both by Locke's mentalistic theory and by the referential theory, takes the form of what we can call a *compositional* theory. Such theories assume that each word possesses a discrete meaning that is specifiable without reference to other words in the language. Lexical meaning is also independent of the roles words play in sentences and, by implication, speech acts. We saw the difficulties that beset this position. The theory of meaning we shall be advancing here could be called an *abstractive* theory since it conceives of the meaning of words as abstracted from a more widely embedded meaningfulness. The meaning of a word is an abstract feature of the meaning of the sentences in which it occurs, not a component that might, as it were, be extracted from its context and exist on its own.

However, our theory will incorporate many elements that appear in traditional compositional theories, not least in our account of the functioning of singular terms, as will become apparent in the next chapter. But it is important to stress that traditional characterizations remain incomplete so long as words are viewed in isolation from the role they play in sentences and, consequently, in utterances. We are maintaining, in other words, that the meanings of singular terms and predicates (as well as other parts of speech) consist in the contributions they make to fixing the meanings of sentences (i.e. the success conditions of those sentences). But this is not tantamount to the claim that a purely "combinatorial" account, one stating that such-and-such combinations of singular terms and predicates yield sentences with such-and-such success conditions, exhausts what there is to be said about their semantical contributions.

One objection against abstractive theories immediately suggests itself. We have already on several occasions adverted to the fact that language is *generative*, permitting the construction of a potentially infinite number of sentences and that a competent language user understands a potential infinity of sentences. This feature comes of the fact that sentences are built up out of standard components, words, and that the meanings of sentences is a function of the meanings of the words. This explains how it is that language users are able to decode the meaning of sentences they have never previously encountered: they are able to infer the meaning of the sentence from the meanings of the individual words. But then surely it would seem to follow, the objection runs, that words themselves have semantical contents and that the meanings of sentences are derivative? For how can the meanings of words be abstracted from the meanings of sentences if the contents of sentences must first be decoded and construed by appeal to the meanings of the words?

Well, words do indeed have their own semantic contents antecedently to any role they might play in the construction of any particular sentence, but this has no bearing on the fact that the semantical content of a word must be defined in terms of its contribution to all the possible sentences into which it might enter. One way of explaining this is to compare the reading of a sentence with the counting up of a pile of money paid out as part of a deal. Every note and coin carries the designated value given by its denomination and the sum total is given by simple addition. Just as the aggregate value of the pile of money is calculated on the basis of the value of each note and coin, so too the meaning of a sentence is 'calculated' by reference to the meaning of each word. Like the words, the monetary units have values independent of and prior to this particular transaction. This does not, however, alter the fact that the value of a note or a coin does not exceed the role it plays in all sorts of actual and hypothetical financial transactions. Notes and coins have no value independent of the transactions in which they figure, which fact becomes all too obvious in a period of hyperinflation. The population loses confidence in the currency and refuses to accept it in exchange for actual goods: in that situation the notes are worth no more than the paper they are printed on.

By the same token, every word in a language has a semantical content which is independent of the concrete situation of a particular utterance. All the same, each word's meaning is given by the contribution that it makes to the determination of the meanings of sentences – namely, their success conditions – in the totality of conceivable utterances in which they might occur.

Chapter 3
The semantics of singular terms

1. We saw in the previous chapter that the sentence is the fundamental unit of semantic analysis. The sentence is the primary bearer of meaning; meaning consists in its success conditions. Amongst the various success conditions, truth conditions (the success conditions of assertions) were shown to play a particularly significant role since the success conditions of other kinds of utterances were specifiable in terms of those of declarative sentences, in conjunction with an indication of their respective forces.

But while they are indeed the primary vehicles of meaning, sentences are made up of smaller, semantically significant units and from these we singled out singular terms and predicates as being of particular interest. The meanings of the latter consist in their contribution to the determination of the success conditions (truth conditions) of the sentence, although there is more to be said about their semantics than is captured by the formula to the effect that the combination of an item from one of these two linguistic categories with an item from the other generates a sentence with determinate success conditions (truth conditions).

In this chapter we offer an account of the semantics of the first of these two types of expression, namely singular terms. The expression 'singular term' includes proper names, definite descriptions and indexicals. Proper names are expressions such as 'Peter', 'Paul' and 'Mary'; 'Johnson' and 'Smith'; 'New York', 'London' and 'France'; 'Mount Everest'; 'Venus' and 'Sirius'; and definite descriptions such as 'the largest city in the world', 'the fastest marathon runner', 'the first house on the right', 'the man standing by the door', and so on. Finally, indexicals (demonstratives) include such expressions as 'here', 'now', 'that', 'there', 'I', 'you', and so on.

As the name suggests, singular terms are expressions that stand for individual entities or that at least is the assumption informing their use. ('Singular' comes from the Latin, 'singularis': single or individual.) Clearly, this does not tell us very much; the next step, then, is to provide an account of what it means to say that an expression stands for something. We are not much enlightened if 'stand for' is replaced by one of the other more or less technical expressions that philosophers have introduced to pick out this relation such as 'refer to', 'denote' and others; these expressions do not so much offer an analysis of the problem as they give it a name. We saw in chapters 1 and 2 that the route to an understanding of this semantic relationship passes via an account of the role it plays in whole sentences, which is complemented in turn by a comprehensive description of the role played by sentences in human communication.

As we saw in the previous chapter, singular terms are used to draw the attention of an interlocutor to some particular item before going on to say something about it. Alternatively, as Strawson puts it, the point of the use of a singular term is to enable the interlocutor to identify the item in question. In the absence of any such conversational setting the use of singular terms is pointless. The conversational situation is always part of an interactive communicative context where what is said may be an assertion about the way things are, a command that a change be brought about, a promise that the speaker will bring about such a change, a question about a given state of affairs, and so on.

We pointed out that it is inconceivable that there should have been a phase in the evolution of language when it comprised merely singular terms used to refer to things and not complete speech acts involving the utterance of whole sentences. If our primordial speaker, Zork, had gone about conferring names on things at a point when complete speech acts had yet to emerge, his behaviour would have been unintelligible to his fellows (and to himself): as unintelligible as it would be for one to attach price tags to things at a time when the notion of buying and selling still lay in the future. Even to call Zork's activity, 'giving things names', betrays a misconception; it would be more correct to say that he places himself in close proximity to a range of objects, points to each in turn and, as he does so, makes a specific vocal sound. The point of this behaviour would have remained entirely obscure.

In consequence, the semantic role of singular expressions cannot be specified without some account of the wider topic of the performance of a complete speech act, which is the utterance of a whole sentence to some end. Within some such account, however, it is possible to get a handle on a particular aspect of what is going on, viz. the speaker's bid to get the listener to identify a particular item. Theories of the semantic role of singular terms, traditionally called 'theories of reference', are required to provide an account of the workings of language that lights up precisely that feature.

2. So how do we bring it about that an expression like 'Greenland' picks out a vast island way up in the North Atlantic, so that our interlocutor knows

what we are talking about when we use it? How do we get the expression 'the Big Bang' to single out a cosmic event which, for obvious reasons, no one witnessed? Or how, for that matter, do we get a perfectly ordinary name like 'John Smith' to refer to John Smith? What, in effect, is the relation between name and reality?

To reply to these questions we shall start by examining a rudimentary theory about the link between names and other singular terms, and the items to which they refer, a theory that commits the error of examining these issues out of context, discussed in chapter 1. The criticisms that this theory encountered furnishes us with an insight into what a more adequate theory would have to deliver. Our approach offers the additional advantage of reflecting the historical progress of philosophical thought, for the successors of the rudimentary theory were the products of a philosophical debate which raged for most of the twentieth century.

The theory we shall examine is one that identifies the meaning of a singular term with its referent in a given context: the object or individual referred to in the context. Let us call this theory the *label theory*. The theory is also known by another sobriquet, coined by Gilbert Ryle, namely the 'Fido'-Fido theory. The gist of either name is the same: the relation between any referring expression and its referent is somehow modelled on the relation between a pet animal and its name. The referent of the name is conveniently accessible to the observer since, in paradigmatic cases, the referent is literally the bearer of the name: a nametag hangs from its collar. Less metaphorically, we can sum up the label theory by saying that on it, the semantics of referring terms would be exhaustively captured by a rudimentary list, one juxtaposing every name or other referring expression with its bearer. Thus:

> The meaning of the word 'Greenland' is Greenland
> The meaning of the word 'Napoleon Bonaparte' is Napoleon Bonaparte
> The meaning of the words 'The king of Sweden' is the king of Sweden
> The meaning of the word 'Fido' is Fido
> and so on.

It is obvious that this theory commits the error we touched upon in chapter 1, viz. that of considering language in isolation from its use, more specifically, that of treating reference in isolation from its function in language. For such a list fails to give any indication as to how this correlation between words and things works in human communication.

3. The weaknesses inherent in the label theory were highlighted through criticisms raised by Bertrand Russell. There is a certain irony in this, however,

since Russell's objections are somewhat technical and do not directly target the failure of the label theory to consider the function of singular expressions in wider contexts of use. Indeed, Russell was inclined to overlook the need for that perspective and in fact subscribed to a version of the label theory, albeit one applying only to an extremely narrow range of referring expressions. Nevertheless, his objections served to point the way to a broader theory that reflected the recognition of the need for a functional account.

Russell's first objection concerns negative existential statements such as 'Atlantis has never existed'. It is obvious that this sentence is both meaningful and true: Atlantis has indeed never existed. But according to the label theory, the sentence cannot both be true and possess meaning. For the sentence to have a meaning, its every constituent must have a meaning. The name 'Atlantis' is a constituent of the sentence and according to this theory the meaning of the name is its referent, namely Atlantis. In consequence, the sentence 'Atlantis has never existed' has a meaning only if Atlantis has existed. But the statement denies that Atlantis ever existed, so if it has meaning it is false. Conversely, if the sentence 'Atlantis has never existed' is true, then Atlantis does not exist. But in that case 'Atlantis' is devoid of meaning, since for the label theory meaning is identical with the referent, and a referent is precisely what the name 'Atlantis' lacks if what the sentence says is true. But if a sentence contains a constituent without meaning, the entire sentence is without a meaning. Thus if the sentence 'Atlantis has never existed' is true, it is devoid of meaning, and so unintelligible. However, the sentence 'Atlantis has never existed' is true, it does have a meaning, and we understand it.

Second, Russell levelled a more general objection against meaningful sentences that contain non-referring singular expressions. Leaving names to one side, let us now turn to definite descriptions as further instances of singular expressions.

Let p be any assertion. Now there exists a logical principle, 'the law of the excluded middle', according to which p or non-p always holds: for any unambiguous sentence it holds either that the sentence is true or that its negation is true – there is no third possibility. But take a sentence such as 'The present king of France is bald'. The sentence is clearly meaningful, but it cannot be true since there is no present king of France. Nor can it be false, since its falsehood would presuppose that there existed a king of France who happened not to be bald. The sentence appears to be neither true nor false. According to the label theory, then, we have here a sentence that is neither true nor false, and which thus violates the law of the excluded middle, a fundamental law of logic.

The remedy proposed by Russell for the resolution of these difficulties is the so-called theory of descriptions. This theory provides an analysis of definite descriptions such as 'the highest mountain in the Alps', 'the northernmost town in Europe', 'the king of France'. According to Russell, a sentence such as 'The present king of France is bald' presents the following logical structure:

There is one entity and only one entity that is now king of France and anything that is now king of France is bald.

Analysed more closely, this structure comprises the following three components:

a) There is at least one entity that is now king of France (the existence condition).
b) There is at most one entity that is now king of France (the uniqueness condition).
c) Anything that is now king of France is bald (the subsumption condition).

The contribution of the definite description to the sentence is reflected in conditions (a) and (b); the description is thus said to be correct if and only if (a) and (b) are fulfilled (which, roughly speaking, means that the definite description has reference); it is incorrect if the conditions (a) and (b) go unfulfilled (which roughly amounts to saying that the description fails to refer).

Note that none of the sentences (a)–(c) are of subject-predicate form. In particular, neither (a) nor (b) or (c) contain definite descriptions – these have been completely eliminated. (If a sentence contains several definite descriptions the analysis obviously has to be repeated until all such have been eliminated.) Russell's analysis may accordingly be characterized as a method by which definite descriptions are eliminated through the grammatical subject-predicate sentences being replaced by an equivalent (if we abstract from the ambiguities of natural language) set of sentences of the form 'There is ...' (or 'There exist/s ...') and 'All ...' (or 'Anything ...').

The grammatical subject in the above sentences – the definite description – has, then, no independent reference, but contributes to the meaning of the sentence only in virtue of the sentential context. The analysis of such sentences exhibits the validity of the principle that sentential elements should be understood in light of the role they play in the sentence as a whole. And, by the same token, the sentential unit should be understood in terms of its communicative function.

According to Russell, the correct logico-semantic analysis of the sentence 'The present king of France is bald' runs as follows:

There exists one entity and only one entity that is now king of France and anything that is now king of France is bald.

For Russell, this sentence is meaningful but false in that it constitutes an unequivocally incorrect existential claim: there is in fact no present king of France so condition (a) goes unfulfilled.

This analysis disposes of the difficulties posed by the principle of the excluded middle: either p or non-p. If we call the above sentence p we can conclude that the sentence's negation, non-p, must be true. And no difficulty is posed by the formulation of a sentence which is true precisely when p is false, and vice versa. It runs as follows:

It is *not* the case that there exists one entity and only one entity that is now king of France and anything that is now king of France is bald.

It is important, however, not to be confused by the fact that there is another reading of non-p which is not true, namely:

There is one and only one entity that is now king of France and anything that is now king of France is *not* bald.

This sentence is false on account of its existential claim.

There is, then, no violation of the law of the excluded middle in this and analogous cases if the existential sentence and its negation are read aright. The sentence 'Either the present king of France is bald or he is not bald' is to be construed as follows:

EITHER it is the case that there exists one entity and only one entity that is now king of France and anything that is now king of France is bald.

OR it is *not* the case that there exists one entity and only one entity that is now king of France and anything that is now king of France is bald.

We have seen how Russell analyses definite descriptions so that the paradoxes generated by them disappear. However, the difficulties attaching to proper names, as illustrated by the problem of Atlantis above, remain. But Russell claims further that his analysis of definite descriptions is applicable to names as well. His point is that names are simply disguised definite descriptions or, better, are convenient abbreviations of definite descriptions. A hint of how this is to be understood emerges once we consider how we would reply in an everyday context to a question concerning the identity of a certain named individual. The teacher asks a pupil: 'Peter, who is Salman Rushdie? Peter: 'A controversial Anglo-Indian writer, whose works include *The Satanic Verses*, a book which so outraged the Islamic world that it led to its author living under the constant threat of assassination.' Here we see how a name is 'unpacked' in terms of a definite description of its bearer. According to Russell, then, names are abbreviated versions of definite descriptions.

4. With this analysis in mind, let us turn to the paradoxes involving proper names. We can begin with negative existential statements such as the sentence 'Atlantis has never existed'. On Russell's thesis, the semantics of proper names, the name 'Atlantis' is simply an abbreviated definite description. It has the following logico-semantic structure (other descriptions of course might be supplied):

> There is one and only one entity that is a continent that was once situated between Europe and America but which later sank into the sea.

That is to say that there is one entity and only one entity that uniquely satisfies the description of a continent that ... and so on. The sentence 'Atlantis has never existed' is simply the negation of the aforementioned sentence, viz.:

> It is not the case that there is one and only one entity that is a continent that was once situated between Europe and America but which later sank into the sea.

Russell is thus able to account for the fact that sentences, such as that concerning 'Atlantis' which contain "empty names", are meaningful without having to resort to the insinuation of mysterious entities (such as, say, "subsistents" à la Meinong, cf. chapter 1) which are thereafter denied existence. It turns out that, properly understood, such sentences are complex existential sentences which are simply false if there exists no unique item of the kind satisfying the description.

Russell's solution marks a step towards a theory that gives us a handle on how it is that we are able to use names in our communication with one another, marking an advance on the label theory. Every name implicitly contains the bearer's individual profile, those characteristics that uniquely identify the bearer. Everyone who knows the meaning of the names 'Greenland', or 'David Johnson' is *ipso facto* in possession of an item of information that uniquely picks out the entities named – that fits each of these two things individually but nothing else in the universe. It is in this way that names 'hook onto' reality. Moreover, the particular information does not merely fit the relevant entity or person; it will often be information of a kind that enables us to track down that item or individual. In principle, anyone acquainted with the meaning of such a name would be able to use the relevant information to go out into the world and find its bearer. So whenever we address one another using name-featuring utterances, we are conveying, in capsule form, information about reality. Moreover it is this information that confers meaning on the name, even though it might prove to be empty.

Before we leave Russell's account of singular terms a caveat needs to be entered for the sake of historical accuracy. Strictly speaking, it is incorrect to suggest that Russell rejects the theory that identifies the meaning of a name with its reference. Russell retained this principle but against the background of the considerations recorded above he drew the conclusion that proper names as we normally understand them – names such as 'Bertrand Russell', 'Zork', 'Napoleon', and so on – are not proper names at all. *Genuine* proper names, logically proper names as Russell called them, are expressions such as 'this', 'I', and other indexicals. The meaning of these expressions really is their reference, according to Russell, and so they are in fact meaningless if what they refer to does not exist. If you point to empty space and say 'This is very sharp', the sentence makes no sense – precisely as Russell's analysis leads us to expect. (We leave it to the reader to devise an example in which 'I'm very happy' is uttered in the absence of any reference for the pronoun!) Regarding *genuine* names, then, Russell holds that their meaning is identical with their reference – on the assumption that real names are not expressions of the type 'Peter' and 'Paul' but, instead, indexicals such as 'this' and 'I'.

5. We have now seen how Russell is led towards a theory that addresses the question of how referring expressions function in human communication, thus improving on the label theory. But for all his critique of it, he concedes to that same theory a certain residual albeit strictly limited validity. By contrast, an alternative proposal for the semantics of singular terms advanced by Gottlob Frege marks a wholly radical break with the label theory inasmuch as Frege introduces a distinction between the meaning of the linguistic expression (*Sinn*) and its reference (*Bedeutung*).

The *locus classicus* for Frege's criticism of the label theory appears in the article 'Über Sinn und Bedeutung' (Sense and Meaning) of 1892. Here Frege points out that the label theory cannot account for the informative (epistemic, cognitive) difference that exists between identity sentences of the type 'a = a' and of the type 'a = b'.

Frege confronts the label theory with the following dilemma. The identity relation expresses a relation between objects or between signs that refer to objects. If we assume the truth of the first disjunct, to the effect that the identity relation is a relation between objects, the label theory cannot distinguish between 'a = a' and 'a = b' in respect of cognitive content. Identity statements of the type 'a = a' are self-evidently trivial. A language user who understands the constituent expressions in 'a = a' will know straight off that the sentence is true. Identity statements of the type 'a = b' are, by contrast, informative, but it is difficult to see how the label theory can account for that fact. Assume that the sentence is true: a is identical with b. Assume further that Jack understands the sentence 'a = b'. According to the label theory, this understanding consists in Jack's knowing of a certain item x that the name 'a' refers to it, and in his knowing of x that the name 'b' refers to it. But if Jack knows that, a moment's reflection suffices for him to realize that the sentence 'a is identical with b' is true. The sentence thus becomes trivial.

Let us illustrate this using Frege's famous example (and, in presenting it, let us follow Frege in not distinguishing between proper names and definite descriptions, subsuming both under the label 'name', liberally construed). The name 'the Evening Star' designates the same celestial body as does the name 'the Morning Star': they are both names of the planet Venus. According to the label theory, the meaning of these names is therefore one and the same, viz. the planet Venus. So if the sentence 'the Morning Star is the same (celestial body) as the Evening Star' is true, there is no difference between the cognitive content of this sentence and that of the trivial statement 'the Morning Star is the same (celestial body) as the Morning Star'. But in actual fact it took millennia for mankind to make the discovery that it was one and the same celestial body that was visible in the morning and evening, respectively. Identity seems to be anything but a banal linguistic fact ascertainable by brief reflection on the meaning of the terms. The label theory cannot, then, explain how a language user who understands identity-statements can acquire fresh information by being told the truth-value of the statement.

A plausible response would be to defend the label theory through appeal to an alternative interpretation, which has it that the identity relation is a relation between signs. The informational content of the sentence 'a = b' consists in the sentence's expressing the fact that the sign 'a' designates the same object as the sign 'b'.

This proposal has difficulties of its own, however. Frege points out that it amounts to a metalinguistic interpretation of identity-statements. This interpretation construes them as statements about linguistic conventions to the effect that the expressions 'a' and 'b' stand for the same entities, rather than as statements about non-linguistic reality: that a is identical to b. That this is a misinterpretation becomes clear if we compare a genuine sentence of identity with a purely linguistic claim. For instance, we are not much enlightened if we are told that 'Tellus' in Latin stands for the same object as the term 'Ge' in Greek unless we also know what that object is. Until we do, we are possessed of an item of information about two languages and not knowledge about the world. But once we are informed that Tellus, and so Ge likewise, refer to the earth, we are enlightened straightaway.

The conclusion that follows from this is that the identity relation concerns individual objects, viz. a relation in which each particular stands to itself and to nothing else. The label theory is thus misconceived: no matter which of the two interpretations the theory uses in accounting for the informational content of identity sentences, it leads to highly implausible results.

How, then, should we account for the fact that we can acquire fresh information by being informed of the truth-value of identity-statements of the type 'a = b'? What is the explanation of the difference in informational content between statements of type 'a = a' and type 'a = b'?

6. For there to be any adequate account of the differential information value of the two sentences, more is evidently needed than the simple pointing out of the fact that there is a typographical difference between the signs. What Frege is looking for is a difference in respect of the mode in which the signs refer to their referents. According to Frege, that difference can only obtain if the difference between the signs is correlated with a difference in the way in which they present their referents.

Frege illustrates the point with the following example:

'Let a, b, c be the lines connecting the vertices of a triangle with the midpoints of the opposite sides. The point of intersection of a and b is then the same as the point of intersection of b and c. So we have different designations for the same point, and these names ('point of intersection of a and b', 'point of intersection of b and c') likewise indicate the mode of presentation; and hence the statement contains actual knowledge.'

('Sense and Meaning', Frege 1892 (1952), p. 57; translation by P. Geach and M. Black. Although Geach and Black translate 'Bedeutung' as 'meaning', to avoid confusion we shall follow the widespread practice of rendering it as 'reference'.)

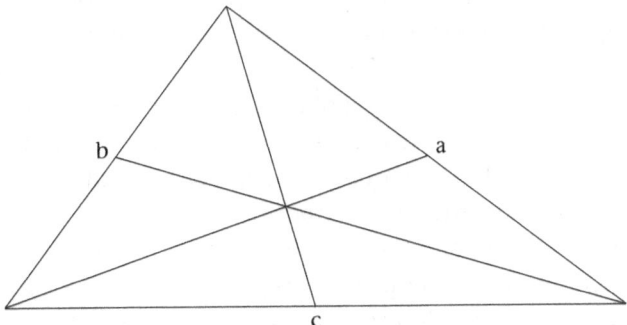

Fig. 3.1   Frege's triangle

Frege is once again using the term 'name' in a liberal sense, to include both proper names and definite descriptions, and so as roughly equivalent to our 'singular terms'. He points out that the two singular expressions in the quotation, 'point of intersection of a and b', 'point of intersection of b and c' have the same reference (*Bedeutung*), viz. the point wherein the lines a, b and c intersect. But these singular terms – which in the present case are definite descriptions – present their references under different aspects.

The ways in which the terms present their references constitute their meanings (*Sinn*). The fact that two terms can have different meanings but the same reference means that identity-statements can be true and informative, as in the case of the sentence, 'the point of intersection for a and b is identical with that of b and c'.

A language user who *understands* the sentence 'the point of intersection for a and b is identical with that of b and c' is, in virtue of his understanding of the singular terms of the sentence, in possession of two definite descriptions which he can use to pick out their common referent. The informational content is cashed out when, in recognizing the truth of the sentence, he learns that the two modes of presentation identify one and the same object. This means that the point presented as the intersection of a and b has the further property of being the intersection of b and c. Likewise with the example above. The individual who understands and believes the sentence 'the Morning Star is the same (celestial body) as the Evening Star' knows that the bright celestial body visible in the east in the morning is the same as that visible in the west in the evening, if that sentence is true.

In his argument for the indispensability of the notion of sense (*Sinn*), Frege identified three levels in the description of language: the expression, its reference and its sense or meaning. Frege applies these distinctions to all types of expression, including proper names in the narrow sense. These too are bound up with a sense and not just a reference (if indeed they have one).

7. Frege characterizes the meaning of an expression in terms of its 'mode of presentation', or the way in which the referent of an expression is presented to the language user. There is a phenomenological point here: we are never *simply* confronted with the various items that are objects for our consciousness but are always presented with them in a particular way; they are presented to us under some description or as perceived in some particular way. It is these modes of presentation that are correlated with the relevant terms as their sense or meaning.

We can elaborate this point by appeal to the way in which we learn the use of a term. Normally, we encounter a term in the context of a description of what it is it refers to, or we are given a non-verbal presentation of its reference. It is this description or mode of presentation that the language user henceforth connects with the term as its sense.

Eight-year-old John was supplied with the reference of the name 'Stratford-upon-Avon' as being Shakespeare's birthplace. 'Dartmoor' was explained as naming the stretch of wild, heather and bracken-covered country where the family stops for a motoring break on their way to their holiday cottage, while 'Eileen' acquired a sense for John through his being taken down through Grandma's garden to the opening in the hedge and being introduced to the nice lady who lives next door. These criteria were ones John was later able to use when he needed to seek out the bearers of the names. Grandma might say: 'Eileen's got some sweets for you'. All John has to do now is to apply what he has learnt. He tears across Grandma's garden to the gap in the hedge that gives access to the house next door where the nice old lady lives. Note that some of these names are given by a description that John has picked up (Dartmoor), others by his learning to recognize a person by his or her appearance and not on the basis of a description (Eileen). It is important to note that when we recognize people by their appearance we typically do so without consulting some verbal description stored in our memory. This is well illustrated by the fact that the witness to a crime may find it very difficult to put words to his recollection of the offender's appearance when helping the police create an identikit, despite being able to identify the individual straight off in court.

8. Frege's concept of sense has two main functions. First, it has a cognitive role: it figures in an account of what the language user understands. The language user's understanding of an expression is precisely his knowledge of the mode in which the expression represents its reference, which is to say, his knowledge of the expression's *Sinn*.

Second, the concept of sense has a semantic role. An expression's *Sinn* mediates the connection between the expression and its referent, in that the expression refers to the object that satisfies the description or the criterion of identity associated with the expression. This is captured by Frege's dictum to the effect that, set against the way the world is, the sense of an expression fixes or determines its reference. Indeed, we can speak of it as an indirect theory of reference. A term's sense fixes its reference through a determination of precisely those characteristics (Frege's 'Merkmale') that need to be satisfied for a thing to be the referent of a name. This contrasts with a direct theory of reference, exemplified by the label theory, where the referential relation between expression and referent does not proceed via a description.

To sharpen this thesis we might say that the sense of an expression constitutes a necessary and sufficient condition for the identification of its referent. We might, for instance, link up the name 'Hans Christian Andersen' with the description 'the author of 'The Ugly Duckling', 'The Snow Queen' and 'The Tinder Box''. The necessary condition runs: if any individual is the bearer of the name 'Hans Christian Andersen', then that individual is the sole author of 'The Ugly Duckling', 'The Snow Queen' and 'The Tinder Box'. The sufficient condition runs: if any individual is the sole author of 'The Ugly Duckling', 'The Snow Queen', and 'The Tinder Box', then that person is the bearer of the name 'Hans Christian Andersen'.

Let us conclude our account of Frege's distinction between *Sinn* and *Bedeutung* by rehearsing two of its major implications. Interestingly, they illustrate how Frege deals with the difficulties that exercised Russell:

a) Two singular terms can have different senses but the same reference, which is to say that two different modes of presentation or sets of identity criteria lead us to the same object. Such instances show how it is possible for identity-statements to be informative since one and the same object satisfies both sets of identity criteria.

b) Singular terms can have a sense and yet lack reference. This occurs when the identification criterion associated with the expression fails to pick out anything at all. The name 'Atlantis', for instance, may be associated with a sense that presents the reference of the name as 'the continent that was once situated between Europe and America but which later sank into the sea.' The name has a sense but no reference since its purported reference has never existed.

9. Frege's theory of the meaning of singular terms solves the problems it was designed to solve but is flawed by certain rather implausible implications – implications which it is not alone in generating since it shares them with Russell's theory. One example is that in every language that contains proper names, a large number of unwanted *analytic* sentences are generated. An analytic sentence is true simply in virtue of the meanings of its constituents: for instance, the sentence 'Bachelors are unmarried' is an analytic sentence because it follows directly from the meaning of the term 'bachelor' that any such individual is unmarried. Take the sentence 'Dartmoor is the stretch of wild, heather and bracken-covered country where we stop for a motoring break on our way to our holiday cottage'. This will figure for John as an analytic sentence. The same holds of 'Atlantis is the continent that was once situated between Europe and America but which subsequently sank into the sea'. It follows that this sentence cannot be informative – which it obviously is. Conversely, a sentence such as 'Atlantis did not sink into the sea' would have the status of a self-contradiction, i.e. a sentence that is false solely in virtue of the meanings of the constituent words. On the face of it, this seems wrong too. If it proved to be the case that somewhere out in the North Atlantic there lay an entire continent (miraculously escaping the notice of modern geographers) and if this continent were the very same as that lighted upon by Greek sailors in the distant past, giving rise to the stories about Atlantis, we would scarcely deny that it was indeed Atlantis.

To remedy such complications John Searle and Peter Strawson, taking their inspiration from Wittgenstein, have proposed that there is not just *one* identifying description attaching to proper names, but a 'cluster' of equal *alternative* descriptions. Today, for instance, we associate not just one description with the name 'Moses' but a cluster of them: the man who led the Israelites out of Egypt, or the man who set down the Ten Commandments, or the man who smashed the golden calf, or the man who divided the Red Sea. (The number of alternatives will often be indefinite.) Moses is now identified as the individual who satisfies a suitably large number of alternative descriptions, but not necessarily all.

This theory reduces the problems of analyticity and entailed contradictions. A sentence such as 'Moses is the man who led the Israelites out of Egypt' no longer counts as analytic; for it has not been established that Moses possesses precisely this property out of the cluster. Consequently, it would be informative to learn that it is this very description out of the entire cluster that Moses putatively satisfies. And there is no longer any absurdity involved in wondering whether someone other than Moses smashed the golden calf.

However, the solution to these problems offered by the cluster theory is less than robust. Granted, the sentence 'Moses led the Israelites out of Egypt' is no longer analytic, but the following sentence remains so: 'Moses led the Israelites out of Egypt or he set down the Ten Commandments or he caused the Red Sea to divide'. And again, this sentence does not appear to be true in virtue of the meanings of the words alone, but would seem to be straightforwardly informative. Certainly, its denial hardly appears to be incoherent.

Finally, there is an objection to the description theory, both in its simple version and in the cluster variant, that has to do with language use in communication. It is inconceivable that each speaker should attach the same identification conditions to the various words in the language. People learn words in very diverse contexts; John associates the name Eileen with Grandma's nice next-door neighbour, while at the baker's on the corner they know Eileen as the old lady who regularly buys chocolate éclairs on Saturdays. This would seem to suggest that we all use names (and arguably other words too) in different senses, and systematically talk past each other in our quotidian exchanges. This counterintuitive result casts doubt on the capacity of Frege's theory to explain how language works. Frege was not unaware of the problem, but he regarded it as a defect to which natural languages are prone and not a flaw in his own theory. While considering such ambiguities tolerable in ordinary language, he insisted on a scientific language being free of them.

10. It is however, possible to repair this defect in the description theory by drawing on ideas developed by Hilary Putnam. Putnam attacks the implicit individualist bias of the classical theory, namely its assumption that the meaning of a word is something known and mastered by each individual language user. Instead Putnam argues that linguistic meaning is a collective and social phenomenon: a word's meaning is determined by the descriptions attached to it by the linguistic community as a whole.

Take names such as 'Plato' and 'Aristotle'. Many people are familiar with these names but without knowing much about their bearers. The descriptions they associate with the names will tend to be rough-and-ready, in the style of 'Greek philosopher living before the birth of Christ'. Speakers do not standardly command sets of necessary and sufficient conditions that govern the identification of their referents, and indeed, associate too little descriptive content with the names to be able to distinguish the one from the other. Nonetheless, such language users are able to deploy the names in sentences, and as used by them these names mean the same as they do when uttered by any respected historian of philosophy. It is clear that by 'Plato' these people mean Plato and by 'Aristotle' they mean Aristotle.

Such examples show that the individual language user rarely commands the necessary and sufficient conditions that must be fulfilled for some particular thing or individual to be the bearer of a name. For all that, when he uses the name he refers to the bearer. This is true not only of personal names but also when the names used are those of countries, towns, animals, places, mountains, rivers, and so on.

Now the nub of Putnam's insight is that it is not the individual language user who is the possessor of identifying knowledge but rather the entire linguistic community. Naturally, within the linguistic community knowledge about various individuals, geographical items, and so on, is very unevenly distributed. Some language users know a great deal about philosophers, including information that enables them to distinguish one philosopher from another. Other language users are comparably genned up about the cities of antiquity; others still about jazz musicians, classical composers, physicists, European royals, and so on. In virtue of this variety in the patterns of knowledge possession there is what Putnam calls a 'linguistic division of labour'. Some language users are purveyors of identifying knowledge about particular philosophers, others about the cities of antiquity, still others possess identifying knowledge associated with the names of jazz executants, classical composers, rap performers, and so on. But everyone who uses the name intends that his use should conform to the use of those in the language community who command the most specialized knowledge. That is to say, the body of language users intend that their use of the relevant name should pick out the same item as it picks out in the context of expert use and that it should do so on the basis of the same *Merkmale* in each case. The difference is that the non-specialist language user is not able himself to specify the distinguishing marks but implicitly defers, as it were, to those in the linguistic community best qualified to be the purveyors of such information. Enriched by this insight, the description theory comes a step closer to a more plausible and realistic description of how names work in our language. This theory is able to account for how it is that, despite our widely divergent epistemic backgrounds, we still speak the same language, assigning the same meaning to the words.

11. Let us consider now an objection to the description theory, one to which even the improved, collectivist variant is vulnerable. The objection is Saul Kripke's and may be illustrated by the following example.

It so happens that the individual known in the history of philosophy as 'Plato', and identified as the author of dialogues that include *The Republic*, *The Laws*, *Theaetetus* and *The Symposium*, was really named 'Aristocles'; 'Plato' was a nickname he acquired later. Giving imagination free rein, let us further assume that at the same time, tucked away in a garret in Athens there was an individual who really had been given the name 'Plato' at birth and who, by some extraordinary coincidence, spent all his time authoring philosophical dialogues that were identical, word for word, to those penned by Aristocles. None of this individual's works has survived, however: as a result of his reclusive life-style, his works and all other information about him were lost after his death.

On Frege and Russell's theories, the name 'Plato' refers in virtue of some definite description specifying the criteria that have to be met for a person in the actual world to count as the referent of the name. Such criteria would inevitably include the individual's being the author of works entitled *The Republic, The Laws, Theaetetus* and *The Symposium*, and, that he should bear the name 'Plato'. The person who in actual fact was given the name Plato – the hermit in the garret – satisfies more of the relevant descriptive criteria than the one named 'Aristocles' and so he would seem to be the individual of whom we speak when using the name 'Plato'. But our linguistic intuitions tell us that 'Plato' refers to the other fellow, the individual originally named 'Aristocles'. The loner in the garret is a complete non-starter as the referent of the name 'Plato'.

12. What implications do these objections have for the semantics of proper names? Surely, Frege and Russell's theory of the indirect reference of proper names passing via a definite description will have to be abandoned. It cannot be salvaged by adding in a thesis to the effect that proper names are not attached to *one* definite description but to a cluster of alternative descriptions, or through a shift from reliance on the individual language user's identifying knowledge to reliance on the knowledge that is possessed by the linguistic community as a whole. For it is possible to recast the objections so as to take account of the more complex descriptions of the meanings of proper names (interminable disjunctions of descriptions). And we can construct examples where not even the aggregated identifying knowledge of the linguistic community contains the means to distinguish one person from another – we did so with the Plato story.

But what, then, is to replace Russell or Frege's theories? Here disagreement reigns and there is, strictly speaking, no fully elaborated theory going, only a raft of proposals for a new theory of the meaning of proper names. We shall give an outline of the most prominent among them in the following.

13. Saul Kripke has argued that proper names refer directly to their bearers without the intermediary of a Fregean *Sinn*; thus, in one sense, heralding a rebranding of the label theory. The idea is that a particular name is attached to its bearer in a name-giving act, formal or informal. At a formal church christening the Jones's latest offspring is given a first name, say 'Leo'. Those attending the ceremony later disperse into the wider community and spread the name by talking about the young baby and its christening. By so doing they add the name 'Leo Jones' to their interlocutors' repertoires. Those thus appropriating it talk to yet others and they too pick up the name, which will end up spreading to large constituencies of language users who need not possess any definite identifying description that fits Leo Jones. But, as used by them, the name continues to refer to Leo Jones in virtue of the causal chain (a communicative chain) that goes all the way back from hearer to speaker to hearer to speaker until finally terminating in the baptismal ceremony. So a language user may rightly be said to use 'Leo Jones' of Leo Jones insofar as he uses the name with the intention of using it in the same way as those from whom he acquired it, and insofar as he does, his acquisition of it belongs to the causal-historical chain tracing back to Leo Jones's baptism.

Significantly, a theory of this kind differs from the label theory in that, instead of being identified with its bearer, the meaning of the name is identified with the historical-causal communicative chain that traces from the original baptism to the acquisition of the name by language users. To some extent this particular theoretical feature parallels the Fregean mode of presentation. There is, however, the crucial difference between them that whereas Frege conceives of the mode of presentation as something cognitive or informative, the historical-causal chain is not cognitive in nature. It represents neither knowledge nor skill (in identifying the bearer of the name) in the language user. For there is no guarantee that the user of a word can remember from whom he got it and whom he would need to contact in order to trace the communicative chain through which the name had passed before reaching him. (Let the reader select an arbitrary name from his repertoire and try to recall from whom he first acquired it.) Arguably, then, the meaning of the name contains an indexical element (i.e. a reference to a historical-causal chain in the actual world) irreducible to pure informational content.

This theory explains why, in our thought experiment, the name 'Plato' attached to the individual for whom 'Plato' was just a nickname and not to the Plato officially so named. For our story comprises a historical communicative chain (historical tradition) continuous with that same Plato and reaching down to the present day. It is this individual's writings that have been transmitted to us together with the name 'Plato'; this legacy has been passed on from one person to another through a time span of almost 2500 years. We supposed that the other Plato disappeared from the chronicle of the world without a trace; there exists no connection between the people who attended the ceremony at which he received the name 'Plato', and those who use the name 'Plato' today. Consequently, the name 'Plato' attaches to Aristocles and not to the recluse in the garret.

14. One species of name-giving ceremony is, then, the baptism or christening. Now the baptismal act, the historical-causal chain and the accession to hearers' repertoires of the relevant name are, however, insufficient to secure the efficacy of the name-giving in the sense of the name's being guaranteed continued use. Such efficacy requires certain background understandings that determine what it is that gets named in a baptismal act: it is precisely the infant that is given a name – not its hair, its nose or itself complete with christening gown so that another name comes into use if it has a change of clothes. The proper alignment turns on the implicit background understandings of the agents, not on the externals of the ceremony itself. For when the child is brought to the font so, too, is its christening attire, which also comes in for a sprinkling of water from the font. Only the background understandings of the participants make it the case that the clothes are not part of what gets baptized.

There needs, then, to be a general concept (a predicate) to pick out the proper object of baptism. The predicates are of the type referred to as 'common nouns' in chapter 1; exemplars include 'infant', 'person', 'cow', 'town', and so on. It is the infant that is christened, not the infant-*cum*-his-christening-gown; a ship gets named, not the-ship-*cum*-the-bottle-of-champagne-smashed-against-its-hull. The predicate is necessary, then, for the identification of the bearer of a name. All the same, that identification does not necessarily enter into the language user's understanding of the name. Let us assume that Jane picks up the name 'Leo' by hearing Leo Jones's mother say 'Leo was purring away happily in the sun this morning'. Jane gets the impression that Leo must be the family cat and so great is her surprise a few days later when her husband happens to mention that Leo next door is soon to start attending a crèche. So is Jane referring to Leo, the baby next door, when she says to her husband that he cannot seriously be talking about Leo? The intuitive answer is yes. But, obviously, this means that the predicate 'human being' does not figure in her understanding of the name since she believes Leo to be a cat. However that may be, Jane has acquired the name 'Leo' via a historical-causal chain grounded in an original baptism in which Leo Jones, and nothing feline, received a name, in that all those present understood perfectly that it was an infant that was being baptized and not a cat. This feature is bound into what Jane signs up to in using the name, but without its figuring in her understanding of the name.

15. But does that mean, then, that there are no constraints on a language user's knowledge of the meaning of a name if he or she is to be said to master its use? The answer is that a certain, unspecified minimum of knowledge is required. Arguably, to understand the name 'Albert Einstein' one would need to know that it was the name of a human being. For other names, a discerning user would need to know that they are names of cities, names of animals, events, and so on. The understanding of the name presupposes some familiarity with the relevant predicates involved. But no sharply delimited set is specifiable since, in contrast to the description theory, there is no sharp cut-off point distinguishing the possession of information that unambiguously identifies the bearer of the name from the failure to have such information. The causal theory allows one to argue that an individual's mastery of a name may be more or less competent or well grounded without prejudice to the claim that the name refers to a particular person. For the connection between name and bearer consists in the causal chain. Jane did indeed refer to Leo Jones when she used the name 'Leo' but her understanding of the name was clearly deficient.

16. Let us look at how the new theory resolves Frege and Russell's classic objections against the label theory.

a) Empty proper names. How does the new theory account for the fact that names without reference occur in meaningful sentences?
   Certainly, the theory resembles the label theory in not identifying the name's meaning with a description. But it also resembles the Frege-Russell theory in not identifying the meaning of a name with its bearer but, instead, with the historical-causal chain of communication, which proceeds from the grounding of the name in a baptism and passing from link to link, underpins the deployment of the name by current language users. So a name without a bearer is merely a name that is associated with a

historical-causal chain, and thereby with a meaning, but without the chain actually reaching back to any bearer.

Bearerless names evolve variously. In a given appellation a description (featuring indexicals) may be used to fix the reference of the name without, on that occasion, any object being indicated. In the nineteenth century, for example, astronomers believed that there must be a planet in orbit between Mercury and the sun whose gravity produced an anomaly in Mercury's trajectory, the so-called perihelion movement. These astronomers dubbed this planet 'Vulcan', computed its position, and then set about trying to sight it using telescopes. But no such planet was ever discovered. Alternatively, a language user acquires the ability to use a name, e.g. 'Santa Claus', through participation in a chain that is empty because the name is attached to a fictive character. Incorporated into the use of the name is the pretence that it designates in the normal way, just as in a theatrical performance where the actor 'acts as though' he is fencing or quarrelling.

b) Informative identity sentences. Here the solution parallels Frege's: the language user apprised of the truth of an identity statement linking two distinct names knows that while discrete communicative chains are associated with each name they home in on one and the same object. The difference here, however, is that the two paths that trace back to the bearer do not consist of information but of discrete historical-causal chains which lead to one and the same object. In certain variants of the position there is an implied predicate under which the items may be identified as being the same.

17. Unfortunately, its merits notwithstanding, the theory outlined above is flawed: it represents a retrograde step in our endeavour to give an account of the workings of names in contexts of use. The theories we have looked at so far each represent an advance on their predecessor in respect of showing how names actually function in communication, and the significance of that use. The label theory identified the meaning of a name with its bearer but left it mysterious how a speaker who uses a name in a sentence brings it about that his hearer identifies its referent. Russell and Frege's answer was that a name contains implicit information which unambiguously identifies a unique referent. But this solution runs into the problem of the heterogeneity of the descriptions that language users associate with the words, with the result that every use of language becomes vulnerable to systematic misunderstanding. We constantly run the risk of talking past one another; indeed, our

doing so is almost inevitable. Putnam's theory of 'linguistic division of labour' repaired this defect by embedding language use in a linguistic community which stands collectively as the repository of the knowledge to which individual language users implicitly defer. Semantic consistency is thus secured.

Now the causal theory of reference delivers an analysis of the semantics of proper names that separates reference from informational or cognitive value. It allows a name to stand for a person or item without its ever being clear how the user is able to convey the relevant information to another, thereby leaving it obscure how this person or thing comes to enter into the interlocutor's thinking about reality. Let us, for example, assume that a researcher in a monastery library finds a fragment of faded medieval parchment on which reference is made to one Joseph whose life was claimed by the Black Death. Obviously, this reference cannot secure a unique identification of Joseph since there were undoubtedly many people named Joseph who died as a result of the Black Death. We have no option, then, but to refer to Joseph as the person by the name of Joseph who was a victim of the Black Death and known to the author of the document. But since the author's identity remains obscure, the reference cannot be traced further.

This leads us to the following point: if the causal theory of reference is correct, then the parchment refers with precise particularity to a person by the name of Joseph and says of him that he died from the Black Death. But the information patently retrievable from the document by the researcher seems to amount to nothing more than the alleged fact that there once lived a person by the name of Joseph who died from the Black Death. *Which* of the many plague-stricken individuals the document refers to is not information to which the researcher is privy. The referential relation (the causal relation) may well pick out a quite specific person from amongst the many victims of the plague; but this identification is not ingredient in the information that the document communicates to the researcher.

Patently, then, the causal theory of proper names drives a wedge between the semantic relationship and informational content: in some situations, names can be said to refer to certain particular entities which lie beyond the cognitive reach of language users, even beyond their collective reach, and thus beyond the compass of their thought. The historian who reads the medieval document understands that there was an individual by the name of Joseph who succumbed to the Black Death, but it seems incorrect to say that there was a particular person (out of the innumerable Josephs who died in very similar circumstances) regarding whom the historian has information and whom he has in mind. None of these Josephs is distinguishable as the particular object of the historian's thought, for there is no recoverable route stretching back from the historian to some particular individual.

In response to these difficulties, various compromise positions have been proposed by Gareth Evans and others, combining features of the descriptive and the causal theories of proper names. The reintroduction of a descriptive element into the analysis of proper names is intended to close the gap between reference and informational content to which the causal theory gives rise. There is no reason to go into the details of these proposals here since they present no theoretical novelty; they constitute an attempt to refine the strands of earlier theories so as better to effect their assimilation to our semantic intuitions. Suffice it to say that in the outworkings of these positions, the theory of proper names (and of other singular terms) has moved steadily in the direction of more comprehensive and more realistic descriptions of that complex socio-linguistic practice into which such terms enter. The narrowness and abstractness of the classical positions have finally been overcome.

However, there have also been more radical responses. Certain philosophers, chief among them Michael Dummett, have criticized the naïve intuitive concept of reference which is used as a standard for the assessment of rival proposals. Dummett would concede, with respect to the example used above, that we might very well find it intuitively correct to say that the name 'Joseph' the historian encounters in the document refers to a particular individual identified as one standing in a particular causal relationship to its author. But he argues that we should reject this conception of reference and accept that reference extends no further than what the means available to the linguistic community – the contemporary linguistic community, note, and not its hypothetical counterpart that comprises both living and defunct language users – is capable of establishing. The attribution of a referential function to a name under conditions where this principle is not met finds its sole justification in the conjecture that someday identificatory information will turn up. In the default situation, the name remains empty. A concept of reference that transcends the compass of language in its role as an instrument of communication and thought is a fiction.

Once such arguments are brought into play, what appear to be reflections on a rather narrow topic soon find themselves embedded in a broader context that embraces the relationships between language, reality and thought in general. While, in order to test several candidate theories, the preceding analyses of the concept of reference appealed to our intuitive ideas about the reference of certain sentences and made those ideas a touchstone, their criterial adequacy is thrown into doubt once they themselves are subjected to scrutiny from broader philosophical perspectives. These latter are exemplified by Dummett's reflections on what kind of knowledge has to be ascribed to a language user for us to be able to say of him that he grasps the semantics of his language. These problems are ones we do not have the space to explore in depth in this book although we shall be touching on them again in chapter 11. Having canvassed the treatments of singular terms and reference advanced in the most recent theories of language, and having noted how the issues surrounding their analysis ultimately link into wider topics involving the relation between reality and thought, we shall leave the discussion at this point.

Chapter 4

Predication

1. In the previous chapter, we examined how singular terms perform their linguistic role, which is that of *identifying* particular entities, typically those existing in time and space, such as persons, geographical locations, and so on. We stressed that such identification cannot occur in isolation, but only in the context of a speech act, the utterance of a complete sentence. Hence, the meaning of singular terms is their contribution to the articulation of the success conditions of the sentences in which they occur, amongst which conditions truth conditions are theoretically salient. We turn now to the roles played by other parts of speech, the most important of which are *predicates*. 'Predicate' is a technical term covering both common nouns and adjectives. In chapter 2, we offered a very general hint of what the linguistic role of predicates is, viz. that of *classifying* objects referred to. Now it is time to examine in detail how that role is performed.

Since the process does not entirely duplicate the parsing of sentences taught at school, we need to begin by giving an account of how, on the standard philosophical approach, sentences are broken down into their semantic components. In the preceding chapter we did indeed proceed much as we would in traditional sentence analysis, for we looked at singular terms, which roughly correspond to what we would pick out as nouns. The next step, on the grammatical analysis, would be to turn our attention to verbs. However, verbs do not figure as an important independent category in philosophical semantics, and so we make no use of that category here. Instead, our focus will be predicates, for verbs are largely absorbed by predicates in our analysis. We shall begin by taking a brief look at how this is contrived.

If we use the verb to classify sentences, one way of sorting them into two classes immediately suggests itself: there are sentences featuring the verb 'is' (including inflections such as 'am/are', 'was', 'has/have been', and so on, and excluding its role in expressing the progressive aspect of other verbs) and there are those which contain all other verbs. The first class is exemplified by such sentences as 'Peter is happy', 'London is bigger than Edinburgh', 'The polar bear is an endangered species', and so on, and the second by sentences such as 'Peter works in the city', 'The president declares war', 'The polar bear feeds mainly on fish', and so on. In the first set of examples a predicate is explicitly attributed to one or more items while in the second set the sentences seem to exhibit a different semantic form. We are not going to worry about the linguistic function of this distinction but need merely to note that it makes no difference to the philosophical analysis of meaning: to that end, all the sentence samples are construed in terms of predicates attributed to certain things and persons. That such a construal is possible becomes clear from the fact that we can convert the above sentences into a form that makes the attribution of a predicate quite explicit: 'Peter is working in the city', 'The president is declaring war', 'The polar bear is mainly fish-eating'. These conversions may not be elegant and may not have exactly the same import as the original sentences, but it is intuitively plausible to say that such transformations can always be performed and that nothing essential to the meaning of the original sentence is lost in so doing.

The philosophical analysis of sentences proceeds under the generally accepted assumption that the variety of syntactical patterns that sentences exhibit may be replaced by one and the same predicative form. Only a few sentence types are exceptions to this claim, such as those asserting existence or identity. Quantified sentences, i.e. sentences of the form 'All ... are ...' or 'Some ... are ...' turn out to be derived from sentences of predicative form, as we shall see in chapter 5. Sometimes, instead of attributing a property to one thing, sentences express relations between entities. These too may be subjected to predicative analysis through the introduction of many-place predicates, such as 'x is the giver of y to z' or 'x is sitting between y, z and r'. The result is sometimes a clumsy locution as with 'Peter is the giver of a kick to Paul' instead of 'Peter kicks Paul'. But nothing in the meaning of the sentence is lost in that rephrasing; or so it is assumed.

All this means that the role of the verb in the sentence is much diminished, and it will not be subjected to further analysis in this book. We are left, then, with the inflections of the verb 'to be' whose function is that of coupling singular terms and predicates in sentences such as 'The polar bear *is* fish-eating', 'Peter *is* drowsy', 'Uncle *is* the giver of the book to James', and so on. This function is traditionally designated the *copula*, which is the Latin for 'coupling'. ('Is' may also be used to express existence and identity but that too lies outside the compass of our current inquiry.) Now in the light of what was said in chapter 2, we are able to see what this 'coupling' amounts to: it consists in predicates and singular terms occurring together in an assertion or some other utterance. So it is more enlightening to say that the word 'is' (inclusive of its inflections) signals the presence of an utterance (an uttered sentence), as opposed to the mere concatenation of singular terms and predicates.

There are further distinctions familiar from the classroom teaching of grammar which go untreated in standard philosophical and logical uses of the term 'predicate'. One is the distinction between *adjectives* and *common nouns* (noted above). The first group includes such words as 'red', 'poisonous', 'hungry', 'democratic', 'old', 'eight-cylinder', 'arthritic', and so on. To the second belong such words as 'stag', 'whale', 'camper', 'screwdriver' *in so far as* they occur in a predicative role. This they do in sentences such as 'The animal killed by the hunter was a stag', 'He arrived in a camper', 'For this job you need a screwdriver'. Common nouns are also known as 'count nouns' which reflects the fact that in using such a term F we can always ask: How many F's are there? – that is, How many dogs/bushes/fire-extinguishers/saucepans/fishes/penknives, and so on, are there? This sets count nouns apart from adjectives, with respect to which the corresponding question hardly makes sense: the query, How many salts/reds/warms are there? allows no precise answer, at least not in the absence of a disambiguating context.

The term 'predicate', then, is employed in philosophical analysis in a way that abstracts from the differences between these parts of speech, and we adopt the same usage in this book. This is not to say, however, that the distinction between adjectives and common nouns is immaterial in all philosophical analyses; indeed, its significance will become apparent later in this chapter. The point here is merely that in our usage of the generic term 'predicate', this distinction is disregarded.

2. In chapter 1, we saw that in philosophy predicates have often been construed on the model of referring terms, which stand for concrete items. This assimilation poses certain difficulties, however, a few of which were touched upon in that early chapter. What might seem to qualify as the likeliest candidates for the referent of a predicate like 'red' or 'rhinoceros' are the members of the classes of red things and rhinoceroses respectively, i.e. the sum total of red things and rhinoceroses existing in the past, the present and the future (the *extensions* of these expressions). But the assignment of this role to predicates would appear to lead to the assignment of the same meaning to all "empty" predicates, i.e. all those that have no application: the class of unicorns becomes identical with the class of mermaids, namely the null set. And yet sentences about unicorns do not have the same meaning as sentences about mermaids. A related problem arises if we say that the term 'blue whale' has the same meaning as 'the largest animal that has ever existed' on the

ground that the two terms pick out the same class. But these two expressions plainly do not mean the same.

Offhand, there would appear to be a ready answer to this challenge. Even though the expressions 'unicorn' and 'mermaid' both stand for the null class, they do not, we might say, mean the same because the two predicates are analytically resoluble into simpler ones, with their several extensions. A mermaid is a creature with the upper body of a woman and a fish's tail while a unicorn is a horse-like creature with a spiralled horn projecting from its forehead. The two predicates are defined, then, by using simpler predicates with non-empty extensions: woman+upper+body+fish+tail and horse+horn respectively. By the same token, the term 'blue whale' does not have the same meaning as 'the largest animal that has ever existed': the two expressions involve disparate simpler predicates with their several extensions. The former expression 'blue whale' involves the predicate 'mammal', whereas the latter expression does not.

The idea here, then, is that were we to break down complex predicates such as 'mermaid', 'mammal', 'bus' into the simpler predicates that enter into their definition, we would always end up with predicates which have a non-empty extension. For ultimately our analysis of complex predicates is bound to lead us to predicates that have been defined through what is called ostensive definition: a particular item is pointed out and the information is provided that it falls under a certain predicate. (As when we say: 'This shade is known as sepia'.) Alternatively, all terms would have to be defined by reference to others, but such a process would lead to circularity and to language never hooking up with the world. It would seem to follow from this that when we analyse complex predicates we will always end up with terms that have positive extensions. For you are only able to point to something in giving its definition if that thing exists – you cannot point to a non-existent item.

On the face of it, this solution sounds plausible. But it loses some of its credibility when we realize that it closely replicates an unsuccessful attempt to solve the corresponding problem surrounding proper names: we recall Russell's theory. It swiftly becomes clear that the problem of "empty extensions" parallels that of "empty names" addressed in the previous chapter; and by the same token, the solution we are considering here matches that offered by Russell's theory, which has it that names are implicit descriptions of what they denominate. The claim that 'unicorn' means the same as the expression 'horse-like animal with a spiralled horn projecting from its forehead' falls into the same category as the claim that the name 'Aristotle' means the same as the definite description, 'the philosopher who was Plato's pupil and the teacher of Alexander the Great'. We looked at the difficulties facing this theory in the previous chapter and have reason to expect a similar theory for predicates to run into the same problems. Indeed, our current predicament is worse, since we are now being asked to define the predicates in question on the basis of simple terms, definable only by ostension. What simple ostensive predicates would jointly capture the full meaning of such terms as 'animal', 'culture', 'politics', 'philosophy', or 'society'? There are scarcely clear answers to be had here.

3. A second difficulty facing the extensional definition of predicates resides in the fact that it makes all sentences that contain predicates true or false in virtue of their constituent words or, to use a technical term, it makes them *analytically true or false*. We normally distinguish between sentences that are true or false in virtue of the meanings of the words, and those whose truth or falsity does not depend on the meanings of the words alone but also on the way the world is. Thus the sentence 'All bachelors are unmarried' is true in virtue of the meaning of the words since it is implicit in the concept of 'bachelor' that they are unmarried. By contrast, the truth or falsity of the sentence 'All bachelors have unhealthy eating habits' is not determined by the meaning of the words, that is, by how 'bachelor' is defined; its truth-value cannot be established through an analysis of the concept of a bachelor but only by an empirical study of bachelor diets.

Now if predicates were to be defined extensionally, the definition of the predicate 'bachelor' would be given by a list of those individuals who are bachelors. Accordingly, a sentence like 'Peter Johnson is a bachelor' would either be analytically true or analytically false in as much as its truth or falsity is determinable by discovering whether the name 'Peter Johnson' figures in the list of bachelors. The same would apply in the case of a sentence like 'All bachelors have unhealthy eating habits', for its truth-value could be determined by checking out the lists defining the predicates 'bachelor' and 'has unhealthy eating habits', respectively, to see whether the individuals registering on the first list also figure on the second.

Finally, the extensional mode of definition is inadequate to the task of giving an account of the functioning of predicates in a language. The specification of the meaning of a predicate by reference to a class of things that exhibit a particular property is adequate so long as all we are interested in is being able to distinguish the predicate in question from other predicates. We can thus specify the meaning of 'red' in contradistinction to 'green' or 'square' by making inventories of red, green or square things respectively. This method does not serve our needs, however, if we want to account for what predicates have *in common as linguistic instruments,* i.e. what their particular function in language is, as distinct from that of definite descriptions and proper names. For it is clear that by making an inventory of the things which have the property red, we are not delivering an explanation of the difference in function between the predicate 'red' and singular terms. We might say 'The meaning of the predicate 'red' is what all the things on the list have in common.' But this tells us nothing about what distinguishes the functioning of a predicate from that of a singular term.

4. In order to overcome these difficulties we will now turn to some expressions in language where there is no temptation at all to think that they refer to "things" (we alluded to such words in chapter 1.). They are words such as 'not', 'and', 'or', 'if-then', and so on. We shall see that our treatment of these expressions furnishes us with a model for understanding the workings of predicates.

To understand how these words function, we shall begin with the word 'not'. It patently does not stand for any concrete item: neither a mental entity in the speaker's mind nor anything existing in the external objective world, nor even in some third realm of Platonic ideas. What, then, is the role in language played by the word 'not'?

The following exchange offers us a hint:

  A: 'It rained yesterday.'
  B: 'No.'

B's utterance in this context has the same meaning as the sentence 'It did not rain yesterday'. This is because the word 'No' relates to the sentence uttered by A and performs, as it were, an operation upon it, namely, the operation of negation. When one sentence is negated, the result is a different sentence whose truth-value is the opposite of the original. If the original sentence 'It is raining' was true, the utterance 'No' is false, and vice versa.

Indeed, sentences containing the word 'not' could be expressed by using the word 'no': instead of saying, 'It will not rain today' we could say, 'It'll rain today, no'. The latter sounds like a variety of pidgin English, which while grammatically non-standard remains understandable and, indeed, wholly unambiguous. In this sentence the word 'no' stands outside the sentence 'It'll rain today' and expresses the operation of negation as performed on this sentence in the same way as in the brief exchange above.

The close connection between the words 'no' and 'not' allows us to analyse the latter in the same way. The function in sentences of the word 'not' is not that of designating or identifying any such entity as "not-ness", but of performing an operation on the sentence in which it occurs.

The applicability of this analysis extends to a large number of the other expressions which, as we saw in chapter 1, neither denote particulars nor are predicates. A word such as 'or' denotes nothing but specifies an operation on sentences. This operation too is definable by reference to the truth-values of other sentences. If we interpose 'or' between two sentences the result is a compound sentence which is true if at least one of its constituent sentences is true and otherwise false.

This relation is made clearer when expressed schematically in a so-called truth table as shown below (Tables 4.1 and 4.2). Furthest to the left above the horizontal line are two sentences symbolized by the letters 'p' and 'q'. To their right is a sentence comprising what are now subsentences conjoined by the word 'or'. The letters in the rows below ('t' = true, 'f' = false) indicate how the truth-value of the compound sentence depends on the truth-value of each of its components. Each row reads from left to right and tells us that if the truth-value of each component is as specified, that of the compound sentence is as shown. Similarly the preposition 'and' expresses a relation between the truth-values of component sentences as illustrated below.

Table 4.1 Truth table for 'or'

p	q	p or q
t	t	t
t	f	t
f	t	t
f	f	f

Table 4.2 Truth table for 'and'

p	q	p and q
t	t	t
t	f	f
f	t	f
f	f	f

These expressions are what logicians call *functional expressions*: they express relationships between sentences. The compound sentence has a truth-value which is a function of – i.e. is dependent on – the truth-values of the constituent sentences. Words like 'not', 'or', 'and' and 'if then' are termed *connectives* because they connect sentences and do so by expressing in each case a relation between the truth-values of the sentences they connect. (This does not strictly apply to 'not' which attaches to a single sentence.)

5. Before going any further we need briefly to remark on the concept of a *function*, which has already been invoked to describe the role of certain linguistic expressions. Basically, a function is a relation between distinct items.

A telephone directory, for instance is (the transcript of) a function, namely the function that assigns phone numbers and addresses to the names of subscribers. The same applies in the case of a pizzeria's list of takeaways, where the assortment of pizzas on offer are listed with their respective prices: the function assigns a price to each type of pizza.

The concept of a function is drawn from mathematics, where it plays an important role: equations, for instance, may be regarded as functions. Equations such as $y = x^2$ are functions uniquely relating one number to another number in accordance with a rule. The equation $y = x^2$ expresses a correlation between a given number x and the square of that number, i.e. the number multiplied by itself. In mathematics the ordering constitutive of a function is referred to as a *mapping* of one group of things onto or into another, and this is sometimes expressed as follows: $f: x \rightarrow x^2$, where the arrow reads 'mapped onto or into'. The ordering in a function may thus be said to have a direction, expressible by means of the arrow. We start with a given value x and correlate it with another value, in this case the square of x. In mathematics the set of elements being mapped is called the function's *domain*, while the set onto which it is mapped into is called the *value range*. In the case of the function $f: x \rightarrow x^2$ the domain might be the set of all numbers with the value range as the set of all positive numbers.

The functions designated by the expression 'not' and 'if then' (and its equivalents such as 'on condition that', and so on) are called *truth-functions*. This is due to the fact that the function's domain and range each consist of truth-values, which is to say that they are simply functions from truth-values to truth-values. A truth-function takes the truth-value of a sentence or of an ordered set of sentences, and maps it onto a new truth-value. Accordingly, the operation 'not' is defined by its assignment of the truth-value true to the value false and the value false to the value true. This formula exhausts the semantic content of the word 'not'.

6. Using this conceptual apparatus, we may proceed to analyse predicates in a way that avoids their construal as names of abstract entities. The idea originated with Gottlob Frege. We simply regard a predicate such as 'intelligent' or 'red' or 'a living being' as a function that assigns the referents of singular terms to truth-values or, alternatively expressed, that makes the referents of singular terms the domain and truth-values the range. The function is invoked when the predicate and the referring expression are conjoined in a sentence. The resultant sentence will be either true or false with each sentence correlated with a 't' for true or an 'f' for false to indicate which of the two obtains. We can say, then, that the predicate 'intelligent' or 'red' or

'mammalian' is specified by this function. We can put this more perspicuously by systematically inserting the referring expressions of the language into the sentence schema '… is mammalian'.

The result is as follows:

	… is mammalian
Einstein	t
Mount Everest	f
Sylvester Stallone	t
Bobby the gorilla	f
Big Ben	f
The world's greatest author	t
And so on.	

The idea informing the procedure is that by taking each thing in the universe, inserting the singular term designating it into this schema and then recording the resultant truth-value (either 't' or 'f'), we get the determination of the predicate's meaning (leaving to one side for the moment predicates with empty extensions).

It is important to recognize what makes this mode of definition different from that criticized in section 3 of this chapter. There each predicate was defined by reference to a list of the items to which it applied. The difference between that and the above schema is that the latter shows how a predicate functions in the context of a sentence: it makes manifest the very character of the predicative function. The predicate interacts with another sentential component, a singular expression, so that they conjointly determine the truth-value, either true or false. This aspect is absent from the traditional extensional approach, which merely yields a list corresponding only to the column on the left side of the above schema. The functional analysis, by contrast, shows what the predicative role consists in: predicates are functions mapping the references of singular terms onto truth-values.

If this account appears somewhat technical, it is worth remembering that, in essence, it is merely a formal way of representing the process of *classifying things*, which is what predicates do. By attaching the labels 'true' or 'false' to sentences that link entities up with predicates, we engage in the business of classification, using language as a means. Classification might proceed without the involvement of language, e.g. by items being sorted into two groups, red things going into the one and non-red things into the other; but linguistic labelling is a very convenient way of achieving the same aim. Recall what was said about the role of predicates in chapter 2: human survival depends on our acquiring the ability to classify things, sorting them into categories such as edible/ toxic, suitable/unsuitable for hut construction, and so on. Predicates serve as linguistic tools that facilitate this procedure.

This observation should prompt the thought that there must be more to be said about predication than what is captured by the purely "functional" or "combinatorial" schema above. There needs to be an account of the conditions that have to be satisfied for predicates to perform their classificatory role. We shall provide elements of such an account below. But first we must attend to some worries surrounding the functional theory just presented. For although this theory disposes of many of the difficulties that were highlighted at the beginning of the chapter, some problems still remain.

7. One of the problems still with us springs from the co-extensionality of expressions such as 'blue whale' and 'the largest animal that has ever existed', as well as 'unicorn' and 'mermaid'. The difficulty is that predicates cannot be determined solely by reference to the *actually existing* things to which they apply. A term such as 'blue whale' cannot be defined by listing all currently existent blue whales, since this in itself does not distinguish them from 'the largest animals that have ever existed': the class of blue whales and that of the largest animals that have ever existed is one and the same. And as regards the other two expressions, there exists nothing whatsoever to which they apply. This would seem to pull us once again in the direction of a Platonic interpretation of predicates, for it would appear that what determines a predicate's meaning is not the contingent concrete things to which the predicate applies but some kind of abstract metaphysical entity rather: Platonic Forms or universals.

Note, in this connection, the affinities between the problem that we are now addressing and that which Frege's distinction between *Sinn* and *Bedeutung* was designed to solve. Frege's problem was that a sentence expressing identity of the type 'The Morning Star is the same (object) as the Evening Star' ought, on a purely referential theory, to be as uninformative as the sentence 'The Morning Star is the same as the Morning Star'. By the same token the sentence 'The blue whale is the largest animal that has ever existed' ought to be no more informative than the sentence 'The blue whale is the blue whale', since on the referential (extensional) theory of meaning they carry identical semantic contents. Philosophers from Plato onwards have advocated a theory of predication that purports to solve the difficulty through the claim that predicates do not refer to concrete things, their extension, but to abstract entities, universals. The thesis has it, then, that the expressions 'blue whale' and 'the largest animal that ever existed' refer to two different universals.

8. But perhaps there's a way of dispensing with the need for such dubious entities. Perhaps it is possible to retain the idea that a predicate such as 'horse' simply picks out those good old quadrupeds that can be ridden on and used to draw carriages, and to drop the whole idea of arcane, otherworldly entities as the Form of the Horse. Of course, the concept would have to designate not only the horses that actually exist, will come to exist or have existed, but also *possible* horses, horses that *would have* existed, on the realization of various hypothetical scenarios. For instance, we should plausibly be able to say that if those superb racehorses Schubert and Mary had produced offspring, these latter would, without doubt, have made first-class racehorses. In making this assertion, we could say that we were referring to possible horses, horses that would have resulted from a breeding programme that was in fact never implemented.

Introducing possible individuals enables us to solve the problem of the extensional coincidence of 'blue whale' and 'the largest animals that have ever existed'. For while co-extensionality does indeed obtain with respect to actually existent beings of these types it is easy to conceive of *possible* creatures belonging to the one class but not the other. It is conceivable that there once existed prehistoric reptiles even larger than the enormous creatures whose fossilized remains have been identified, larger even than the blue whale. The class of possible beings envisaged as the largest animals ever to exist is thus distinct from the class of blue whales. Obviously, then, the term 'blue whale' and 'the largest animals that have ever existed' have different meanings.

This approach to the problem has been taken up with enthusiasm by a number of philosophers who, adopting its core intuitive idea, have elaborated an ambitious and complex semantic doctrine, commonly referred to as 'possible world semantics'. This doctrine is thought to hold the key not only to the status of universal predicates but also to that of modal terms, psychological attributions, and other items which, as we shall see, create difficulties for extensional semantics. This semantic theory, with its attendant metaphysical picture, deserves a chapter all to itself. We shall take a closer look at it in chapter 7.

9. Here we shall turn our attention to an alternative proposal purporting to solve the problem of the semantics of predicates. It agrees with the preceding account in holding that only particulars exist and that nothing universal in

nature confers semantic content on general terms such as 'red', 'cucumber', and so on. But the proponents of this alternative approach are deeply sceptical of the notion of 'possible entities' featured in the account sketched out above. They regard such posits as sheer metaphysical constructions which, instead of shedding light on the workings of language, assume that these are already well illuminated. They maintain instead that whatever universality there is owes itself entirely to human powers of *abstraction*. Predicates such as 'red', 'cucumber', and so on, are the result of the operations of the human capacity of abstraction on the similarities obtaining among individual items. Consequently, what these predicative terms really designate is an element inherent in the process of cognition, namely, *general concepts*. In a sentence like 'The sun is red', 'the sun' refers to a celestial body whereas the term 'red' refers to nothing in the physical world but to an element in human thought, namely the concept 'redness'.

This purported solution, traditionally called *conceptualism*, may be seen as a refinement of the theory of ideas championed by Locke and his fellow empiricists. As in Locke, meaning is seen as essentially mental, figuring as a constituent of human thought. Still, this theory marks an advance in sophistication on Locke's somewhat naïve version, which conceived of ideas as images in the mind. Here concepts do not count as objects at all but as capacities or powers rather, manifested by those who possess them. To possess a concept is to possess a particular intellectual skill. The cognitive skill an individual evinces in his grasp of the concept 'red' consists in his ability to pick out red things, to classify items as red or otherwise – e.g. by sorting them into piles of red and non-red things respectively.

Thus conceptualism also offers an answer to the question of the special role of predicates, as against that of singular terms. It starts with the uncontroversial observation that predicates serve to *classify* things, in particular those things designated by singular terms. In the sentence 'The sun is red', the singular term 'the sun' identifies a particular celestial body and the term 'red' classifies this item as one belonging amongst those that have the same colour as sunsets, freshly boiled lobsters, ripe tomatoes, and so on.

Construing predication as classification is hardly controversial and might not even appear to distinguish conceptualism from the functional theory (in the mathematical sense) sketched above. But while the functional theory conceives of classifications as finished sorting operations, representing, as it were, the *outcomes* of the process of classification, conceptualism focuses on the activity itself, or rather the capacity to engage in it. An attractive feature of this theory is that on it such classifying capacities are themselves particular – Peter has a distinct capacity to classify red things which is distinguishable from Paul's and Vera's ability to do the same. Were he to suffer a stroke, Peter might lose his capacity while Paul and Vera would retain theirs. Conceptualism is thus able to avoid the quagmire into which Locke descended by declaring certain ideas in themselves to be general. A concept is general in *application* only in the sense of being applicable to a vast number of things, and potentially to an infinite number. Another attractive feature of conceptualism is that it apparently explains the differential meanings of the predicates 'blue whale' and 'the largest creature that ever existed'. For the power to classify things according to whether or not they are blue whales is clearly different from the ability to classify things according to their size.

All the same, a problem arises for conceptualism at precisely this point. For the relevant taxonomizing capacity cannot cover *actually* existent things alone, but must take in possible things as well, otherwise the account will be wanting. If we have to explain what it is that enables someone to grasp the difference between the sentences 'Bess is a unicorn' and 'Bess is a mermaid', it avails us nothing to appeal to a capacity to classify existent unicorns and mermaids since there are no such entities. Dividing the world's contents up into those things that are mermaids and those that are not would be to replicate the separation of things that are from those that are not unicorns: the first class will be empty and the second would contain everything that exists. To account for the individual's understanding of the relevant sentences we need to be able to refer to his capacity to classify *possibles*. But then, of course, we are back with the notion of possible things. Conceptualism is not, after all, an alternative to the account which deals in hypothetical entities or possibles, but would seem rather to presuppose it.

There exists a traditional theory of general terms that may profitably be viewed as a distinctive version of conceptualism. This theory is *nominalism*, a position first developed in the context of medieval debates about the existence of "universals" (general ideas). According to nominalism, there exists no universal entity in which all particulars denoted by one term e.g. 'horse', participate. There is simply the fact that all such items are referred to by the use of the same expression, 'horse'. Language use alone, then, possesses universality.

If it is maintained that an individual's mastery of a general concept resides exclusively in his capacity to use the appropriate linguistic term, nominalism follows from conceptualism. This contrasts with the broader definition given above, which takes in non-linguistic acts of classification. In any event, nominalism is vulnerable to the same objection as that raised there: in order to solve the problems attaching to the co-extensionality of such expressions as 'blue whale' and 'the largest animal that has ever existed' the application of these terms has not only to be general but must also extend to *potential* members of these classes. It is not enough that the term 'blue whale' denotes a class of entities, namely, all the blue whales that have existed, exist today or will exist in the future, since it is very likely that this class has the same extension as the expression 'the largest animals that have ever existed'. To show that these expressions have different semantic contents it is necessary (and sufficient) to refer to *possible* or *hypothetical* items that show up the differences.

Moreover, the nominalist's purported solution is threatened by circularity. For on his account, the only universality to be had is that governing the use of the same word tokens, e.g. 'horse'. But there does not exist just one individual word 'horse' used by all language users (speakers of English) in the sense, say, of its being inscribed on some sort of official plate, needing to be procured from the authorities and displayed in some way every time a speaker wishes to say something about horses. The term 'horse' is in itself a universal entity which comprises all the particular uses of the word that have been made by individuals in the past plus those that will be made in the future. But then we have to ask wherein the generality of the word 'horse' consists. Does it consist in the fact that utterances of the word participate in a universal entity, the Form of the Word 'Horse', or can the nominalist's explanation also do duty here? This latter has it that the only feature all utterances of the word 'horse' have in common is our using the same word, the word (expression) "the word 'horse'" to describe those utterances. Now if we opt for this account we shall never arrive at an explanation that goes to the root of the problem, for the nominalist will go on introducing new universal words without the universal use of each of these words ever being explained.

10. We shall leave the discussion about the relationship between extension and meaning for the time being; we shall be returning to it in chapters 6 and 10. Instead we now return to the functional or "combinatorial" model of predication set out in section 6. As already indicated, that model does not *exhaust* what can be said about predicates; in particular it fails to take account of the fact that predicates come in several different varieties and that some of them have distinctive features that go beyond what is captured by such formal analyses. These features will only become apparent on a closer examination of the conditions of use of the various classes of predicates.

Let us begin by looking at a class of predicates which, in their conditions of employment, have certain features in common with proper names: we have in mind the so-called *natural kind terms*, an important focus in the work of Hilary Putnam and Saul Kripke. 'Natural kind' terms designate types of entity whose differentiae as a particular species of thing are given by the natural order. The most perspicuous examples are biological species comprising individuals which not only look alike but are related in virtue of their descent from common ancestors and interbreeding. Thus, terms such as 'horse', 'beech', 'Tyrannosaurus rex', figure as natural kind terms. But chemical substances too constitute natural kinds with 'water', 'coal', 'alcohol', and so on, all counting as natural kind terms.

The possession by natural class terms of special semantic properties was a feature vividly demonstrated by Hilary Putnam using the following thought experiment. Take a natural class term like 'water'. An obvious way of defining '… is water' would be '… is a colourless liquid without taste or odour which freezes at 0 degrees Celsius and boils at 100 degrees Celsius'. But let us now imagine that an expedition leaving earth for outer space arrives at a remote planet where the party comes across a liquid, which, initially, they take to be water. It exhibits all the qualitative properties of water: it is colourless and odourless, freezes at 0 degrees Celsius and boils at 100 degrees Celsius. We can envisage this liquid being as much like water as anything could be, and can go on to imagine the planet populated by humanoid beings for whom water plays the same role as it does for us: it is in their taps, they drink it, and die if they have to go without it for any length of time.

Now imagine further that a chemical analysis reveals that this substance does not have the chemical structure H_2O but another, which we shall call XYZ. If this happens the expedition will conclude that they had been mistaken: the observed substance was not water but merely something closely resembling it. This conclusion shows that the nature of water is determined by its underlying structure, and not by its observable surface properties such as colourlessness, odourlessness, and so on. Or, more accurately: the characterization of water is given by the underlying nature of that colourless, odourless liquid *found here on earth*. Our use of the term 'water' enters into a practical nexus with a particular complement of the colourless and tasteless liquid occurring in the universe, namely, that encountered on earth, and which exhibits a particular molecular structure, H_2O. Consequently, any superficially similar liquid discoverable elsewhere in the universe is water if and only if it shares the chemical structure of the colourless and tasteless liquid found *here* on earth. We can pinpoint it further: the word 'water' as we use it today traces back, via a chain of communication, to the original linguistic practice of employing the term 'water' *here* on earth. That practice involved exemplars of liquid with the formula H_2O, and not XYZ (even though at that point the two would have been indistinguishable to language users). This is why 'water' refers to H_2O, not XYZ.

Notice the parallel to the way in which proper names function on Kripke's account, which we examined in the preceding chapter. For all his lack of familiarity with any description that uniquely fits Napoleon, a language-user using the name 'Napoleon' refers to a particular individual. This is because his use of the name traces back to its use by those capable of identifying Napoleon – indeed, ultimately to those who were present when he was given a name. The language-user connects up to those individuals via an unbroken causal chain of communication. Similarly, a person on earth refers to H_2O, not XYZ, whenever he talks about water, despite his being incapable of telling them apart. Again, his reference owes itself to a chain of communication going back from his use to those individuals who were the first to coin the term 'water'. Their use of the word was aimed at picking out a particular liquid here on earth, which, as we know, is H_2O.

Natural kind semantics distinguishes a very important group of terms in natural languages that designate kinds of things which we believe to share the same underlying structure. However, these specific natures are not ones we have always been capable of recognizing and their recognition was certainly beyond the powers of our distant forebears who originally named the various sectors of reality. For although we pick out natural kinds by focusing on their surface properties, such as water's lack of taste and odour, we do not judge these features to be definitory of the relevant natural kind terms. Instead, we seek to identify the specific underlying structure and make whatever this proves to be determinative for the use of the term. But note that it is only the structure as correctly identified that qualifies for that role: should we subsequently discover our determination of the underlying structure to be erroneous, we modify the characterization of the concept accordingly. Thus even today, it would be incorrect to say that 'water' is *defined* as *meaning* the same as 'the liquid constituted by one oxygen and two hydrogen atoms (H_2O)'. For were scientists to discover that the chemical composition of the liquid found in rivers, lakes and oceans had been misidentified since it proved not to match the formula H_2O, we would not declare water to be non-existent: we would say that we had discovered that the formula for water is not H_2O – which of course we would be barred from saying had water been *defined* as H_2O.

The affinity between the determination of natural kind terms and the semantics of proper names, then, may be expressed by saying that the former perform the function of picking out a natural kind just as proper names do particulars (a person, material object, geographical location, and so on.) A natural kind is picked out by being that which is traceable through a communicative chain going back from a given utterance of a natural kind term (like 'water') until arriving at the point where this term was first introduced into the language. (It must always be borne in mind that the utterance of a term cannot be understood in abstraction from the context of the utterance of *complete* sentences.) This feature sets natural kind terms apart from such simple universal predicates as 'red', 'bent', and so on. The semantic content of these latter is captured by their functional or combinatorial aspect; in other words, once we have specified, in terms of a schema like that appearing in section 6, how they contribute to the determination of the truth-conditions of sentences in which they occur, there is nothing further to be said about their meaning.

11. We have repeatedly made the point that an acceptable semantic model for the various parts of speech must be *abstractive*: it must specify the meaning of words in terms of the contribution they make to the determination of the success conditions of sentences of which they are constituents. This is not to say, however, that a specification of meaning is always accomplishable solely by means of a functional schema of the kind given in section 6 of this chapter. Not all words in the language have meanings, i.e. truth-value contributions, that are *exhaustively* accounted for by such a schema; the meanings of most words have aspects that go beyond what is capturable by some formal regimentation. The meaning of the word 'not' is indeed exhausted by a simple truth table, but the same does not apply in the case of names such as 'Napoleon Bonaparte' or predicates such as 'water'. To explain how they contribute to the truth conditions of the sentences in which they occur, a more elaborate account needs to be given.

The distinction is illustrated by the fact that the semantics of singular terms contrasts with that of predicates whose semantic role is exhausted by a formal functional analysis, with natural kind predicates figuring as a hybrid form. In a sentence such as 'The Eiffel Tower soars up' the meaning of the expression 'Eiffel Tower' is, as we have seen, dependent on the existence of a chain of communication going back to a particular existing thing, namely, a particular architectonic structure in Paris. In their semantics, proper names such as 'Plato', 'the Eiffel Tower', 'Paris', and so on, feature distinctive references to reality, inasmuch as these expressions are in part defined by their being ingredient in a linguistic practice in which the terms are traced back to a name-giving ceremony or similar determination of meaning that involved contact with the named item. No analogue to this is found in the meanings of abstract predicates such as 'spherical' or 'thousandfold': their meaning is specifiable without reference to any localized object or class of objects in the world. The expression 'spherical' would be meaningful irrespective of whether there had ever existed spheres in the world; its meaning is given in terms of an abstract mathematical definition. The semantic status of natural kind terms such as 'water' and 'electric' lies somewhere in between these two groups. They presuppose no *particular* existents since water is a substance widely dispersed across this planet, and any of the separate occurrences of the liquid would have served equally well in the naming ceremony. All the same, 'water' and other natural kind terms are defined relative to the particular sorts of thing found on our planet as distinct from what might be found in other regions of space.

To avoid any misunderstanding, it needs to be stressed that the *truth* of a sentence naturally presupposes the existence of items corresponding to its semantic constituents. The distinction elaborated above concerns only the meanings of expressions. For a sentence of the form 'a is spherical' to be true, something must exist that possesses the property of sphericity. The point to note is simply that the *meaning* of the sentence may be specified without reference to any particular thing or class of things that satisfies the predicate 'spherical'. Moreover, it may be true that human beings could never come to acquire certain simple predicates – the colour blue, for example – in the absence of experiencable blue things. But this is a fact of epistemology, not of semantics. It is moreover a contingent fact, since it is at least coherent to imagine a world in which the names for portions of the colour spectrum were innate.

12. The earlier sections may have left the reflective reader somewhat mystified. For it begins to look as though reality is constituted of entities designated by singular terms (and perhaps natural kind terms), period: nothing is designated by predicates of the type 'red' or 'spherical'. This is indeed the view that certain philosophers urge us to adopt: only singular terms carry existential import, and such terms refer only to individuals. A philosopher of this persuasion is Willard Van Orman Quine, who prefers, however, to express the point in terms of the ontological commitments carried by the quantified sentences which would replace singular terms in a fully regimented logical idiom. There is never any need when seriously engaging in metaphysics to refer to properties and relations and so accord them the status of existents. This austere metaphysical picture would seem to stand in stark contradiction to manifest aspects of our experience, however. For there is no separation in our experience between the way in which a particular thing – a rose, say – presents itself to our sensory appreciation and the way in which a thing's strictly universal properties – the rose's redness, its configuration or

its fragrance – is present to us. Both are equally palpable and observable. But in the analysis given above, the latter is robbed of all existence, only the rose itself is real.

However, such mystification would result from confusing the workings of certain linguistic categories with an ontological thesis, a thesis about what the world comprises. The above account deals with the functioning of singular terms, natural kind terms, and strictly universal predicates, in language. It is not an account of the constitution of the world – of what sorts of things are to be found in it.

We anticipated this point in the previous chapter when we pointed out that names are not self-standing but presuppose a complete language in which whole sentences are uttered. It is impossible to conceive of a tribe that only uses proper names and never whole sentences: it is impossible to conceive of the application of names such as 'Margaret Thatcher' or 'Albert Einstein' without their being embedded in a complete language. But it does not follow from this that those two individuals did not exist antecedently to names being conferred upon them. The analysis set out above concerns language, not the reality it describes.

The same thing applies in the case of strictly universal predicates. We will now elucidate this point by means of a less trivial example. We will provide a brief sketch of an alternative way of describing the world, one not reliant on distinctions between singular terms, natural kind terms and strictly universal predicates – which distinctions produce a world occupied solely by particulars and nothing else. The point of the exercise, which borrows heavily from the writings of Peter Strawson, is to throw further light on the interrelated semantic roles of singular terms and predicates.

13. Consider such terms as 'gold', 'snow', 'coal', 'water', 'rain', and so on. In traditional grammars these are often referred to as 'mass terms', which are neither singular expressions nor predicates. A singular term denotes a particular individual thing of a given type, in contradistinction to others of that type. This does not hold of a term such as 'gold': it refers to anything that qualifies as 'gold'.

But nor is it correct to regard it as a predicate. For 'gold' is not a common noun like 'dog' or 'bush'. As noted previously, in the case of common nouns we can always ask: How many F's are there? But we cannot similarly ask: How many 'golds' are there? Our question has to be: How *much* gold is there? This explains the differentia of 'mass terms': they apply to masses and quantities, not numerable items.

Mass terms are also distinct from adjectives such as 'yellow' or 'heavy'. Gold is distinguished by various properties but is not itself a property. Offhand, there might appear to be a case for regarding gold as a complex property in which the simpler properties of yellowness, weight, malleability, and so on, are simply fused. But such an idea conflicts with the fact that while things are made of gold, it hardly makes sense to say that an item of jewellery is made of yellowness, weight and malleability.

Why do we use mass terms? The answer is given by what the simple test shows: that what falls under common nouns is countable, whereas what falls under mass terms is not. The referents of common nouns are clearly bounded individual items, typically defined by their possession of a definite shape (and partly by size). To be a dog, a carrot, a motorbike, a tree, is to be distinguished, *inter alia*, by the possession of a particular shape: a shape outlining a functional whole, an integral individual entity. A horse is a creature with a clearly identifiable physical form. If a horse or a car is split in two, it loses not only its characteristic shape but also most of its functions. A bisected horse is not the sort of thing that can pull a cart, and a car in two halves will not take one very far. This means, then, that the question of how many specific exemplars are present at a given time and in a given place is one to which a definite answer can always be returned.

The same plainly does not apply in the case of 'coal', 'snow', and so on. True, it is not difficult to introduce terms indicating a sort of measure when referring to gold, coal, snow, and so on, as the referents of mass terms and as specifying rough amounts: we speak of a *lump* of gold, a *seam* of coal, and so on. But there is no natural boundedness here because there is no characteristic form. The boundedness displayed by a lump of gold represents no functional unity that is forfeited if cleavage takes place. Split a lump of gold in two and the result is every bit as much a case of lumps of gold as the original was – even if each has a lesser value.

But while mass terms are in practice linked to particular kinds of phenomenon, they can also be applied to other things albeit, typically, without the same degree of naturalness. Take the terms 'cow' and 'bull' which are patently common nouns. English also includes the term 'cattle', which is a mass term. 'Cattle' is used of cows and bulls when they occur in large numbers and thus designated they manifest, en masse, features similar to those picked out by mass terms. For even though cows and bulls present their own characteristic physical integrity, which is enough to secure an unequivocal answer to the question 'How many?', we have the option of regarding them as an aggregate in circumstances where the exact number of individual exemplars present is of no consequence. What we have in such cases is first and foremost a 'herd of cattle', displaying nothing more in the way of natural size or configuration than lumps of gold do. Notice too how we can shift from the mass term 'cattle' to a common noun by referring to 'a head of cattle' even as we refer to 'a lump of gold'.

Properties too are describable using mass terms. Instead of conceiving of properties as abstract general entities qualitatively inherent in concrete items, we can identify them directly by using mass terms. Instead of saying that there were many red things present we might say that there was a lot of red to be seen. We use this mode of description when we say things like: 'This painting needs some red to offset the subdued tones'. In making that remark, we are referring not to red daubs or other red *things* but to red as such. (Obviously, 'mass term' is not a good name for these qualitative terms. For red, in contrast to what is designated by typical mass terms like 'gold' and 'snow', is not a massy entity. But we will retain the term here to highlight the connection between the logical character of such terms and typical mass terms like 'gold'. We will refer to the former as 'qualitative mass terms' to signal the distinction.)

A crucial difference between qualitative mass terms like 'red' and 'flat' and the corresponding predicates lies in the way in which we pick out or identify what they designate. When using mass terms we identify these entities by virtue of their localization in space. Let us imagine an interior designer who on surveying a room remarks 'We need a splash of white here to create a more harmonious balance'. On this description no discrimination is made among what white *item* might secure the desired harmony: whether it be by the introduction of a white sofa, a white carpet, a white painting or simply a pool of white light produced by a spotlight. In mass term vocabulary, these are all specified in the same manner, by reference to 'a splash of white here'. By contrast, when using a predicate vocabulary we have to say that there are different *things* that are white and that the white object in the corner is different from its predecessor since now the white sofa has been replaced with a white rug. In consequence, a predicative vocabulary runs into certain difficulties in cases in which the white in question is the effect of a spotlight, for then there is no white *item*. Contrariwise, if the difference is merely that some other white object now occupies the corner, in the vocabulary of mass terms the situation remains unchanged: it is still the case that 'there's a splash of white in the corner'. No discrimination is made between the individual white *items*, because here whiteness is not conceived of as a property inhering in particular items but as a feature of reality in its own right. (Of course, 'splash' is a count noun, but this does not compromise the status of 'white' as a mass term.)

The point we are concerned to bring out here is that so long as we are using a language that operates only with mass terms, colours are just as concrete as that which singular terms designate in a richer language. When we say 'there is a splash of white here' we are talking about a feature of reality which is observable and touchable; it can even be moved as when we alter the angle of the spotlight. There is no reference to abstract objects such as the class of all white things or to the 'property of whiteness'. It is, then, not an inherent feature of colours or analogous features of reality that they are abstract in themselves: they are so as a result of the way we categorize them in language.

Once we move from a lexicon comprising mass terms to one including singular terms and predicates an asymmetrical transformation of the two categories of mass terms occurs, with those such as 'gold', 'cattle', and so on, falling into one group and purely qualitative instances into another. The former get carried over into the class of common nouns such as 'cows' or 'bulls' and 'lumps of gold' which may then enter into the composition of singular terms such as 'the dappled bull over there' or 'Daisy the Cow'. These terms apply to concrete things that may be pointed to and touched. Qualitative mass terms, by contrast, are transformed into (qualitative) predicates, ontologically dependent on the items whose properties they are. Pointing to the property as such, for instance redness, or hardness is no longer an option; they have become abstract entities with no location in space. But one can point to the concrete red *thing* whose property redness is. It is this relation of dependence that comes to expression in the claim that (strictly universal) predicates simply stand for functions while singular terms stand for concrete items. This is a feature of subject-predicate language, however, and not of reality.

It is possible, then, to describe reality on a simple level prior to any distinction being drawn between items denoted using referential terms and the abstract properties inhering in them to which predicates refer. Reference and predication arise through a logical transformation of this simple level of description. This point serves to remind us that reference and predication are linguistic functions and not features of non-linguistic reality.

14. In this chapter our aim has been to account for the meaning of predicates by considering the role they play in whole sentences. The notion of truth conditions, and the way predicates contribute to their determination, played a crucial role in our story; but it turned out that an adequate picture of predication and, in particular, one capable of doing justice to the differences

between various kinds of predicates, required our advancing beyond a purely functional, Fregean account.

In what concerns the ontology of predication, we have examined attempts to specify the semantic content of predicates without drawing on anything other than the objects to which the predicates apply, and so without assigning to the predicates themselves distinct referents, with "universals" as the prime candidate.

It turned out, however, that the meanings of predicates are not susceptible of determination solely by means of a list of the concrete, existent items to which they apply. The semantics of an expression such as 'blue whale' cannot be specified by cataloguing existent blue whales since any such list fails to distinguish the term from the expression 'the largest animal that has ever existed': the list of blue whales and that of the largest animals (belonging to the same species) that have ever existed is one and the same. We need to consider *possible* animals as well. Now patently, we can certainly imagine a dinosaur larger than the blue whale. This is sufficient to show that it is purely accidental that the two predicates 'blue whale' and 'the largest animal that has ever existed' apply to the same things, and it becomes immediately clear that they have differing semantic contents.

To an influential modern school of semanticists, this is not only a demonstration of the inadequacy of extensionalist semantics, but actually points the way to a better theory of predication. The proposal advanced from this quarter enjoins us to take seriously the notion of possible items falling under a concept, extrapolating it up to the idea of an entire world populated by possibles. Hence we get the programme referred to as 'possible world semantics'. We shall return to this programme again in chapter 7 and subject it to critical scrutiny.

Chapter 5

Theories of truth

1. The concept of truth has lain at the heart of the analysis of linguistic meaning presented in the foregoing chapters. It is now time to sharpen our focus on this concept, which has been the subject of intense critical scrutiny in recent philosophy. We shall be examining the most important amongst the many theories of truth framed by philosophers throughout 2500 years of grappling with the problem. If the credentials of none prove sufficiently cogent, it would seriously compromise the viability of a theory of meaning based upon the concept of truth.

It is important to be clear about what is meant by a theory of truth. A theory of truth is a theory of what truth is or, alternatively, of what something's being true consists in. It is not a theory of how truth is arrived at or of what the criterion for success is on that score; such questions belong to epistemology, whereas questions about the nature of truth are part of metaphysics and the philosophy of language.

The question of the nature of truth can in turn be understood in two ways. It may be construed as a question about what 'truth' or 'true' means. Or, alternatively, it may relate to the essence of truth, with the suggestion that this is something other and deeper than what is captured by a dictionary definition of the term 'true'. In themselves, dictionary definitions offer scant enlightenment. An analogy (one echoing our discussion of natural kinds in chapter 3) will illustrate this. If you ask what water is, you may be requesting a dictionary definition of the term 'water' and be satisfied with the answer that it is 'a colourless, odourless, tasteless fluid found on or near the surface of the earth'. But the question could equally well be a request for a more exact, chemical specification of what water is, in which case you would want to be told that water is a chemical compound whose molecules are composed of two hydrogen atoms and one oxygen atom (H_2O).

The theories of truth that we shall be looking at in this chapter most closely approach the definition of water that gives the specification H_2O. Now obviously, this is an analogy that must be handled with caution since truth is not a chemical substance, nor is it similarly formulaic. But there are parallels all the same. When science specifies H₂O as expressive of the constitution of water it is because the assumption that it has this composition enables us to explain its chemical and physical properties. By the same token, in seeking to answer the question about the nature of truth, we are after a characterization of the notion that will elucidate the totality of contexts in which we refer to it in language and thought: we want one that explicates the features that truth evinces in these contexts. Truth, as we shall understand it here, is a property of sentences or sentential utterances. In other words we shall prescind from 'truth' as a property in other senses, as when we speak of 'true friends' or 'true love'.

The contexts relative to which truth is characterized can hardly themselves be exhaustively specified without appeal to the notion of truth. So fundamental is the latter that it is impossible to descend to an even deeper level to identify other, simpler and more primitive concepts in terms of which truth can be defined. It would be futile, then, to insist on the non-circularity normally required of competent dictionary definitions. This does not mean that every characterization of truth will be devoid of content, for any such characterization involves other concepts that contribute substantively to its characterization: truth links into a conceptual framework that helps elucidate it. Nor is this approach undermined by the fact that that framework is incapable of exhaustive definition without appeal to truth itself.

We distinguished between the question of what truth is and that of how truth is established, which is to say, how it may be ascertained which sentences or beliefs are true. The two questions are not identical: it is perfectly possible to conceive of a theory of the nature of truth without that providing any guide as to how truths are ascertained. This holds of the correspondence theory, as we shall see below. Conversely, the separation does not preclude answers to one question also serving as answers to the other. The coherence theory of truth, for example, returns parallel answers to the two questions, as do the pragmatic theory of truth and the consensus theory. All the same, the two questions remain discrete.

2. There are certain properties attaching to the concept of truth which are so uncontroversial and intrinsic to it that they can be said to impose constraints on any analysis of the concept. The most important of these is expressed by the equivalence thesis, which specifies that the declaration that a sentence is true is equivalent to its assertion. More formally, it says that for any sentence p, 'p' is true, if and only if p. (It would be more correct to say for any sentence p, the result of putting that sentence into quotation marks is true, if and only

if p.) Thus: 'The sunset is red' is true if and only if the sunset is red; 'Ostriches hide their heads in the sand' is true if and only if ostriches hide their heads in the sand; and so on.

There is a notable property attaching to truth that the equivalence thesis brings out. For it highlights the fact that truth may be predicated of a sentence ad infinitum and any resultant sentence will be equivalent with the original sentence. If 'p' is equivalent to 'it is true that p', 'p' must also be equivalent to 'it is true that it is true that p', and to 'it is true that it is true that it is true that it is true that p', and so on. Irrespective of how many times the "truth predicate" is added to a given sentence, only one sentence will have been asserted. This is known as the 'iterability' of the truth predicate: it is always possible to 'iterate' the predication of truth and the result of so doing is equivalent to the initial assertion of the sentence. We shall see that this trivial property of the truth predicate is not without potency: it exposes certain dubious theories of truth.

Another important feature of the concept of truth, and so a feature that a theory of truth must be capable of explaining or, at the very least, of not contradicting, is the circumstance that we (normally) aim at attaining true conceptions of reality and eschewing false ones. This might seem so obvious as neither to need nor admit an explanation. But as we shall see in what follows, there are theories of truth that are able to explain this and ones so framed that this feature becomes inexplicable.

We shall consider six different theories of truth: the correspondence theory, the coherence theory, the consensus theory, the pragmatic theory, the semantic theory and the redundancy theory.

3. The classical theory of truth is the *correspondence theory*, which has it that the truth of a sentence consists in its correspondence with reality.

On a commonsense understanding of it, this theory can scarcely be contested. For to say that a sentence "corresponds with reality" need only be a roundabout way of saying that it is true. There is no constraint on the speaker making that claim to have any very precise idea of what it means for a sentence to "correspond with reality". But by the same token, no light is shed by it on the concept of truth. The challenge to the correspondence theorist will inevitably be to give a substantive and non-trivial characterization of what this correspondence consists in. To what, then, does a true sentence correspond, according to correspondence theorists? The traditional answer has it that the sentence corresponds to a *fact*. That the sentence 'It's raining' is true means that it corresponds to the fact that it is raining. Generalized, it follows that a true sentence 'p' corresponds to the fact that p.

But for all its commonsense credentials, this theory has been the subject of vigorous attack. The contention has sounded that it is completely vacuous and so bereft of any explanatory power. The problem, according to its critics is that there simply is no class of things or phenomena that is captured by the term 'facts'. When someone says 'It is a fact that Labour was returned to office with a huge majority', the speaker does not commit himself to the existence of a special class of items, *facts*, to one of which the sentence about Labour happens to correspond. He is simply saying that the sentence is true, albeit somewhat emphatically. Instead of saying 'It is a fact that Labour was returned to office with a huge majority' he might have said 'It is indisputable that Labour was returned to office with a huge majority'.

The existence of this link between facts and sentences is brought out by the circumstance that facts cannot be individuated other than by reference to the sentences that purport to express them. There is no way of identifying the fact that Labour was returned to office with a huge majority than precisely by using the locution 'The fact that Labour was returned to office with a huge majority'. For instance, you cannot literally point to a fact in the same way as you might point to a thing or person in indicating the reference of a proper name. A person who says 'Allow me to point out to you the fact that …' does not do any pointing at all but utters a sentence which identifies the fact.

According to its critics, the theory of truth as correspondence with the facts results from a misconceived idea of how language functions in clauses such as those beginning 'It is a fact that …' Philosophers have assumed that this locution picked out a rather special sort of entity in the world, whereas properly understood it is a linguistic device by which the speaker expresses a high degree of confidence about what he is saying, and this is its sole function. Philosophers have not, then, uncovered a special sort of item in the world – facts – that may be used to explicate the concept of truth.

4. The difference in the relationship obtaining between facts and sentences on the one hand, and that between names and things on the other, arguably points us towards a different and more apt formulation of the correspondence theory. Perhaps our mistake has been to start from the relationship between a whole sentence and reality, whereas it might have been a better strategy to focus on the constituent parts of a sentence and study the relations between these and the world.

The theory of meaning in the earlier chapters might provide the ground plan for such a theory. There we divided sentences up into singular terms and predicates and discussed how each sentential component connected to reality. Perhaps the concept of truth might be characterized through predicating it on these sets of relations.

To illustrate this line of thought, we do well to begin with simple subject-predicate sentences of the type, 'The house is red'. On any particular occasion of utterance, the word 'house' refers to a particular house whose identity is provided by the context. The house in question can be identified and pointed out independently of the use of this particular sentence. In other words there exists a segment of reality to which the term 'the house' can be said to correspond: the term refers to it. In chapter 3 we gave a detailed account of this referential relation.

But what about the predicate 'red'? We have already seen that predicates have extensions, the counterparts of the referents of singular terms. The extension of the word 'red' is the class of red things. Now it might feel intuitively right to say that the predicate 'red' corresponds to reality if and only if reality is able to muster a non-empty extension for the expression. But this is hardly an appropriate response to the question being addressed here. For it would mean that the predicative part of the sentence 'The house is red' and that of the sentence 'Poppies are red' correspond with the same aspect of reality. And this is not satisfactory from the point of view of the correspondence theory. The correspondence theory presupposes that the predicate 'red' in the sentence 'the house is red' corresponds to some concrete aspect of the-house's-being red, something getting no mention in the sentence 'Poppies are red'.

What we want is a way of getting the individual redness of the house to figure in the truth conditions of the sentence. A solution to this quandary has been presented in the form of the so-called 'trope theory'. According to this theory, properties of things are individual entities, as individual as the things they inform. Two apples on a branch might be so close to each other in colour as to be indistinguishable in this respect; all the same, the redness of one apple is not the same redness as that possessed by the other. If one of the apples gets eaten, its redness is no more, but the other one and its individual redness – its individual instance of redness – remains. This item is the *trope*.

So the solution proposed here is as follows. The truth conditions of the sentence 'The house is red' consists in the item referred to by the term 'the house' being somehow linked to the item (the trope) referred to by the term 'red', which is the house's individual redness. The truth conditions of the sentence thus involve a connection between two independently specifiable items. In identifying the individual instance of redness, we do not have to refer to it as the redness of the house, thus making our sentence a mere verbal truth; we might, for instance, identify the expanse of colour by pointing to it, or by giving its spatial coordinates.

Unfortunately, this simple solution will not work. The chief problem from our point of view is that the trope theory fails to deliver a general account of the logical form of subject-predicate sentences. Trope theory leaves us with a stratum of subject-predicate sentences for which no analysis has been provided. This is, of course, the stratum of sentences describing the tropes themselves. Take the sentence, 'This trope is red', which must certainly be recognized as legitimate by the trope theorists. How are the truth conditions of this sentence to be specified? Are we to say that the trope's being red consists in its being associated with a further trope, which furnishes the first trope with its colour? We are clearly into an infinite regress. The standard answer from trope theorists is that the link between a trope and its property is just a simple, unanalysable fact. But this answer is patently ad hoc; and anyway, if it is valid, it is hard to see why it failed to deliver an analysis of the original sentence, 'The house is red'. Why not say that the truth condition is just the fact of the house being red, and draw a line under the discussion at that point?

5. To advance to a better answer we need to go back to the simple language described in chapter 4, namely, the language of mass terms. As our discussion revealed, there are aspects of reality describable in this language and they are present whenever sentences such as 'the house is red' is assertible; there is something one can point to in any such situation, namely 'this red', where the red in question is not picked out as the property of a thing but is apprehended as an independently existing feature, as when someone points to an instance of water and says, 'this water'. It is beyond question such things exist. They can be photographed, touched and measured; they can also be destroyed or painted over.

It might be objected that each time there is something referable to as 'this red', there is, indispensably, a *thing* that is red; so the mass term is not independent of language that refers to things and predicates properties of them. This objection, however, is misconceived; it is not a conceptual truth that there must always be some item that is the bearer of those features of reality we describe in qualitative mass terms. Admittedly, given the way the world is, that is most often the case in our environment, but there are exceptions. You can point to the sky above the horizon just after the sun has set and exclaim 'Just look at that beautiful red!' without pointing to any *thing* that is red – no more than we talk about a *thing* when we say that the sky is normally blue.

So we get the following preliminary result: a plausible reading of the correspondence theory is possible if we conceive of the relevant correspondence as obtaining not exclusively at the level of sentences and of facts, but as obtaining between the components of sentences and their relations to items in the world that figure as the constituents of facts. To deliver such a picture, we need to have recourse to the language of mass terms.

It is no objection to this account that it does not provide a synonymous analysans of subject-predicate discourse. Obviously, a sentence such as 'There is red on this house' is not strictly equivalent to the sentence 'The house is red'. But the purpose of the account was not to establish semantic equivalence, but merely to point to certain facts in the world upon which subject-predicate facts supervene and without which they would not obtain. Obviously, in describing the latter in terms other than those of subject-predicate we are offering an alternative with a slightly different import. But the cost of insisting on equivalence of meaning would obviously be the delivery of a vacuous theory, which would, trivially, identify the truth-conditions of the sentence 'The house is red' with the house's being red.

Thus the correspondence theory can be invested with plausible content if we view correspondence between language and reality as obtaining not, primarily, at the level of the sentence, with sentences purportedly referring to a special class of thing, namely facts, but instead at the level of terms. In a sentence, both the singular term and the predicate have correlates in reality, namely a particular thing that the singular term refers to, and a particular aspect that may be picked out by means of mass terms.

In previous chapters, we were concerned to make the point that neither reference nor predication can be understood independently of their function in complete sentences. We stressed the fact that we can think of reference achieved by means of a singular term concatenated with a predicate characterizing the relevant referent as constitutive of a complete speech act. Two implications follow. First, that the correspondence theory proposed here should not be construed as operating exclusively at a sub-sentential level; the sentential level and the sub-sentential level (the level of reference and predication) are inextricably interwoven. Second, as we have already pointed out, the concept of truth is incapable of determination without appeal to concepts which, in their turn, involve that of truth. Speech acts are defined in terms of their success conditions, central among which are truth conditions. Now, conversely, we define the concept of truth by means of the concepts of reference and predication which are bound up with that of assertion and hence of truth.

That this relation of interdependence does not deprive the proposed correspondence theory of content is owed to the fact that the theory appeals to a broader conceptual scheme. For instance, the characterization of the semantics of singular terms contained more than the mere claim that singular terms contribute to the determination of the truth-values of sentences in a way capturable by a functional schema alone. An account was also provided of what it means to identify an individual object as the referent of a singular term, an account involving, amongst other things, reference to a causal-historical chain of communication and a community of language users. In the previous chapter we were likewise engaged in describing how the application of a predicate presupposes a particular setting involving the world, language and a community of language users, a setting whose description drew upon a rich vocabulary, far exceeding the bare notion of truth.

Finally, a brief remark is called for to prevent misunderstanding. In attempting to discover what corresponds to the predicate in a true sentence, the aim of our search is not that of chapter 4 where we sought to identify the *meaning* of predicates. Obviously the meaning of a predicate cannot be determined by anything that corresponds to it in the sense just proposed for a predicate has a *general* meaning not exhausted by anything connected with it on particular occasions of use. We saw in the previous chapter, however, that the meaning of a predicate cannot be determined even when we appeal to its full extension: to achieve an adequate determination we must also include hypothetical or possible instances. Whether this mode of definition is satisfactory from a broader metaphysical perspective is an issue we leave open for the present.

6. Has the theory of truth sketched here general validity? It might be suspected that it only applies to simple subject-predicate sentences of the type 'The house is red'. What sort of extension would the analysis require if it were also to embrace negative sentences, say? To what does a sentence such as 'The house is not red' correspond? Let us imagine that the house is yellow; does the predicate in that sentence, '... is not red', correspond to the colour yellow? Even if we return an affirmative answer, we would have to say, in the same breath, that it does not correspond to the colour yellow in the same way as does the predicate in the sentence 'The house is *yellow*'. It looks as though 'corresponds to' means something different here.

We are given a hint of how to solve this problem by the observation we made in chapter 4 to the effect that the word 'not' appearing in a sentence does not stand for something in the way a name does. Consequently we must abandon the idea that a sentence such as 'The house is not red' corresponds to reality in the manner of 'The house is red'. For there is a component of the sentence, namely the word 'not', which is essential to the sentential meaning, but to which nothing in the world corresponds. In that same chapter we noted the sentential role played by 'not': that of bringing about a change in the sentence's truth condition. The sentence 'not p' is true when 'p' is false, and false when 'p' is true.

This suggests an answer to how we should construe the correspondence of a negative sentence with the world. We can simply say that the sentence 'non-p' corresponds with reality precisely when 'p' does *not* correspond with reality. Thus we are not giving any independent characterization of what it means to say that a negative sentence corresponds to reality but are defining it relative to the correspondence of the relevant positive sentence; it represents the negation of this positive correspondence.

The analysis of correspondence for the word 'not' can be straightforwardly generalized to apply to the other connectives dealt with in chapter 4. Take the disjunction, 'either p or q'. Of this sentence too it must be conceded that it fails to correspond to reality in the way that 'p' or 'q' do. Both the sentence 'New Labour is in power' and the sentence 'Either New Labour is in power or the Tories are in power' is true if it is the case that New Labour is in power; but it is obvious that the latter disjunctive sentence does not correspond to reality in the same way as does the former. The solution is again to define correspondence for 'p or q' relative to the correspondence relation obtaining for 'p' or for 'q': 'p or q' corresponds with reality if 'p' corresponds with reality or 'q' corresponds with reality, or if both do. The analysis can be straightforwardly extended to cover other connectives such as 'if then' and 'and', and the same goes for other expressions in the language. (A later section dealing with Tarski's theory of truth will show how this is achieved technically.)

Another issue concerns the question of whether the proposed analysis is transferable from sentences which deal with a concrete subject matter to more abstract kinds. What corresponds with the sentences of mathematics? And what corresponds with subjunctive conditionals such as, 'If the Soviets had not backed down in the Cuba crisis, a nuclear world war would have ensued'? And how about modal statements such as, 'It is possible that there existed dinosaurs even larger than the blue whale'? And how can we fit the statements of ethics, or aesthetics, into the correspondence mould?

There are two main routes that we can proceed down. One is to adopt a staunchly realist interpretation of sentences of these kinds. This means that we see them as relating to an independent reality which they purport to reflect. In chapter 7, we shall be examining the notion of possible worlds, held by many philosophers of language to deliver the metaphysical foundation of such a realist interpretation of some of the sentential categories mentioned above.

The other route involves the denial that in using sentences of these categories, we are engaging in truth-making at all, strictly speaking. Statements in ethics and aesthetics do not purport to report facts about the world but are uttered with other ends in view, such as that of guiding action. Nor do counterfactual conditionals and modal statements purport to describe reality but express aspects of our epistemic condition.

These are large issues and we cannot treat them adequately in this book. The point we want to stress here is that in applying a theory of truth to these categories of sentences, what is up for assessment is not only one proposed definition of truth, but also certain everyday assumptions as to which parts of our discourse have a truth-making remit (assumptions that have not gone unchallenged by philosophers). These two issues must be treated in tandem. Our conjecture is that, in the picture eventually to emerge, a suitably refined correspondence theory of truth will have a secure place and will contribute to the identification of those parts of discourse that are properly construable as truth-making.

In conclusion, two brief comments on the correspondence theory: first, the theory offers a simple and convincing explanation as to why we want to be in possession of true conceptions of reality. For if such beliefs correspond with reality and so yield information about it, they are useful instruments in the navigation of the environment in which we are set and conduct our lives.

Second, it must be emphasized that the correspondence theory is not a theory about how truth is discovered. The correspondence between thought/language and reality is an immensely abstract relationship which holds no key as to how it may be established or demonstrated. The correspondence theory is a theory about what truth consists in and not an epistemological theory offering an account of how truth is discovered.

7. The correspondence theory's traditional rival is the *coherence theory*. The coherence theory was born of the scepticism felt by some philosophers about the likelihood of a satisfactory description of the relationship existing between sentences and reality that the correspondence theory presupposes. Instead, the coherence theorists formulate truth as a relation between sentences. To say that a sentence is true is to say that it fits with the largest set of sentences between which agreement obtains.

We can illustrate this line of thought as follows. Let us imagine that everyone is asked to write down on slips of paper all the sentences they believe to be true – one sentence per slip. We then proceed to sort these slips of paper so that all the ones that are mutually consistent, those that can be true simultaneously, go into the same pile. We will discover that there are many ways in which the sentences can be assembled into piles. And we will further discover that the size of the piles varies according to how we conduct our sorting. Let us for instance imagine that we are occupied with that part of a pile that has to do with European history in the twentieth century. If, by mischance, we put a slip into this pile on which it says that the Germans did not murder a large number of Jews during the Second World War (as certain ultra-radical historians have claimed) there will be innumerable other slips of paper that have to be left out: namely, all those on which the survivors of the massacres tell of their experiences, or on which the allied soldiers who freed the survivors recount what confronted them, or slips describing footage presumed to have been shot in the camps, and so on. These sentences are ineligible for inclusion in the pile because they contradict the original sentence. We now realize that our pile would swell if we simply reject the slips that deny the Holocaust, and admit all the others. This is precisely what the coherence theory invites us to do: we are to seek to assemble our slips in such a way that we get the largest pile possible. The resultant pile represents the truth. For an individual sentence to be true is for it to belong to this maximal pile.

A standard objection against the coherence theory is that it admits of no distinction between truth and fiction. According to the coherence theory, if an author creates an imaginary world as Tolkien does in his books, the sentences delivering the narrative depict a reality, or would do if Tolkien's descriptions of this fantastical realm were more comprehensive than the existent descriptions of the actual world.

We have, however, already rebutted this objection in virtue of the way we specified the coherence theory. Coherence should not be construed as a relation between sentences in general but between sentences that are in fact believed. But very few readers actually believe in the sentences in Tolkien's works. In consequence, the existence of comprehensive fictional universes does not threaten the coherence theory of truth.

This answer sparks a fresh question. According to the coherence theory as just formulated, what is required of us is not that we assign truth to the sentences that cohere with most others, but only to those sentences that cohere with sentences which one already believes. But if this process is ever to get off the ground there have to be sentences that a person believes independently of their coherence being established. On plain commonsensical conceptions of truth there is no doubt that such sentences exist and which they are: they are sentences believed to be true because affirmed by the deliverances of our senses. If a person directs his gaze to a tree directly in his visual field in broad daylight, he can scarcely avoid forming the judgement that there is a tree before him, he has no choice in the matter and no theoretical reflection is going to help him. Nor does he need to start wondering whether the sentence coheres with other sentences to which he gives credence.

The critical question, however, is whether the coherence theory is able to account for this fact. Sensory observation consists in a thing causally affecting us (through our sense organs) in such a way that it gives rise to a conception of how the world is constituted. Now this sounds like a theory that fits very neatly with a correspondence conception of truth, for it says that there is a real world out there and that the truth of any given sentence consists in its agreement with that world. But then truth can no longer be said solely to reside in the connections between sentences: the additional claim has is that sometimes people interact with reality in a way that induces particular conceptions of the world in them. Thus in their attempts to save the coherence theory, its exponents have moved a considerable distance in the direction of the correspondence theory.

The coherence theory also illustrates the fact that truth cannot be defined without appeal to concepts which imply truth in and of themselves. The coherence theory enjoins us to identify the largest possible set of mutually compatible sentences among the set of sentences that we believe. But what does 'sentences that we believe' mean? It can hardly mean anything other than 'sentences we believe to be *true*'. The concept of truth is already implicit in the definition of truth. In fact, circularity enters into the coherence theory in the very characterization of the theory's identifying concept. That a set of sentences is coherent means, at minimum, that the conjunction of all or some produces no contradiction. And this in turn, according to the standard definition in logic, means that it is possible for all these sentences to be *true* together.

As we saw with the correspondence theory as set out above, such circularities are not necessarily fatal. Fatality threatens only if the circle is very tight through truth's being defined exclusively in terms of another concept x, with this concept being defined exclusively in terms of the concept of truth. If, instead, the circle is capacious and rich in conceptual content, the characterization of the concept of truth may well be substantive, its circularity notwithstanding.

The coherence theory also offers a rationale for our high valorization of truth. The advantage of being possessed of true conceptions is that it aligns the agent's conceptions with those of the majority who entertain conceptions about some given matter. But even though this is one part of the advantage offered by true theories it is not all of it or even the most important part. The most important consideration is that the agent's conceptions comport with reality itself. This is an advantage even if it means that these conceptions are occasionally at odds with those of others. But this distinction is one that the coherence theorist obviously cannot draw.

In conclusion, it is important to point out that the coherence theory patently combines a definition of truth with a particular conception of how truth is cognized. The coherence theory offers a prescription for the identification of truth and for checking out that truth is what has been identified: briefly, a list of the largest number of mutually compatible conceptions regarding a given matter has to be compiled. The account that comprises the totality of these conceptions expresses *the truth*. Thus, the coherency theory is best seen as providing an answer to the epistemic question as to how truth is ascertained.

8. We now turn to another theory of truth, the *consensus theory*. Historically, this theory was given its first formulation by Charles Sanders Peirce. He writes:

> 'The opinion which is fated to be ultimately agreed to by all who investigate it is what we mean by truth.' (Peirce 1931–58, §5.407)

> 'Truth is that concordance of an abstract statement with the ideal limit towards which endless investigation would tend to bring scientific belief ...' (Peirce 1931–58, §5.565)

From a systematic perspective the consensus theory, as we shall see in a moment, may be accounted a further elaboration of the coherence theory. As a variant of the latter, the consensus theory is indispensably vulnerable to the criticisms set out above. On the other hand, it evinces certain interesting properties which make it worthy of separate study.

The coherence theory presented above defines truth on the basis of the connections between the sentences that people *believe*, not just those they might formulate. To arrive at the consensus theory we must add to this, first, the proviso that the people in question comprise all those who have an opinion on the matter (this liberal principle may be replaced by reference to a particular group, say, a group comprising those with specialized knowledge). Second, we must stipulate that truth is not defined by reference to the mere coherence obtaining between these beliefs but precisely by a *consensus*. It turns on *agreement* in beliefs, which means that each of the parties to the consensus is cognizant of the fact that he has the same belief as the others and is aware of the additional fact that those others too are similarly cognizant. A consensus is not a chance coincidence between people's beliefs but a coincidence that is mutually acknowledged by them.

Third, and most important, the coherence theory holds that the consensus in question is not necessarily one that actually obtains but that it is conceptualizable as a hypothetical agreement which the individuals concerned (the constituency of experts, say) *would* reach had they unlimited time and unlimited resources at their disposal. This amplification is necessary given the consideration that, without it, truth would be a somewhat paltry affair: the set of questions that mankind has actually investigated and reached consensus on is a vanishingly small quotient of the topics that might be addressed and on which we believe there to be a truth of the matter. There is probably no consensus about the number of hairs on the Pope's head or the shortest distance measured in centimetres between the White House and the Kremlin. And yet we still believe there to be a truth of the matter; no one happens to know what it is.

The need for the claim that there is a truth of the matter resides not least in the fact that concepts of truth and reality are closely interknit: the real is what is picked out by true sentences. But according to the consensus theory, the real is what attracts a consensus. In consequence, reality threatens to be a much more tenuous thing than we had ever imagined. For, as we normally conceive it, there are infinitely many things in the world that are real even in the absence of any consensus concerning them. There is, for instance, no consensus as to whether there is life elsewhere in the universe. But it would appear obvious that either there is life elsewhere in the universe or there is not, irrespective of whether there is a consensus one way or the other.

On the face of it, Peirce's version of the consensus theory takes account of this objection. Peirce maintains, as the above quotation indicates, that for a sentence to be true it is not required that there exist a consensus about its truth. It is sufficient that there *would* be a consensus if researchers with unlimited time and resources at their disposal were put on the job. (In this way the question of whether there is life elsewhere in the universe would be decidable were it possible to dispatch a space expedition to investigate.) This standpoint has been refined by Jürgen Habermas, who has reflected on what constraints should be imposed on the hypothetical scientific procedures putatively able to settle the issue. In particular, Habermas stresses the importance of the absence of the distorting influence of constraining power relations between the participant agents, and adds that issues of truth should not be left to specialists but should ideally involve a discussion between all rational agents. A related theory, but without Habermas's concern with universal dialogue, has recently been advanced by Richard Rorty.

The problem with this solution is that it presupposes a degree of decidability in respect of scientific questions that is dubious to say the least. Questions of historical fact, for instance, make this very clear. For, notoriously, there remain major unresolved conundrums in history studies; it is reasonable to assume, for instance, that historians will never agree about who was responsible for the assassination of J.F. Kennedy. According to the consensus theory this means that there is no truth of the matter. This result, however, seems patently absurd.

As we shall see, the consensus theory somewhat paradoxically substitutes for the intuitive concept of truth construed as agreement with a realm of palpable reality something much more vague and indeterminate – namely whatever, subject to diverse hypothetical and idealized conditions, would be the findings of a scientific enquiry. But if one is convinced that, with infinite time and resources to pursue the investigation, there would indeed be answers to such scientific questions, it would ultimately be because one had made an assumption to which on the consensus theory one is not unqualifiedly entitled: for what is being implicitly presupposed is that there exists an independent reality and that this reality is one that scientific enquiry, aided by unlimited resources, would be capable of bringing to light. But then a correspondence notion of truth to the effect that there exists an independent realm of reality is obviously being presupposed, with the corollary that in the final analysis a scientific investigation will arrive at conclusions that correspond to this reality. But such an assumption lies beyond the reach of the consensus theory.

9. The *pragmatic theory of truth* is the creation of a group of American philosophers working at the close of the nineteenth century, the so-called Pragmatists. The pragmatic movement in America comprised John Dewey, William James, and Charles Peirce, the originator of the consensus theory.

It is slightly misleading to speak of *the* pragmatic theory of truth since it is scarcely possible to find a formulation that Dewey, James and Peirce would all be prepared to endorse. Besides, the pragmatist philosophers are not renowned for their conceptual precision; there are innumerable non-equivalent formulations of the theory in each of these writers. Accordingly, the pragmatic theory of truth referred to here is very much a standardized version and not one that in its entirety can be attributed to any of the school's protagonists.

The following formulation from James will serve as a point of departure:

> *"The true'*, to put it very briefly, is only the expedient in the way of our thinking, just as *'the right'* is only the expedient in the way of our behaving. Expedient in almost any fashion; and expedient in the long run and on the whole of course; for what meets expediently all the experience in sight won't necessarily meet all farther experience equally satisfactorily.' (James 1907 (1975), p. 106).

The key idea informing the pragmatic theory of truth is that truth is that set of beliefs which will produce the most advantageous consequences. The pragmatic theory starts out from the circumstance, presumably not denied by any theory of truth, that there is an advantage to believing truths rather than falsehoods. It is without doubt conducive to the success of all human endeavours that they are preponderantly based on a correct conception of reality rather than a false one.

The pragmatists point out the difficulties inherent in any attempt to give an explanation of this fact. The adherents of traditional truth theories such as the correspondence theory will say that true belief corresponds with reality and therein resides its merit. But we have already seen that it is rather difficult to confer a precise content on this notion of 'correspondence'. James, at least, did not think it could be done.

Instead, the pragmatist claims that our concept of truth is simply the concept of sentences belief in which yields positive consequences. We should abandon any attempt to explain why this is so and simply acknowledge that certain sentences are 'good to believe' and these we call 'true'.

The classic argument against the pragmatic theory of truth is the availability of persuasive counterexamples. Let us assume that Anthony holds the belief that the influenza virus is readily killed off by the ingestion of garlic in sufficient quantities. So he makes garlic a dietary must and gets through the winter without ever catching the flu. The explanation for this is that those with whom he is in contact are careful to give him a wide berth so as to avoid being overwhelmed by the smell of garlic: his risk of contagion is thus considerably reduced. But does this consequence make Anthony's belief that garlic is the antidote to the influenza virus true? It would seem to be a highly counterintuitive conclusion.

James stresses, however, as we saw in the above quotation, that it is expediency or utility in the long run that counts. And one might claim that in the long run the futility of Anthony's strategy will come to light. Sooner or later Anthony will come into contact with people who are partial to the smell of garlic, making no attempt to keep their distance; and sooner or later he will catch flu from one of them. Ultimately, an untrue theory will show itself to be inexpedient.

But perhaps there are false beliefs that will never be exposed as such. Let us for example assume that belief in a benevolent deity is useful to those who subscribe to it: they receive impulses to live better lives and accept the vicissitudes of human existence with greater serenity than others. But does this automatically make the belief in a higher being true? Most people will be disinclined to grant that it does. They may even say that it is precisely the function of the concept of truth to articulate the distinction between what is actually the case and what are agreeable illusions into which humanity is content to be lulled, as, say, religious doctrines that promise eternal bliss.

Granted, examples may be found of beliefs that are self-fulfilling. But these examples belong to such a narrow category that they disconfirm rather than confirm pragmatism as a general theory of truth. Ahead of a match, a professional boxer may boost his confidence by telling himself that he is a far better boxer than his opponent; he might even undergo hypnosis to reinforce this belief. His newly acquired conviction imbues him with such bullishness that in the event he proves to have the edge on his opponent and wins the match. So here we see how a particular belief is capable of producing certain consequences that make it true. But this is quite clearly a special case. It does not apply to the generality of beliefs – such as the belief that there is a stone in my shoe or that the sun is farther away from the earth than the moon.

The example given also suggests that the pragmatic theory of truth leads to relativism. What is useful for one person to believe is not necessarily useful for others. This consequence is one James accepts completely. He writes:

> '[My critics] forget that in any concrete account of what is denoted by 'truth' in human life, the word can only be used relatively to some particular trower. Thus, I may hold it true that Shakespeare wrote the plays that bear his name, and may express my opinion to a critic. If the critic be both a pragmatist and a baconian [one who ascribes to Bacon the authorship of the plays attributed to Shakespeare] he will in his capacity of pragmatist see plainly that the workings of my opinion, I being what I am, make it perfectly true for me, while in his capacity of baconian he still believes that Shakespeare never wrote the plays in question. But most anti-pragmatist critics take the word truth as something absolute.' (James 1909 (1975), p. 147f.)

Let us conclude by pointing out a positive feature of the pragmatic theory of truth: it explains why we seek truth. For if the true is essentially the useful, it is obvious that truth-seeking is worthwhile.

10. The *semantic theory* of truth, originated by the Polish-American logician Alfred Tarski, is an extensional definition: it defines a concept by listing the things that fall under it. For example an extensional definition of the concept 'capital of a Scandinavian country' comprises the list 'Stockholm', 'Copenhagen', 'Oslo'. An extensional definition of truth would likewise consist of a list of the items that possess the property truth. Since, according to Tarski, sentences are the bearers of truth-values the definition of truth comprises a list of sentences.

It is evident, however, that a problem arises when extensional definition is transferred from examples such as 'capital of a Scandinavian country' to a concept such as 'true sentence'. While the fact of which cities in the Scandinavian countries are capitals is firm and known beyond doubt, there are many sentences where the truth-values are highly disputed, or which are just simply beyond the range of human cognitive powers. To this class belong such sentences as, 'Lee Harvey Oswald was the sole assassin of John F. Kennedy', 'Before the Big Bang, another universe existed governed by natural laws quite different from the ones we know today', or, 'A million years ago, lightning struck the place where Buckingham Palace is now situated'. A theory of truth merely comprising a list of true sentences would require continual adjustment with some sentences having to be removed and others being added, and it would surely suffer from substantial gaps consisting of sentences where the truth-value could not be established. The way to circumvent this difficulty is to enter not only the sentences that are known to be true, but also all the other sentences formulable in the language *correlated with a specification of the circumstances under which they are true*. In other words, rather than the bare statement of a true sentence (e.g. 'France is a republic'), the definition should amplify it with a description of the circumstance which makes it true. The definition will contain a sentence of the form 'France is a republic' is true under the circumstances in which France is a republic. Or, more concisely put, "France is a republic' is true if and only if France is a republic'. For any sentence in the English language, the truth definition for English must correlate an instance of it with its truth condition.

Consonantly with this, Tarski specified a material adequacy condition on any extensional truth definition for a given language (the so-called convention T). For every sentence S in language L the definition must entail a theorem of the form 'S is true in L if and only if p', where 'p' is a sentence that 'S' denotes, or some other sentence that shares the same meaning. (Following Tarski, such theorems are called 'T-sentences'.) The above example is an illustration of the most perspicuous form such a theorem can take, an instance where the language in which the theory is formulated contains the language for which truth must be defined. Here the name 'S' will be a sentence inside quotation marks and the T-sentence says of it that it is true if and only if ..., with the *same* sentence without quotation marks replacing the dots. (A sentence inside quotation marks is a name of the same sentence appearing without quotation marks.) We recognize here the 'iterative property' that we mentioned at the beginning of the chapter, a property whose possession acts as a minimum constraint on any conception of truth.

We have previously noted that extensional definitions of concepts exhibit the defect of being unable to distinguish between those that are co-extensional such as the concepts 'blue whale' and 'the largest animals that have ever existed'; for any list of blue whales doubles as a list of the largest animals that have ever existed. We mentioned too that this difficulty might be surmounted by the introduction of *possible* members into the extension of the concept. Now this difficulty would seem to be circumvented in Tarski's theory. Instead of comprising a list of true sentences, Tarski's definition is composed of a set of formulae, capable of generating all the sentences in the language and juxtaposing them with their truth conditions. The primary reason for this is that Tarski's theory is intended to apply to infinite languages, i.e. languages comprising an infinite number of well-formed sentences. For such languages, a finite list would obviously fail to capture the content of the truth predicate. So Tarski's definition may be said to specify not merely the sentences actually articulated, but possible sentences too.

The definition takes the form of a so-called *recursive* theory, which comprises a collection of principles or formulae from which certain sentences (or other entities, for example numbers) may be derived. The theory may then be applied to these same sentences (or numbers) which in turn generate new ones, and so on indefinitely. We can compare it to a computer program which produces a certain output. This same output can be fed back into the computer as new input, with a resultant output that can be reused to prime the computer, and so on. In this way a finite theory (a finite computer program) is capable of generating an infinite output.

However, Tarski's definition does not fully resolve the problem arising from the fact that an extensional definition can accommodate only a limited number of examples of the defined concept. Granted, what it yields is a definition of the potentially infinite number of true sentences in a single language. But, first, it does this on the basis of a purely extensional definition of the terms 'reference' and 'satisfaction', which appear as lists of names and predicates. Second, truth is not a property of one particular language or of a determinate finite set of languages. Truth is not a language-specific property, but has equal application to all languages both actually existent and possible. In consequence, the concept of truth is not exhausted by a Tarskian definition of truth given for an individual language, or for all that exist, have existed or will come to do so. Here the problem of extensionality rears its head again: every extensional definition is limited on one dimension or another.

11. Significantly, Tarski saw the matter differently. He considered it entirely misconceived to attempt a general, abstract, definition of the term 'truth'. On his view, any such would be bound to lead to paradoxes. Let us briefly examine this problem.

We can formulate the following meaningful, self-referential and false sentence in English:

   A. This sentence is a French sentence.

We can also formulate the following meaningful and true sentence:

   B. Sentence A is false.

Finally, using the same semantic elements we can formulate the sentence:

   C. Sentence C is false.

But is sentence C true or false? Assume that it is true. In that case what it says about itself is correct, and since it says that C is false, it must be correct that C is false. Assume instead that it is false. Since the sentence says of itself that it is false, what it says is correct. In other words, the sentence is true. So we find ourselves faced with a paradox. If the sentence is true, it is false, and if it is false, it is true. The joint result is a contradiction: sentence C is both true and false.

One might take the view that such sentences represent a harmless structural defect in the language – of the sort that allows us to formulate nonsense sentences in the style of 'colourless green ideas sleep furiously'. But Tarski cautions against such complacency: the possibility of formulating paradoxes in language shows that the language is incoherent and needs remedying.

Tarski shows that such paradoxes arise in a language if the following two properties are true. First, it admits self-reference and the application of the predicates 'true' and 'false'. Second, the laws of logic hold. If we are to avoid paradoxes, one of these two properties must be forfeited. Since dispensing with the laws of logic hardly seems advisable, it is the first property that must go. In particular, it is important to make it inadmissible for sentences to predicate the words 'true' or 'false' of themselves or of other sentences in the same language.

This means, then, that the truth definition for a given language must always be formulated in another language. (This does not exclude the existence of substantial overlaps between the two). The language defined (the object language) must not encompass the semantic vocabulary applied in its description, including the term 'true'. Now it follows from this, according to Tarski, that no general definition of truth can be given. Truth can only be defined for a concretely specified, precisely regimented language. In consequence, Tarski does not account it a defect in his theory that it cannot deliver a general definition: no such definition is even possible.

The constraint that a language must be absolutely well defined itself in order to admit a well-defined concept of truth implies, further, according to Tarski, that it is doubtful whether truth is definable for natural languages such as English and French. For natural languages do not obey rigidly specified rules of syntax, capable of delivering a completely unambiguous answer to the question of whether the sentence is well formed. Natural languages have evolved via a historical process, with all the indeterminacies such a process spawns. Tarski's definition applies, rather, to formal languages and mathematics. His definition has application, then, to the language of predicate logic, i.e. the formal language in which logical relations between subject-predicate sentences and those derivable from them are formulated.

12. In what follows, we shall attempt to illustrate the core idea informing Tarski's theory through focusing on an exceedingly simplified example. It involves not the language of predicate logic but a simplified language, L, closely analogous to it.

Let us first rehearse the definitional technique: it involves defining truth recursively, i.e. defining truth for simple linguistic expressions and on that basis defining truth for increasingly more complex expressions. Terminologically, the definition set out below takes a slightly different form: the simplest expressions that are defined are not 'truth' but the two terms 'satisfaction' and 'reference'. Truth is then defined on the basis of these. This move is motivated by the fact that these simpler concepts diverge sufficiently from the concept of truth (which applies to sentences) for it to be terminologically advantageous to have particular terms for them. We already have a designation for one of these relations, namely 'reference', while 'satisfaction' is a term of art introduced by Tarski.

We begin by specifying the elements of the language. It is a finite language with very few components. It comprises the following:

The names: 'Søren Kierkegaard', 'Niels Bohr', and 'Karen Blixen'.
The predicates '... is famous' and '... is red-headed'.
The connectives 'not', 'and', 'or' and 'if ... then'.
The quantifiers 'all' and 'some'
The variables 'x', 'y' and 'z'.

We next define the referential relation. That we do by enumerating the items in the language L that have reference, namely, names, correlated to those things to which they refer:

'Søren Kierkegaard' refers-in-L to Søren Kierkegaard.
'Niels Bohr' refers-in-L to Niels Bohr.
'Karen Blixen' refers-in-L to Karen Blixen.

We will recall that these sentences serve to *define* the term 'reference' (or better: 'reference-in-L'). They do not express the fact that a given name stands in a previously known referential relation to a given thing. They say instead that the expression 'reference-in-L' is defined by the relation in which the names 'Søren Kierkegaard', 'Niels Bohr', and 'Karen Blixen' stand to Søren Kierkegaard, Niels Bohr, Karen Blixen, respectively. We are presuming that the language comprises no elements other than those just specified. The domain of objects for our simple language thus comprises only the "objects" Søren Kierkegaard, Niels Bohr and Karen Blixen.

Next we define the expression 'satisfaction' for the predicates in L:

The predicate '... is famous' is satisfied by an object if and only if the object is famous.

The predicate '... is red-headed' is satisfied by an object if and only if the object is red-headed.

Next we define truth for simple sentences of the form 't is λ' in the language:

> A sentence 't is λ' is true-in-L if and only if the predicate λ is satisfied by the object to which the name t refers.

Thereafter we define truth for sentences containing connectives:

> A sentence of the form 'Not p' is true-in-L if and only if p is not true-in-L.

> A sentence of the form 'p and q' is true-in-L if and only if p is true-in-L and q is true-in-L.

> A sentence of the form 'p or q' is true-in-L if and only if p is true-in-L or q is true-in-L.

> A sentence of the form 'If p then q' is true-in-L if and only if p is not true-in-L or q is true-in-L.

Finally, we define truth for sentences with *quantifiers*. Quantifiers are expressions such as 'all' and 'some', i.e. expressions indicating how many objects from the domain we are talking about. First, we must introduce a technical vocabulary: we say that a sentence is "open" if it contains one or more variables that are not bound by any quantifier. An "open sentence" is, strictly speaking not a sentence at all but an expression which becomes a sentence when combined with one quantifier (or more) or by a name replacing the variable. The following are open sentences:

> x is famous
> y is red-headed

Like sentences proper, open sentences may be complex, which is to say they may contain connectives. The following are complex open sentences:

> x is famous and y is red-headed
> If y is red-headed, then Niels Bohr is famous
> y is red-headed or y is not red-headed

Such open sentences are transformed into proper sentences if a name replaces the variable (several names if there are several variables). The sentence thus produced is true-in-L, insofar as the object/objects for which the name or names stand satisfy the predicate or predicates in question (cf. the definition above). An open sentence is likewise transformed into a proper sentence if the variable is bound by a quantifier, i.e. if to the open sentence an expression is added of the form 'For all x, it holds that ...' or 'For some x it holds that ...'

Now, finally, we are in a position to define what truth is for sentences with quantifiers. (In the following 'Φυ' stands for any open sentence in which the variable υ occurs):

> A sentence of the type 'For all υ it holds that Φυ' is true-in-L if and only if for every name t which replaces υ in Φυ, it holds that the resultant sentence Φt is true-in-L.

> A sentence of the type 'For some υ it holds that Φυ' is true-in-L if and only if for at least one name which replaces υ in Φυ, it holds that the resultant sentence Φt is true-in-L.

We have now given a definition of 'truth', or 'true' in the language L, since we have characterized truth for each of the admissible sentence types in this simple language.

We can illustrate this by means of an example, namely a quantified sentence of the type 'For some x ...' and where Φ is the sentence 'x is famous'. We have the sentence, 'For some x, it is the case that x is famous'. This sentence is true-in-L if there is at least one name in L such that a sentence that is true-in-L results when this name is substituted for 'x' in the open sentence 'x is famous'. This means, in turn, (cf. the definition above) that the object to which the name refers to must satisfy the predicate '... is famous'. So 'For some x it is the case that x is famous' is true if and only if Søren Kierkegaard or Niels Bohr or Karen Blixen is famous – that is, if and only if for some x (in the domain) x is famous. Hence we have an instance of the T-schema. We see here how we arrive at the quantified sentence's truth condition by regressing from the quantified sentence to the truth condition for a simpler sentence and finally to reference- and satisfaction-conditions for names and predicates in the language L. This shows how the truth conditions of complex sentences are constituted out of the semantic contributions of simpler constituent sentences and expressions.

At this point, the reader might be tempted to conclude that Tarski's definition is a mere collection of truisms. This impression owes itself in part to our omission of the definition's technical refinements. Further, the language in which the theory is couched (the so-called 'metalanguage') in our simple version contains the language the theory is about (the 'object language'): both are English. It is indeed truistic to say that the predicate '... is famous' is satisfied by famous things. But it soon becomes much less trivial when we insert an object language, French, say, discrete from the metalanguage. It is not trivial to say that a thing satisfies the French predicate '... est fameux' if and only if it is famous.

13. The question of how the semantic definition of truth relates to the correspondence theory has long been a topic of vigorous philosophical debate. Tarski himself was somewhat ambiguous on this front since on the one hand he suggested that his truth definition might be seen as a version of the correspondence theory and, on the other, that it was a critique of both that and other philosophical theories of truth. In any case it is clear that Tarski must be opposed to the correspondence theory qua general definition of truth since, as we have seen, he held that no such definition was possible. Moreover, Tarski thought that there were special problems attaching to truth definitions for natural languages, which definitions the correspondence theory aspired to deliver.

That said, there are clearly points of similarity between the semantic definition of truth and the correspondence theory. Tarski's definition specifies, for every sentence in a (regimented, formal) language, how the world must be for that sentence to be true; it might also be said that it specifies the situation to which the sentence corresponds. And beyond that, it demonstrates how the truth condition of the sentence is constituted via the contributions of the sentential components, singular terms and predicates. This means that reference and satisfaction conditions play as pivotal a role in this theory of truth as they do in the version of the correspondence theory outlined in the foregoing account. A significant difference is, however, that Tarski remains silent on the specifics of these relations: they are defined solely in extensional terms, in the form of lists of singular terms and predicates. By contrast, in our account, we sought to show how a fuller picture, not least of the referential relation, might be elaborated, and how it contributes to a more substantive version of the correspondence theory.

14. But can we accept Tarski's definition of truth? The charge is often levelled against it that, whatever Tarski might have thought, it remains a serious deficiency in it that it does not offer a general characterization of the con-cept of truth but only definitions for individual languages. In fact, Tarski's definition is even more restricted and less informative than would initially appear. For

Tarski's definition, in our simplified version, will almost certainly give the reader the impression that even though the definition comes in a language-relative form, it implicitly delivers a general prescription for the formulation of a theory of truth for language. And indeed, that was how we presented the theory: we said that an extensional theory of truth is created by the formulation of a set of principles which recursively generates the sentences of the given language, and conjoins them with specifications of their truth conditions. However, it needs to be pointed out that, according to Tarski's principles, any such formulation is inadmissible. For in such prescriptions, expressions such as 'truth conditions' are given without reference to any particular language. In other words, truth is referred to generically, which circumstance opens up for the formulation of the truth paradox. According to Tarski we are not permitted to formulate (or even tacitly extrapolate to) a general theory of truth, nor even a general prescription for how one might be framed.

This consequence is very difficult to swallow. It is intuitively absurd to think of talk about truth *per se* as somehow illicit, so that we are barred from saying that there is a property common to English and French sentences when they are true. Truth is alleged to be something quite different for, say, English and French sentences, respectively; any attempt to pin down what the relevant concepts of truth have in common leads to paradoxes and is prohibited. It is hard to be persuaded that paradox is avoidable only through strict compliance with the principle that truth must be formulated for each language individually. Without seeking to contest Tarski's claim that paradoxes pose a problem for actual languages, it surely has to be argued that those convinced that truth is susceptible of a general characterization of truth need not submit so readily.

Moreover, Tarski's truth definition is unsatisfactory insomuch as it leaves the basic notions of reference and satisfaction undefined. These are specified purely extensionally, in the form of lists of names and predicates, respectively. Using names and predicates as a (generically) undefined input, Tarski's truth definition demonstrates how truth-values are produced when items of these kinds are combined in sentences. This results in the kind of purely combinatorial (functional) account of truth and meaning whose inadequacy we have been at pains to expose. In order to characterize both truth and meaning, we need to invoke features of the workings of singular terms and of predicates that go beyond their interaction in sentences. We need to say something about how particulars are identified, about communicative causal links, about the linguistic division of labour, and so on; in brief, we need the kind of account that was the burden of chapters 3 and 4.

This is not to deny that Tarski's truth definition works admirably for the formal languages of logic and set theory. But when we set up formal truth definitions in these areas, what we are after is not the elucidation of the general concept of truth, but just a grasp of it that suffices to investigate the logical form of a language, i.e. the notion of logical consequence in that language. This is a restricted, and legitimate, purpose. However, when as philosophers we engage with the question about the nature of truth, we set our sights higher.

15. Tarski's ambition was to develop a theory of truth which would recursively generate all the sentences of a particular language, juxtaposed with their truth conditions, on the model of the sentence, 'S is true iff p'. The technicalities of the recursion are irrelevant for the specific characterization of truth delivered by the definition; in a sense, the substantive content of the definition is provided by the constraint that any sentence derived from the definition satisfy the Tarski condition. That condition, in effect, captures the intuitive notion of truth.

Tarski's logical machinery applies only to formal languages, and no one has any precise idea of how to frame it for natural languages since there is at present no prescription for the generation of their truth conditions. One option might be to disconnect the two aspects of Tarski's project, viz. the constructive part and the constraint.

Indeed, many philosophers have recently advanced proposals to this effect, but the idea itself antedates these and traces back at least as far as to Frank Ramsey. The idea is simply to say that truth is exhausted by the Tarski constraint, as applied to any meaningful sentence in the language. According to any such theory, we can dipense with the predicate 'true' since, instead of stating of a given sentence p, that it is true, we can simply assert p. Hence the theory is called a *redundancy theory* of truth. Often, what has been proposed is a "disquotational" form of the theory, which says that the defining feature of truth is its licensing of the passage from a quotation to an unquoted sentence.

There are difficulties with this theory of truth, however, some of which it shares with Tarski's account, while others are unique to it. Here is a difficulty not shared by Tarski's theory. According to a purely disquotational theory, we can always replace any occurrence of the term 'true' by the disquoted sentence. But it might be retorted that we often use the term 'true' to refer to sets of sentences or utterances in omnibus fashion, when specification of the individual sentences in disquoted form is not an option, as, for instance, when we say, 'Everything that George Washington ever said was true', or in

'The logical consequences of true sentences are always true'. (Tarski's theory is not hit by this objection since it is not purely disquotational, but only uses the disquotation constraint as an adequacy criterion for acceptable definitions.)

A related difficulty pertains to the role of truth in explaining the practical usefulness of some of our beliefs in contrast to others, for instance, the striking success of projects based upon accepted scientific theories as opposed to those reliant on various magical procedures. The obvious answer to this is that those scientific beliefs are indeed *true* while the magical beliefs are false. There is no way that this general insight can be explained in purely disquotational terms, if for no other reason than the sheer lack of any compendious way in which all truths can be referred to, other than precisely as all truths.

16. We have now examined a number of traditional theories of truth: the correspondence theory, the coherence theory, the consensus theory, the pragmatic theory, Tarski's "semantic" theory and the redundancy theory. Of these the correspondence theory seemed best able to able to "fight its corner" whereas the others showed themselves to be beset by serious difficulties. The correspondence theory appears to be capable of defending itself against the recurrent criticism that it is impossible to characterize the special agreement that ostensibly holds between true sentences and reality. Such a characterization is available if a sentence is viewed as composed of parts, in particular, of singular terms and predicates, whose relation to reality (not least in terms of reference) can be characterized in ways that go beyond the fact that their combination yields a well-formed sentence with a certain specified truth condition.

It must be conceded, however, that we were able to achieve this because we abandoned the notion of a definition of truth in the strict sense. A strict definition is *inter alia* subject to the non-circularity constraint, which precludes appeal to terms that are determined by the concept being defined. We violated this rule by relying heavily on concepts of reference and of predication not fully graspable independently of the notion of truth. Nevertheless, the concept of truth is so fundamental as to be incapable of any strictly independent definition. The best one can hope for is success in furnishing an adequate account of the concept and its role in human language and thought, an account that ultimately involves the concept of truth itself. All the same, such an account will be informative in virtue of involving other concepts and showing their connections to the concept of truth, as the above discussion sought to show.

Chapter 6
Davidson's programme

1. In the preceding chapters we have been occupied with the idea that linguistic meaning may be explicated in terms of the concept of truth. But how is this idea to be developed into a concrete, comprehensive theory of the truth conditions of sentences and, by implication, of their meaning? How can the coupling of truth and meaning be brought to yield an account of how the semantic content of natural languages is constructed? This is a question to which the American philosopher Donald Davidson has offered a response by presenting what is in many respects a radically new approach to the theory of meaning.

2. The most perspicuous way of describing Davidson's strategy is to compare it to the construction of a computer program capable of simulating the human ability to speak and understand a natural language such as English, French or Danish. If we were to succeed in creating a computer program so powerful that it was able to simulate the competence of a human language user, the claim that we had thereby acquired a model of the knowledge that a language user commands would be a plausible one. The primary knowledge here is, of course, knowledge of meaning – the semantics of the language.

Thankfully, we need not address the vexed issue here of whether a computer capable of simulating the linguistic skills of a human speaker could be said to understand the language and thus, in a certain sense of the word, to possess consciousness. We can avoid this problem simply by confining our investigation to the question of whether a computer is able to simulate human linguistic competence through being capable of generating the same linguistic output as a human speaker. The simulation of understanding does not itself constitute understanding; as little as a computer simulation of the landing of a plane does the landing of a plane.

The philosophical task consists, first, in specifying the precise skill that we want the computer to possess. What is it exactly that the language user does that we want the computer to mimic? What aspects of a language user's competence are relevant and which are extraneous? (A human language user hearing someone speak may be able to identify his or her social status. But this is hardly relevant to the present enquiry.) The philosopher's contribution is to analyse the requirements an adequate program must meet, and to articulate them in the form of a list of adequacy conditions.

That much accomplished, we approach the programmers with our requirements and ask them to construct a programme that meets them. If the programmers succeed in developing a programme that satisfies these constraints and so makes it possible for a computer to simulate the user of a natural language in the relevant respects, we shall have achieved our aim. According to Davidson we shall have acquired not just a programme for an arbitrary natural language but, further, answers to general questions about the shape a theory of meaning for a natural language should take. On his view, this is all that we can expect in the way of an answer to our question about the nature of linguistic meaning and the functioning of natural languages.

As may already have been apparent, we are using the word 'programme' in two senses: to refer both to a programme which states the meaning of the sentences in a particular language, and to the notion of a programmatic statement about the form such computer programmes should take and what we can learn from the programming exercise. There is the same doubleness in our use of the term 'theory of meaning' inasmuch as the word refers in part to a theory for a concrete language, and in part to the notion of a general philosophical account of linguistic meaning.

3. What invests language with meaning? According to Davidson we have the answer if we know how to construct a theory (here conceived in terms of a computer programme) which satisfies two constraints. i) The theory must be able to provide an interpretation of all the utterances that a language user might produce – actually or potentially. ii) The theory must be verifiable independently of any detailed prior knowledge of the language users' communicative intentions. This is Davidson's way of preserving the theory from the taint of circularity mediated not least by semantic concepts or their cognates figuring in the workings of the theory. Our ambition is not simply to shed light on the semantics of this or that particular language but to illuminate the concept of meaning as such. Such an ambition would be compromised if the theory made implicit use of the concepts it purports to elucidate. We shall examine these constraints more closely in what follows.

The requirement that the theory should give an interpretation of all actual as well as possible utterances in a language is in itself trivial: it is simply the constraint that the theory should be able, comprehensively, to account for its domain of objects. What *is* of interest is what this constraint entails with regard to the theory's construction. That task is not solved by reference to a mere translation manual comprising a list of the sentences of the language in question juxtaposed by a specification of their meaning. Such a theory, for French, would contain sentences of the following form:

'La neige est blanche' means the snow is white in French.

'Haut les mains!' means hands up in French.

And so on. Obviously, this would be the simplest solution if the language in question were finite, containing a finite number of sentences. This feature is characteristic of railway signal systems, road signs and semaphore. A finite theory would also suffice if, qua tourist, one needed only to master a limited segment of a natural language. But it is of no use at all if the aim is to furnish a complete theory for a natural language.

A distinguishing feature of natural languages is their *generative* character: they permit the construction of a potentially infinite number of meaningful sentences using a finite list of words and rules of syntax, so that users are capable of formulating and understanding a corresponding potential infinitude of sentences on the basis of finite acquisition. He or she has heard a certain finite number of sentences, acquired a certain vocabulary and implicitly grasped the grammatical rules through example and correction. This enables the individual to understand an infinite number of sentences he or she has never heard before.

These considerations furnish us with the following information about the theory we are after: if the theory is to be complete it must, first, be able to state the meaning of every sentence formulable in the language in question, the theory's object language. (The theory is naturally not required to specify the meaning of every sentence in every language!) Second, the theory must resemble natural languages in respect of being learnable by a finite being. This means, *inter alia*, that its computer version must be storable in a finite computer with finite storage capacity.

It further implies, third, that the theory must exhibit the structure of the language. To give the theory a finite form we need to identify the semantic structure of the sentences of the language in question. We need to establish what allows sentential elements to occur in a plurality of sentences, how they contribute to the meanings of these, what syntactic structures recur in the various sentences, and how the structures contribute to the meanings of the sentences. Beyond that, exhibiting the semantic structure of the sentences is relevant to the question of what logical inferences are possible and how they are to be drawn; more precisely, what inferences may be drawn solely on the basis of the logical *form* of the sentences, irrespective of the non-logical terms that fill in the form. Using the customary terminology, this is to say that the semantic structure of the sentences must reflect their *logical form*.

4. After having secured the general form of the theory, Davidson next considers the question of the theorems. The theorems are the inferences derivable from the axioms of the theory and take the form of sentences which, in one way or another, specify the meaning of the corresponding sentences in the object language. Returning to our computer analogy the question is: What should the computer's output look like? What do we want to appear on the screen as output when our input is an arbitrary sentence from the object language?

A first natural response is to require that for any sentence in the object language, the theory yield a theorem that says what that sentence means. If the object language is French and the metalanguage English, for the French sentence 'La neige est blanche' the theory must imply a theorem of the following type:

'La neige est blanche' means in French that snow is white.

(It is important to specify the language to which the sentence belongs since a sentence composed of the same alphabetical characters and spaces in identical sequences may belong to several different languages and have different meanings in those languages.)

This can be expressed more formally as follows. Let 'S' be the name of a sentence in the object language L and let 'p' be a sentence in the metalanguage which means the same as S in L. This means that 'p' is possibly S itself (if L appears as part of the metalanguage) or a translation of S in the metalanguage. Our initial answer, then, was that for every sentence S in L the theory should entail a theorem of the form:

S in L means that p.

This answer is of course correct inasmuch as the theory tells us what we want to know: it tells us what S means. But it is less than felicitous if we want a general theory of linguistic meaning, and not merely a theory of the meaning of the sentences in this or that particular language. We want an account of what it is we do when we state the meaning of a word or sentence. And in that regard we are not much enlightened by being told that a sentence *means* such and such. It is patently circular to explain meaning in terms of meaning. Meaning is a concept that needs to be *explained* by our theory, not a concept the theory can avail itself of in the delivery of such an explanation.

The task before us, then, is to find a substitute for the expression 'means-in-L that'. We know that the theory for any sentence in L must entail a theorem of the form:

S in L * p

where 'p' is S itself or a translation of S into the metalanguage, and where '*' is as yet an unidentified filling which in a non-circular way replaces the expression 'means that'.

We can now proceed to investigate what we should substitute for '*' in 'S in L * p'. One option might be a reference to the speaker's communicative intentions (which we have already encountered in chapter 2 and shall meet again in chapter 8):

S in L is used by speakers to communicate that p.

However, this proposal runs into similar circularity problems. The theory needs to be capable of empirical verification independently of knowledge of the meanings of the object language. But to identify the communicative intentions of the speakers of the object language – at any rate the more complex intentions – we need to understand their utterances, which is to say, sentences in their language. Such intricate intentions cannot be accessed otherwise than through attending to the speaker's account of his or her intentions. So reference to the communicative intentions of L-users fails to qualify as an apt substitute for the expression 'means that'.

Davidson next replaces the intensional idiom 'means that' with an extensional filling: 'is * in L if and only if', so that the form of the complete theorem is now:

S is * in L if and only if p.

Now we recognize that '... is * in L' is a truth-predicate for W (provided that 'p' means the same as S). That is, our dummy predicate is co-extensional with the Tarskian predicate '... is true in L' since S will satisfy either of these predicates on condition that p.

This makes it a natural thought to substitute 'true in L' for '* in L', thus giving the theorems of our semantic theory the following standard form:

S is true in L if and only if p.

In the new formula, S is the name of a sentence in the object language and p is a sentence in the metalanguage used to express the truth condition for S. This formula is not vulnerable to the charge that it uses expressions that it is incumbent on the theory to explain: it contains a connective familiar from propositional logic – 'if and only if' – and of course the concept of truth raises philosophical problems of its own. But shedding light on the latter is not specifically part of the remit of a theory of meaning (Davidson might disagree with this; see below).

The constraint on our theory can now be formulated as follows. We want a theory, *in casu* a computer programme, which, on a finite basis and for every sentence S in the object language, implies a theorem of the form 'S is true if and only if p', where the sentence in the object language is substituted for S and where a sentence is substituted for p which is true precisely when S is true. So what we are after is a computer programme which is capable of stating in English, say, the meaning of every possible well-formed French sentence, and imposes the constraint that the programme be finite and match each of these sentences with a theorem of the form: S is true if and only if p, where S is a French sentence, and where p is the English sentence which has the same truth condition as S. For instance, the theorem for the sentence 'La neige est blanche' will be the following:

'La neige est blanche' is true if and only if and only if snow is white.

5. We have now specified the general form of the computer programme that we have asked our programmers to make up for us. The rest is sheer technical know-how, so at this point the philosopher can sit back and let the programmer get on with the job.

Now Davidson contends that the philosophical and logical literature already contains the materials for such a theory (= a computer programme). We have only to consult Tarski's truth definition, discussed in the previous chapter. Indeed, the connection was just waiting to be made: the theorems we want our theory of meaning to generate are ostensibly very similar to those required of a theory of truth according to Tarski (the so-called T-sentences). It is equally clear that the general constraints that Tarski imposes on a theory of truth for a particular language mirror those Davidson imposes on any theory of meaning. The theory of truth, then, must generate all the sentences in the language on the basis of finite resources and, for each sentence, must correlate it with a specification of its truth condition.

Let us briefly recall how a theory of truth achieves this, according to Tarski (or, more accurately, how it is achieved in our simplified version of Tarski's theory given in chapter 5). First, two concepts are defined that are simpler than the concept of truth, namely satisfaction and reference. They are defined by means of sequences taking the form of lists of predicates and referring expressions along with a specification of their satisfaction conditions and referents. Next, a definition is given of 'truth' for simple sentences, where a predicate is concatenated with a referring expression. Finally, a definition is given of what truth means for truth functions and for quantifiers, that is to say, expressions of the type 'All x are ...' and 'Some x are ...' (The reader may find it helpful to refer back to chapter 5 to refresh his grasp of these points.)

Tarski's theory furnishes a recursive definition of the concept of truth by taking sentences of the language constructed out of simpler elements and correlating them with a specification of their truth conditions. But on Davidson's view this must be the equivalent of the delivery of a specification of the meanings of the sentences. For the meanings of sentences are their truth conditions; and here, for every sentence in the language, we get a sentence that specifies what is the case when the sentence is true. In other words, Tarski's extensional truth-definition doubles as an extensional theory of meaning for a given language. And, more – it arguably offers a general insight into the nature of linguistic meaning inasmuch as it yields a general prescription for the construction of a theory.

6. Davidson concludes that a theory of meaning for a language L, so constructed that it is structurally equivalent to a (recursive) definition of truth-in-L of the type formulated by Tarski, constitutes an adequate theory of meaning for L. It shows how the meanings of the infinitude of sentences formulable in the language depend on the meanings of the words. Davidson's constraint on an adequate theory proved to be equivalent to Tarski's convention T, and since a Tarskian (recursive) definition of truth-in-L satisfies convention T, a theory of meaning for L so devised as to have the same structure as a recursive definition of truth-in-L, would naturally also satisfy Davidson's adequacy constraint.

A Tarskian elaboration of a theory of meaning for L also satisfies the constraint that forbids the use of (undefined) semantic concepts. Admittedly, a recursive definition of truth-in-L contains, as we saw above, an important semantic concept, namely satisfaction (and in our simplified version, reference, too). But since satisfaction (and reference) is extensionally defined, the constraint excluding undefined semantic concepts in the conceptual apparatus of the theory has been met. In any case, satisfaction and reference are conceptual adjuncts which enable us to generate the theory's "meaning-specifying" sentences – the theorems – but without appearing in these themselves: in the theorems, the T-sentences, only the expression true-in-L appears.

Finally, a Tarskian elaboration of the theory of meaning meets the constraint that the theory should give the meaning of every sentence belonging to the language's potential infinity of sentences on the basis of the meanings of the expressions figuring in it.

Other candidates for a substitution for '*' in the formula 'S in L * p' might also conceivably meet the adequacy constraint; but according to Davidson we do not know of any that do. The most natural candidate for an adequate theory of meaning for L is, therefore, one that contains a recursive definition of truth-in-L.

7. So far so good. There are, however, two important differences between Tarski's definition of truth and Davidson's theory of meaning which arguably pose certain problems for Davidson.

First, Tarski takes the concept of meaning for granted and, accordingly, as constitutive of the foundation for the definition of truth: in Tarski's definition of truth, 'p' is specified as S itself or a translation of S – an expression which is identical in *meaning* to S. But Davidson cannot make similar use of the concept of meaning in his definition when the aim is precisely that of formulating a theory of meaning.

Second, Tarski's definition of truth is formulated for a formal language, namely the language of predicate logic. Davidson's aim, by contrast, is the delivery of a theory of meaning for natural languages and so he needs to adjust his theory to accommodate natural language with its inventory of names, indexicals, non-extensional contexts and other expressions which have no counterparts in predicate logic. We shall take a closer look at these differences and the problems to which they give rise in what follows.

Tarski's aim is to give an extensional definition of truth-in-L and in pursuit of this end he can take meaning for granted: either L is contained in the metalanguage or the metalanguage contains translations of L. Davidson's aim, by contrast, is to give a theory of meaning for L and so he cannot take meaning for granted. The simplest way out of this difficulty would simply be to reverse, as it were, the direction in which the truth definition is read. Every definition can be read in two directions depending on which of the two expressions figuring in it the reader is already conversant with. If he is familiar with neither, the definition will be uninformative. A definition such as:

A bachelor is an unmarried man

for example, will be read from left to right by a person who knows what an unmarried man is but not what a bachelor is; he now learns what the word 'bachelor' means. Conversely, it would be read from right to left by a person who knows what a bachelor is, but is in the dark as to what an unmarried man is: he now learns what 'unmarried man' means.

The theorems in Tarski's theory of truth might be treated similarly. They might plausibly be read not as a definition of 'truth' but as a specification of truth conditions (predicated on a recognized concept of truth) for the sentences in a given language (and also as a prescription for how truth conditions might be specified for any language). For example, instead of taking the example "'Snow is white' is true if and only if snow is white' to be (an element of) a definition of truth, it might be taken as a specification of the truth condition for the sentence 'Snow is white' on the assumption that we already know what truth is. However, that is not quite the route Davidson takes. To do so would be to presuppose that there existed an alternative, acceptable concept of truth that might be inserted into Tarski's formulas. But according to Davidson this is not the case: Tarski's truth definition is the only adequate definition going and the traditional theories such as the correspondence theory and the coherence theory all lead to unsatisfactory results.

Davidson is now faced with a problem: he wants to use Tarski's definition to define both 'truth' and 'meaning'. In other words, he wants to read the definition both ways – he seems to be placing himself in the position of the individual who knows neither what 'bachelor' nor what 'unmarried man' means but expects to be enlightened about both at once by reading the formula 'A bachelor is an unmarried man'. To be sure, Davidson believes that there is a way out of this difficulty. He starts from the claim that the concept of truth, in line with the concept of meaning, is so fundamental that it is impossible to penetrate beneath it to define it in terms of something even more basic. In common with other basic concepts, it resists explicit definition. Instead, it has to be defined through being brought into systematic relations with a suite of basic concepts that work together to produce a description of reality. That reality, here, is human behaviour, thoughts, intentions and utterances. On this approach, we can define the concepts of truth and meaning, respectively in conjunction with others such as 'action', 'intention', 'preference', and so on, in one go. These concepts are in part defined by their own logical interconnections – as articulated by Tarski's extensional definition – and in part by their joint embedment in a complete description of human behaviour.

Davidson uncovers the roles played by these concepts by investigating the process designed to discover which theory of meaning, constructed according to Tarski's model, reflects the language use of a particular speech community. We make the assumption that we have no prior knowledge whatsoever of the community's language or their conception of reality. In other words, the process involves what in the jargon is known as 'radical interpretation'. We are not confronted, then, with the manageable task of having to set up a theory of meaning for a language with which we are familiar – French, say – where all we need to do is to draw on our command of the two languages to formulate theorems such as "La neige est blanche' is true in French if and only if snow is white'. (Here we offer only a brief sketch of radical interpretation since we shall be returning to the phenomenon in greater detail in chapter 10. We confine ourselves to the discussions of those features relevant to the elucidation of Davidson's argument.)

Our present task, then, is that of constructing a theory of meaning on the model of Tarski's theory of truth and for a totally unknown language. As we now know, it consists in working up a theory whose axioms entail theorems that systematically correlate sentences in the object language with their truth conditions as specified in the metalanguage. An obvious way to go about this is to correlate the sentences which we hear the foreign speaker utter with a description of the circumstances under which they are uttered. For it seems natural enough to imagine that the circumstances under which they are uttered constitute the sentences' truth conditions.

There are, however, problems with this project, and ones that highlight how closely interwoven truth is with the other concepts operative in the interpretative process. We can only derive the truth conditions of sentences from the situations in which they are uttered if we assume that the speaker has a broadly veridical conception of reality. For if the speaker's grasp of the nature of his environment is pervasively defective, this fact will be reflected in his utterances. We are thus constrained to adopt a methodological principle, the so-called *principle of charity*, which enjoins us to ascribe true beliefs to others unless we can explain how they came to be mistaken. We also need to make certain assumptions about the desires and intentions of these language users; if they are intent on deceiving their interlocutors, their sentences will hardly reflect their true understandings. We must likewise make certain assumptions about what matters to them since this will be decisive for the kinds of utterance they produce. If, for example, as votaries of an exacting deity the natives' actions are, in every last detail, subject to religious prohibitions and taboos, their utterances will doubtless often turn on the niceties of the application of these sacred injunctions.

We shall not pursue this topic further here but refer the reader to the more comprehensive treatment in chapter 10. The crucial point is Davidson's contention that truth is one concept in a conceptual web that includes others such as meaning, intention, desires, thoughts; and, further, that the best account of the concept of truth is arrived at by describing this web in all its variety and showing how it can be used to describe human speech, agency and thought.

8. We can briefly compare Davidson's concept of truth with that advanced in chapter 5. There are certain affinities but also important differences. We agreed with Davidson that the concept of truth is a fundamental concept that cannot be explicitly defined in terms of a stratum of yet lower-lying concepts – for there are none. Instead, the concept is implicitly defined via a mutual interplay with other basic concepts. Particular importance was attributed to the notion of reference. We argued that the concept of reference makes it possible to assign a particular content to the traditional correspondence theory of truth. Davidson denies, however, that the concept of reference plays any significant role in the definition of truth. This is surprising since the concept of the satisfaction conditions of a predicate is crucial here and this concept, as Davidson himself makes clear, can be regarded as generic to reference. But the point he is concerned to make is that satisfaction is no more than a theoretical adjunct, a technical device enabling the construction of an elegant recursive theory of truth. The term does not in itself refer to anything in observable reality (here, speakers' linguistic practice). This is evidenced, according to Davidson, by the fact that the concept of reference does not appear in those parts of the theory that are directly descriptive of reality, namely the theorems (T-sentences). As against this, we have argued that the concept of reference is not without intrinsic content even though it is not characterizable in complete independence from a theory of truth. Relevant here is the notion of a causal link between the speaker and the item referred to, discussed in chapter 3. Besides, the conception of reference as a species of activity through which items are identified – by their being pointed to, or by the specification of properties unique to them – makes it a genuine element in language games, not just a theoretical adjunct. It is an activity that is part and parcel of linguistic practice and so not confined to the theories of language devised by philosophers. In everyday use too we put questions such as

'Whom are you talking about?' and receive in reply a pointing out of, or a specification of, the relevant individual.

9. Tarski's ideas about the definition of truth were originally intended for formal, artificial languages, so if these ideas are to be applied to utterances in natural languages, Tarski's principles need to be modified accordingly. By the same token, natural languages must in some respects be adjusted to Tarski's model. Let us note a couple of points where such modifications are necessary if Davidson's programme is to be carried through.

First, in artificial and formal languages sentences may be straightforwardly regarded as truth-bearers, and there is no need to distinguish between the truth-values of sentences and the truth-values of their contextual use in utterances. But in natural languages sentences vary in truth-value in virtue of containing indexical expressions: one and the same sentence can vary in truth-value depending on where and when it is uttered. (Consider such sentences as 'It is Tuesday today' and 'It is snowing here'.) Tarski's model needs modification if it is to be applicable to sentences in natural languages; the modifications will consist in truth's being characterized relative to a time (t) and a language user (NN) so that we get T-sentences exhibiting forms such as:

> S is true-in-L as uttered by U at time t, if and only if it is the case that p is near U at time t,

where 'S' is a description of a sentence L with indexical content and where 'p' is S itself or a translation of S in a metalanguage. An example would be:

> 'It's snowing here' is true-in-L as uttered by U at time t if and only if it is the case that it is snowing near U at time t.

Second, natural languages must be brought into line with the formal language for which Tarski developed his definition of truth. This applies, as already noted, to the predicate calculus. Formal languages are developed to clarify certain logical features of everyday speech; but it is a familiar fact that differences obtain between formal language and ordinary language. One such difference concerns universally quantified sentences, i.e. sentences such as 'All rhinos are vicious'. In predicate logic these are expressed by means of a formula which rendered into English runs 'For all x, if x is a rhino then x is vicious'. According to the conventions of predicate logic such a sentence is true if no rhinos exist. From the perspective of ordinary language, this is highly counterintuitive. In this respect ordinary language stands in need of modification if it is to be congruent with the language of predicate logic.

10. Tarski has expressed scepticism about the possibility of constructing definitions of truth for natural languages, partly on account of their muster of adverbials and various non-extensional contexts. Davidson has, therefore, to show that Tarski's truth definition can be modified to accommodate the idioms of natural languages. We shall now turn to Davidson's attempt at tackling two of these problems: adverbials and the non-extensional contexts exemplified by indirect speech.

Davidson is primarily interested in presenting the logical form of sentences, the semantical structure relevant to the entailment relations of sentences – what they entail and are entailed by. Precisely this aspiration runs into trouble when the theory has to tackle *adverbials* in natural language. Take, for example, the expression 'at St Ives in the morning' in the sentence:

Deirdre swam at St Ives in the morning.

This sentence entails the following sentences:

Deirdre swam.

Deirdre swam in the morning.

Deirdre swam at St Ives.

The problem is that we are unable to give an account of the relevant entailments if we give a standard analysis of the sentence using the two singular terms 'Deirdre' and 'St Ives' and a two-place predicate (a relational expression) '... swam in the morning at ...' Viewed from the perspective of predicate logic, the predicates '... swam' and '... swam in the morning' and '... swam in the morning at ...' are wholly discrete and unrelated expressions. Predicate logic cannot 'discern' that the first predicate is, so to speak, contained in the second and the second in the third, and that therefore entailment relations obtain between them. This is due to the fact that these predicates are generated, the one from the other, by adverbial modification, an operation not admitted by predicate logic. Davidson has proposed the escape route that consists in our regarding the sentence as featuring an existential quantifier that ranges over events. The logical form of the sentence then becomes the following:

> There exists an event x such that x was brought about by Deirdre, x was a swimming, x was brought about in the morning and x was brought about at St Ives.

If there does indeed exist such an event, then by using ordinary predicate logic we are able to infer that there also exists an event, brought about by Deirdre and which was an instance of swimming and further that there was an event which was an instance of swimming brought about by Deirdre in the morning and brought about at St Ives. So doing allows entailments to and from such sentences to be formalized in predicate logic, which circumstance, beyond being prerequisite to Davidson's programme, represents a strengthening of predicate logic generally.

The drawbacks to this technique are, first, that quantification over events requires an event ontology, mediated by the constraint that we regard events as a class of existents. This, however, is hardly a major problem since in everyday contexts we do not scruple to talk about sea battles, football matches, speech acts and rock concerts, all of which are events, not entities. Another problem is that not all adverbial modifications are captured by Davidson's analysis. Suppose that one evening, as an antidote to insomnia, Lucinda starts reading *A Thousand and One Nights*. Her reading, that is, is meant to induce sleep. The hours pass, and she manages to read the whole book before finally falling asleep. We would describe this by saying 'Lucinda read the book quickly, but fell asleep slowly.' Analysis of this sentence implies that there exists an event that is both rapid and slow: rapid qua reading-of-a-book but slow qua falling-asleep. The analysis thus entails the self-contradictory claim that one and the same event is both rapid and slow. Finally, the analysis cannot be applied to "attributive adjectives". An example is the term 'intellectual' in the sentence 'Rambo is an intellectual dwarf'. We cannot infer from this sentence that Rambo is a dwarf, and certainly not that Rambo is an intellectual. Unfortunately, Davidson's analysis permits both these inferences.

11. Like Tarski's definition of truth, Davidson's theory of meaning is extensional. This means that the theory conforms to the principle that in any given sentence we can use other words that share the same reference or extension interchangeably without any modification of the sentence's truth-value. In consequence, Davidson's theory may be expected to run into serious difficulties when applied to certain idioms of natural language known not to conform to the principle of extensionality. One of these is indirect speech.

Consider the following sentence:

1. Galileo said that the earth moves.

If the extensionality principle is to hold for this sentence we must be able to substitute expressions with the same extension (reference) without the sentence undergoing a change in truth-value. Now consider the following fact:

2. The earth is the only planet in the solar system where television programmes are produced.

'The earth' and 'the only planet in the solar system where television programmes are produced' are, then, co-extensional expressions, and we should be able to make the substitution in (1) which yields the following sentence:

3. Galileo said that the only planet in the solar system where television programmes are produced, moves.

The problem is that (1) and (2) are true while (3) is obviously false: (3) does not report what Galileo said. In consequence, given a blanket application of the extensionality principle to the sentences of natural language, invalid inferences result. We note, then, that ordinary language contains contexts for which the extensionality principle does not hold. Such contexts include, e.g. 'NN believes that', 'NN hopes that', 'The symbol S means that' and suchlike.

The extensionality principle returns a simple answer to the question of how words contribute to the truth-value of the sentences in which they appear in extensional contexts. The contribution of the constituent words to the truth-value of the sentence is simply a function of their references and extensions. But how are we to account for the contribution of the constituent words to the truth-values of sentences where the words occur in non-extensional contexts?

Any solution to this problem will have to meet the following two constraints in order to be acceptable to Davidson. It will have to conform to the extensionality principle while blocking the above inference from (1) and (2) to (3), and will have to render an account of an inference from (1) to, for instance:

4. Galileo said something.

Let us look at how Davidson honours these constraints. Assume that in Rome on 12 April in the year of our Lord 1633, at three minutes past three local time Galileo uttered the Italian sentence 'Eppur si muove' (which we translate into 'The earth moves') and that the reader of this paragraph at this present moment in time utters the sentence 'The earth moves'. On that assumption, the reader and Galileo have said the same thing. This idea paves the way for Davidson's account of indirect speech.

According to Davidson the locution ' says that' is to be read, in terms of its logical form, as a three-place predicate which picks out a speaker (in casu: Galileo), an utterance produced by that speaker (in casu: Galileo's utterance of 'Eppur si muove'), as well as a reference to an utterance by a person who formulates the sentence in indirect speech (for example, our subsequent utterance of the sentence 'The earth moves') viz.:

> There exists an utterance x produced by Galileo such that our subsequent utterance brings it about that Galileo and we say the same thing. The earth moves.

Davidson goes on to abbreviate this so that our utterance of 'The earth moves' now assumes initial position:

> The earth moves. Galileo said that.

The point, according to Davidson, is that the logical form of what appeared to be one grammatical sentence ('Galileo said that the earth moved') uncovers the fact that semantically speaking, there are two. This move enables Davidson to retain the extensionality principle for the first sentence, which specifies the content of the segment of direct speech: we can substitute coextensional expressions to our hearts' content without the sentence undergoing a change in truth-value. By the same token, this solution enables Davidson to account for the fact that such substitutions affect the truth-value of the other sentence – namely, if it happens that the substitutions make it the case that we and Galileo are no longer saying the same thing. Finally, the account permits the inference (4): Galileo said something, from the sentence 'Galileo said that'.

But does the move not implicate Davidson in the use of the concept of meaning in his semantic analysis, a use outlawed by the constraints that he himself has formulated? For on the face of it, the claim that we and Galileo say the same thing seems to rely on the concept of meaning, in that here 'say the same thing' does not mean to use the same words (for Galileo spoke

Italian and we speak English) but rather to use words that have the same *meaning*.

On this subject, Davidson notes that his analysis of the expression 'says that' applies solely to the logical form of the expression, not to its content. The content of the sentence is the business of the object language; the blame cannot be laid at Davidson's door if a usage includes expressions about which we for philosophical – or scientific – reasons may be sceptical. If a language such as French, for instance, contains the word 'sorcière', the theory for this language has to use matching words in the relevant T-sentence such as "Il y a des sorcières' is true if and only if there are witches'; but this is not to say that the linguistic theory is committed to the existence of witches. In the same way, the expression 'says the same thing as' is simply part of the language for which the theory was formulated, but is not a component in the theory's own conceptual apparatus.

We are thus led to the following definitive account of a sentence containing indirect speech, formulated as a theorem in a theory of meaning:

'Galileo said that the earth moves' is true-in-English if and only if there exists an utterance of Galileo's such that my subsequent utterance makes it the case that we say the same thing. The earth moves.

Whether this theorem is true will depend on the following statements expressing empirical facts:

5. That Galileo actually uttered the sentence 'Eppur si muove'.

6. That it is possible to set up an empirically verifiable T-theory for Italian which respects the principle of charity and which implies the following theorem:

'Eppur si muove' is true-in-Italian if and only if the earth moves.

(This is not strictly accurate since what the sentence means is 'It moves'. However, here we shall go along with Davidson's construal of the example which presupposes the present reading. Incidentally, the correct reading would bring us face to face with certain problems of Davidson's theory which we will discuss in section 13).

And finally:

> 7. That the speaker subsequently actually utters the sentence 'The earth moves'.

By means of this analysis we can, first, account for the fact that the sentence 'Galileo said that' becomes false if we let 'that' refer to the utterance of a sentence that is achieved by substituting for the expression 'earth' another co-extensional expression in the sentence 'The earth moves'. For example:

> The only planet in the solar system where television programmes are produced moves. Galileo said that.

For even if 'The only planet in the solar system where television programmes are produced moves' results from a legitimate substitution in the sentence 'The earth moves', it is not the sentence that an empirically verified T-theory observing the principle of charity would use to formulate the truth condition for the Italian sentence 'Eppur si muove'. Second, we can also block the problematic inference from (1) and (2) to (3) above. Given the sentences:

> The earth moves. Galileo said that,

and

> The earth is the only planet in the solar system where television programmes are produced,

we can infer at most the following unproblematic conjunction:

> The only planet in the solar system where television programmes are produced moves. Galileo said something.

As noted above, language exhibits a large number of non-extensional contexts such as 'believes that', 'hopes that', and so on. According to Davidson, all of these create problems of the same type as those which, as we have noted, attach to the expressions 'says that' and 'means that'. Davidson is sanguine about the prospects for accounts of these expressions on the lines of that given for 'says that' in indirect speech contexts.

12. We shall now turn to some of the difficulties that Davidson's project, for all its merits in comparison with traditional theories of meaning, still has to face. The problems mostly relate to the constraints that the theory shares with many others that work within the parameters of an extensional framework.

In virtue of its form, the following expression is a T-sentence:

(S) 'La neige est blanche' is true-in-French if and only if grass is green.

This T-sentence is true. It is true that grass is green and it is also true that the sentence 'La neige est blanche' is accounted true by French speakers. The two sentences thus have the same truth-value and precisely this is what the connective 'if and only if' indicates regarding the two sentences it conjoins. But (S) is patently unacceptable as an account of the *meaning* of the French sentence 'La neige est blanche'. 'Grass is green' sheds no light at all on the meaning of 'La neige est blanche'.

On the face of it, Davidson would seem to have an answer to this challenge. On any full-fledged theory of meaning for French, a sentence such as (S) would not stand alone (as in a translation manual) but would be derivable from simpler parts of the theory, primarily the axioms which determine the conditions for the satisfaction of the two predicates 'x est blanche' and 'x est la neige'. These two predicates will recur in countless other T-sentences, including those sentences which if used to speak about grass or greenness in the metalanguage would be false. In consequence, possible errors in the axioms that fix the meaning of the predicates are easily detectable. Using the same two axioms, the theory would, for instance, entail the following defective T-sentence:

(S*) 'Celui est blanc' uttered by NN here is true-in-French, if and only if what NN is pointing to here is green.

In the middle of a snowy landscape in the company of a Frenchman, we have no difficulty in establishing that (S*) is wrong. We point to the snow and say 'Celle-là est blanche' and he nods in agreement, but obviously what we are pointing at is not green. Or we point to luminously verdant beechwoods in May and say 'Celui est blanc' and note that the French speaker shakes his head. Thus the theory of truth which implies (S*) is evidently wrong and we can accordingly not count on (S), which follows from the same theory, being correct.

More generally, the answer is that these sentences can be ruled out as specifications of meaning since they are not derivable from a well-constructed and empirically-grounded theory of meaning. Obviously, meaning cannot, then, be specified solely through appeal to T-sentences in the theory, but requires the additional fact that T-sentences are derivable from the theory's axioms. This circumstance must be added in as further information if the theory is to be able to specify the meaning of a particular language.

Indeed, further reflection reveals that yet greater amplification is required, including the proviso that the theory should so reflect the linguistic practice of a group of language users as to make the majority of their assertions true. This proviso is the principle of charity, to which we shall return in chapter 10.

But is this constraint compatible with the extensionality principle? To say that language users assert something is to say that they commit themselves to the truth of something's being thus and so. But this involves an inherently non-extensional idiom. To commit oneself to its being true that the earth moves is, for instance, not the same as committing oneself to its being true that the only planet where television programmes are produced, moves. But this means that non-extensional elements enter into the specification of the theory of meaning.

Davidson is aware of the problem and has offered the defence that the theory itself – the revised Tarski model – is extensional; the non-extensional element only insinuates itself into the "contextual remarks" about the theory. This is correct but looks uneasily like an attempt to duck the issue. Inasmuch as these "contextual remarks" contain information that is necessary for the theory's claim to deliver a characterization of linguistic meaning, the difference between what the theory says in and of itself and what the "directions for use" say, is altogether irrelevant.

13. But might it not be possible to apply Davidson's analysis of indirect speech to those very sentences that constitute the contextual remarks and thus show that they do not violate the extensionality principle? We could, in other words, neutralize the sentences of the type 'The natives assert that ...' by converting them into an extensional form by using Davidson's prescription as set out in section 11.

The observation is correct and so Davidson's theory comes to hinge on the viability of the analysis of indirect speech. Its validity has been disputed and here we will adduce but one difficulty out of many – a difficulty that Davidson himself has pointed out, though without having delivered a satisfactory solution to it. Let us take a variant of the example we have been using to illustrate Davidson's theory, namely the sentence that runs:

There exists a planet of which Galileo said that it moves.

According to Davidson, this sentence should be analysed as follows:

It moves. There exists a planet of which Galileo said that.

In a sentence such as 'There exists a planet of which Galileo said that it moves', the expression 'of which Galileo said that it moves' gives a more precise specification of the expression 'planet'. The word 'it' refers to 'planet', exemplifying the referential relationship known as anaphora. Such a sentence is thus intrinsically *self-referential*, but this feature is lost when the sentence is split up into two ostensibly independent parts in Davidson's analysis. Forfeited too is what the sentence properly refers to. Davidson's analysis of indirect speech is in default here.

The point becomes clearer if we express it in quasi-logical notation. The logical form of Davidson's paraphrase is as follows:

x moves. ∃x (x is a planet & Galileo said that).

Here, the first 'x' is not bound by the quantifier. Hence, it is not properly tied up with the second element in the analysis, and is not stricly speaking a complete sentence at all, but merely a sentence form.

The debate about Davidson's theory of meaning is far from closed and it would be premature to claim that it cannot be strengthened in a manner that would invest it with the resources to tackle this and other difficulties. But we shall not pursue these issues further here. At this point we can merely conclude that Davidson's proposal is the best truth-based, generative theory of meaning for natural languages currently on offer. However, it faces as yet unresolved problems in handling non-extensional contexts. In the next chapter, we shall consider various proposals for dealing with such contexts.

Chapter 7

Intensional semantics

1. In the previous chapter, we looked at Davidson's programme for the development of a theory of meaning for natural languages. In particular, we examined Davidson's answer to the challenge posed by adverbials as well as his attempt to account for indirect speech ('saying that'-contexts). In so doing, we also noted the problems to which these proposed solutions give rise. 'Saying that'-contexts provide one example of the apparent non-extensionality encountered in natural languages, others of which include locutions such as 'It is necessary that …' and 'NN believes that …' Since it is more than a little questionable whether Davidson's paratactic method resolves the problems presented by these contexts, this chapter will be devoted to the consideration of an alternative solution, one purportedly delivered by so-called intensional semantics.

Let us begin by clarifying what we understand by the terms 'extensional semantics', 'extensional contexts' and 'extensional language', which to this point have been used in a relatively non-technical sense. With that clarification in place, we will turn our attention to the puzzles arising in non-extensional contexts, pointed up by Frege in "Sense and Meaning", and which present a challenge to any purely extensional semantics. This will take us to this chapter's chief focus, the semantic theories advanced in the twentieth century that purport to deliver a systematic account of non-extensional contexts – so-called intensional semantics.

2. An extensional semantics involves no semantic properties of names and predicates other than their respective references and extensions, and no semantic properties of sentences other than their truth-value. We shall use the expression *semantic value* to cover the truth-values of sentences, extensions of predicates and references of names. The extensional approach is informed by the *compositionality principle* and the concomitant *substitutability principle*. The *compositionality principle* says that a sentence's semantic value (truth-value) is a function of the semantic values of its constituents (the references of names, extensions of predicates, or component clauses). Once these last

mentioned elements are fixed (for example in an interpretation or a value assignment) the truth-value of each sentence formulable in the language will likewise be fixed (in accordance with the semantic rules for quantifiers and logical constants).

Suppose that 'Huxley' refers to Aldous Huxley, and that the predicate '... is/was an Englishman' pairs Englishmen with the semantic value true, and everything else with the value false, thus:

Reference ('Huxley') = Aldous Huxley

Extension ('... is/was an Englishman') = {<Aldous Huxley, true>, <Shakespeare, true>, <Karen Blixen, false>, <Hans Christian Andersen, false> ...}

Then the truth-value of 'Huxley was an Englishman' is a simple function of the constituents' semantic values inasmuch as the function with which the predicate is associated maps the semantic value linked to the name 'Huxley', namely Aldous Huxley, onto the value true.

The compositionality principle implies another, namely, the *substitutability principle*. This principle states that in extensional languages, one co-referential expression may be substituted for another *salva veritate*. Whether the expression is a clause forming part of a complex sentence, or a predicate, a relational expression or a singular term, it can be replaced by an expression with the same truth-value, extension or reference without that substitution affecting the truth-value of the sentence in which the substitution occurs. A sentential context in which the substitution of co-extensional expressions may be performed *salva veritate* is called an *extensional context*.

Davidson's proposal for a theory of meaning for natural languages is patently conceived as an extensional theory. First, the theory of meaning is based on the Tarskian definition of truth. Second, the axioms are constructed for the non-logical constants in a Tarskian truth theory for a particular natural language by pairing extensions: the singular terms of the object language are paired with references, just as predicates and relational expressions are paired with extensions – both using the (supposedly) co-extensional singular terms, predicates and relational expressions of the metalanguage. And finally, to the logical expressions of the object language are assigned precisely the semantic rules that a Tarskian truth definition assigns to the logical expressions of a classical first-order language. Note, in conclusion, that Davidson's solution for the account of contexts with indirect reference (saying-that contexts) is conceived as an extensional solution.

The chief virtue of an extensional semantics is that it renders the semantic contribution of every category of expression transparent. It also makes transparent the logical form of sentences, i.e. the logical implications of those sentences that follow from their form (as opposed to those generated by the particular terms occurring in them). For instance, the Tarskian definition of truth (or, more generally, a Tarskian model theory) provides an account of logical consequence, i.e. formal validity for first-order languages. Such languages exhibit a clear and unambiguous syntax. Atomic sentences are constituted by singular terms and predicates; other sentences are formed through the introduction of truth connectives, quantifiers and variables. Formal validity is solely a function of syntactic form (logical form) and is quite unconnected with the particular names and predicates that occur in sentences. The semantic validity of arguments is explicated by reference to the dependence of the truth-values of sentences on the truth-values of their constituents. Consequently, an argument is valid if the conclusion is true in every interpretation in which the premises are true, i.e. if it is impossible that there should exist a model which assigns semantic values to linguistic constituents with the result that the premises are true and the conclusion false. Here we are reckoning only with the semantic values of names, predicates and relational expressions.

The crucial question, however, is whether or not a semantical theory for a natural language can be developed within the framework yielded by the compositionality principle and the substitutability principle. In the preceding chapters, we have repeatedly come across problems posed by the ostensibly non-extensional contexts of natural language which hint at a negative answer to this question. In this chapter, we shall examine those contexts in a more systematic manner to decide whether the obstacles to an extensional treatment are genuine or only apparent. We shall also investigate whether the virtues of extensional semantics – perspicuity and clarity – may be retained if its defining principles are abandoned.

3. In his celebrated article 'Sense and Meaning', Frege introduced a string of puzzles aimed at persuading us that linguistic expressions do not merely have a reference (*Bedeutung*) – if indeed they do – but that they also have a sense (*Sinn*). We encountered some of these puzzles in chapter 3, which dealt with the reference of singular terms. If we want to account for the contribution made by singular terms to the informational content of identity sentences, we need to recognize, Frege argues, that in addition to references, singular terms also have senses. For otherwise the informational content of a sentence of the type 'a = b' is the same as that contained in sentences of the

type 'a = a'. Further, according to Frege we ought only to assume that linguistic understanding consists in knowledge of the senses of expressions and not necessarily in knowledge of their semantic values: references, extensions and truth-values.

But Frege's article raised other problems too: those that arise when the tripartite conjunction comprising the thesis that the meaning of an expression is identical with its reference, the compositionality principle and the concomitant substitutability principle are confronted with an array of other sentential functors of natural languages and their capacity for producing meaningful sentences. It is to the problems generated by such constructions that we shall now turn.

Let us start by looking at modal contexts which appear in connection with the sentential functors 'it is necessary that ...' and 'it is possible that ...' (In the substitutions discussed below we shall follow Frege in regarding descriptions as names.) Consider the true sentence: 'The Morning Star is a planet'. Since the expressions 'Evening Star' and 'Morning Star' have the same reference, the substitutability principle allows us to substitute the one for the other so that we get the sentence 'The Evening Star is a planet', which is likewise true. The underlying presupposition is that the truth-value of a sentence is purely a function of the semantic values of its constituents.

But consider now the following substitution. It is obvious that the sentence 'Necessarily, the Morning Star is identical with the Morning Star' is true. Now the terms 'the Evening Star' and 'the Morning Star' have the same reference. According to the substitutability principle we should be able to use these two terms interchangeably and so get the true sentence: 'It is necessary that the Evening Star is identical with the Morning Star'. However, this sentence is not obviously true. For instance, was it not in God's power so to create the world that the planet we observe in a certain region of the sky in the evening was not identical with the planet we see in a different region of the sky in the morning? The truth-value of the resultant sentence is, then, not construable as a function of the semantic values of its constituent parts. If it were, the sentence would have been true.

It becomes clear, then, that the substitutability principle does not apply in modal contexts. And since this principle follows from the compositionality principle, a further corollary is that the truth-values of sentences featuring modal contexts cannot be construed as functions of the extensions of their constituents. It would seem that neither the substitutability principle nor the compositionality principle apply in modal contexts. This has the consequence that the modal sentence constructions of natural languages cannot be accounted for within the framework of a purely extensional semantics.

Let us next turn to so-called 'propositional attitude contexts', which are those presented by sentence constructions through which we ascribe cognitive states to others and ourselves. These contexts are mediated by expressions such as 'believe that', 'know that', 'hope that', 'fear that', 'wish that', and so on. Consider the following sentence: 'Jones believes that the Evening Star is identical with the Evening Star'. Since the terms 'the Evening Star' and 'the Morning Star' are co-referential we would tend to assume that the resultant substitution 'Jones believes that the Evening Star is identical with the Morning Star' is likewise true. But it need not be. To see this, think of Jones as an unenlightened Babylonian who, according to Frege, would be unaware that the Evening Star is one and the same entity as the Morning Star.

The problem with the truth-value shift that occurs when co-referential expressions are substituted for one another does not only apply in the case of singular terms. The problem also arises for co-extensional predicates and sentences with the same truth-values. Here is a classic example. Assume that the sentence 'Jones believes that Otto is an animal with a liver' is true. The predicates '... is an animal with a liver' and '... is an animal with kidneys' are co-extensional. By substitution we get 'Jones believes that Otto is an animal with kidneys'. But if we cast Jones as a boy who believes that only mammals have livers and only poultry have kidneys and conjoin this to his belief that his pet rhino, Otto, is a mammal, the result of the substitution is false.

The problem is replicated in the case of the intersubstitutability of sentences with the same truth-value. Assume that the sentence 'Neil Armstrong believes that Lee Harvey Oswald killed J.F. Kennedy' is true and that the following two sentences have the same truth-value: 'Lee Harvey Oswald killed J.F. Kennedy' and 'The moon is made of green cheese'. Given those assumptions, 'Neil Armstrong believes that the moon is made of green cheese' ought on the substitutability principle to be true. But that it is utterly untrue is something of which Neil Armstrong has a surer grasp than most people.

Again, we may note that each of these examples apparently violates the compositionality principle. The truth-values of sentences in attitude contexts are not functions of the semantic values of the constituent expressions: references, extensions or truth-values. Were that so, the substitution of co-extensional expressions would not occasion shifts in truth-value. Consequently, the propositional attitude contexts of natural languages apparently fall outside the framework of an extensional semantics.

We recall that we are using the designation 'non-extensional context' as a generic label for all those sentential contexts in which the substitution of co-extensional expressions may give rise to changes of truth-value, whereas the designation 'extensional context' is applied to those contexts where the substitution of co-extensional expressions does not give rise to such problems. Note too that the set of non-extensional contexts includes types other than modal contexts and those governed by propositional attitudes referred to above. To this class belong also counterfactual sentences, contexts of explanation, and others.

Thus we seem to be forced to conclude that there are certain contexts of natural language that we cannot account for within the framework of a purely extensional semantics that builds on the extensionalist compositionality principle. Such was not Frege's conclusion, however. Frege held that these exceptions to the extensionality principle were only apparent.

4. Frege's proposal for the solution of the problem of the substitution of co-extensional expressions in non-extensional contexts is best elucidated if we start from his argument for the thesis that the reference of a sentence is its truth-value. Frege argues in 'Sense and Meaning' as follows: if, in a sentence, we substitute for one expression another which has the same reference but a different sense, the truth-value of the sentence is left unchanged but its sense is altered. After the substitution, the sentence expresses a different thought but its truth-value remains the same. Frege concludes from this that the sentence's truth-value is perforce its reference while the thought it expresses is its sense.

Frege's solution to the problem of substitution in non-extensional contexts is similarly grounded. Take a sentence like 'Necessarily, all bachelors are men' and let us, in our contrived example, assume that '... is a man' and '... is a regular reader of *Playboy*' are, in fact, co-extensional. Substituting the one for the other, we get the sentence: 'Necessarily, all bachelors are readers of *Playboy*'. But we can conceive of God creating a world in which, when it comes to bachelors' self-reported reading habits, actions (albeit unexpectedly) do indeed match words: none of them read *Playboy*. This means that our substitution of co-extensional expressions in this instance mediates a change in truth-value. The only way of explaining the change in truth-value has to be that the predicates have different senses.

If, on the other hand, we substitute for each other two expressions that have the same senses – e.g. the predicates '... is a bachelor' and '... is an unmarried man', thereby getting the sentence 'Necessarily, all unmarried men are men', the sentence retains its original truth-value. There is no way in which God could have created a world in which unmarried men are not men. This argues for the claim that the truth-values of non-extensional contexts at sentence level are a function of their senses rather than the extensions of their constituents. This is ultimately the gist of Frege's conclusion, but he couches it differently. Wanting to retain the compositionality principle (to the effect that the truth-value of a sentence is a function of the references of its constituents) Frege frames his conclusion as follows: expressions occurring in non-extensional contexts undergo a switch so that their customary ('direct') references are replaced by *indirect* references, given by their customary senses. In consequence, the reference of an expression occurring in non-extensional contexts is its customary sense, with the inevitable result that the truth-values of sentences containing non-extensional contexts are a function of the customary senses of the constituents. (This applies, of course, only if the operators governing the whole sentence create a non-extensional context; those parts of the sentence outside their scope contribute in virtue of their customary references.)

Frege's solution thus allows him to retain the substitutability principle, to the effect that co-extensional expressions can be intersubstituted *salva veritate*, but now subject to the caveat that expressions in non-extensional contexts no longer refer to their customary references. Linguistic expressions occurring in non-extensional contexts refer instead to their senses, which thus become their indirect references. The net result is that in non-extensional contexts intersubstitutability is restricted to expressions that have the same sense (and possibly only if they have the same sense for the individual language user whose propositional attitudes are being addressed). In consequence, we are restricted, in non-extensional contexts, to substituting synonymous expressions for each other.

5. Frege's account of non-extensional contexts is problematic, however. First, what kind of entity is a Fregean sense? This ontological question is one that Frege answered by claiming that some kind of Platonic realm must be assumed, furnished with such entities, graspable only in thought. But most philosophers since Frege have regarded senses, thoughts, possible states of affairs, propositions and the like with considerable scepticism and rejected them in favour of an increase in ontological parsimony. However that may be, we shall return to such ontological issues in our final chapter.

Second, even if, for the sake of argument, we assumed that there existed such things as Fregean senses, they would hardly be of any use in the formulation of theories of meaning for natural languages. As Davidson has pointed out, the one use to which Fregean senses cannot be put is that of functioning as meanings in a theory of meaning. For instance, the sense of a sentence is a function of the senses of its constituent parts. The meaning of the sentence 'Venus is high in the sky' is a function of the sense of the name 'Venus' and that of 'is high in the sky'. If we take the sense of 'Venus' as an argument, the sense of the predicate '... is high in the sky' yields the sense of 'Venus is high in the sky' as a value. But this is obviously a vacuous account. We enquire after the meaning of 'Venus is high in the sky' and get the answer, the sense of 'Venus is high in the sky'. The systematic nature of the account is to no purpose. (Cf. Davidson, 'Truth and Meaning'.) The explanations become no less circular if we thereafter ask for an account of the senses of the constituent words. For we get the answer that their senses are simply the contributions they make to the senses of the sentences of which they are parts.

The upshot is that Fregean senses are redundant and should surely yield to referents in the construction of a systematic theory of meaning for a natural language. Compare the Fregean account with an extensional semantics for first-order language in Tarskian mode. Once the references of the first-order language are fixed, the semantic rules for the other expressions will systematically (by recursion) determine the semantic values for every well-formed sentence formulable in the language. Moreover, such a semantics provides us with a basis for the testing of the validity/invalidity of inferences: an inference is valid insofar as the existence of any interpretation (the ascription of references and extensions) on which the premises are true and the conclusion false can be ruled out.

We are faced with a choice, then. On the one hand, we can opt for acceptance of the ontological parsimony of extensional semantics and thus the rejection of those parts of natural language that generate non-extensional contexts; or at least ban them in scientifically respectable settings. This is Quine's solution. But under that scenario, the outlook is bleak for those sciences that operate with sectors of language that are irreducible to purely extensional contexts – namely, the humanities and psychology insofar as the latter is neither behaviouristic nor a pure brain science. Alternatively, we might make allowance for the high quotient in natural languages of apparently non-extensional contexts, but reinterpret them as extensional according to Frege's formula. The price exacted here is our having to countenance a metaphysical morass of obscure entities such as Fregean senses, which are arguably ill-qualified to serve as a foundation for a science of semantics.

6. There might be a third way, however. To introduce it, we need to put technicalities aside for a while and cast our minds back to a highly dramatic episode in twentieth century history.

During the Cold War of 1945–90, politicians and military strategists on both sides of the iron curtain speculated on what the outcomes of a "hot" war might be. To that end, they developed various instruments of analysis with which to explore different scenarios. What would happen if the USA launched a pre-emptive nuclear strike with the Soviet Union mounting a counterattack a couple of hours later? What would happen if the Soviet Union was the aggressor and America responded after a few hours' vacillation? The idea was, then, by adjusting certain specific parameters and holding others constant, to reach reliable estimates of the respective scenarios.

Let us now exploit this line of thinking in the interests of an issue as irenic as the references of designated terms on different future scenarios. To whom, then, in the context of the war game sketched above, do the words 'the winner' and 'the loser' refer? Well, it depends on which of the two articulated scenarios one has in mind. Let us say, for instance, that the winner, under the first scenario where USA is the aggressor, is the USA itself, while the Soviet Union is the winner under the second scenario, where it is cast as the aggressor:

Scenario 1: the USA is the winner; the Soviet Union is the loser.
Scenario 2: the Soviet Union is the winner; the USA is the loser.

This means that the references of the terms 'the winner' and 'the loser' are interchangeable, depending on which of the scenarios we are talking about. We can say that the references of the terms are a function of outcomes under the respective scenarios:

Ref. ('the winner') under scenario 1 is the USA, Ref. ('the winner') under scenario 2 is the Soviet Union,
Ref. ('the loser') under scenario 1 is the Soviet Union, Ref. ('the loser') under scenario 2 is the USA.

This may be expressed in terms of functions, i.e. the term 'the winner' is used in accordance with the following function:

{<scenario$_1$, the USA>, <scenario$_2$, the Soviet Union>},

while the term 'the loser' is used in accordance with the following function:

{<scenario$_1$, the Soviet Union>, <scenario$_2$, the USA>}.

We will use the expression 'the intension of a term' (as against its extension) about functions from scenarios to the term's extensions in the various scenarios. The intension of the term 'the winner' is thus a function from scenarios to extensions of the word in the respective scenarios.

Int. ('the winner') = {<scenario$_1$, the USA>, <scenario$_2$, the Soviet Union>}.

And similarly for the term 'the loser':

Int. ('the loser') = {<scenario$_1$, the Soviet Union>, <scenario$_2$, the USA>}.

7. Let us turn again to the Fregean dictum: the sense of an expression determines its extension, given the way the world is. What Frege has in mind here is the sense of an expression as being something like a 'mode of presentation' of its reference, which, given the way the world is, "picks out" the object or objects in question. If, for example, with the name 'J.F. Kennedy', we associate the description 'the US President in the year 1962', then the reference of that name is plainly the individual who in the actual world satisfies the description by being the President of the USA in 1962.

But let us take a closer look at Frege's dictum. Instead of construing the meanings of names as rules or algorithms which in some sense "pick out" the object that satisfies the description in virtue of being its extension, we can construe them as regular mathematical functions. The sense of an expression, thus understood, is a function which, given the world as its argument, determines a particular semantic value. Pursuing this line of thought, we get the sense of an expression's figuring as a function which takes a given world, a scenario, a situation, or more generally an index as an argument, delivering as a value the expression's extension in the relevant world, scenario, situation or, more generally, at the relevant index. On that reading, the senses that we associate with the words 'the winner' and 'the loser' are quite simply their respective intensions.

Note that we specify the intension of an expression by specifying what it refers to in the various scenarios. So it is not Fregean senses but references/extensions at the various possible worlds or in the various scenarios that figure in this kind of semantics: intensions are thus functions from possible worlds to the respective expressions' semantic values (references, extensions, truth-values) at those worlds. An intensional semantics, then, is *pro tanto* a generalization of an ordinary extensional semantics.

8. We will now apply this line of thought to the various types of expression, names, predicates and sentences, so that these too are ascribed intensions, i.e. functions from scenarios to extensions under the relevant scenarios. But first, here are three of the Cold War's worst scenarios.

We construe a scenario as a total description of the way in which events in the world might conceivably unfold. Our Cold War scenarios will thus all involve the actual world's presidents, high-ranking generals, lieutenants, military units and their full complement of hardware: fleets of ships and aircraft, tanks, atom bombs and conventional bombs – just to mention some of the most important sorts of materials. The various scenarios will thus be distinguished simply in terms of what happens under them, how they play out.

Over the course of the summer and early autumn 1962, the Russians sent missiles, manpower (at least 20,000 men, perhaps 40,000) and military hardware to Cuba, and embarked upon the installation of launch pads in San Cristobal, Guanajay and Sagua la Grande. Reports were coming in from Danish observation posts in the Øresund and from agents in Cuba that led the Americans to initiate monitoring activities in Cuba. On 29 August fears were confirmed. A U-2 surveillance plane returned to base with photographs which clearly showed that the Russians were in the process of setting up missile installations near San Cristobal. Further, U-2 flights confirmed that the installation of launch pads was under way at other locations in the island.

J.F. Kennedy summoned his team and inaugurated top-secret crisis meetings to discuss what the American response should be. Although three scenarios were articulated, in effect only two were considered. In fact, the staff divided into two groups and each group worked on a complete scenario. The first and patently most alarming of the two ran as follows:

1. Kennedy and his people ignore what the Russians are doing. The Russians, for their part, set up missile launch pads capable of homing in on targets throughout the USA and ones stretching down into the northern part of South America. With the entire region under threat and under cover of the missile shield, Nikita Kruschev and Fidel Castro start exporting communism to South America. The Democrats are accused of adopting a passive stance and lose the mid-term election. The Republicans come to power – and with them the military hawks. Kennedy and his administration are thus out of office and a worldwide war is brewing.

This scenario alarmed most of those present at the crisis meetings. They turned to consider a second:

2. Kennedy and his staff put the American forces on high alert whereupon they bomb the missile bases and invade Cuba, toppling Fidel Castro. But since the air force chiefs cannot guarantee a 100 per cent effective bombing campaign, considerable collateral damage must be contemplated as a result of error, in addition to the risk of missile attacks on Washington, the Pentagon and New York from the few launch pads that would survive

the onslaught. Given the major loss of life among the Russian soldiers at the installations, USA finds itself in open war with the Soviet Union. Nikita Kruschev accordingly mounts a blockade of Berlin and attacks American bases and missile installations in Turkey and Italy.

Finally, a third and less confrontational scenario is elaborated:

> 3. Kennedy and his staff mount a blockade of Cuba and demand that the Russian missiles be removed. Nikita Kruschev stops the overseas deliveries to Cuba and receives confidential assurances that the Americans will neither invade Cuba nor attempt to depose Fidel Castro and that later they will destroy their missile installations in Turkey and Italy. This ensures that Kruschev's decision will not look like a climb-down in the eyes of the Russian hawks. The Americans escalate the arms build-up in Florida. The Russians, perceiving the seriousness of the threat, dismantle the installations and ship both personnel and material back to Russia.

After some hesitation most of the decision-makers favoured the third scenario over the second, since the third, albeit confrontational, is less aggressive and yet leaves open the option of tightening the screws should the Russians oppose the blockade and persist in the installation of launch pads and the positioning of missiles. The bombing of the missile installations and an invasion might then be considered. The downside of this scenario was that the Russians might try to breach the blockade established by the American fleet and could be expected to retaliate by mounting a blockade of Berlin and threatening to attack bases in Turkey and Italy.

How would the Soviets react? After his television address to the nation in which he informed Americans about the missiles in Cuba and the imminent blockade, Kennedy conjectured that the Russians would bomb Turkish bases and mount a blockade of Berlin. In the event, history unfolded largely along the lines of the third scenario.

9. To illustrate intensional semantics, we will now construct a simple language consisting of names, predicates, connectives and two modal operators (in the first instance omitting quantifiers and variables). We set out the lexis of the language and its rules for the construction of well-formed formulae. This is followed by an account of the semantics of the language: we assign to the language's names and predicates intensions, i.e. references and extensions relative to the three scenarios and specify the semantic rules for connectives and modal operators:

Names: 'Kennedy', 'J.F.K.', 'Kruschev', 'Castro'.

Predicates: '... remains in office', '... mounts a blockade', '... invades another country'.

Connectives: '~', 'v', '&', '→' and '↔'.

Modal operators: 'it is necessary that ...' and 'it is possible that ...'

Syntax: If t is a name and if λ is a predicate, then λt is a well-formed formula. If Φ and Ψ are well-formed formulae, then '$-\Phi$', '$\Phi \vee \Psi$', '$\Phi \& \Psi$', '$\Phi \rightarrow \Psi$', '$\Phi \leftrightarrow \Psi$', 'it is necessary that Φ' and 'it is possible that Φ' are well-formed formulae. Nothing else is a well-formed formula.

Semantics: The intensions of the names and the predicates are fixed in the style of the designations 'the winner' and 'the loser', while the references of the names remain constant from scenario to scenario (s_1, s_2, and s_3 will henceforth designate the respective scenarios).

Int.('Kennedy') = {<s_1, John F. Kennedy>, <s_2, John F. Kennedy>, <s_3, John F. Kennedy>}.

Int.('J.F.K.') = {<s_1, John F. Kennedy>, <s_2, John F. Kennedy>, <s_3, John F. Kennedy>}.

Int.('Kruschev') = {<s_1, Nikita Kruschev>, <s_2, Nikita Kruschev>, <s_3, Nikita Kruschev>}.

Int.('Castro') = {<s_1, Fidel Castro>, <s_2, Fidel Castro>, <s_3, Fidel Castro>}.

To whom does 'Kennedy' refer under the three scenarios? Why, to the John Fitzgerald Kennedy of the actual world, no less. The difference is simply that in each of the scenarios the surrounding world pursues a different course. And to whom did the American hawks refer by the name 'Kruschev' when discussing and comparing the possible outworkings of each of the scenarios? Why, to none other than the actual world's Nikita Kruschev. So too with the name 'Castro': the staff referred to the Fidel Castro who to this very day remains president of Cuba.

In considering the intensions of the predicates, let us begin by recalling the semantic contributions of predicates in ordinary extensional semantics (cf. chapter 4). There we have a domain of objects. The names refer to these, and the semantical role of predicates is to be true or false of them according as they fall within the predicate's extension. The predicates are thus assigned extensions in the form of sets comprising the objects of which they are true, which is to say that they are assigned functions from objects to truth-values: (n-place-predicates are assigned functions from n-tuples to truth-values.) As, for example, with the predicate '… is a human being':

> Ext.('… is a human being') = {<Kennedy, true>, <Kruschev, true>, <Castro, true>, …},

i.e. functions of the form: <e, t>, where 'e' stands for the object and 't' stands for a truth-value.

Note that we are cheating slightly here. If the domain is the real world with its rich inventory of objects, running through the entire extension is not an option, and so we use the ellipsis symbol ('…') to indicate the obvious continuation of the list. The alternative would have been to deploy a more narrowly circumscribed domain. We shall shortly be taking the same liberties again when we give the intensions of predicates relative to the three Cuban scenarios. Since we have chosen to let each of the scenarios represent total world histories, the domain for each of the scenarios is the inventory of the actual world and, again, since such domains are unsurveyable, we indicate continuation by means of the ellipsis symbol.

This has the following consequence for the shape of the intensions of the predicates: the intensions map scenario-indices onto extensions under the relevant scenarios. Since the extensions of the predicates are themselves functions linking the objects in the domain to truth-values, the predicates' intensions accordingly take the form of functions from scenarios to functions from the objects of scenarios to truth-values:

> Int.('… remains in office') = {<s_1, <Fidel, true>>, <s_1, <Nikita, true>>, <s_2, <J.F.K., true>>, <s_3, <J.F.K., true>>, <s_3, <Fidel, true>>, <s_3, <Nikita, true>>, …}.

> Int.('… mounts a blockade') = {<s_2, <Nikita, true>>, <s_3, <J.F.K., true>>, …}.

> Int.('… invades another country') = {<s_3, <J.F.K., true>>, …}.

The predicates' intensions work out as follows: in the worldhistory described under scenario 1 the predicate '... remains in office' is true of Fidel Castro and Nikita Kruschev but false of Kennedy; the predicate as applied in the history described under scenario 2 is true of J.F. Kennedy and false of Fidel Castro and Nikita Kruschev; and in that described under scenario 3 it is true of all three heads of state. (Remember that we are cheating: we are proceeding as though the domain only involved these three individuals even though the predicates are defined for all objects.)

We will now assess the sentence 'Kruschev mounts a blockade' under scenario 2. Since the extension of 'Kruschev' in scenario 2 is Nikita Kruschev: $<s_2$, Nikita$>$, and since '... mounts a blockade' in scenario 2 has as its extension a function that maps Nikita Krushchev onto the value true: $<s_2$, $<$Nikita, true$>>$, the sentence is true in scenario 2:

Ext.('Kruschev mounts a blockade')(s_2) = true.

Next, let us look at the rules for connectives. Let 'p' and 'q' be any well-formed formulae. Then:

'~p' is true in scenario i, if and only if p is not true in scenario i.

'p v q' is true in scenario i, if and only if p is true in scenario i or q is true in scenario i.

'p & q' is true in scenario i if and only if p is true in scenario i and q is true in scenario i.

'p → q' is true in scenario i if and only if p is false in scenario i or q is true in scenario i.

If a sentence p is not true in a scenario, it is false in that scenario.

Finally, we need to formulate semantic rules for the modal operators: 'it is possible that ...' and 'it is necessary that ...' The method we adopt involves reference to the breakthrough achieved by Leibniz – later echoed in the work of Carnap and Kripke. Let us imagine that prior to creation God carefully considered the world histories he or she might choose to realize. Whereas Kennedy's staff pondered the three Cuba-crisis scenarios, we can imagine God contemplating not just three but each and every possible world scenario, prior to opting for the creation of the best of them all: the actual world as we know it.

To get an intuitive fix on the notion of a necessary truth, we can think of it as a truth expressible by a sentence that is true irrespective of which scenario God chose to realize. The sentence '2 + 2 = 4' is an example. Irrespective of which out of the many possible scenarios God actually elected to realize, '2 + 2 = 4' would have been true in that scenario. The sentence operator 'it is necessary that ...' may be taken to mean that a sentence of the form 'it is necessary that p' is true if and only if p is true in all possible scenarios. Consequently, if something is necessarily true in one scenario it is true in all:

> 'It is necessary that p' is true in a scenario if and only if p is true in all scenarios.

By the same token, we intuitively understand a possible truth as one expressible by a sentence that is true just in case that sentence is true in just one of the many world scenarios God might have realized. The sentence 'grass is blue' is, for instance, a possible truth because grass is indeed blue in one of the (mildly psychedelic) world scenarios whose realization God entertained. We may accordingly construe the sentence operator 'it is possible that ...' such that 'it is possible that p' is true if and only if p is true in at least one scenario:

> 'It is possible that p' is true in a scenario if and only if p is true in at least one scenario.

It is worth noting that while Rudolf Carnap figured importantly among those who worked with possible worlds – or, as he called them, state-descriptions – it fell to Saul Kripke to revolutionize possible world semantics by introducing the *accessibility relation*. The accessibility relation introduces structure into the field of the possible worlds, linking them up with each other in specific ways. This relation is important to our formulation of the semantic rules for necessity and possibility operators for it is the imposition of restrictions upon the accessibility relation that determines which possible worlds are interlinked or mutually "accessible". Such restrictions play an important role, e.g. in a temporal logic where the future but not the past is accessible to the present. The various modal logics are elaborated according to the kinds of restrictions imposed on the accessibility relation. That relation is definable as reflexive, symmetrical, transitive or serial, or as a combination of these. The rules as formulated above assume that we are working with a model in which all worlds are mutually accessible, i.e. a so-called S5 model where the accessibility relation is an equivalence relation. All the above-mentioned relations are satisfied.

If we introduce the accessibility relation into the formulation of definitions for the necessity operator and the possibility operator, respectively, the definitions take the following form: 'It is necessary that p' is true under a scenario i if and only if for all scenarios j that are accessible from scenario i, it holds that p is true under scenario j. Similarly: 'It is possible that p' is true under scenario i if and only if there exists at least one scenario j which is accessible from scenario i such that p is true under scenario j.

10. We will now illustrate how an intensional semantics functions by examining a couple of modal logical fallacies by reference to our scenarios:

> Necessarily, either Kennedy remains in office or Kennedy does not remain in office. Therefore, necessarily Kennedy remains in office or necessarily Kennedy does not remain in office.

The premise is true in our model. In scenario 1 'Kennedy remains in office or Kennedy does not remain in office' is true because the right-hand disjunct 'Kennedy does not remain in office' is true. In scenarios 2 and 3 'Kennedy remains in office or Kennedy does not remain in office' is true because the left-hand disjunct 'Kennedy remains in office' is true in both scenarios. Finally, the whole sentence 'Necessarily, either Kennedy remains in office or Kennedy does not remain in office' is true since the embedded disjunction is, as we have seen, true in all scenarios of the model. The conclusion, however, is false in our model. A disjunction is false if its disjuncts are false and in our model each of the disjuncts of the conclusion is indeed false. The left-hand disjunct 'Necessarily, Kennedy remains in office' is false because 'Kennedy remains in office' is false in scenario 1 and the right-hand disjunct 'Necessarily, Kennedy will not remain in office' is false because 'Kennedy does not remain in office' is not true in scenarios 2 and 3. Our model, then, evinces a counterexample that shows that the inference is invalid: its premise is true in the model and its conclusion is false in the model.

Let us look at another modal logical fallacy:

> It is possible that Kruschev mounts a blockade and it is possible that Kruschev does not mount a blockade. Therefore, it is possible that Kruschev both mounts and does not mount a blockade.

As before, the premise is true in the model. A conjunction is true only if both its conjuncts are true. And that is precisely the case here: 'It is possible that Kruschev mounts a blockade' is true because there is a scenario under which 'Kruschev mounts a blockade' is true, namely scenario 2; while 'It is possible that Kruschev does not mount a blockade' is true, namely under scenarios 1 and 3. The conclusion 'It is possible that Kruschev both mounts and does not mount a blockade' is false under each of the scenarios, however. In scenarios 1 and 3 the left-hand conjunct is false and in scenario 2 the right-hand conjunct is false. In consequence, this model too is a counterexample to the above inference.

11. We now return to the issue of the intersubstitutability of co-extensional expressions in modal contexts. We consider the following substitution:

Necessarily, Kennedy mounts a blockade if and only if he mounts a blockade. Kennedy mounts a blockade if and only if he remains in office. Therefore necessarily, Kennedy mounts a blockade if and only if he remains in office.

Let us assess the substitution on the basis of scenario 3. Here the sentences 'Kennedy mounts a blockade' and 'Kennedy remains in office' are co-extensional (they are both true); that is, the second premise is true. Since it also holds that the sentence 'Kennedy mounts a blockade if and only if Kennedy mounts a blockade' is true in each of the three scenarios (it is a pure tautology), the sentence 'Necessarily, Kennedy mounts a blockade if and only if Kennedy mounts a blockade' is obviously also true. We now substitute for 'Kennedy remains in office' the one occurrence of 'Kennedy mounts a blockade', which delivers the sentence 'Necessarily, Kennedy mounts a blockade if and only if he remains in office'. This sentence, however, is false, for while the sentence 'Kennedy mounts a blockade if and only if Kennedy remains in office' is true in scenarios 2 and 3, it is false in scenario 1. Our scenarios thus constitute a counterexample to substitution: the substitution of co-extensional sentences cannot always be carried through *salva veritate* in modal contexts.

Moreover, the model shows that two predicates can be co-extensional in one of the scenarios (e.g. '... remains in office' and '... invades another country' in scenario 2) but not co-intensional: they are not co-extensional in all three scenarios. The model also shows why we cannot substitute co-extensional predicates (in the style of 'animal with a liver' and 'animal with kidneys') for each other in modal contexts *salva veritate*.

We have thus constructed a semantic model which allows for the counter-examples to the thesis of the intersubstitutability of co-extensional expressions, in casu sentences and predicates within modal contexts. But it is plausible to maintain that within the model we are able to substitute co-intensional expressions for each other *salva veritate*, e.g. the names 'Kennedy' and 'JFK':

> Necessarily, Kennedy is identical with Kennedy.
> Kennedy is identical with JFK.
> Therefore: Necessarily, JFK is identical with Kennedy.

Two names have the same intension if they have the same reference under all possible scenarios. In our model a name behaves like what Kripke calls a *rigid designator*: the name refers to the same object in all scenarios, i.e. at all possible worlds in which the name refers. Notice that names and definite descriptions behave differently in modal contexts. Take, for instance, the name 'Kennedy' and the description 'the president who mounts a blockade'. The latter would refer to Kruschev in scenario 2 and to Kennedy in scenario 3, but would be without reference in scenario 1. Names are thus rigid designators while descriptions are flaccid designators.

12. It is possible, then, to elaborate a semantics for language which contains modal and other non-extensional contexts. Moreover, we have done so by retaining important elements of the model-theoretical approach that we encountered in our account of Tarski's definition of truth in chapter 5. The models and model structures of intensional semantics are just a shade more complex. Where extensional languages only need models that operate with just one world, intensional semantics commands models that contain one or more worlds (or index situations), and an accessibility relation. But the complexity does not detract from the inherent perspicuity of this kind of model. The model shows in systematic detail how the truth conditions of non-extensional sentences are composed of the semantic values of their components. The basic idea is that a sentence has its semantic value not simply in virtue of what happens at one world but of what happens at other possible worlds. This is to say that the semantic value of a sentence at a possible world or index depends not only on the semantic values of the constituent expressions at that possible world/index but equally on those semantic values they have at possible worlds accessible from the world in question. For instance, the sentence 'Necessarily, 2 + 2 = 4' is true at the actual world not just because '2 + 2 = 4' is true at the actual world but because '2 + 2 = 4' is true at all

possible worlds. By contrast, the sentence 'Necessarily, the number of planets is 9' is false at the actual world. Granted, the sentence 'The number of planets is 9' is true at the actual world, but there are possible worlds at which the sentence is false, and a sentence is only necessarily true if it is true at all possible worlds. With this development of the basic idea of the model-theoretical approach, a Tarskian definition for a first-order language arguably qualifies as a borderline case of intensional semantics: namely, as an intensional semantics for a one-world model.

13. With our Cold War example fresh in our mind, we can go on to give a general description of a so-called possible world semantics for a first-order language. This is a language consisting of names, individual variables, predicates, connectives: 'not', 'and', 'or' and 'if ... then', the existential and the universal quantifiers as well as the modal functional expressions: 'it is necessary that ...' and 'it is possible that ...' (we skip the formal syntactical specification of the language in question).

A model (<D,I,R>,F) consists of a model structure and an interpretation. The model structure: <D,I,R> involves a domain D, a collection of objects and the values true and false and a collection, I, of possible worlds or index situations with one of their number highlighted as the actual world or index situation. (We are cheating slightly by letting the domain of objects be the same for all indices. But this does not rule out other distributions at the various indices.) R is the so-called accessibility relation, which specifies the relations that obtain between the various indices. Interpretation F is a function which ascribes semantic values to the non-logical constants of the language in each of the model's worlds or index situations and specifies semantic rules for the logical expressions of the language. The interpretation is thus a function that assigns extensions to all non-logical expressions on each index. But such functions can straightforwardly be transformed into an assignment of intensions.

The intensions assigned to names are ones which for each index specify the reference of the name at that index. Similarly, predicates are ascribed intensions which at each index specify a function from the objects of the index into truth-values at the index. The sentences are assigned intensions which for each index specifies the truth-value at that index.

The semantic rules for the logical expressions (the usual logical connectives and the new modal operators) take over the job of recursively assigning semantic values to the complex expressions of the language in accordance with the rules for the construction of well-formed formulae. Each world or index situation constitutes a way in which the objects in D can be arranged.

Concretely, a model may take the form indicated below. The description is recursive, and subject to the caveat that its base of value assignments to the language's non-logical constants merely describes the *form* that value assignments would take in a concrete model. (Instead of writing 'F(X) at world i' we write 'F(X)(i)' which reads: the semantic value of the expression X is at world i ...)

NAMES: For each name and for each index i (at world i) in the model there will be a value description of the form:

F(t)(i) = the object which F links to the name t at world i.

If we imagine that names are rigid designators, the intension of the name will be a constant function, i.e. t will be linked by function F to the same object at all indices (at all possible worlds) just in case the object is in the relevant index domain. (For instance, F links 'Kennedy' to John F. Kennedy at all the worlds where John F. Kennedy exists.) However, if the name t is a flaccid designator, e.g. a definite description, the function F may link t to different objects according to the world. Thus, in some worlds the expression 'the US president in the year 2002' links up with George Walker Bush, in others with Al Gore.

PREDICATES: (For ease of exposition, we shall restrict ourselves to one-place predicates.) Here too it holds that for every predicate and for every index i (world i) in the model there will be a value assignment of the form:

F(λ)(i) = the set of objects that at world i satisfies predicate λ (which is identical with λ's extension at world i).

F applied to predicate λ is thus a complex function that ascribes λ to an extension at each of the worlds/indices of the model.

SENTENCES: We are now able to specify the form for a recursive definition of the truth of atomic sentences in the following way:

F(λt)(i) = true if and only if F(t)(i) is an element of F(λ)(i),

i.e. a sentence λt is true at a world i if and only if the object which F links to the name t is an element in the set of objects which F links to the predicate λ

at the world i. F(λt) is thus a complex function from t's and λ's extensions in the various worlds to the sentence λt's truth-value at the respective worlds.

Every sentence formulable in the language will, in virtue of the interpretative function of the model, be linked to a function from possible worlds to truth-values (namely the relevant sentence's intension). This holds not only of the language's atomic sentences but also of the complex sentences, viz., by using the following semantic rules:

NEGATION: F(~p)(i) = true if and only if F(p)(i) = false (not true).

CONJUNCTION: F(p & q)(i) = true if and only if F(p)(i) = true and F(q)(i) = true.

DISJUNCTION: F(p v q)(i) = true if and only if F(p)(i) = true or F(q)(i) = true.

THE CONDITIONAL: F(p → q)(i) = true if and only if F(p)(i) = false or F(q)(i) = true.

THE UNIVERSAL QUANTIFIER: F(∀υΦυ)(i) = true if and only if for every name t substituted for υ in Φυ it holds that F(Φt)(i) = true.

THE EXISTENTIAL QUANTIFIER: F(∃υΦυ)(i) = true if and only if for at least one name t substituted for υ in Φυ it holds that F(Φt)(i) = true.

The following are the semantic rules for the modal operators, where 'p' is any well-formed formula:

THE NECESSITY OPERATOR: F(it is necessary that p)(i) = true if and only if for all worlds j, such that iRj (world j is accessible from world i) it holds that F(p)(j) = true.

I.e. 'it is necessary that p' is true at a world i if and only if for all possible worlds j that are accessible from world i it holds that p is true at world j.

THE POSSIBILITY OPERATOR: F(it is possible that p)(i) = true if and only if for at least one world j, such that iRj, it holds that F(p)(j) = true.

I.e. 'it is possible that p' is true at world i if and only if there is at least one world j which is accessible from world i such that p is true at world j.

We can now define validity and semantic consequence for our modal language relative to a possible world semantics:

> A formula p is valid in a modal logic if and only if the formula is true at all worlds in every model within the constraints of the relevant modal logic (i.e. all depending on which restrictions we impose on accessibility relation R).

> An inference is logically valid within a modal logic if and only if the conclusion is true at every world in every model constructable in terms of the relevant modal logic's resources in which the premises of the inference are true.

14. We have now examined possible world semantics and seen how its resources may be deployed to account for substitutions in non-extensional contexts, more precisely modal contexts ('it is necessary that ...', 'it is possible that ...' and cognates), as well as having noted that possible world semantics allows a systematic and compositional account of sentences' truth conditions. It thus retains the chief technical virtue of an extensional semantics. But can possible world semantics also account for logical inferences and the substitution of expressions that involve the other types of non-extensional contexts? Such might include those featuring propositional attitude ascriptions. Precisely this species of non-extensional context has proved particularly intractable. The potential of possible world semantics is thus aptly tested by an examination of its capacity to accommodate propositional attitude ascriptions. We shall accordingly focus on the problems that these contexts pose for any (candidate) accounts of their logical form, which is to say, the semantic structure in virtue of which the substitution of expressions and logical inferences are valid. Finally, we shall turn to a couple of the proposed solutions that exploit possible world semantics.

We begin with a characterization of propositional attitude ascriptions. Propositional attitudes are mental states such as the belief that p, a wish that p, a fear that p, and so on. These are all intentional states with specific contents, and they typically figure in the explanation and understanding of human action. However, the issue of the constitution of propositional attitudes qua mental states belongs to the philosophy of mind and so will not receive further treatment here.

What philosophy of language is concerned with is the *ascription* of propositional attitudes: meaningful sentences through which we attribute propositional attitudes to ourselves or to others. It is the account of the logical form of these sentences that is in focus here. Ascriptions of propositional attitudes consist in two-place predicates: '… believe(s)/wish(es)/hope(s) …' that denote the relevant attitudes; 'NN' that designates the subject or subjects to whom the attitude is ascribed; and finally the noun phrase 'that p' which designates the proposition that is the object of the attitude. We use the term 'proposition' in an ontologically neutral sense, assuming no commitment as to the nature or ontological status of propositions. Loosely formulated, a sentence of the type 'NN believes that p' is true just in case the subject to which 'NN' refers has the relevant attitude to the proposition named by 'that p'. The task of the philosophy of language is to render an account of the logical form of such ascriptions: namely, to state what semantic contributions are made by the immediate context into which the 'that'-clause is embedded.

If it is to deliver the goods, a theory of meaning for sentences that ascribe propositional attitudes must, at a minimum, meet the following requirements.

First, the theory has to account for the logical validity of substitutions and inferences in contexts featuring propositional attitude ascriptions.

Second, it must be compositional and systematic. Compositional, in that on the basis of the contributions of the constituents, the theory has to be able to account for the meanings of the ascriptions. And systematic, in that the theory has to figure as part of a theory of meaning which specifies the truth conditions for every sentence formulable in the language, including sentences that ascribe propositional attitudes.

We can now turn to the task itself. Consider a sentence such as the following:

Rudolf believes that Otto is an animal with kidneys.

As we know, the predicates '… is an animal with kidneys' and '… is an animal with a liver' are co-extensional. But, as we have already seen, we cannot in every case substitute the one for the other in our sentences without mediating a change in truth-value. This phenomenon is readily explicable with the help of possible world semantics. Two expressions may well be co-extensional in the actual world, but if they have different intensions (i.e. different extensions in other possible worlds), they cannot be blanketly substituted for one another *salva veritate*, and especially not in non-extensional contexts.

This would seem to argue for the identification of the meaning of an expression with its intension. We went on, then, to suggest a rule to the effect that co-intensional expressions may be substituted for each other in non-extensional contexts. This rule is valid for modal contexts, but does it also hold for contexts in which propositional attitude ascriptions are made?

Consider the following sentence:

Rudolf believes that Ludwig is drawing an equiangular triangle.

Now it is a necessary truth that all equiangular triangles are equilateral and vice versa. This is due to the fact that the predicates '... is a equiangular triangle' and '... is an equilateral triangle' are co-intensional: they have the same extensions in all possible worlds. We might imagine, then, that we would be able to substitute these terms for each other, *salva veritate*. So we make the appropriate substitution and get the sentence:

Rudolf believes that Ludwig is drawing an equilateral triangle.

The problem is, of course, that we can easily specify a model on which the first sentence is true, and the predicates are co-intensional, but where the second sentence is false. For Rudolf may not be acquainted with the concept of an equilateral triangle, or he may be under the misconception that it is one thing for a triangle to be equiangular but quite another for it to be equilateral.

But the objection might be raised: were Rudolf only to stop to think, would he not discover that the two concepts are co-intensional? Surely, the objection would continue, the substitutability rule could be modified so as to apply only to idealized cases. But such a move would shift the focus of the enquiry away from the meanings of propositional attitude-ascribing sentences to an epistemological question about a priori knowledge. To show that the introduction of idealizing caveats into the account of linguistic meaning solves no problems, we offer another example:

'Ludwig is drawing an equiangular triangle' means in English that Ludwig is drawing an equiangular triangle.

And, after substitution of co-intensional expressions:

'Ludwig is drawing an equiangular triangle' means in English that Ludwig is drawing an equilateral triangle.

Obviously, the first sentence is true whereas the second is false. So the sentences must have different truth conditions.

The upshot, then, is, first, the disappointing news that there are apparently non-extensional contexts where not only co-extensional expressions but also co-intensional expressions prove not to be blanketly intersubstitutable *salva veritate*. This holds, as the examples show, of ascriptions of propositional attitudes, indirect speech contexts, 'means that' contexts and others. Borrowing a term from M.J. Cresswell, we shall call them *hyper-intensional* contexts. But beyond that, the above examples show that not merely extensions but also intensions are insufficiently discriminating to function as the meanings of linguistic expressions. All tautologies, for example, are assigned the same sense since they express one and the same constant function from all possible worlds to the value true.

So the question now is whether an intensional semantics commands the resources to account for the substitution of hyper-intensional contexts. We shall consider two variants. They are distinguished by their determinations of propositions – namely, as unstructured and structured, respectively.

15. Let us begin with unstructured propositions. According to R. Stalnaker, propositions are construable as functions from possible worlds to truth-values. Beliefs are a-linguistic or language-independent and, consequently, their contents are not dependent on linguistic structure. A belief may be said to be true if the actual world is an element in the particular proposition's truth set. This means that all tautologies/necessary truths express the same proposition: namely, the constant function that maps all possible worlds onto the value true. Whether you believe that $2 + 2 = 4$ or that the sum of the angles of a Euclidian triangle is 180 degrees amounts to the same thing. In both cases you hold a belief that is true at all possible worlds. And to that extent, the two beliefs are indistinguishable.

Stalnaker's proposal is, then, to make the proposition that is the object of an analytical belief *metalinguistic*, namely the proposition that the corresponding sentence expresses a function from all possible worlds to the value true. According to Stalnaker, if Otto has the belief that $2 + 2 = 4$, it should be construed as the belief that, at all possible worlds, the sentence '$2 + 2 = 4$' has the value true. This makes the proposition contingent, namely, on the belief as to whether an arbitrary sentence expresses a function from all possible worlds to the value true. This serves to block the substitutability of co-intensional expressions. Granted, sentences such as '$2 + 2 = 4$' and 'the sum of the angles of a (Euclidean) triangle is 180 degrees' are co-intensional, but since the contributions of these sentences to the truth conditions of sentences that ascribe propositional attitudes are to be regarded as metalinguistic, the contributions of their respective truth conditions are plainly different, in that they now relate to two different sets of linguistic conventions.

The truth condition of the sentence 'Otto believes that 2 + 2 = 4' is the following:

'Otto believes that 2 + 2 = 4' is true if and only if Otto believes that the sentence '2 + 2 = 4' is true at all possible worlds.

Whereas the truth condition of the sentence 'Otto believes that the sum of the angles of a (Euclidean) triangle is 180 degrees' is:

'Otto believes that the sum of the angles of a (Euclidean) triangle is 180 degrees' is true if Otto believes that the sentence 'the sum of the angles of a (Euclidean) triangle is 180 degrees' is true at all possible worlds.

That different truth conditions are involved is clear from the consideration that Otto would give an affirmative answer to the question about the sentence '2 + 2 = 4' but, unfortunately, might reply in the negative to the question regarding the truth-value of the sentence 'The sum of the angles of a (Euclidean) triangle is 180 degrees'.

For all the surface seductiveness of this metalinguistic solution, it faces a new set of problem. Consider the following sentences:

(a) Otto believes that 2 + 2 = 4.
(b) Otto believes that two plus two equals four.
(c) Otto croit que deux et deux font quatre.

All three sentences ascribe the same belief to Otto, but in Stalnaker's account we get three different sets of truth conditions:

(a') Otto believes that the sentence '2 + 2 = 4' is true at all possible worlds,
(b') Otto believes that the sentence 'two plus two equals four' is true at all possible worlds,
(c') Otto believes that the sentence 'deux et deux font quatre' is true at all possible worlds.

The account, then, is too fine-grained. Where (a), (b) and (c) can be said to ascribe the same belief to Otto, (a'), (b') and (c') ascribe different beliefs to him. Otto may well have learned arithmetic but is as yet unacquainted with

Arabic numerals, and is completely innocent of French. In consequence, (b') is true of him while (a') and (c') are false. This state of affairs results from the fact that the account is relative to the particular language referred to in the stipulation of truth conditions.

One response to this might be to require that the truth condition should be specified with reference to a sentence in the subject's language which is functionally equivalent to or translatable into the sentence that specifies the propositional content in the ascription of the propositional attitude. But by so doing, the problem of the theory's taking of an idiolectic, not to say highly idiosyncratic, turn is compounded by the problems it has in accounting for translatability and functional equivalence.

However, we shall take our leave of Stalnaker at this point. Stalnaker's concern is primarily the issue of propositional attitudes as they relate to epistemology and the philosophy of mind – and not that of their *ascription*, which remains the remit of the philosophy of language.

16. Let us turn, then, to the other variant, the structured propositions argued for by Rudolf Carnap and David Lewis. Two tautologies like 'All equiangular (Euclidean) triangles have angles whose sum is 180 degrees' and 'All equilateral (Euclidean) triangles have angles whose sum is 180 degrees' are indeed indistinguishable inasmuch as they are true at all possible worlds, but if we look at the propositions they express as compositional, i.e. as functions of the intensions of their constituents, there would seem to be a difference in the ways in which these propositions are respectively constructed. The proposition expressed by the first sentence exemplifies a function of the intension of the term 'equiangular', whereas the proposition expressed by the second sentence is a function of the intension of the word 'equilateral'. The intensions of these two expressions are clearly different: there are equilateral figures that are not equiangular and vice versa.

The meaning of a sentence should not, then, be simply identified with its intension (that is at most the meaning of the sentence in a crude sense, albeit fully adequate for certain purposes) but needs in addition to be identified with the structure of the intension, which is to say its composition. This enables the propositions to be further differentiated in respect of their constituents or sub-constituents. All in all, we get an account of sentence meaning that is more fine-grained. As a result, two sentences have the same meaning if their intensions are compositionally identical – or intensionally isomorphic as Carnap puts it.

For tautologies such as '2 + 2 = 4' and 'All (Euclidean) triangles have angles whose sum is 180 degrees' may indeed be co-intensional but they are not intensionally isomorphic: their intensions are structurally disparate, since they do not have the same meaning in the fine-grained sense.

The downside to this proposal, however, as Lewis observes, is that on this analysis, two sentences such as '2 + 2 = 4' and 'It is not the case that 2 + 2 is not = 4' will be assigned different meanings. However, this is a result Lewis is prepared to accept. But the sentences '2 + 2 = 4' and '4 = 2 + 2' also have to be assigned different meanings inasmuch as the compositional structures of their respective propositions are different even though containing the same expressions. But putting this to one side, and in order to consider an example, let us accept the theory and submit the thesis that two expressions can be substituted for each other *salva veritate* insofar as they share the same compositionally structured intensions.

Does this solve our problems in respect of substitution in hyper-intensional contexts? Consider the following two sentences:

Hans believes that Bob Dylan recorded *Time out of Mind*.

Hans believes that Robert Zimmerman recorded *Time out of Mind*.

Since the names 'Bob Dylan' and 'Robert Zimmerman' are rigid designators they share the same intension, and since both names are simple constituents occupying the same position in both sentences, the sentences must be intensionally isomorphic. It might be thought, then, that the two sentences have the same truth-values. But that they do not is plain from the fact that Hans only recently became a card-carrying Dylan fan and unaware that the singer's original name was Robert Zimmerman.

One solution might be to include sentential constituents in the compositional structure of propositions. On this proposal, the proposition expressed by a sentence might be a function of both the constituent expressions (syntax) and the constituent expressions' intensions (semantics). But once again we run into the problems of the metalinguistic solution: the dependence of truth conditions on the existence of particular languages. The sentences 'Otto believes that two plus two is four' and 'Otto croit que deux et deux font quatre' would accordingly be assigned different intensional structures, despite the deliverances of our intuitions to the effect that they have the same meaning. In common with the other metalinguistic solutions, this proposal proves to be too fine-grained.

So what is the correct account of the logical form of hyper-intensional contexts – *in casu*, the ascription of propositional attitudes? The disappointing answer is that, at present, there seems to be no generally accepted account, and all those on offer – including more elaborate versions of those referred to above – are beset by serious problems. Still, this much may be said: a satisfactory solution needs to feature a component that differentiates the meaning content of expressions in hyper-intensional contexts over and above what is extensionally and intensionally given, and which thus, in some sense or other, assumes the role assigned to Frege's 'mode of presentation', though without the introduction of Fregean senses or the reduction of the difference to concrete linguistic differences as given, say, by different sentences or their token utterances.

17. It has now been shown that it is possible to construct an intensional semantics whose central conceptual crux is that the semantic values of expressions – and, accordingly, their compositional contribution – do not depend solely on their semantic values in the actual world but also on their values at other possible worlds. This line of thought can even be extended so that linguistic expressions are not simply assigned semantic values relative to possible worlds (or situations) but are also relative to vectors of indexicals which, for instance, relativize the semantic value of an expression to a possible world, time, place, speaker, items singled out through the use of demonstratives, a discourse segment, an infinite sequence of things (cf. Lewis 1972, p. 176).

As an example let us take a look at indexicals and demonstratives, which raise thorny problems for theoretical semantics. They have been examined by David Kaplan who has tried to accommodate his analysis within a possible world semantics.

Suppose that both Napoleon Bonaparte and Sid Schlutz, an inmate at the asylum for the insane, utter the sentence, 'I am the Emperor of France'. Of these sentences, one is true, the other false, thereby conveniently demonstrating that, in one sense of 'meaning', they have different meanings. Still, the two sentences consist of identical elements embedded in an identical syntactic framework and hence must have the same meaning, in another sense of 'meaning'. The task is to elucidate what those two senses are, and to spell out the difference in terms of possible worlds.

Intuitively, we might want to explicate the latter, shared type of meaning for the indexical term 'I' along the lines of:

'I' refers to the speaker.

This is almost right, Kaplan agrees, but it is open to a fateful misreading, according to which it is equivalent to, "'I' refers to the speaker, whoever that is'; or, in our technical terminology, 'In any possible world w, 'I' refers to the speaker in w'. The same approach applies to other indexicals; for instance, the meaning rule for 'here' would go as follows:

In any possible world w, 'here' refers to the place of utterance in w.

On this analysis, however, the sentence 'I am here now' will come out as necessarily true since it would be true in all possible worlds, or as Kaplan phrases it, under all circumstances of evaluation. But intuitively, the sentence is not necessarily true, since if Willie utters the sentence, 'I am here now', he does indeed speak truly, but there would seem to be no logical or metaphysical compulsion to the fact reported: surely, Willie might just as well have been busy elsewhere.

The way to fix the meaning rules is to construe them, not as giving the meaning of the terms, but as singling out the reference of the indexicals relative to a specific context of use. In more precise terms, the rules do not assign a fixed intension to the terms, but specify an intension as the value of a function that takes the respective reference in the context as an argument. (An intension, we remember, is a function from a possible world – a situation of evaluation – to an extension.) In the case of indexicals such as 'I' or 'here', the value of the intension-function, *once fixed by the context*, is a constant: if Willie utters the sentence, 'I am here now' and we evaluate this sentence across various possible worlds, the person we examine in all these worlds is Willie, and the place is the same place as that in which Willie uttered the sentence.

This analysis captures the two levels in the semantic functioning of indexicals, of which the first comprises that which is common to all uses of the term, i.e. the meaning rules stated above (under the proper interpretation) while the second comprises that in which they differ, i.e. the identity of the item singled out by the use of an indexical in context. Thus, both the identity of meaning and the difference in import between the two utterances of 'I am the emperor of France' above have been accounted for. The first semantic element, Kaplan dubs 'character', the second he calls 'content', adding that it is roughly equivalent to our familiar old notion of intension.

This analysis may be captured in the apparatus of possible worlds. The context of an utterance is a quadruple consisting of a world, an agent, a time, and a place <w, a, t, p>. Indexicals are taken to be directly referring to the objects in the context in which they are uttered. Suppose that Willie utters 'I am here now' in context $c:<w_3, a_8, t_2, p_{45}>$, then 'I' refers to a_8 at c, 'here' refers to p_{45} at c, and 'now' refers to t_2 at c.

The circumstances of evaluation are the worlds we already know from possible worlds semantics. But now the worlds are a bit more complex, consisting of a tuple with two parameters: worlds and times $<w, t>$. A circumstance is called the home-circumstance of a context if it consists of the same values of the parameters w and t as occurred in the context. Thus the home-circumstance of context c above is $<w_3, t_2>$.

The character of an indexical is a function that takes an object in a context and delivers a constant function as its value. That is, characters are functions of the following type: $<c,<<w, t>, e>>$, where c is a context and w and t are worlds and times and e is an entity in c, e.g. the speaker, the place, the time, or the world of c. So the character takes c as an argument and delivers the constant function $<<w, t>, e>$. This function is our familiar old intension which for any dyad of a world and a time $<w, t>$ delivers the same entity e from the context c as its constant value. For example, if 'I' refers to a_8 in c, then 'I' refers to a_8 in all circumstances of evaluation whether a_8 exists in the world of the circumstances or not; if 'here' refers to a certain place p_{45} in c, then 'here' refers to p_{45} in all circumstances of evaluation whether p_{45} is a place there or not. The character of 'I' thus takes a context, $<w, a, t, p>$, as argument and delivers an intension of the form $<<w_i, t_j>, a>$, for all values of i and j. Thus, at the circumstances consisting of the world w_{118} and time t_{26} 'I' as uttered in context $<w_3, a_8, t_2, p_{45}>$ still refers to a_8.

The character of 'I' as spoken in a different context, say, $< w_{77}, a_9, t_{38}, p_{80}>$, delivers intensions of the form: $<<w_i, t_j>, a_9>$, for all values of i and j. The same goes for 'here' and 'now'. We can thus represent the character of the different indexicals as follows, for all values of i and j:

Character('I') = {$<<w_1, a_1, t_1, p_1>, <<w_i, t_j>, a_1>>$, ... , $<<w_m, a_n, t_o, p_p>, << w_i, t_j >, a_n>>$, ...}.

Character('here') = {$<<w_1, a_1, t_1, p_1>, <<w_i, t_j>, p_1>>$, ... , $<< w_m, a_n, t_o, p_p>, << w_i, t_j>, p_p >>$, ...}.

Character('now') = {$<< w_1, a_1, t_1, p_1>, <<w_i, t_j>, t_1>>$, ... , $<< w_m, a_n, t_o, p_p>, << w_i, t_j>, t_o>>$, ...}.

By way of illustration, let us evaluate the sentence 'I am here now' in terms of the above apparatus, beginning with the evaluation at the utterance's home-circumstance. Suppose that Willie is a_8, then as he utters 'I am here now' in c he is clearly in the place p_{45} at time t_2 in world w_3, so the sentence is true at its home-circumstance.

Next we evaluate the utterance in a circumstance $<w_{12}, t_{75}>$ different from its home-circumstance, where a_8 no longer is at the place p_{45}, and where t_{75} is a time later than t_2. The character of 'I' as uttered in $<w_3, a_8, t_2, p_{45}>$ delivers a constant function: Ext.('I')$(w_i, t_j) = a_8$ for all values of i and j; the character of 'here' as uttered in the same context delivers Ext.('here')$(w_i, t_j) = p_{45}$ for all values of i and j, and the character of 'now' as uttered in the same context delivers Ext.('now')$(w_i, t_j) = t_2$, again for all values i and j. So 'I am here now' as uttered by Willie in $<w_3, a_8, t_2, p_{45}>$ is true at a circumstance of evaluation if and only if Willie is at place p_{45} at time t_2 in the world of the respective circumstance. But we assumed that $<w_{12}, t_{75}>$ is a circumstance in which Willie is not at place p_{45} at time t_2; indeed, Willie might not even exist in the world of this circumstance. So the sentence 'I am here now' as uttered by Willie in c does not come out as true at this circumstance. Hence, in conformity with our intuitions, it is not rendered as a necessary truth.

Finally, a brief look at demonstratives. Demonstratives such as 'that', 'this', 'these', and 'those', unlike indexicals, may be used to refer in a context only when they are supplemented by a demonstration which can take the form, e.g. of a pointing, a sweeping hand gesture, or a description of some kind, such as 'the big green tomato over there'. The demonstrative refers to the demonstrated object.

For the investigation of demonstratives Kaplan introduces a device called the 'dthat-operator'. The operator 'dthat[ ]' is a generalized demonstrative which takes a demonstation or a description of an item in a context as its argument and delivers an intension as its value. (The demonstration is represented within the square brackets.) Thus, like character it delivers a constant function as its value: the demonstrative plus its demonstration in a context delivers the item directly referred to in the context as its extension in all circumstances of evaluation. The demonstrative 'dthat[woman standing at the door]' as uttered by Willie in context c as above refers to, say, Willie's wife, and it continues to do so in all other circumstances of evaluation, no matter who or what happens to be standing at the door in these circumstances. So the utterance of 'dthat[woman standing at the door] might not have been standing at the door' in context c is true just in case there is an accessible circumstance in which Willie's wife, as singled out in the context c, is not standing at the door.

A demonstration thus has features in common with a Fregean sense, i.e. a way of presenting an object, since the demonstration presents the object in a particular way: from this or that perspective, by this or that description, and so on, although the demonstration merely serves to fix the reference in the context. Kaplan can thus do full justice to the informative nature of true identity statements made by means of demonstratives, such as 'dthat[woman in the mirror right in front of me] is identical with dthat[woman standing at the door]'. (This point has affinities with the account of the informational content of identity statements given by the causal theory of reference, cf. chapter 3.)

Kaplan's theory, however, also shares features with Kripke's thoughts on rigid designation (see chapter 3) and with Putnam's demonstration of the indexical element in natural kind terms (see chapter 4). A name refers in all possible worlds to the same object to which it refers in its "home" world. 'Aristotle' refers to the actual Aristotle in all the worlds in which he exists. Similarly, a natural kind term refers in all possible worlds to whatever belongs to the same kind (same liquid, same kind of animal, same kind of stuff) as the kind originally pointed to in its "home" world, i.e. the actual world. As we saw in chapter 4, 'water' refers in all possible worlds to liquids that are of the same kind as the liquid pointed out as water *here* in our actual world.

18. Possible world semantics has succeeded in making linguistic meanings less obscure than they were on the Fregean theory of sense. The propositions or intensions expressed by sentences are to be understood as functions from possible worlds to truth-values – or purely as a set of possible worlds, the so-called truth set. The abstract concepts with which predicates are associated are construable as functions from possible worlds to extensions in such. The individual sense with which a name is associated is construable in terms of constant functions from possible worlds to one and the same object – insofar as it exists in the relevant possible world. (Empty names are construable as partial functions, which is to say, as functions that are undefined at the actual world.) In this way, possible world semantics, although intensional, displays the same perspicuousness as extensional semantics. The semantic modes of operation of the various parts of language are exhibited clearly and systematically.

David Lewis has formulated a powerful functionalist argument for the claim that intensions are indeed senses as a truth-conditional account construes that notion. Lewis characterizes the role played by meanings and shows that intensions meet precisely this characterization:

'In order to say what meaning *is*, we may first ask what a meaning *does*, and then find something that does that.

A meaning for a sentence is something that determines the conditions under which the sentence is true or false. It determines the truth-value of the sentence in various possible states of affairs, at various times, at various places, for various speakers, and so on'. (Lewis 1972, p. 173)

The role of senses is to fix truth conditions or the contributions made by subsentential expressions in fixing truth conditions. The intensions of the various linguistic expressions achieve precisely this: the intensions of sentences fill out the role of the senses of sentences inasmuch as they fix their truth conditions by fixing their truth-values relative to different indices; equally, the intensions of the expressions that are constitutive of sentences fill out the compositional role of contributing to the intensions of the sentences of which they are parts (as shown in detail above).

The possible world account is adequate from a cognitive perspective as well. What does his knowledge of the intensions of his language enable a language user to do? Turn him loose in a possible world (which means: acquaint him with all the facts about this world and other worlds in the model) and he would be able to determine the truth-value of any well-formed sentence formulable in the language. This is tantamount to saying that this language user can do precisely what any language user cognizant of the truth conditions of the sentences can.

However, possible world semantics has problems of its own, not least that of adequately accounting for the cumbersome ontology that is concomitant upon it. How should we construe the concept of possible worlds? When it is a case of the logician's interest in having semantic models at his disposal to investigate logical consequence and to produce proofs of soundness and completeness for the various modal logics, anything at all can serve as a possible world – from arrangements of tables and chairs to abstract set theory models. For the construction of so-called canonical models the logician unblushingly avails himself of syntactically specified maximally consistent sets of sentences to serve as models of possible worlds in which those very sets may be given an interpretation that shows them to be semantically consistent. The function of the interpretation is essentially as follows: $F(p)(i)$ = true if and only if p is an element in W_i where W_i is a syntactically specified maximally consistent set of sentences while $F(p)(i)$ = false if and only if p is not an element in W_i.

The logician is as ready to use the states of the temporal sequences of computers as semantic models for the various modal logics when showing the various meta-properties of modal logics. This goes for epistemic, temporal, dynamic or deontic logics. Just so long as the model is well ordered and otherwise behaves just as it should, everything is fine. But that answer will hardly satisfy the philosopher in metaphysical mode. The philosopher's query takes the following form. What is the ontological status of the so-called possible worlds and their cognates? A lot turns on this question. If the concept of possible worlds is to play a crucial role in a theory of meaning based on a possible worlds semantics, it avails us nothing simply to regard possible worlds as heuristic fictions (i.e. a purely instrumentalist interpretation) for then no real content is given to possible world semantics or, by implication, to the concept of linguistic meaning and linguistic understanding. The concept requires more substance than that.

Thus in the final analysis, the fate of intensional semantics hangs on the resolution of certain profound issues in metaphysics. We cannot address these widely ramifying problems in this chapter, however. Instead, we shall examine them more systematically in our closing chapter.

Chapter 8
Speech acts

1. The earlier chapters identified the most important among the various constituents of sentences and examined their semantic roles. The concept of truth occupied a central place in our analysis since the semantic role of any linguistic component consists in its contribution to the determination of the truth conditions of sentences. In seeking to identify the type of contribution made by each linguistic category, we discovered that it was possible, and indeed necessary, to characterize the distinctive contributions in ways that went beyond a purely "combinatorial" account which specifies, in the form of a mathematical function, how singular expressions and predicates combine to generate truth-values. It turned out that a satisfactory account would involve a broad array of further concepts that would put flesh on the bones of the structure we have elaborated. The preceding chapter explored the further resources which the notion of a 'possible world' provides.

The truth-based mode of analysis builds on our reflections in chapter 2, where the aim was to show that the concept of truth plays a pivotal role in fixing linguistic meaning. Linguistic meaning is a matter of the relation of language to reality, as mediated by users' knowledge of the language. The concept of truth captures a crucial aspect of this nexus between world and language.

We arrived at the role of the concept of truth in chapter 2 via an analysis of the various acts performable through language use: giving commands, asking questions, asserting, promising, requesting, and so on. It turned out that the capture of the success conditions of such acts is essential to a correct characterization of their contents. When these success conditions pertain to assertions, *truth conditions* are seen to assume a particular significance among them. But the importance of truth conditions in semantics extends beyond their role in characterizing the meanings of assertions. The success conditions for other types of linguistic act are specifiable with reference to the success conditions – which is to say, the truth conditions – of assertive sentences.

After our excursus into Davidson's programme in chapter 6, we can now put a more precise gloss upon this point. When we are dealing with a natural language with its infinitude of sentences, a theory of meaning, in order to be "systematic", must be able to account for the way that the meanings of any well-formed sentence is built up out of the meanings of the component terms: the *generativeness* of language must be done justice to. It transpires that we can make some headway with this task if we take truth as the core notion, adopting Tarski's truth definition for the purpose. This was the essence of Davidson's programme, which uses a Tarskian truth theory to recursively generate the truth conditions of any assertive sentence in the object language.

By contrast, no one has any inkling of how to devise a generative theory specifying the semantics of non-assertive sentences, if this is to be a strict counterpart to Davidson's theory for assertions. Such a theory would somehow correlate quoted non-assertive sentences of the object language with unquoted sentences, of the same mood, in the metalanguage. The result is unikely to be even grammatical. Instead, we have to resort to a theory which proceeds via a theory of truth. Given a Davidson-style theory which correlates quoted assertive sentences with their truth conditions, we might derive the sought-for theory by taking the T-sentences which are the output of Davidson's theory and transforming them into meaning-specifying theorems of the desired kind. This might be achieved by first transforming the quoted sentences into sentences of the chosen non-assertive moods by the appropriate syntactic transformations (change of word order, and so on). Next, the truth conditions stated on the right-hand sides of T-sentences would be reformulated as success conditions of the appropriate kind.

For many kinds of speech acts, it would be fairly straightforward to do this. There are obvious systematic connections between the syntactic form of the assertion, 'The door is closed' and the order, 'Close the door', and similarly for promises, optatives and yes-or-no questions pertaining to the state of closure of the same door. (Chomskyan generative grammar spells out these similarities by analysing all these syntactic forms as transformations of a postulated "deep structure".) In the same way, there are systematic affinities between the truth conditions of an assertion and the success conditions of the orders, questions and promises that are syntactically derived from it. When we turn to other non-assertoric moods, the situation is admittedly less simple. For instance, the open question, 'Why did Richard Nixon leave office?' is grammatically related to the sentence, 'Richard Nixon left office', but its success conditions are not derivable from the truth conditions of the latter in any simple way. Still, even if a theory of the suggested kind is bound to be fairly complex, it seems to be our best bet. In this way, the meaning of assertions, based upon truth as its core notion, and the recursive meaning theory pertaining to it, comes to assume a privileged position in the theory of meaning.

In this chapter, we shall be dealing with the semantics of non-assertive utterances (and with that of assertives as well); but we shall not be trying to work out the details of the kind of theory suggested above. This would be a job for linguistics rather than the philosophy of language. Instead, we shall be doing something that is preparatory to the development of such a theory, viz. to provide a general characterization of the various kinds of sentential moods, i.e. of the different forces with which sentences may be uttered. We shall be examining that which distinguishes assertions, promises, orders, questions, and so on.

In so doing, we shall resume the project that was first addressed in chapter 2, i.e. representing linguistic meaning in terms of use. The analysis of the use of language showed that truth played a central role in this area, and for a couple of chapters we focused on this notion which as it were was distilled out of the initial, broader notion of language use. Now we shall be going back to the richer notion of use again, and be dealing with the nature of speech acts in their full breadth. In the meantime, we have acquired some more precise tools with which to describe language, and we shall be adding a couple more as we go along. We conclude the chapter by considering how language viewed as a structure fits together with language viewed as practice.

2. A person who produces linguistic utterances performs an act susceptible of many different levels of description. The analysis presented here combines contributions from such figures as John Austin, Paul Grice and John Searle.

In the following we shall be describing speakers' performance of *speech acts*. Two preliminary remarks are in order. First, these "speech" acts need not necessarily involve *spoken* language, or indeed language at all, but may equally well consist of writing, gestures, signs or other forms of communication. But, following customary usage, we shall be deploying the term 'speech acts' as a generic term. Second, in what follows we shall be referring to the various acts a language user performs by or in the utterance of a sentence. Strictly speaking, it would be more accurate to speak of different *aspects* of one and the same act; most of these "acts" cannot be performed separately but, given their nature, are performed as concomitants to some other types of speech act. But any comprehensive description would soon become too circumstantial, so here too we shall follow common usage and refer to these features as independent acts.

At the most basic level, in performing a speech act the speaker is articulating particular sounds capable of phonetic description. But he does more than that: he utters sounds that are linked to signs constituent in a sentence where they play specific semantic roles. Most notably, his utterance will often involve an expression that performs a purely referential function – it identifies the item the sentence is about – as well as one performing a predicative function, through which something is said about the item first identified (the specific character of these functions has been fully described in the preceding chapters).

These functions are performed by means of what we call a *locutionary act* (from the Latin *locutio*, speech or utterance). Consequently, the two individuals in the following dialogue perform the same locutionary act. A: 'Has Prince Charles abdicated his right to the throne?' B: 'No, Prince Charles has not abdicated his right to the throne.' They both refer to the same person – one Prince Charles, and in the same way, and both predicate the same thing of him, namely abdication.

3. But while, in the above dialogue, A and B are talking about the same subject, it is equally clear that they are saying different things about it. A's words constitute a question; B's a statement or an assertion. Questions and assertions are examples of the types of *force* that may be grafted onto one and the same locutionary act. Following Austin, this is called *illocutionary force* (from the words 'in'+'locutio') and points to the fact that asking and asserting are things we do *by or in* the utterance of certain words over and above the locutionary act. By uttering the words 'It's raining' we perform the illocutionary act of assertion (that it is raining) regardless of whether anyone believes us; in uttering the words 'Is it raining?' we ask (whether it is raining) regardless of whether anyone knows the answer and, if they do, whether they are prepared to disclose it to us.

Let us now turn to a number of linguistic acts and analyse them at the illocutionary level. There prove to be many different types of illocutionary force and, by implication, of illocutionary acts. Here are some examples:

1. Christopher is going to sell the car soon.
2. Is Christopher going to sell the car soon?
3. Sell the car soon, Christopher!
4. If only Christopher would sell the car soon!
5. I Christopher promise to sell the car soon.

There is a sense in which all these sentences are about the same thing – namely Christopher and the prospective selling of a car; they are the vehicles of the same locutionary act. But it is also clear that they say very different things. We have already looked at the first two. The first sentence is an *assertion*: It is being asserted that Christopher will soon sell the car. Sentence 2 is a *question* and is aimed at getting the interlocutor to produce an assertion to the effect that Christopher will soon sell the car, or one making the opposite prediction. Sentence 3 is a *command* or a *request* urging or entreating Christopher to sell the car, and is followed by one (sentence 4) expressing the wish that Christopher should sell the car. Finally, we have sentence 5 which is a *promise* that Christopher will soon sell the car (i.e. a promise made by Christopher that he will soon sell the car).

4. Indeed, there are locutions in everyday discourse whose precise point is to make this dual structure visible. Sometimes we need to make the illocutionary power of our utterances explicit if misunderstanding is to be avoided. Often, too, in everyday discourse, more is implied than is actually said. What is implied is often part of the overall message we seek to get across to our interlocutor. But sometimes we are concerned not to imply more than we actually say and have to amplify our utterance to make this explicit. Wife to husband: 'It took you a very long time to take that letter to the post!' Husband: 'Are you implying that I stopped off for a pint on the way?' Wife: 'Not at all, I only said (viz. asserted) that taking that letter to the post took you a very long time'.

Conversely, one can highlight the nature of a speech act by making its character explicit in its very performance. This occurs, for example, when marriage vows are made in a church wedding service. The groom says: 'I Giles take thee Anthea to my wedded wife, to have and to hold from this day forward; and thereto I plight my troth.'

Expressions in which the illocutionary force of a speech act is made explicit are called *performatives*. The expressions 'I assert that ...', 'I hereby declare ...', 'I swear by all that's sacred that ...' are all performatives. Performatives also come in more specialized versions such as 'I hereby name this ship 'North Cape Voyager'; 'We hereby congratulate you on your new appointment'; 'The defendant is hereby sentenced to four years' hard labour', and so on.

Note that performatives are not *descriptions* of a process or act, functioning as accompaniments to either of the latter, but constitute the very execution of the act they might appear to be describing. The President's wife who utters the words 'I hereby name this ship North Cape Voyager' is not describing something that is going on parallel with and independently of her utterance; her utterance *is* the act of naming, or an indispensable part of it. The man who says 'I promise to quit smoking' is not *describing* an independent activity, the making of a promise, but is making the promise by uttering the words.

5. A third and final level in the description of speech acts comes as an answer to the question, 'What did the speaker hope to achieve by saying what he did?' when the enquiry concerns the consequences that go beyond what is expressed by the locutionary and illocutionary acts. As a rule, speakers' utterances are informed by multiple and complex intentions. In uttering the sentence 'It's going to rain soon' in a particular situation, the speaker's intention may be to remind another person to take an umbrella with him, to indicate that the garden furniture should be taken in, to predict that the tennis match will probably have to be cancelled, and so on. By putting a question such as 'When did you stop beating your wife?' one's intention may be to infuriate the addressee, diminish him in the eyes of others, imply that one possesses compromising information about him, and so on.

All such consequences are called *perlocutionary consequences* and the corresponding acts *perlocutionary acts* from the words 'per' (Latin: through) + 'locutio', i.e. the consequences of a speech act which are achieved *through* the utterance and which go beyond its purely locutionary and illocutionary consequences.

We can formulate a more precise criterion for the difference between illocutionary and perlocutionary expressions by drawing on the notion of performatives. We start from the fact that illocutionary acts are performed *in or by* the utterance of a linguistic expression (a sentence); there is, as it were, nothing further that needs to occur after the utterance has been produced for the illocutionary act to be complete (assuming an appropriate social setting including a hearer capable of understanding what is said). That the completion of the illocutionary utterance lies in the utterance itself means that in the course of the performance of such an act the speaker would always be able to say, 'I *hereby* perform the following linguistic act: ...' with the specification of the act filling the blank. These will include such locutions as 'I promise that ...', 'I assert that ...', and so on. The resulting sentences will have the following form: 'I hereby perform the following linguistic act: I promise that/assert that/ask whether ...' Obviously, these expressions are only more elaborate ways of saying 'I promise that ...', 'I assert that ...'; they are simply cumbersome versions of ordinary performatives. Every illocutionary act would thus be performable through the utterance of a performative expression of the form, 'I hereby perform such and such a linguistic act'.

Now the point to note is that the same does not apply in the case of the *perlocutionary* effects typically effected by linguistic means and whose mediation is typically what is most important in our sights. In conversation with others, we are often interested in having them accept some particular version of how things are, an account of some matter that we are giving them: we give it to them, that is, in order that they should believe it. But that we do not bring about this belief merely through an illocutionary act is made clear by the fact that we could not achieve our aims by means of a performative. A salesman who said to his customer, 'I'm hereby getting you to believe that this washing machine is superior to its competitors' would not succeed in his project and would be regarded as slightly mad. There is no such thing as getting people to believe things simply by declaring that they do so. It is possible that their coming to believe what one says is *causally mediated* by what one says; but they do not believe it *in virtue of* the speaker's declaring that they do.

Notice the contrast with the illocutionary act. A salesman who says, 'The Fixflux washer is the brand leader' has thereby asserted or claimed that Fixflux is superior to all other models. His assertion does not figure as an effect produced by the words he utters but is constituted by the words themselves (set in an appropriate social context). Such illocutionary effects reside in the uttering of certain types of sentences and are not causal consequences of them.

This shows that the notion of an illocutionary act, as originally defined by John Austin, conceals an ambiguity of which Austin was well aware: among the perlocutionary effects of a speech act are some which, as it were, merely consummate the illocutionary act, while others go beyond this. For instance, among the perlocutionary consequences of the utterance 'Close the door' might be the fact that the door is subsequently closed by the individual so commanded, and, further, that the latter suffers embarrassment. The former effect naturally qualifies as the consummation of the command, since it is what anyone issuing the command standardly wants to see effected. Still, it is a perlocutionary effect, since it is not achieved *in and by* the enunciation of the command. After all, the command might not be obeyed. The other effect, the infliction of embarrassment, might be an intended consequence of the command on a particular occasion, but is not standardly intended, and could hardly be called the consummation of that speech act. In the light of this, it would probably be convenient to have separate terms for these two kinds of perlocutionary effects. However, none such is in standard use, and we would not want further to encumber an already complex terminology by proposing one here. So we restrict ourselves to pointing out that the distinction exists.

6. With this theoretical conceptual apparatus in place, we may proceed to make use of it in explicating the concept of 'meaning' relevant to the analysis of speech acts. We will examine what is involved in saying that a person meant such-and-such by what he said, or that a sentence or some other locution means such and such. Key to this analysis is the idea of a person's *meaning* something by an utterance being primary and basic. The concept of *sentence meaning* turns out to be secondary. A sentence derives its meaning from a person's use of it to communicate speaker's meaning.

We will begin by analyzing the formula 'By producing utterance U, S meant that p' where U is a particular utterance produced by speaker S in a particular situation. (For example, a concrete utterance of the words 'It's raining' produced at a particular time by a particular individual.) What are we saying about speaker S when we so describe his agency? We shall begin with *assertions* since assertions, as we have seen, take theoretical priority amongst speech acts.

One seemingly plausible analytical schema is: 'S utters U which in S's language means that p'. For example, 'By producing the utterance U Hubert meant that it is raining' means that Hubert's utterance belonged to the general type (namely, 'Il pleut') which in Hubert's language (namely, French), means that it is raining. The problem with this proposal is that it presupposes the existence of a conventional medium of communication, a language. But the existence of such a conventional medium must be rooted in one that is not conventional. A conventional medium of communication can only have arisen as a conventionalization of something already in existence. There must be some more fundamental notion of communication, logically and historically, a notion embracing what is common to both conventional and non-conventional means of communication. It is this more basic notion in whose pursuit we are presently engaged (which of course does not prevent our wanting to subject conventionalized means of communication to a thorough investigation too, but that is for later).

To reach this pre-conventional level, we need to focus on the situation where an individual communicates his message by means of a non-linguistic device, improvised for the occasion.

So let us briefly return to the fable recounted in chapter 2 about the origins of language. We saw how, in a concrete situation, our notional ancestor Zork, by using a bear-style grunt to warn the other members of the tribe of the presence of a bear, set in motion a process which would lead to the evolution of a rudimentary form of language. There the process was initiated by an intended warning; here we shall focus instead on the pivotal speech act of assertion. If Zork's utterance is an assertion – the assertion that a bear is in the vicinity – his communicative intentions may be cast as follows:

1. Zork intends that his tribespeople should recognize that there is a bear nearby.

2. Zork intends that his tribespeople should recognize that he is emitting the bear-style grunt to achieve the effect referred to in 1.

3. Zork intends that his tribespeople should acquire the belief (recognition) referred to in 1 as a result of the belief (recognition) referred to in 2.

There are, then, three levels in the reaction that Zork seeks to elicit from his tribespeople. For us to be able to say that Zork *meant* something by his emission of the grunt it must, first, be Zork's intention that on hearing the grunt his tribespeople should form the belief that there is a bear close at hand. But, second, more is required. For if Zork emitted the sound with the intention that his cohorts should take it to be the grunt of a real bear and not realize that the sound was produced by Zork in order that they, on hearing it, should draw the relevant conclusion, it would not be plausible to say that the sound had a meaning at all. The sound would enter into no *communication* whatsoever. It is imperative that the hearers understand that the sound is one produced by Zork with the intention that they should hear it and draw the relevant conclusion. And third, they must actually draw the conclusion Zork wants them to draw.

We can now go on to formulate a more general analysis of assertion inasmuch as we bear in mind that 'utterances' may be any species of sign, not just linguistic signs. In essence the analysis is that formulated by Paul Grice:

1. S utters U, intending that hearer H should believe that p.

2. S intends that H should believe that S has uttered (produced) U with the intention stated in 1, i.e. that H should believe that p.

3. S intends that H should believe that p as a result of the belief that S has uttered (produced) U with the intention that H should believe that p.

7. At first glance, this analysis would seem to carry a measure of plausibility, but it is problematic nonetheless. To illustrate the problems and to bring them into sharper focus we shall consider an example taken from everyday discourse. Consider the following dialogue enacted in the Jones's household on Mr Jones's arrival home late one night, befuddled by drink (the germ of the example is owed to Stephen Schiffer):

> Husband: 'I know you're not going to believe this, but I've been hard at it at the office all evening.'
> Wife: 'You're lying! You've been out on a binge again.'

On Grice's analysis, the husband's utterance is aimed at getting his wife to believe that he has been working late at the office, and he intends that she should believe this since that was his aim in making it. But as he himself confesses, he has no confidence in his chances of securing this outcome. Indeed, an utterance such as the husband's ought almost, on Grice's analysis, to qualify as a contradiction, since on the face of it he would seem to be trying to persuade his wife of something of which he in the same breath acknowledges that he cannot persuade her. But in fact there does not seem to be a contradiction.

By the same token, the wife's retort ought strictly to qualify as even more deviant. For on the Gricean analysis her utterance is aimed at getting her husband to believe that he is lying and that he has been out drinking. But it is surely beyond doubt that he knows this all too well, and unless his wife suspects him to be suffering from amnesia *she* too is perfectly aware that *he* knows this, and so it can hardly be her intention to enlighten him. In other words, we seem to be faced with a brace of counterexamples to Grice's analysis. We are presented with utterances that are fully intelligible and standard but which, on the assumption that the analysis is correct, ought to strike us as deviant.

There is another more theoretical line of reasoning with the same thrust. Meaning something by an utterance is something one does *by or through* the articulation of certain symbols; a speaker who has produced an utterance does not have to wait for other things to happen in the world for his utterance to be invested with semantic content (provided that a minimal social context is in place). This indicates that the feature of the speech act that fixes speaker's meaning is the illocutionary act (plus the locutionary act). This means, in turn, that those features of the speech act that define what the speaker means must be capable of explicit expression in the form of a performative (as we saw in section 5). It is clear, however, that the above analysis cannot meet that constraint. Let us return to Jones's statement: 'I've been hard at it at the office all evening'. On the Gricean analysis, Jones's meaning is fixed by his intention to get his wife to believe that he has been working at the office. It is obvious that this intention cannot be realized via a performative taking the form of 'I hereby induce in you the belief that I have been at the office working hard all evening'. This utterance from Jones's lips would not secure his aim and would probably only serve to exacerbate his predicament.

8. There are many ways in which the analysis might be modified to take account of such counterexamples. One that immediately suggests itself is the claim that the intended effect of saying something is only that hearers shall *understand* what the speaker means, not that they should necessarily believe it: whether they do so or not is another matter and not a question of language. Their so believing is a perlocutionary effect that has nothing to do with speaker meaning.

Unfortunately, this proposal runs the risk of circularity: we are out to define speaker meaning in terms of a certain intended effect in the hearer. But we obviously get nowhere if we go on to characterize these effects as the hearer's understanding of what the speaker meant. The situation is not improved if we try to spell out the speaker's intentions more explicitly: we still get a formula to the effect that the speaker intends the hearer to grasp the speaker's intention to get the hearer to grasp the speaker's intention to get the hearer to ...

The circularity involved here is pernicuous and not to be confused with the innocuous iteration characteristic of all analyses of meaning in the Gricean tradition. Such analyses involve a hierarchy of intentions where the intentions at the higher levels refer to intentions at the next lower levels. However, at the bottom of the hierarchy is an intention which does not refer to any prior speaker intention, but to some independent state. On Grice's analysis, this state is a belief in the hearer. But such an independent state is lacking in the present proposal.

Let us attempt a fresh start, building on the principle yielded by the distinction between illocutionary and perlocutionary effects and the performative test that reveals the real illocutionary effects. What must an illocutionary act consist of for this principle to hold? What types of action are performable *by and through* the utterance of an assertion? A response offered by John Searle has it that it is an act whereby one vouches for the *truth* of the utterance – i.e. not assuming the responsibility for making it true (as is the case with promises) but assuming responsibility for the sentence's being already and independently true. To assert that p is to take on a particular truth condition or to be committed to p's being the case.

What does it mean to say that we "take on a truth condition" or that we are "committed to the proposition that p"? It means that we assume a responsibility to ground and make a case for the proposition should doubt arise. 'You said the petrol tank was full, but I can see that it's almost empty.' 'But I filled it up yesterday' or 'The gauge showed the tank to be three-quarters full last time I looked at it', and so on. If we cannot support the statement and if it turns out to be incorrect, we have to withdraw it and admit to being mistaken. (Very often liability has a practical dimension. If others have based their plans on information you have provided that later proves to have been unreliable, some reparation would seem to be called for. However, this would appear to follow from some general ethical principle about compensating those harmed by one's actions, and not to be an outcome related to language.)

We arrive, then, at the following analysis of the concept of a speaker meaning something (namely that p) by an utterance of the type 'assertion':

S means that p by uttering U if and only if

> 1. S utters U with the intention of committing himself to its being the case that p.
>
> 2. S intends that his utterance of U shall give a hearer H grounds to believe (recognize) that S has uttered (produced) U with the intention of committing himself to its being the case that p.
>
> 3. S intends his utterance of U to give H grounds to believe (recognize) that S has uttered (produced) U with the intention of giving H grounds to believe (recognize) that S has uttered (produced) U with the aim of committing himself to its being the case that p.

This analysis may seem complicated but in fact it is simply a regimentation of the communicative situation described in our account of Zork's protolanguage, viz. chapter 2. Points 2 and 3 in the analysis, which introduce the *grounding* constraint, follow from certain considerations that were already in play in the above example involving protolanguage speakers. A person can only be said to mean something by an utterance if he has given the hearers grounds to believe that such a meaning is intended. *If*, instead of uttering the characteristic and familiar bear-style grunt, Zork had emitted the rarely registered sound produced by female bears when suckling their young, and *if* Zork was aware that his tribespeople would not pick up on this sound, it would not be correct to say that Zork *meant* anything by emitting it. For then Zork would have been without any legitimate expectation that his fellow tribesmen would be capable of figuring out his communicative intent. Point 2 of the analysis takes account of this by requiring that the utterer produce grounds for H to believe (recognize) that the utterer had this intention. And according to point 3, the utterer so conveys these grounds that the hearer has reason to believe that he expressly intends their recognition as such.

Note too that it does not follow from this analysis that the hearer actually understands the grounds. A speaker has made an assertion in virtue of having said something that *would supply a hearer with grounds* provided that he grasped them; but it is not assumed that this is always the case. Once again we are alerted to the fact that when a language user makes an assertion, he performs an action on his own account; to qualify as such, his assertion is not contingent upon the astuteness of his hearers.

9. Certainly, this analysis of assertion solves the original problem. However, it raises a difficulty of its own. Human language must be assumed to have evolved out of signal systems which our early forebears used to warn one another of dangers, to draw attention to sources of food, to maintain contact among members of the group, and so on. These were the features our fable about Zork and his cohorts sought to capture. The intentions informing their protolinguistic utterances must, in other words, have been of the type, 'I want my tribespeople to understand that there is a bear nearby'. They would scarcely have been of the type 'I want my fellows to understand that I am committed to the fact of there being a bear nearby – i.e. that I am prepared to offer evidence that there is a bear nearby; and if there proves not to be, I shall explicitly withdraw my assertion'. This constitutes a thought so sophisticated and abstract that it is hardly plausible that it should have lain within the capacities of our distant ancestors.

Perhaps the difficulty can be resolved by supplying a more detailed evolutionary story. Human language did indeed evolve from more primitive signal systems among our forebears. And these signal systems typically had functions such as that of alerting the tribe to propinquitous predators. The purposes that these people bound into their utterances were doubtless of the form, 'I intend that the others should be alert to the fact that there is a bear nearby'. However, once a language is set up with this function, other and more abstract communicative intentions can be built upon it, with the original motivations lapsing. For at a later point, say, a member of the tribe, recognizing his inability to persuade his fellows of the proximity of a bear, still emits the bear warning so as not be reproached later with failing to raise the alarm. And by the same token, one person will tell another something of which he knows the other already to be aware, in order to advertise the fact that he shares this knowledge. (This was the case with the little domestic episode above. The wife wanted her husband to know that she was not taken in by his fabrications but was fully clued-up, rather, on the nature of his most recent activities.)

With the introduction of these more abstract intentions, the need arises to modify the definition of utterer's meaning: we have to say that the point of uttering p is not necessarily to get the hearer to believe that p but, minimally, to commit the utterer to its being the case that p. Naturally, in most communicative situations the speaker will have wider-reaching aims. But they are not what *defines* utterer's meaning. Such intended effects are now purely *perlocutionary*.

10. We saw above some of the constraints that have to be met for us to be able to say that a person means something by an utterance (of the category *assertion*). However, they fall short of yielding an exhaustive, generic characterization. We will now give a more comprehensive analysis of the conditions that have to be met for the act of assertion to count as having been brought off. We shall then extend the analysis to other types of speech acts.

Up until now, we have talked about speech acts which exhibit different moods as agreeing in their success conditions but diverging with respect to illocutionary force. This manner of description has served us well so far but, evidently, leaves the notion of illocutionary force unanalysed. The key to any such analysis is once again the notion of certain conditions which the act must satisfy, but now construed more broadly so as to take in not only what we have so far referred to as success conditions but, further, conditions that must be presupposed if the action is to get off the ground at all; or, to use Austin's expression, if it is to be *happy*. What we need to do now is to present a full analysis of speech acts exhibiting different moods by appeal to the full complement of conditions that have to be satisfied for such acts to count as having been happily and successfully performed.

From now on, we shall use the term 'success conditions' to refer to this broader class of conditions. This leaves us in need of a term with which to pick out the narrower class of conditions previously denoted by that term; for this type of condition remains theoretically central in the characterization of linguistic meaning in that it demonstrates the semantic affinities between assertions, commands, questions, wishes, and so on, that turn on the same content (i.e. involve the same locutionary act). These prove to have identical, or at least overlapping, success conditions of the privileged kind while diverging with respect to other conditions. We shall henceforth refer to the privileged class of conditions as *fulfilment conditions*.

Overall, the analysis offered here follows that formulated by Searle (Searle 1970) albeit slightly modified. It is aimed at analytically capturing the standard or normal case of the speech act in question, although it has sufficient resources to handle such borderline and somewhat anomalous cases as those we examined in section 7 above. The main difference from the standard Searlian analysis is the inclusion of the fulfilment condition (which is, however, familiar from Austin's original analysis of speech acts).

We begin with assertions, listing the conditions that have to be met, in typical or normal cases, if an assertion is to be successful:

1. *It is the case that p.*
This is the fulfilment condition.

2. *S utters U with the intention of committing himself to its being the case that p.*

3. *S intends that his utterance of U shall give a hearer H grounds to believe that S has uttered U with the intention of committing himself to its being the case that p.*

S intends that his utterance of U shall give a hearer H grounds to believe (recognize) that S has uttered (produced) U with the intention of giving a hearer H grounds to believe (recognize) that S has uttered (produced) U with the aim of committing himself to its being the case that p.

This element corresponds to elements 2 and 3 of the analysis in section 8 above.

4. *S believes that p is the case and has good grounds for believing this.*

5. *H does not already know that p, or it is at least not obvious that S knows that p.*

6. *Normal conditions for communication obtain.*
This means that the hearers are able to hear what the speaker is saying and to recognize his intentions. The hearer must not be severely

hearingimpaired, chronically or acutely deranged, and so on. We saw above that a person may be said to perform an assertion even though in a borderline case these conditions go unsatisfied. But the conditions listed above characterize the *normal* communication situation.

Condition 1 captures the fact that in the normal case, an assertion is considered infelicitous or unfulfilled if things are not as the assertion says. This does not mean that somebody who asserts what is false has not made an assertion, but precisely that his assertion must be deemed infelicitous. Compare this with the case of someone going out to hunt lions. If he fails to shoot a lion, we must deem his efforts unfulfilled. But we are naturally not forced to conclude that he was not hunting lions after all. In the same way, someone may aim at asserting what is true, fail in the endeavour but still be taken to have made an assertion.

Condition 1, by the way, is not encompassed by condition 2, which only states that S *intends* to be committed to the condition stated in 1. (We are saying that 1's *being a condition* of successful utterance does not follow from condition 2, not making the obvious point that the *satisfaction* of 1 does not follow from the satisfaction of 2). The two are distinct. An inmate in a psychiatric hospital might utter the sentence, 'I am Napoleon Bonaparte', thereby intending to commit himself to the fact of his being Napoleon Bonaparte, but without succeeding: no one takes him seriously. That is, not only do they not believe his claim to be true, they do not even recognize it as a claim. Moreover, we mentioned above that S might well believe that p without intending to get H to believe this since S knows that H already holds this belief. This does not alter the fact that, standardly, H is not already apprised of the fact that p and so the utterance counts as *one conveying the information* that p is the case.

In his analysis (of which ours is a slightly modified variant) Searle calls condition 2 the *essential condition* because it defines the kind of act each speech act essentially is. Condition 4 is called *the sincerity condition* while comdition 5 denotes the *preparatory condition*. This division is a useful tool to describe what happens when we utter a sentence. Take the assertion 'Great Britain is a monarchy'. The essential condition captures what a speaker literally *asserts* in and through the utterance. A person who utters this sentence is committed to the truth of Great Britain's being a monarchy; this is what he asserts in uttering the sentence.

The preparatory condition points out circumstances not directly asserted by the speaker, but *suggested* by what he says. If one person says to another 'Great Britain is a monarchy', his making this utterance suggests that the second individual was previously unaware of this – so utterances of this type are likely to trigger mildly indignant reactions in the style of 'You know, I really don't need to be told that'. We shall return to this issue in section 13.

The sincerity constraint captures what the speaker *expresses* through his utterance, i.e. the information about himself that the utterance also conveys. A person who says that 'Great Britain is a monarchy' thereby gives expression to the belief that Great Britain is a monarchy. It may of course be the case that he is saying what he knows to be untrue and so does not himself believe what he is saying. However, this has no bearing on the fact that the assertion of the sentence is conventionally taken to be the expression of the belief that things are as the sentence says they are.

The sincerity constraint highlights the circumstance that every utterance, irrespective of content, reveals something about the utterer. An utterance is an act whereby, given the background of certain assumptions about the situation in which he finds himself, the speaker seeks to achieve an end. Therefore every linguistic act is simultaneously expressive of the desire motivating the speaker's communication and the assumptions that make up the background context of the speech act. This applies, as we have just seen, to the most abstract of speech acts, the assertion. It applies much more obviously to such speech acts as commands, invocations, requests, entreaties, and so on, for in those the speech act is patently partially expressive of the speaker's state of mind. We shall see below that there are speech acts whose entire thrust is the expression of the speaker's intentions and desires.

11. Let us now undertake a corresponding analysis of another type of linguistic act – promising. In all essentials, it conforms to the foregoing analysis (and hence to the standard analysis offered by Searle), but certain of the constraints are amplified:

1. *S performs action A, subsequently to uttering U.*
This is the fulfilment condition.

2. *S utters U with the intention of committing himself to do A.*
This is the essential condition.

3. *S intends to produce in H the knowledge that the utterance of S is to count as placing S under an obligation to do A.*
S intends that his utterance of U shall oblige him to do A through H's recognition that S uttered (produced) U with the intention of undertaking to do A.

The need arises for four further conditions not appearing in the analysis of assertions:

> 4. *The utterance U refers to a future action to be performed by S.*
> This captures the fact that one can only promise to do something in the future, and not in the past, and one can only promise to do something on one's own account, not on that of others. In consequence, one can only promise to get others to do something insofar as they are in one's power or subject to one's authority.
>
> 5. *H prefers the doing of A to the omission of A.*
> This takes account of the fact that one cannot coherently promise someone to do something that the latter would prefer not to be done. Insofar as a speaker commits himself to the performance of an act that the hearer would prefer left undone the speech act is a *threat*, not a promise. This is a preparatory condition.
>
> 6. *It is not obvious that S would perform the act in the normal course of events.*
> One cannot meaningfully promise someone to do something that the latter knows one would do anyway. This is also a preparatory condition.
>
> 7. *S intends to do A.*
> This is the sincerity condition: in uttering a promise, S expresses an intention to do as promised.

Finally, a condition which also occurs among those that define assertion:

> 8. *The normal conditions for communication obtain.*
> The content of this constraint is the same as above.

In parallel with the case of assertion, condition 1 captures the fact that in the normal case, a promise is considered unfulfilled and defective if it is not kept. This of course does not mean that somebody who fails to keep his promises did not make a promise after all, but precisely that his promise must be deemed unfulfilled. This condition is obviously not encompassed by condition 7, since somebody may fail to keep his promises for reasons of incapacity, rather than insincerity. As a matter of fact, the two conditions are two-ways independent, since somebody may have planned to break a promise and still perform the promised act. Jack may promise Jill to be at the High Roller Bar on Sunday night, later decide to stand her up, then forget about the whole thing, go on a binge on Sunday night and just happen to stumble into the High Roller Bar at the agreed hour.

In conclusion, let us examine the speech act of 'commanding':

1. *H performs action A, subsequently to S's utterance of U.*
This is the fulfilment condition.

2. *S utters U with the intention of getting H to perform action A.*
This is the essential condition.

3. *S utters U intending to get H to realize that S wants to get H to perform act A. S intends that H perform the act A as a result of H's recognition that S wants him to perform this act.*

4. *H is capable of performing act A and S knows that H is capable of performing this act.*
One cannot meaningfully command a person to do something if one knows that the action lies beyond the range of his capacities. This is a preparatory condition.

5. *It is not obvious that H will perform A in the normal course of events.*
One cannot meaningfully command a person to do something that one knows the individual will do anyway. This too is a preparatory condition.

6. *S wants H to perform act A.*
This is the sincerity condition. By issuing a command, S expresses the desire that act A be performed.

7. *The normal conditions for communication obtain.*

The same point applies as before: condition 1 does not mean that a disobeyed command is not a command, but only that it is unfulfilled.

12. There are countless other types of speech acts: asking, greeting, congratulating, thanking, warning and many more. We cannot go into them all here but will simply note that according to Searle all such speech acts fall within the scope of the five types: assertions, directives, commissives, expressives and declarations.

Assertives are speech acts in which the speaker commits himself to some state of affairs' obtaining. Assertions, which we looked at above, fall into this category as does suggesting, insisting, assuring, affirming and many others. As indicated, the difference between these various assertions turns most significantly on the degree of the speaker's commitment to some state of affairs' obtaining.

Directives are speech acts in which the speaker seeks to get the hearer to perform some act. Above we examined commands, which fall into this category. Others include requests, coaxings, prayers, invitations, advisings, questions, challenges, pressurizings and many more.

Commissives are speech acts where the speaker commits himself to performing some act. Promises are the classic example of a commissive, but this category also includes threats, guarantees, oaths, and so on.

Expressives are intended to give expression to the speaker's psychological state. To this group belong apologies, congratulations, thanks, cheers, and so on. With such utterances, the speech act is exhausted by what in other cases is merely a secondary aspect. We saw above that the other types of speech act all involved a sincerity condition, which captured what the speaker reveals about himself in describing reality, issuing a command, putting questions, and so on. In expressives this aspect constitutes the entire speech act. A person who says 'Congratulations!' or 'Welcome!' does not describe the world but simply gives (conventional) expression to an attitude towards the addressee. While the attitude need not be sincerely held, the utterance remains an expression of it.

Declarations are speech acts through which a change is brought about in the world (apart from something's being said). Examples include appointing, christening, declaring war, dismissing, giving notice, marrying, and so on. By uttering the sentence 'You are hereby appointed scoutmaster' the utterer appoints a particular individual scoutmaster. Again, the sentence is not the description of an action whose performance accompanies the utterance but, in and of itself, constitutes the appointment, and likewise for other members of this category.

One important difference between kinds of speech act can be highlighted by appeal to the notion of *direction of fit*, introduced by John Searle. *Assertives* evince the word-to-world direction of fit, since the world has priority and the "word" (the assertive sentence) must be made to conform to it; conformity with the world, as it were, is the target at which the sentence is aimed. *Directives*, on the other hand, evince the world-to-word direction of fit, since here the "word" (the directive sentence) has priority, and reality has to be brought into line with it. The order is given to dig a trench, and the soldiers must modify the world so that it conforms to that order. The same holds of *commissives*: you promise your wife to mend the hole in the fence, and are thus committed to modifying reality so that it conforms to those words. *Declarations*, in virtue of their utterance alone, change the world to fit the words but, according to Searle, only do so provided some worldly preconditions are already in place: you can only appoint someone scoutmaster if you have the authority to do so. Hence Searle prefers to say that directions have both the word-to-world and the world-to-word directions of fit. Finally, *expressives* have no direction of fit at all. If you congratulate someone, you are not modifying reality to suit your words, nor selecting your words to suit reality, although you are presupposing that your addressee has something to celebrate.

13. In the introduction, we touched upon the traditional distinction between semantics and pragmatics, where the former captures the relationship between language and reality, the latter that between language and language users. Semantics was supposed to comprise everything that has to do with meaning. We now recognize the need to redraw the distinction: meaning is a component in both sets of relations. The meaning of the utterance 'I promise to shut the door' is defined both by its relation to a particular door, and by the commitment undertaken by the speaker with respect to his interlocutor. The assertion, 'The door is shut', might relate to the same door and might be addressed to the same hearer but its distinctive meaning springs from the different commitment that the speaker makes in uttering it. The two sentences involve the same locution, but perform two different illocutionary acts.

The compass of semantics, then, has been shown to extend to certain aspects of sentence use – those aspects involving other-directed agency: to make commitments with respect to the undertaking of certain actions, to convey information, and so on. Still, not everything we bring about through our utterances is intuitively part of their meaning; as we saw above, many *perlocutionary* aims are not. Hence we need to redraw the boundaries of semantics to encompass the former kinds of use and exclude the latter. Let us turn to some examples of such purely pragmatic aspects.

We have seen, then, that if Peter says to Paul 'Great Britain is a monarchy' he has *asserted* that Great Britain is a monarchy, i.e. he has committed himself to its head of state being a hereditary sovereign. Peter has further *suggested* or *insinuated* that Paul did not know this. This insinuation is not the same as an assertion. If Paul should indignantly retort, 'Actually, I happened to know that', Peter can truthfully reply, 'I never said that you didn't'. In so saying he is formally correct: his utterance was indeed not equivalent to the utterance 'Paul does not know that Great Britain is a monarchy'. But it would seem clear that Peter has insinuated that Paul was not cognizant of this well-known fact about Britain's constitution. How can this difference between what is said and what is suggested or insinuated be further explicated?

Paul Grice argues that conversation and communication are subject to certain general constraints that are in fact quite commonsensical and uncontroversial. In very general terms, they require that what a speaker says should be appropriate to the situation of communication. A more specific sub-principle has it that one should make one's contribution relevant to the topic under discussion; there should be neither too much nor too little information. Conversation proceeds under the presupposition that both parties seek to comply, *inter alia*, with this maxim. If we now consider the brief exchange above in the light of these constraints we must assume that Peter believes that his remark provides Paul with relevant information. This is an assumption he can make only if he believes that Paul is unaware of the fact that Great Britain is a monarchy. Consequently, Peter insinuates that Paul suffers from a knowledge deficit in this regard. Or, more plainly: one only tells people things they do not know, and by telling Paul that Great Britain is a monarchy Peter insinuates that he did not already know this. Grice refers to this species of inference drawn from verbal exchanges as *conversational implicatures*.

The difference between what is said and what is "implicated" is that whereas what is said is what the speaker is committed to, given the meanings of the language's lexicon and the sentences formed out of them, what is implicated is not derivable from the meanings of the uttered sentences themselves. It results, rather, from the conversational context, i.e. the fact that the sentence was uttered by one person to another in a particular situation, and the presupposition that the speaker would not bother to utter the sentence unless he saw a point in doing so. Paul's ignorance naturally does not follow from the sentence 'Great Britain is a monarchy' itself. If one were to explain to someone who did not speak English what this sentence means – i.e. what follows from the sentence if it is true – Paul would obviously not figure in the explanation; he in no way enters into its truth condition. By contrast, something about Paul does follow from the circumstance that Peter, in a one-on-one setting with Paul, finds it worthwhile to utter the sentence 'Great Britain is a monarchy' – namely, that Paul was unaware of this (according to Peter). Peter's insinuation is, in other words, a conversational implicature.

Here is another example. Peter and Paul are discussing whether to appoint Oscar to a highly responsible post requiring intellectual and moral qualifications of the first order. Peter asks Paul what Oscar's credentials are and Paul replies that 'He has beautiful handwriting'. This response would immediately be taken to imply that Oscar lacks the requisite qualifications. Peter assumes that Paul complies with the maxim that one restrict one's contributions to those relevant to the context, in casu ones regarding qualifications relevant to the appointment. Since the sole qualification mentioned by Paul is patently irrelevant, the implicature must be that Oscar's credentials include no relevant qualifications. But again, this is not something directly asserted in the uttered sentence but merely something suggested or implicated by it.

Finally, we turn to an example illustrating a different kind of illocutionary force. The bank manager says to one of the bank's important customers: 'This bank can promise you that the Inland Revenue will never learn of this little currency transaction.' To which the customer replies: 'But I'm not out to fraud the tax authorities!' What is in play here is the preparatory condition for promises to the effect that a promiser only promises to do things he assumes that the promisee wants done. And by his utterance the bank manager implicates that the customer wants to defraud the Inland Revenue. Now this is not something he directly asserts by his utterance, for it is precisely a promise and not an assertion. The idea of fraud, however, is implicated and it is against this implication that the customer remonstrates.

The kind of language use illustrated above goes by the name of 'indirect speech acts', since a speech act is performed through another, separate linguistic act. Not all indirect speech acts are as ad hoc as the examples just given. Indeed, some of them are very much part of the standard repertoire of speakers. Let us take a well-worn example, the remark 'Can you reach the salt?' as uttered by one of the guests at supper. Grammatically, it is a question, but would be taken by everyone as a request for the salt; hence, the request is an indirect speech act. Once again, the operative mechanism is conversational implicature. The utterance, taken at absolute face value, would seem to be completely without point and so one that sins against Grice's conversational constraints: in most situations where this utterance might be made it would be perfectly obvious whether or not the salt is within the reach of the addressee. This raises the suspicion that something else is going on. Perhaps the speaker is indeed respecting the principles governing conversation but in unobvious ways. He might be after something other than information about the salt's whereabouts relative to the addressee. Given the context, a fair guess would be that he wanted to season his supper.

Thus, there is still room for a distinction between semantics and pragmatics in the description of language. But now it must be drawn in terms of a different criterion, and will be relocated in the process. Conversational implicatures are defined as pragmatic by the fact that they cannot be derived from the syntactic and lexical form of the sentence alone; to infer the implicated or indirect information, features of the context of the utterance must be invoked. The rationale of marking a distinction of this kind is transparent: the principles of meaning generation which are based upon linguistic form alone are likely to be more rigorous than those which draw heavily upon the context. To the extent that we aim at a systematic theory of semantics, we are well advised to exclude those parts of communication that are not amenable to strict formal treatment. (As we shall see in chapter 9, these distinctions have been challenged in recent work.)

Thus the modified distinction between semantics and pragmatics is designed to save us from the dangers inherent in the admission that a theory of meaning is indeed a theory of use, viz. the prospect that we might have to deal with every aspect of use in our theory. The distinction allows us to define certain features of use as of no concern to our theory, and to concentrate on certain narrower aspects of speech acts which are more amenable to systematic treatment.

14. Throughout the foregoing account, we have referred to the conditions needing to be met for a person to mean something by an utterance without presupposing that these utterances necessarily belong to a language, i.e. a conventional, public instrument for the performance of communicative acts. The point is one that was highlighted at the outset: it is essential that meaning per se be communicable independently of a conventionalized language. For the conventions that define a natural language such as English must be seen as springing from an earlier non-conventionally established mode of communication.

A comparison between language and money sheds light on this: money arose from earlier forms of exchange not involving money. This practice constituted barter, with one good being exchanged for another of equal value. Gradually an understanding grew up that certain specific goods, namely precious metals, were especially well suited to barter: their durability recommended them over less appropriate items such as fresh fruit or fish. Precious metals were also distinguished by their compactness relative to value which made them easily transportable from one place to another. These precious metals (especially gold and silver) originally took the form of a chain or something similar, separable into bands or rings according to the measure a particular transaction required. Later they appeared in standard units bearing an authoritative stamp (often that of the monarch) that attested their weight and thus their value. Only slowly did the realization dawn that it did not matter whether the coins themselves were intrinsically worth their designated value. So long as people accepted them in exchange for goods it was irrelevant that they were worth less in metallic terms, or were even completely worthless; worthless pieces of paper can indeed serve as a valid means of payment. Thus evolved a purely conventional monetary system.

Despite the absence of any well-founded idea as to how the process actually evolved, language is most plausibly conceived of, then, as having arisen from an earlier form of communication that was not conventional. As with the pre-monetary economy, there existed, arguably, a pre-linguistic form of communication. The transition from pre-linguistic to linguistic communication simultaneously marks the transition from meaning as a property of *persons*, to a property of *signs*. A convention to the effect that persons who utter certain standard signs thereby express a particular communicative intent is the same as a convention to the effect that these signs have a particular meaning. Admittedly, one might be able to say that a pre-linguistic sign used by a person in a particular context means such-and-such *in that context*. It makes sense to say that the grunt Zork used in the fable meant that his fellows should watch out for the bear. But that construal governs only a particular sound token, used in a concrete context. It is only when a permanent convention surrounding that imitative grunt is set up that the grunting noise, as such, and in general use, *means* that a bear is close at hand.

The concept of a speaker's meaning with his utterance is thus primary with respect to the meaning of the uttered sign in the linguistic system. It does not count as an objection to this account that *in an established language* linguistic meaning is primary relative to what any individual utterer means by what he says. A sentence such as 'The beechwoods are green' has a conventionally fixed semantic content and it is because it does that anyone who seeks to make a veridical statement in English about the colour of the beechwoods in spring may safely have recourse to this sentence. The meaning of the expression is primary relative to any particular use and grounds that use. This does not, however, conflict with the fact that, *historically*, it is use that comes first and convention later; convention is a conventionalization of actual use. What starts as common use becomes a norm for *correct* use, and so determines usage.

Equally, no argument for the primacy of linguistic meaning relative to users' meaning can be educed from the fact that linguistic meaning goes far beyond individual instances of use, i.e. the set of sentences actually uttered. It is correct that language qua system allows the construction of an infinitude of sentences, each with its conventional semantic content, and that only a finite fraction of such sentences are ever uttered. But this simply means that when a conventional language becomes established the conventionalization of meaning is not restricted to sentences already uttered. What gets conventionalized is a general structure capable of generating an infinite number of sentences, each with its associated semantic content. In chapter 6 we sketched one candidate explanation of this productivity.

Is it not, however, a problem for this conception that there are semantic contents that it seems impossible that any human being could grasp in the absence of a language? No sense can be made of the idea that at some historical point in time predating the emergence of language people possessed the relevant thought content and that only later did they produce a language in which to express it. Consider the pinnacles of human achievement within science, mathematics and philosophy – Einstein's theory of relativity, Bohr's quantum mechanics, Newton's differential calculus, Kant's critique of pure reason, Gödel's incompleteness theorems – and then judge whether any human being might have been capable of such thoughts without a language in which to articulate them. Obviously, no one could. Does this not contradict the above account, which presupposes that thought, in the form of communicative intentions, is prior to language? Not when these things are set in a historical evolutionary context. We have to envisage language emerging first as an instrument for the communication of simple thoughts and intentions of the sort that human subjects can entertain independently of language possession. Our fable illustrated how the evolution of a protolanguage enabled the mediation of very simple intentions turning on food and threatening predators. Once language proper is in place, thoughts involving higher levels of abstraction are possible, ones that would remain inconceivable in the absence of language. They conduce to increased linguistic sophistication, which in turn enables yet more sophisticated thinking.

Mathematics is a case in point. Good mathematical notations allow us to think mathematically, to elaborate proofs without necessarily focusing on the content of the symbols (which is why "mindless" computers are capable of producing mathematical proofs). The notation allows the elaboration of clear definitions of the basic concepts and perspicuous rules for how one sentence may be derived from another. With that notation in place, it is simply a matter of sitting down and doing the proofs. Mathematical truths are too abstract to be encompassed in thought without the support of something as tangible as a set of symbols.

15. But what does it really mean to say that language is a *convention*? Convention is sometimes associated with the idea of something being introduced as the result of human agreement or decision. But it is clear that only a very narrow sector of language is constituted in that way. Or, more accurately,

very little of interest to us here is the result of consensus or decision. There are indeed rules governing the notational aspects of language – there are dictionaries that explicitly fix the correct spellings of words. But there is no corresponding authoritative source for the semantic aspect of language. A dictionary of contemporary English is not a set of official rules to which all speakers of English have to conform. It is a *description*, rather, of an actual practice. Finally, it is also clear that language could never have emerged in tandem with an explicit set of rules since language is required for their formulation.

David Lewis has proposed an alternative analysis of convention to solve this puzzle. Lewis points to the fact that we speak of a "convention" when within a community there exist mutually conflicting ways of achieving an end and the need arises to settle upon a common, coordinated method. Lewis seeks to elucidate the situation where this coordination comes about in the absence of any explicit agreement or decision. Borrowing from Lewis, then, but simplifying somewhat, we can say that a convention is a practice conformed to by all because each person knows that everyone else conforms to it, and because there is a general interest in the predictability and coordination of human actions that results from everyone acting in the same way. Here there might be said to exist a *tacit* or *implicit* convention.

So much about conventions in general. But what distinguishes the convention that defines language? Lewis's answer to that question runs as follows (where P is a population and £ is a language):

> There prevails in P at least a regularity of truthfulness and trust in £. The members of P frequently speak (or write) sentences of £ to one another. When they do, ordinarily the speaker (or writer) utters one of the sentences he believes to be true in £; and the hearer (or reader) responds by coming to share that belief of the speaker's (unless he already had it), and adjusting his other beliefs accordingly.

Note that the fact that a language L is, conventionally, the language spoken by a particular group does not, on Lewis's analysis, mean that it serves as the sole vehicle for all verbal communication. Now this would seem to be correct: the claim that among inhabitants of the UK there is a convention to the effect that English is the standard medium of communication does not exclude occasional recourse being had, say, to French words and sentences. The regnant conventions do not stipulate that only English sentences may be uttered but rather that when they are uttered the speaker must be prepared to vouch for their truth. That said, it is indeed correct that English would hardly qualify as the language spoken by UK citizens if it were not the overwhelmingly dominant language. All the same, trying to set up some sort of minimum standard for its quotient of use is hardly going to prove a fruitful endeavour.

We have reached the point where we are able to reformulate the conditions for saying and meaning something in language L. Once again, the analysis set out below deals only with assertions. Discussions conducted in the foregoing make it unnecessary to rehearse the reasons why that analysis qualifies as primary and as capable of providing a foundation for the analyses of speech acts involving other moods.

S performs a successful act of asserting that p by uttering U, which belongs to language L, if and only if:

1. It is the case that p.

2. S utters U with the intention of committing himself to its being the case that p.

3. S intends his utterance of U to give a hearer H grounds to believe (recognize) that S has uttered (produced) U with the aim of committing himself to its being the case that p.

4. S intends that his utterance of U give hearer H grounds to believe (recognize) that S has uttered (produced) U with the intention of giving H grounds to believe (recognize) that S has uttered (produced) U with the intention of committing himself to its being the case that p, in virtue of H's knowledge of the rules for the language L.

5. It is a convention in S's social group concerning the language (linguistic system) L that a speaker does not utter U unless he can vouch for its being the case that p.

16. In the foregoing discussion of speech act theory we have progressed towards an analysis which locates the concept of truth at the core of the definition of meaning as related to speech acts. For a speaker to mean something is for him to commit himself to the success conditions of his utterance, amongst which, from a theoretical perspective, truth conditions are primary. We supplemented this with elements from David Lewis's account of what it means to say that a speech community uses a particular language as a vehicle for communication, an analysis in which the concept of truth (in the form of

truthfulness) also played a central role. Indeed, there is a matching between the concept of truth as the linchpin of the account and what was said about the concept of meaning in chapters 3, 4 and 6; the two are closely interknit. It remains to show how the two treatments of the concept of meaning, rather than being in contention, go to make up a coherent and complete picture. Here again we follow David Lewis's account.

We have just seen what it means to say that a language is the language spoken by a particular social group, namely, that within the speech community there is a convention governing the truth conditions of sentences in this language – and not just the set of sentences actually uttered, i.e. actual speech in aggregate, but all the sentences construable using the words and the grammatical constructions permitted by that language. What we have in focus, then, is language qua system, both syntactic and semantic: more precisely put, language qua infinite correlation of sentences – those characterized as well formed – with their truth conditions. For it is to such truth conditions that a user of a particular language is committed in uttering a sentence, according to Lewis's definition of linguistic convention.

This conception dovetails with the linguistic model presented in chapter 6. That model was that of a language qua system of principles or formulae (we compared it to a computer programme) with the potential to generate all well-formed sentences and to correlate them with their truth conditions (for assertions): it is, in essence, Davidson's adaptation of Tarski's model. We see how the two analyses of language – the formal, semantic model built on the concept of truth, and speech act theory – go hand in hand. In sum, Lewis's speech act analysis has it that a speech community speaks a language if its members accept a convention about truth in this language, agreeing only to utter true sentences in it. This means that there is a system of rules constitutive of a language, L, which is definitory of both well-formed sentences and their truth conditions and that for every well-formed assertive sentence in this language, speakers take on a commitment to the relevant truth condition in uttering that sentence.

Thus language is primarily a social practice, what Ferdinand de Saussure calls *parole*, speech. More precisely, it is a communicative practice which consists in persons uttering particular sounds with the aim of producing particular effects in one another, typically in what each believes about the world, beliefs freighted with implications for future action. In pursuit of these ends, they avail themselves of a language, now in the sense of a system of words and rules governing their use (*langue*, in Saussure's terminology). These symbols are combined to form larger units, sentences, and every sentence is correlated with the conditions for its successful utterance. The primary success conditions, from a theoretical point of view, are *truth conditions*. A person who utters a constative sentence expressly commits himself to the satisfaction of the sentence's truth condition. Construed qua semiotic system, language is potentially infinite; every natural language contains an infinitude of possible well-formed sentences. So language is not properly described as a list of sentences correlated with their conditions of successful utterance but should be characterized, rather, as a structure of formulae with the potential to generate all well-formed sentences in the language (this is the grammatical-syntactic aspect of the language). Correlated with each sentence is the set of its success conditions; they comprise the semantics of the sentence.

Chapter 9
On the borderline between linguistics and philosophy: recent developments in the theory of meaning

1. In chapter 2, we introduced the idea that meaning is use, an idea which occasioned a revolution in philosophy of language. The chief originator of this idea, Ludwig Wittgenstein, took this insight to extremes, implicitly denying the traditional distinction between semantics and pragmatics. This is a radical position, since it would seem to imperil the very possibility of a systematic theory of meaning. This was indeed the conclusion that Wittgenstein drew, at least to the extent that a systematic theory must also be *general*. The reason is that the purposes for which human beings use language – 'perlocutinary effects', as we have now learned to call them – are endlessly numerous and varied. Hence they resist capture in a general theory of language.

In chapter 8, we examined the way in which the insight that meaning is use has been accommodated in post-Wittgensteinian philosophy of language. Austin, Grice, Searle and others attempted to domesticate this notion and to build it into a theory of meaning which would not break radically with the tradition. To equate meaning with use is tantamount to viewing language as a particular kind of action (speech acts), and the strategy was to capture the meaning of linguistic expressions in terms of the success conditions which speakers impose upon their acts. It turned out that the resulting model would split the speech acts into (at least) three different subsidiatry acts, the locutionary act, the illocutionary act, and the perlocutionary act. This division conforms to the tradition in drawing a distinction between semantics and pragmatics. This distinction gets shifted, however, since semantics is no longer simply, in the manner of Morris, a matter of the relationship between language and the world. Meaning now also comprises parts of what the speaker does vis-à-vis his listener in uttering a sentence, be this asserting, asking, ordering, begging, and so on. This counts as part of the meaning of a sentence as long as it is encoded in the sentence, to be inferred from it in a formal manner. The distinction between semantics and pragmatics is now no longer drawn in terms of the difference between the relation of language to reality, and to speakers and hearers, respectively, but rather in terms of aspects of communicated content that can be computed rigorously purely on the basis of the sentence uttered, and aspects which can only be inferred, in less rigorous ways, by drawing on the context in which the sentence was uttered. This way of drawing the boundary, for instance, places Grice's implicature firmly on the pragmatic side.

This distinction has not gone unchallenged, however. In recent times, a group of linguists and philosophers of language have argued that meaning is never formally encoded in sentences, to be extracted in rigidly specifiable ways. Hence they advocate another shift in the line of division between semantics and pragmatics. But lurking behind this proposal is a yet more serious challenge, viz. one which would undermine the role of truth as the core notion in a theory of meaning. These issues are the topic of this chapter.

2. Now the truth-conditional theory of meaning is not a theory that purports to explain how speakers construct sentences, nor does it concern the way in which hearers go about interpreting them. These are matters for cognitive psychology, not for semantics. This applies *mutatis mutandis* to candidate proposals for the construction of such theories – Davidson's, presented in chapter 6, is a case in point. For although Davidson's theory is designed to satisfy the generative capacity constraint and thereby formally demonstrate how sentences are generated, it is not intended to provide a description of how speakers actually construct the sentences they utter, nor of how hearers decode them.

Still, the bipartition of the theory of linguistic messages into a strictly formal, recursive part (semantics) and a non-formalizable part (pragmatics) suggests a duality in the ways in which language is construed. The strictly semantical aspects constitute a code, and grasping their content *may* indeed consist in a formal process of decoding. The kind of recursive theory that Davidson devised arguably shows that, at least in principle, it is open to a hearer to get at the meaning of a particular sentence via some species of "reverse engineering": the construction of the T-sentence for the sentence requiring decoding would *eo ipso* supply him with the relevant truth conditions (the outcome, in a homophonic theory being trivial, of course). As for the other, non-semantical aspects, a cognitive grasp of them involves inferences of a completely different kind in which the context of utterance plays an essential role. We have already investigated one such inferential form in our presentation of Grice's theory of implicature in chapter 8.

Recently, this purported dichotomy in how linguistic utterances are to be understood has been called into question; and, since the split in the theory of interpretation flowed from a corresponding cleavage in the theory of meaning, the rebuttal of the former will tend to raise doubts about the latter. The claim being advanced is that some features that, offhand, seem to relate to meaning, more specifically to *sentence* meaning (as against Gricean implicatures), and which as such belong to semantics, are in fact manifestly drawn from features of the context of utterance, and in non-formalizable ways. It would seem, then, that they too are eo ipso pragmatic. In consequence, the distinction between semantics and pragmatics needs to be redrawn. To some authors these considerations have seemed to argue for an even more dramatic conclusion, namely, one rendering the very idea of meaning as given by truth conditions insecure.

The theory was given its first systematic presentation by scholars working at the interface of philosophy of language and linguistics, with its initial explicit articulation appearing in the writings of Bach and Harnish. The full-dress version of this idea, however, is to be sought in Sperber and Wilson's book *Relevance*, where the authors seek to locate the discussion within the framework of cognitive science, more precisely the theory of information processing.

3. Sperber and Wilson begin by pointing out that even traditional semanticists are prepared to admit that, strictly speaking, sentence meaning cannot be computed merely on the basis of the sentence, qua complete linguistic unit, alone: the phenomenon of *indexicality* requires that features of the situation of utterance be taken into account. The assumption operative in traditional semantics, however, is that indexical reference can be dealt with solely in formal and rule-governed ways, calling for no derogation from the process of decoding. Sperber and Wilson illustrate the initial plausibility of this claim with the following sentence:

1. I'll come tomorrow.

This sentence contains two indexical referential devices, 'I' and 'tomorrow'. To get at the meaning of the sentence, these devices have to be decoded by appeal to the context, using the following two semantic rules seriatim:

For 'I', substitute a reference to the speaker.

For 'tomorrow', substitute a reference to the day following the day of the utterance.

These are formal and mechanical rules of interpretation, such as could easily be accommodated, for example, by a Davidsonian theory of meaning. As a matter of fact, Davidson himself shows how this can be done in a manner closely related to that proposed by Sperber and Wilson. In "Truth and Meaning", Davidson specifies the T-sentence appropriate to an indexical sentence:

2. 'I am tired' is true as (potentially) spoken by S at t if and only if S is tired at t.

However, Sperber and Wilson quickly move on to examples that are more troublesome for the code theorists:

3. He's got egg on his tie.

4. That's interesting.

English grammar specifies that the referent of 'he' must be male and that the referent of 'that' must be non-human. But these are very weak constraints, leaving an infinite number of items as possible referents of these terms as they figure in the utterance. Without further amplification, these sentences lack fully determinate meanings. But the processes that afford such determination of meaning will patently be *contextual*, *informal* and hence *pragmatic*.

But might we not deal with the problem by drawing upon the utterer's communicative intentions as part of the context? That is, might not the following T-sentence be offered, construed on analogy with 2 above:

5. 'He's got egg on his tie' is true as (potentially) spoken by S at t if and only if the person whom S had in mind at t had egg on his tie.

The problem with this is that, unlike 2, it does not actually deliver the information that singles out the relevant individual. This is clear from the fact that it is not by means of that formula that S would identify him: so doing would be blatantly circular and empty.

Lexical and structural ambiguity constitutes a further problem. Consider the following sentence, again culled from Sperber and Wilson:

6. Jones has bought the *Times*.

This sentence admits of (at least) two interpretations: on one Jones has bought a copy of the newspaper, on the other Jones has bought the company which publishes the newspaper. Only context can decide the matter. One contextual factor would be connectedness to the conversation in which it occurs; the first interpretation, for instance, would be the natural choice if the talk turned on some news item reported in today's *Times*. A consideration of the truth of the claims advanced – similarly, of course, a contextual factor – would also be taken into account: other things being equal, interpretation should strive to reflect the truth of assertions rather than their falsity (cf. chapter 10). The upshot once again is that sentence *meaning* is only determinable *pragmatically*.

It might be objected that all we can properly require of a theory of meaning is that it provide a specification of the truth conditions of each of the possible readings of the sentence, corresponding to each of the senses of the lexically ambiguous term (this is the strategy adopted by Davidson). The decision as to which of them is the correct one on any particular occasion of use is a task for hermeneutics, not a problem for the theory of meaning. In our concrete example, all we should be asking of the theory of meaning is that it provide a reading of the sentence with either interpretation of 'the *Times*' substituted along the following lines:

7. 'Jones has bought the *Times*' is true iff
a) Jones has bought a copy of the newspaper called the *Times*
or
b) Jones has bought the company which publishes the newspaper called the *Times*.

Unfortunately, this strategy is only helpful so long as a determinate number of disjunctive construals are in play. But this is not always the case. The point may be illustrated by the following example from Sperber and Wilson where indeterminacy remains, even after indexicality and lexical ambiguity have been accounted for:

8. Peter's bat is too grey.

The sentence meaning of 8 remains indeterminate until it is made clear not only whether 'bat' means the flying mammal or a baseball bat, but also in what respect it is too grey. Is its excessive greyness related to the rules of regulation baseball? Or is it too grey to stand out against the team colours? Or perhaps too grey to be easily distinguishable from the bats of the opposing team? No finite list of alternatives is going to be exhaustive. Only non-formalizable inferences based upon contextual information will decide the issue.

The same point could have been made in respect of sentences 3 and 4 above. There is no finitely specifiable list of items that would exhaust the possible references of the terms 'he' and 'that' in those sentences.

Without suitable supplementation and disambiguation, none of these sentences is capable of conveying any determinate meaning. This comes out in our hesitation, whatever contextual information we may possess, in attributing particular truth-values to the sentences so long as such indeterminacies remain. But ridding them of indeterminacies proceeds through contextual, non-formalizable and hence *pragmatic* inference. In consequence, the demarcation between semantics and pragmatics dissolves at this point.

4. Sperber and Wilson advance a general theory of these processes of pragmatic interpretation. Their proposal is rooted in cognitive science or rather, more precisely, in the science of information processing. Their approach may fairly be described as "economical" inasmuch as they site information processing in a cost-benefit framework: our cognitive system is so organized as to seek out and store maximally useful information at the lowest possible cost in terms of information processing.

The operative notion driving these inferences is that of *relevance*. Sperber and Wilson define this notion in a relatively technical manner which combines the twin dimensions of informational gain and information processing cost. We need not go into the details since here a commonsense, intuitive understanding of the idea will suffice.

Since communication involves information processing, it too is governed by the general "economical" principles obtaining in this domain. Spoken communication ranks high among the priorities of our cognitive economy. Processing them is not an option but occurs instantly and automatically: when somebody within earshot utters a sentence in our native language, we cannot help registering and parsing it. There is apparently a general built-in presumption in the human cognitive system to the effect that such communication is relevant, i.e. that it repays the expenditure of cognitive energy involved in its construal.

Sperber and Wilson cast this principle in a more precise form as follows:

The presumption of optimal relevance
a) The set of assumptions {I} which the communicator intends to make manifest to the addressee is relevant enough to make it worth the

addressee's while to process the ostensive stimulus.
b) The ostensive stimulus is the most relevant one the communicator could have used to communicate {I}.
(Sperber & Wilson, 1986, p. 158)

This presumption is capable not only of explaining why people take speech very seriously, but can even serve as a premise for the inferential processes by which a listener interprets a given communication. The point may be illuminated by a non-linguistic example, borrowed from the authors. Mary and Peter are sitting on a bench in the park, when Peter spots William, an acquaintance of theirs but also, unfortunately, a terrible bore. To warn Mary of the looming threat, Peter leans back somewhat demonstratively, i.e. in a manner that is clearly attention seeking, not least because it has no obvious practical point. This signals that the movement may have a communicative purpose but does not in itself show what communicative content is intended (the *informative* intention, in Sperber and Wilson's terminology).

To identify that content, Mary must rely on condition (b) which provides that the ostensive stimulus employed by the speaker is the most relevant one available to him in that context. This means, Sperber and Wilson argue, that the addressee may safely take the first supposition that occurs to her, namely that to the effect that the speaker wishes to communicate something, as one capable of satisfying condition (a). She does not have to worry that she might later think of a hypothesis equally capable of satisfying that condition with the ambiguity thus produced. For if there were further equally eligible suppositions, that fact would constitute an infraction of condition (b) since it would mean that, given the economy constraint governing the use of intellectual resources, instead of selecting the most relevant stimulus in Sperber and Wilson's sense the speaker would have gone for one capable of effectually disambiguating the situation. Since this is not what he did, the listener may safely assume that the supposition that most readily suggests itself is also the one intended. So when Mary's attention, activated by Peter's exaggerated attitude, is immediately drawn to William, now in plain view, she may safely assume that this is precisely what Peter wanted her to notice.

So much for non-verbal communication. But it is the central thrust of Sperber and Wilson's position that verbal communication is not essentially different from this. Verbal communication too is an ostensive-inferential process, relying substantially upon the assumption of optimal relevance in order to function as a premise for inferences about the speaker's communicative intentions. There is no formal process of decoding involved. True, Sperber and Wilson do not deny that there is such a thing as coded information.

But they stress two things: (1) Even when the signs are coded, the information conveyed by them only makes sense within an overarching ostensive-referential framework. This wider framework is needed, for instance, to establish whether the coded sign used is indeed meant as a sign, rather than a means of testing a recording device, or the performance of a recital, and so on; (2) The coded information needs supplementation by other elements if a full-fledged truth-bearing message is to result.

It is instructive to contrast Sperber and Wilson's position with Grice's theory of conversational implicature. Grice argued that there is a general presumption that conversational contributions are maximally informative, and his notion of informativeness is of course close kin to Sperber and Wilson's notion of relevance. However, the occasional apparent disappointment of this presumption sets off inferential processes in the hearer which allow implicit messages, so-called conversational implicatures, to be inferred. These belong to the pragmatics of sentences, not to their semantics.

Sperber and Wilson, on the other hand, argue that the use of such inferential rules, and of the notion of relevance in particular, is not restricted to those occasions where the appropriate presumptions are ostensibly infringed. The notion of relevance plays a role in all communication; notice for instance its role in establishing the proper interpretation of sentence 6 above. Moreover, as we have seen, Sperber and Wilson insist that these inferential processes serve to specify *sentence meaning*, and not only the broader message.

5. Sperber and Wilson argue that meaning (sentence meaning) is only partly fixed by the sentence uttered, and hence not recoverable from it by any formal process of decoding. Rather, meaning is fully determined only through a process of non-formal inference based upon the cognitive notion of relevance. This conclusion, if correct, would collapse the distinction between semantics and pragmatics: the determination of (sentence) meaning turns out to be a matter of pragmatics.

It is important to stress that it is indeed *sentence* meaning and not only speaker meaning that is fixed pragmatically, for it is commonly conceded that speaker meaning is determined contextually and pragmatically. When for instance we hear the utterance, 'Can you reach the salt?' we infer, on the basis of pragmatic reasoning (conversational implicature), that the speaker meant 'Would you pass the salt, please?' This poses no problems for traditional semanticists, since they have the notion of sentence meaning to fall back upon as the object of formal, semantical specification. They will claim that the sentence 'Can you reach the salt?' is decodable in the strict sense, and constitutes the literal content of the utterance, whereas the "indirect speech act" of asking for the salt is merely implicated. It is this position that Sperber and Wilson attack.

The issue here concerns the prospects for the elaboration of a formal, recursive theory of semantics, using the concept of truth conditions as the core notion. Recognizing that aspects of communication intuitively belonging to meaning are apparently fixed by contextual, non-formal reasoning, we may decide to abandon that idea. The loss incurred by so doing will depend upon the degree of rigour exhibited by the alternative, pragmatic theory. But these may, after all, prove to be largely terminological issues.

A weightier implication lies in the fact that Sperber and Wilson's analysis threatens to undermine the whole idea of sentence meaning's being a matter of truth conditions. Truth conditions emerge solely as determinants of the meanings of interpreted sentential utterances from which indeterminacies have been removed. Take the example used above:

9. Peter's bat is too grey.

Until we have determined the standard against which the bat is deemed too grey, there is no way in which we can attribute truth conditions to this sentence. As we have seen, however, such disambiguation is based upon an understanding of the undisambiguated sentence and its role in the context in which it occurs. But this means that undisambiguated sentences must already have a *meaning* if there is allegedly something there to understand. (Let us call this *basic* meaning.) But this meaning cannot be a matter of truth conditions, since these are not yet fixed.

If there are such things as basic meanings not defined in terms of truth conditions, then what are they? Sperber and Wilson's concrete proposal identifies them as *semantic representations* (Sperber & Wilson, 1986, p. 193). Semantic representations are described as "incomplete logical forms", i.e. formal schemata with certain logical properties; such properties are required if semantic representations are to play a role in inferential processes, such as serving to turn the logical form into fully truth-evaluable entities. Examples of logical forms include open sentences in the predicate calculus. While permitting certain logical operations, such sentences are not bearers of truth conditions since they can only be turned into truth-definite items by the insertion of names or the addition of quantifiers. In the above instance, the semantic representation would contain a blank to be filled in by some specification of the standard against which Peter's bat is deemed too grey.

6. Sperber and Wilson do not make it very clear how, in more concrete terms, these "semantic representations" are to be understood. There is a worry that their proposal might be pushing semantics back into something akin to the psychologism of seventeenth century philosophy of language. Meanings would seem to have been re-lodged, inaccessibly, in the utterer – if not in his "breast", then at least in his brain. We would have been returned to the identification of meaning with the speaker's "ideas", although these latter have now been endowed with newfangled names culled from modern cognitive science. For "semantic representations" may be given a psychological reading: they are mere stages in the mental process of figuring out the truth conditions of sentences. As such, they are the elusive posits of a speculative cognitive theory. In the context of everyday communication, such items are as private and inaccessible to third persons as are subjective "ideas in the mind".

Sperber and Wilson could alleviate this worry, of course, by adopting a staunchly intersubjectivist interpretation of semantic representations, linking them to identifiable behavioural criteria; but they show little interest in such epistemic concerns. Nonetheless, there are others working in the field who have taken similar ideas in a patently objectivist and indeed formalistic direction. Among them are Kamp and Reyle, building upon earlier work by Kamp and Heim.

Kamp and Reyle's theory is aptly named *Discourse Representation Theory* since that appellation embraces two distinctive features of their programme: first, where traditional semantical theories take the sentence as their unit of semantic analysis, Kamp and Reyle see larger segments of discourse as the natural unit. Second, in drawing upon the locus of an utterance to disambiguate its semantic content, Kamp and Reyle focus exclusively upon con-*text* in a literal sense, i.e. as that which is delivered to a sentence by the segment of discourse in which it is nested.

The title of Kamp and Reyle's main work is *From Discourse to Logic*, and this title well captures the authors' ambition to generate a set of principles of interpretation that permits the analysis of stretches of discourse in a natural language, thereby transforming them into logical forms that are furnished with a semantics, namely the standard semantics of predicate logic.

In this way, the project exhibits some affinity with Davidson's. For Davidson's objective too is the derivation and representation of the semantic conditions of the sentences of natural language through their transposition into the formulae of predicate logic enriched with non-logical vocabulary. The Tarskian framework deployed to this end crucially involves the logical apparatus and the semantics of the predicate calculus. One important difference between Kamp and Reyle's project and Davidson's is precisely the former's focus on extended segments of discourse, with their interpretation encompassing such contextual aspects as derive from this source. It is to this latter feature that Kamp and Reyle's project owes its name of "Dynamic Semantics", since meaning is something that is built up incrementally in the process of interpreting ever longer textual segments. Another important difference is that Davidson's theory is *synthetic*, recursively generating every sentence in the object language along with its meaning (truth conditions), whereas Kamp and Reyle's theory is *analytic*, offering principles for the parsing and interpretation of sentences or strings thereof that serve as input.

Since Kamp and Reyle analyse only texts, the notion of a context of interpretation refers only to *textual* embedding, with non-textual features dropping out of the frame. This enables a vast simplification in the rules that transform natural language sentences into logical forms, and makes it possible to give the theory an air of semi-formality. (Only semi-formality, since some of the rules of interpretation both allow and enforce a discretionary element.)

According to Kamp and Reyle, the route from discourse to logic proceeds via a sequence of steps. Given a text, i.e. a set of linearly ordered sentences, the procedure enjoins, first, the grammatical parsing of the individual sentences. The grammar here adopted for that purpose is essentially a phrase structure grammar as defined by Chomsky. However, in the interests of increased scope, this basic grammar is supplemented with numerous additional rules.

The second step concerns semantic interpretation proper. This consists in the transformation of the syntactical parsings into so-called Discourse Representation Structures (DRSs). DRSs may be seen as the sentences or formulae of an artificial language exhibiting a transparent semantical structure. They consist of two components: (1) The *universe* of the DRS, which is the set of discourse referents, i.e. the terms figuring in the Noun Phrases of the syntactic structures; (2) a set of *DRS conditions*, which consists in the information supplied about the Noun Phrases occurring in the Verb Phrases of the sentences.

The third step in the translation is the transformation of DRSs into formulae of predicate logic. In fact, this step is but a short one for, as Kamp and Reyle readily concede, their DRSs turn out to approximate very closely to the formulae of predicate logic; indeed, they might be considered merely notational variants of such formulae and as such they share the standard model-theoretic semantics of the predicate calculus. In this way, sentences and sentential strings of natural language are ultimately anchored in a familiar semantical model with well-understood properties.

Kamp and Reyle's main achievement is not to have devised a formalization of certain fragments of natural language and their translatability into the formulae of the predicate calculus. Their true contribution resides unquestionably in *the rules that effect the transformation* of sentences of natural language into logical formulae. This is where the real work of semantical analysis takes place.

The restriction of Kamp and Reyle's project to the interpretation of sentences in a purely verbal context marks a crucial contrast to Sperber and Wilson's project, where the objective is to interpret sentences as employed in a full material and social context. This restriction, with the simplifications attendant upon it, allows Kamp and Reyle to come close to the kind of formal theory (namely, one involving rigorous "decoding") which Sperber and Wilson dismiss. Hence the challenge posed to the Davidsonian ideal by this kind of theorizing is relatively minor.

What the two approaches share, however, is the idea that at the most basic level, meaning is the property of items that do not (yet) possess truth conditions. Discourse Representation Structures and their close kin, formulae in the predicate calculus, would seem to qualify as "semantic representations" in Sperber and Wilson's sense: they are not yet bearers of truth conditions, but they exhibit propositional form. They are, then, amenable to inference and to other logical manipulations that would convert them into fully "truth evaluable" items. Consequently, it would appear that meaning is not identifiable with truth conditions. And by stressing the formal status of such semantic representations, identifying them, for all practical purposes, with the formulae of the predicate calculus, Kamp and Heim are able to sidestep the charge that, through foregoing the identification of meaning with truth conditions, semantics has once again become psychologistic, and essentially private.

7. Above, we presented claims put forward on behalf of what have been termed 'pragmatic theories of meaning'. These claims have ignited a lively debate, the details of which cannot be pursued here. In part, the claims pertain to issues which are not strictly germane to our present concerns, such as the question of where the boundary between semantics and pragmatics should be drawn; as noted earlier in the chapter, there is a suspicion that these issues are largely terminological.

What is of interest in the present context is something on which there seems to be a general consensus among the combatants, viz. the idea that sentences may be meaningful without being "truth-evaluable", with the corollary that their meaning cannot consist in their truth conditions. We hope that the plausibility of this claim has emerged from the above discussion. But whatever its credentials, to some participants in the debate it represents a major departure from philosophical orthodoxy.

A modicum of scrutiny reveals, however, that the departure from truth-conditional semantics inherent in this conclusion constitutes only a very slight deviation, for there is virtual unanimity that both sentence meaning and speaker meaning are determined by truth-conditions. What is specific to these new approaches is their perception of these two levels of meaning as derivative upon a more elementary stratum of meaning which we have called *basic meaning*. Basic meaning is not a matter of truth conditions, since sentences are not "truth-evaluable" merely in virtue of possessing basic meaning.

From a logical point of view, however, the principled difference between traditional truth conditional semantics and "truth conditional pragmatics" is quite marginal. We can still, with Frege and Davidson, describe meaning as a function from sentences to truth conditions, or, alternatively, as a function from sentences and contexts to truth-values. Nothing has been educed beyond the fact that this function is rather more complex than hitherto assumed. It may be seen as the conjunction of several part-functions, of which the first transforms the sentence into its referentially disambiguated counterpart (i.e. token-reflexive expressions are replaced with non-indexical expressions), the second so reconfigures this representation that lexical and structural ambiguity is pruned away (giving us sentence meaning, in the conventional sense), a third processes the resultant representation further, ridding it of indeterminacies through "completion" or "expansion" (as in sentences 6 and 8 above) before, as part of the final phase, the illocutionary force of the sentence is captured by a set of success conditions that jointly yield *speaker* meaning. Meaning is still a matter of a functional correlation between sentences and success conditions (in particular truth conditions), but now one more complex than normally envisaged. (We saw in chapter 7 how Kaplan took a step in this direction with his theory of indexicals and demonstratives).

We recall that the canonical characterization of meaning in truth-conditional semantics says that meaning, for sentences, is their truth conditions, and for subsentential expressions, their contribution to the fixing of such truth conditions. This formulation accommodates the obvious yet important point that subsentential linguistic elements, such as singular terms and predicates, although meaningful, do not have truth conditions. Instead, such elements possess meaning by virtue of their contributions to the fixing of the truth conditions of sentences. What is required now is the extension of this analysis to take in whole sentences as well. It needs only a very slight reformulation of the above slogan to accommodate the pragmatist criticism of traditional truth-conditional semantics: we might say that *meaning is the contribution of the sentence and its parts to fixing the truth conditions of utterances, i.e. the truth-value of those sentences in varying contexts of utterance*. This definition leaves open the possibility that sentences too may lack truth conditions while remaining meaningful in virtue of the contribution they make to fixing the truth-value of utterances.

8. Let us now turn to another theory of meaning, evolving on the borderline between linguistics and philosophy, whose deviance from standard truth conditional theories is much more radical. It springs from a collaboration between the linguist George Lakoff and the philosopher Mark Johnson, and comes as part of what is known as "cognitive semantics", which again is part of a broader endeavour known as "cognitive linguistics". This enterprise may be seen as representing a partial return to the classical "ideational" semantics of Locke and the British empiricists: the informing idea is that the workings of the human mind form an essential constituent of the phenomenon of meaning. According to the cognitive theorists, this is an aspect of semantics that has been overlooked in standard accounts. The chief culprits here are the truth theorists, who have focused blindly upon the abstract referential relations of language to an independent reality while neglectful of the way in which the mind processes that reality. What they have all failed to recognize is that linguistic meaning is anchored in common cognitive human processes.

There is one significant difference between the modern cognitive approach and the empiricist ideational semantics of old: the former lays emphasis on the *embodied* nature of cognitive processes. In large measure, thought is here conceived of as the extension of purely bodily patterns of reaction and conceptual frameworks as derivative upon features of the body qua instrument of agency and situated in space. This conception is a far cry from the characteristic disembodiedness associated with classical empiricism. Moreover, modern cognitivists consider the mind's meaning-generating processes to be largely unconscious, an idea which would have struck the classical empiricists as nigh on incoherent. Still, the common features are undeniable.

9. Let us begin by giving an account of the cognitive processes thought to underpin language use before going on to investigate how this apparatus poses a challenge to traditional truth-conditional semantics.

The phenomenon that tends to be flagged up as offering the key to cognitive processing is *categorization*. Two aspects of categorization have been specially singled out for attention, the "prototype effect" and the phenomenon of "basic level primacy".

Let us first remind ourselves of some features of the traditional, logical theory of classification which, in all essentials, goes back to Aristotle. On this conception, classification is accomplished by specifying the necessary and sufficient conditions for an object to belong to a given kind. Some properties on the list are generic ones, shared by other kinds, while others are more specific and constitute the differentiae which distinguish a particular entity from other members of its genus. Thus, famously, a man is a "rational bipedal animal" on an Aristotelian classification.

There are at least two points of interest that follow from this account. The first is that, once it satisfies the necessary and sufficient conditions for membership of the relevant kind, any one specimen is as good an exemplar of that kind as any other. The second has to do with relationships between levels. As seen from the perspective of logical or taxonomic purposes alone (as opposed to various metaphysical concerns), there is no reason to give priority to any one level of classification over others.

As it happens, both assumptions about the nature of human taxonomizing are contradicted by recent empirical research. A pre-eminent figure here is Eleanor Rosch. In the first place, Rosch has demonstrated the existence of so-called "prototype effects". This is a reference to the phenomenon of people considering certain members of a class to be "better members" than others. They will even be prepared to make fairly precise relative assessments of this "goodness", precise enough to enable the setting up a metric of goodness, and systematic and intersubjectively generalizable enough to be of theoretical interest. For instance, amongst birds, robins are consistently described as better specimens than eagles, penguins and ostriches; amongst chairs, desk chairs are better than rocking chairs, barber chairs or beanbag chairs.

The "basic category" effect is the observation that, in the strictly logical hierarchy into which classes and things may be ordered, there is a particular, intermediate level that is somehow psychologically salient. That is the level at which identification of items in the everyday world is first achieved by the young child, the classification of things is most easily stored in the memory, things have (in natural languages) the shortest names and classification coincides most closely with characteristic behavioural reactions to the things categorized. Basic level categories include such exemplars as 'dog', 'chair', 'car', and so on. The superordinate and subordinate levels typically have longer, often composite, names in natural languages, such as 'mammal', 'furniture', 'vehicle' and 'retriever', 'rocking chair', 'sports car'. They are also less accessible to the cognizing mind. Reaching the superordinate levels involves some effort of abstraction, while acquisition of the subordinate categories requires skill of discrimination often possessed only by experts.

The "prototype effect" and the basic category phenomenon are purely empirical phenomena, and their theoretical accountability remains debatable. Many cognitive scientists have adopted a very straightforward explanation, to the effect that the prototype phenomenon reflects the way in which classificatory information is stored and processed in consciousness (or the brain), namely in the form of a paradigmatic icon – a representative of the kind deemed most closely to approach the prototype. In the case of birds, the stored icon would be that of a robin, or something close to it. But the originator of prototype theory, Eleanor Rosch, has explicitly denounced such interpretations as too simple-minded. There is no justification for thinking that these effects are so readily accounted for.

10. George Lakoff is similarly critical. His project is aimed at developing a general cognitive theory of human categories that will account for these features. The chief element in his theory is what he calls *Idealized Cognitive Models*, or ICMs, which combine aspects of Charles Fillmore's frame semantics, Ronald Langacker's cognitive grammar and Gilles Fauconnier's theory of mental spaces. What Lakoff adds to this is a specific theory of metonymic and metaphoric concept formation, developed in collaboration with Mark Johnson.

In general, an ICM is an organized and idealized cluster of information about the natural or social world. Take Fillmore's example of 'bachelor' as an illustration. A bachelor is defined, in terms of simple necessary and sufficient conditions, as an unmarried man of marriable age. But this term is employed within a web of general but somewhat idealized information about the society in which unmarried men live. This web specifies that people normally live in some sort of a social network, not in total isolation; that bachelors are not committed to stable relationships with women partners; that men are heterosexual; that men do not marry before the age of 18, and so on.

This background information mediates considerable uncertainty when it comes to the labelling of certain individuals who are technically classifiable as bachelors but fail to satisfy one or other of the background assumptions.

This applies, say, in the case of men who have entered into long-term cohabitation with a woman but without official certification, for homosexuals who have no intention of marrying, for a young boy abandoned in the jungle and reaching marriable age away from any contact with other people, and so on.

The net result, then, is that we are able to account for (parts of) the prototype structure of the term 'bachelor' by reference to an underlying cognitive model that delivers the biological and socio-cultural parameters for the conceptions of marriage, sexuality, and so on, regnant in our culture.

11. Lakoff's main contribution to cognitive semantics, however, is the theory of the metaphorical structuring of concepts developed in collaboration with Mark Johnson. Lakoff and Johnson define metaphor as the phenomenon of understanding and experiencing one kind of thing in terms of another (Lakoff & Johnson 1980, p. 5). The idea is that we often organize a conceptual field by projecting into it a conceptual structure derived from another field. Typically, the field subject to the imposition is an abstract one – that of the emotions, for example – whereas the source of the projection is a concrete field, often one which is readily accessible to the senses, and hence better understood. Evidently, not all conceptual areas can be structured by means of such transfers; there have to be some non-metaphorical concepts to provide the structure for the metaphorical ones. According to Lakoff and Johnson, the basic level of categorization is an example of such non-metaphorical concepts.

Lakoff's favourite example of a metaphorical construct involves spatial terms such as 'up-down', 'in-out', 'front-back', 'central-peripheral', and so on. They are derived from the way our bodies are situated in space, and are related to our elementary observation of ourselves as bodily creatures so situated.

Lakoff and Johnson present a rich variety of descriptions of various sectors of reality and human existence which are structured by the metaphorical transfer of such directional categories. Here are a few that relate to human emotion (Lakoff & Johnson 1980, p. 15):

I'm feeling *up*. My spirits *rose*. You're in *high* spirits. I'm feeling *down*. I'm *depressed*. He's really *low* these days. My spirits *sank*.

Lakoff and Johnson capture the essence of that metaphorical polarity in the formula, HAPPY IS UP, SAD IS DOWN (we follow the convention of typing conceptual metaphors in upper case), and proceed to explain the rationale underpinning this metaphorical transfer. This has it that there is a characteristic drooping posture that goes along with sadness and depression, while a positive emotional state typically results in an erect, upright posture. Hence the up/down orientation of those moods.

Here is another cluster of related metaphors, expressive of numerical size or volume (*ibid*, pp. 15–16):

> The number of books printed each year keeps going *up*. His draft number is *high*. My income *rose* last year. The amount of artistic activity in this state has gone *down* in the past year. The number of errors he made is incredibly *low*. His income *fell* last year.

The common principle of these metaphors is MORE IS UP, LESS IS DOWN. Their non-metaphorical basis is the fact that when more of a substance or of physical objects are added to a container or pile, the level will go up in a literal physical sense (*ibid*).

Lakoff and Johnson go on to list further metaphors which are structured by the UP-DOWN opposition whose general tenor is expressed by such formulae as CONSCIOUS IS UP, UNCONSCIOUS IS DOWN; MORE IS UP, LESS IS DOWN; HAVING CONTROL OR FORCE IS UP, BEING SUBJECT TO CONTROL OR FORCE IS DOWN; FORESEEABLE FUTURE EVENTS ARE UP; VIRTUE IS UP, DEPRAVITY IS DOWN.

12. So far we have seen how the new cognitivist approach implies certain minor modifications of the traditional semantic picture. It has been shown how classification, and classificatory terms, exhibit a more complicated logic than the simple Aristotelian picture would suggest, and how, rather than serving as a merely stylistic embellishment, metaphor is the result of pervasive conceptual transfers from one field to another. This does not call for a radical modification of traditional semantics – at most for some redrawing of the boundary between semantics and pragmatics. For the pervasive influence of metaphor might simply be an indication that less of our semantic content is coded and more left to informal processes, than might be thought.

Lakoff and Johnson want to go further than this, however. They want to challenge important aspects of the philosophy of language, chief among them being the very idea of meaning as a matter of truth conditions.

In *Women, Fire and Dangerous Things*, George Lakoff sketches out an entire alternative theory of meaning. The basic idea is that linguistic expressions get their meanings by being associated, directly or indirectly, with our pre-conceptual bodily experience. This association is typically mediated by ICMs. These conceptual models are the primary bearers of meaning:

'Meaningfulness derives from the experience of functioning as a being of a certain sort in an environment of a certain sort. Basic-level concepts are meaningful to us because they are characterized by the way we perceive the overall shape of things in terms of part-whole structure and by the way we interact with things with our bodies. ... Natural metaphorical concepts are meaningful because they are based upon (a) directly meaningful concepts and (b) correlations in our experience'. (*op. cit.*, p. 292).

Next, Lakoff links this kind of understanding to the understanding of linguistic expressions:

'A *sentence is directly understood* if the concepts associated with it are directly meaningful'. (*ibid*)

So what we see emerging is a psychologistic, cognitivist theory of meaning: the primary locus of meaningfulness is identified as certain conceptual structures, closely bound up with human experiences and cognitive operations, and with meaning accruing to language through the latter's being the vehicle of their expression.

This is fairly nebulous stuff, and to those who are accustomed to the precision characteristic of the best versions of truth-conditional semantics, it will appear something of a retrograde step. Still, whatever cogency the account possesses comes from the critical part of Lakoff's argumentation, where he attempts to show that a traditional truth-based semantics is impossible. In part, this is predicated upon a rejection of the traditional objectivist or correspondence theory of truth. Lakoff introduces a rival, *constructivist* conception of truth, according to which truth is relative to the way in which we conceive of reality and describe it in language.

From the point of view of its Lakoffian counterpart, the traditional conception of semantics can be shown to be circular. It seeks to define meaning in terms of truth but in fact it works the other way round: truth is, at least to some extent, defined by the meanings with which we invest our words.

Lakoff deploys several argumentative strategies to establish this conclusion, but one of them may be seen as spun from the position known as conceptualism, which we discussed in chapter 4.

According to conceptualism, the correlates of general terms are not found in nature but are imposed upon it: nature is not pre-structured into particular kinds and types, as essentialism would have us believe. Instead, we perform conceptual dissections upon reality, and by so doing segment it into types and kinds. These claims amount to a moderate conceptualism, so long as it is acknowledged that the conceptual carving up undertaken by us is prompted by objective similarities in nature. Nature's inventory does indeed display objective similarities and dissimilarities; but we enjoy a certain latitude in concept formation since we are free to select which similarities shall inform the conceptual underpinnings of our language, both in light of our interests and in part as constrained by certain physiological features of our make-up.

This is the point where Lakoff and Johnson go a step further. According to them, similarities are not discovered, but are, at least sometimes, ones we *make*. This is the case for those large segments of our conceptual system that are structured by metaphorical transfer. We can illustrate this point by adducing one of Lakoff's favourite examples, mentioned above, namely the use of spatial terms to structure the more abstract parts of our cognition of the world.

On p. 113, Lakoff and Johnson ask rhetorically: 'For example, what possible similarities could there be that are shared by all of the concepts that are oriented UP? What similarity could there be between UP, on the one hand, and HAPPINESS, HEALTH, CONTROL, CONSCIOUSNESS, VIRTUE, RATIONALITY, MORE, and so on, on the other?'

The answer we are invited to return is "None". And we are urged to draw the further conclusion that similarity is here created by the imposition of the metaphor, rather than recorded in it. In creating similarity, this conceptual manoeuvre creates fact, or reality, viz. the fact that certain things are similar and hence belong to the same category. The strong form of conceptualism they advocate borders on metaphysical *projectionism*.

But the correct answer would seem to be that there are all the similarities, analogies, and so on, which Lakoff and Johnson take such pains to spell out for us in earlier parts of the book, and which were mentioned above. For example, the systematic way in which human emotions are described in terms of the metaphor HAPPY IS UP, SAD IS DOWN is based upon characteristic drooping posture that goes with sadness and depression, while a positive emotional state typically results in an erect, upright posture. This constitutes an objective link with MORE IS UP, LESS IS DOWN, since the increase or diminution of a pile of stuff will result in the elevation or the lowering of its surface. This is indeed what Lakoff and Johnson impress upon us in chapter 4 of that book.

However, the authors face a dilemma here. In order to persuade us that language is indeed structured in systematic ways by certain dominant metaphors, they have to show in detail that *the same image* occurs and recurs in various linguistic constructions. If this cannot be shown, the use of the same expression is merely a terminological accident, a case of pervasive homonymy. The authors argue vigorously against precisely this possibility (Lakoff & Johnson 1980, pp. 110–11). But so arguing debars them, ipso facto, from denying these similarities and connections later on.

It is, of course, true that the ground of classification may not be sets of similarities in a simple perceptual sense. But then no serious theory of concept formation, or of linguistic classification, ever claimed that things are grouped together merely because they present themselves to the senses as similar. It has been recognized ever since Aristotle that metonymic and other, objective, relationships obtaining between things may serve as bases for classification. (Aristotle referred to terms thus connected as *paronymous*). Aristotle noted that both a body and a complexion are referable to as "healthy", but that the latter is so called because of its (metonymic) relationship to the former; there is no likeness between a healthy body and a healthy complexion. Austin made the same point in 'The Meaning of a Word' (Austin 1961, p. 71), as Lakoff mentions elsewhere (Lakoff 1987, p. 17f.).

Thus, Lakoff's claim that metaphorical language and conceptual segmentation create similarities and hence facts, does not hold water. What we can say is that language tends to highlight certain similarities, or metonymic connections, and suppress others. This does not count as a transformation of reality but is merely a change in our cognitive relation to it.

13. Once Lakoff and Johnson's criticism of truth-conditional semantics is seen to have no force, attention shifts back to their own positive suggestion, whose shortcomings are plain to see.

In particular, their account seems to be open to the objection levelled against its historical precursor, viz. the empiricist, ideational conception of meaning of the seventeenth century. With such emphasis on human experience and cognitive processing, meaning threatens once more to become incurably subjective and inaccessible to the community at large. Meaning is located in human minds in virtue of being a product of their cognitive processes. Indeed, Lakoff and Johnson align themselves with those very aspects of Locke's empiricist metaphysics and philosophy of language from which later philosophers have been eager to distance themselves. As an example of the way in which the mind's cognitive processes transform reality, they mention the phenomenon of colour. Colour, they insist, is not an objective property of reality, but rather a feature of our cognitive representations thereof (Lakoff & Johnson 1999, p. 23ff.) The upshot would seem to be that colour predicates belong to a private idiom, not to public, intersubjectively valid language.

The authors would no doubt dismiss such a conclusion as symptomatic of our thraldom to the baneful dualism of objectivism and subjectivism informing Western thought that they believe themselves to have overcome with their "embodied realism". According to embodied realism, colours are neither subjective nor objective but what are called 'interactional', i.e. they somehow emerge on the interface between physical reality and embodied human cognitive systems. This is not the place to discuss this metaphysical nicety. In the present context, we must confine ourselves to asking Lakoff and Johnson to address the following dilemma: either they must grant that colours are intersubjectively accessible, out there for all language users to see and point out to each other, in which case there is no obstacle to including them in the truth conditions of sentences such as 'The rose is red', and to handling them in the standard truth-conditional manner. Or else they must insist that colour does not enjoy that species of publicity, in which case a truth-conditional account is (perhaps) ruled out, but at the cost of rendering meaning private and inaccessible. The same goes for all meanings that are somehow the product of cognitive processing. According to Lakoff and Johnson, this applies to all meanings (classifications) with the exception of those representing "basic categories". In consequence, large tracts of linguistic meaning are placed beyond our common cognitive compass, which would seem to be a *reductio* of the theory.

Chapter 10
Theory of interpretation

1. The theory of interpretation leads us into an epistemological aspect of the philosophy of language in that interpretation is accounted as much a part of epistemology as of philosophy of language. In any case, it is such a vital part of the latter that no book on the philosophy of language would be complete without a discussion of this topic.

Interpretation theory is concerned with the principles governing the interpretation of linguistic material. As such, it is related to the theory of textual exegesis that commonly goes under the name of hermeneutics. The correct interpretation of religious texts has doubtless exercised minds as long as there have been religions with written traditions, but a discrete scholarly discipline with this as its subject matter emerged only in the seventeenth century. Hermeneutics was originally a handmaiden of theology, meeting that subject's need for a rigorous methodology to guide scriptural interpretation. Later, with the recognition of the need for a rational, rule-governed procedure to guide the interpretation of legal instruments, law too drew on hermeneutics. In the eighteenth century the scope of hermeneutics was expanded to take in fiction and stands today as a discipline subsumed by, or constituting a strand of, literary studies.

There is, however, a crucial difference between the content of traditional hermeneutics and the theory of interpretation that has grown up in analytical philosophy. Hermeneutics typically addresses the task of interpreting a given text in a language which is essentially familiar to the interpreter; the interpretive task may be set by the fact that the text is, say, fragmentary so that there are lacunae to be filled, or by the fact that the time span separating text and interpreter mediates differences in word meaning in some instances. By contrast, analytical philosophy of language, represented by such figures as Willard Van Orman Quine, Donald Davidson and David Lewis, has set itself a task that is essentially more basic, one called *radical interpretation*: it consists in the interpretation of texts (or spoken utterances) formulated in a language of which the interpreter has no prior knowledge. For the sake of exemplary vividness we are invited to envisage the task facing an anthropologist whose work takes him to a remote island whose inhabitants have never been in contact with the outside world, and whose language, in consequence, has gone unrecorded and unstudied.

This way of radicalizing the problem is generic to an entire philosophical approach. When philosophers have questioned the foundations and nature of our knowledge they have typically framed their enterprise in radical terms. They have not asked themselves what, in some practical context, would count as a convincing justification for this or that particular claim, or how, in practical terms, we might seek to settle a question; instead they have looked for the ultimate justification of all our everyday beliefs, including the underpinnings of our everyday modes of justification. Methodological scepticism can be said to underlie this whole approach. The same applies, then, in the case of radical interpretation. So too when the question concerns the basis for the knowledge that comes to expression in a person's ability to understand what others are saying, the problem gets cast in a radical form.

2. Consider, then, how an anthropologist might set about working up a radical interpretation of a completely alien language. Our reflections in the foregoing chapters about the nature of linguistic meaning offer a pointer as to how he might proceed. For we saw that verbal meaning turns on the success conditions of sentences, especially the truth conditions of assertions. This would seem to indicate that the prime task of the anthropologist is to identify the truth conditions of the sentences he hears. Now given that the meanings of sentences are determined by their truth conditions, the anthropologist, by pursuing this route, will eventually arrive at a grasp of what the sentences mean. The first correlation of language and reality is, then, at the level of sentences. So once the anthropologist has established the relevant truth conditions, he can go on to lay bare the internal structure of the sentences, identifying the various linguistic components that collectively fix their truth conditions. Typically, he will be looking for singular terms and predicates while remaining open to the possibility that this particular language does not have that structure – that it operates on the basis of mass terms or other linguistic categories. Indeed, anthropology and linguistics have recently been engaged in a lively debate about whether certain American Indian languages in fact lacked the subject-predicate structure familiar to us from Indo-European languages.

On the completion of this process, the anthropologist will be able to compile a dictionary of the vocabulary of the foreign language, complemented by a syntax: he will, in other words, have secured an overview of the elementary building blocks of the language and an understanding of how they are put together to form well-formed sentences. Notice that this analysis is prerequisite to a proper understanding of the language. The anthropologist needs to get beyond the "translation manual" stage, which involves learning by rote whole sentences and their translations, and thus becoming acquainted with only a finite number of sentences. A complete mastery of a language implies the ability to grasp a potential infinitude of sentences, which in turn presupposes a familiarity with the general *principles* that permit the construction of infinitely many sentences.

It is clear, then, what the anthropologist's preliminary steps must be: he has to record the natives' utterances and the situations under which they are uttered in order to frame hypotheses about the features of the situation that constitute their truth conditions, i.e. those to whose obtaining the utterer thereby commits himself. Borrowing Quine's famous example, we imagine that the anthropologist hears the expression 'Gavagai' uttered in a situation where a rabbit runs past, patently observed by the utterer. The anthropologist is strongly prompted to translate the utterance into 'rabbit', or rather, since we are probably witnessing a complete speech act, an assertion: 'There's a rabbit'. Since it is at this point unclear whether the native is speaking a mass-term language the anthropologist has to remain open to the possibility of the correct rendering being one that exhibits that feature, such as, say, 'Here comes some rabbit'. (We shall see in chapter 11 that there are indeed philosophers who hold that such indeterminacy in the interpretation of the internal structure of sentences is ineradicable in principle.)

A moment's thought reveals that the uncertainty of radical interpretation is not limited to this subtle linguistic variety. There are countless other possible translations of the sentence 'Gavagai': 'Here comes our next meal!'; 'Unfortunately, the open season hasn't yet begun'; 'Darned annoying that we're not allowed to catch more rabbits'; 'That confounded beast eats all my carrots'; and so on. What a person says in a given situation is not merely a function of that situation alone but involves that person's aims and interests, all of which are determinants of the perlocutionary act he performs. Every utterance about a given situation represents a reading of it that is partly self-selecting in the light of the utterer's interests: the utterance varies according to these interests.

But the utterance does not depend on the utterer's interests alone; it depends too on his knowledge and his experience of the situation. In our candidate renderings of 'Gavagai' it was presupposed that the utterer's observation is veridical or, as we might tend to say, matches that of the anthropologist. But this is far from certain. Perhaps the utterer is severely myopic and thus mistaken about what he is observing – in which case the correct translation might be: 'Is that a rabbit or a cat?' or, 'What long ears that dog has!'

The anthropologist must also take account of cultural differences. The natives may believe that rabbits bring bad luck so that on seeing a rabbit they utter an incantation to ward off misfortune. An apt rendering might be: 'May the evil eyes of the beast not light on me!' (Recall our custom of saying 'Bless you!' when someone sneezes. An anthropologist from a different culture might well conclude that 'Bless you!' means 'That was a sneeze.' In fact, the expression originated as a blessing to preserve the sneezer from the plague.) Alternatively, the natives might entertain the belief that the souls of the dead inhabit rabbits, in which case they would treat the latter reverentially. On that scenario the aptest rendering might be, 'My father's soul indwells in that rabbit' or 'I salute you, Honoured Forebear!'

Certain points emerge from these considerations. First, it becomes clear that any interpretation of a piece of language is essentially embedded in the interpretation of native behaviour overall. It is impossible to work out what people are saying without at the same time working out what they would be likely to say. And what they are likely to say depends on the nature of their chief concerns – both in terms of long-term aims and of whatever is currently occupying their attention. As already noted, primary among our communicative aims is the bringing about of certain effects in the world – having others share our understandings of states of affairs and act upon them. The effects that we seek to produce in hearers mesh with those aims in whose pursuit we are engaged. So it is the natives' interests and aims, then, that need identifying if we are to be able to interpret their utterances. Viewed systematically, linguistic meaning is an abstraction extracted from human activity as a whole. To interpret language we need to understand and interpret this whole.

Given, too, that their individual aims are intimately interwoven with their conception of the world, it becomes clear, second, that any identification of the natives' purposes requires the wholesale decoding of their culture. Even the most private and sequestered acts such as going to confession or praying in seclusion can only be understood against the background of a comprehensive conception of reality. The anthropologist must acquaint himself with this worldview and acquire a grasp of the natives' conceptions of gods, ancestors, taboos, magic elixirs, and so on. Without it he will have no inkling of what is going on, nor, by implication, of what is said. Do the natives believe, say, that human souls inhabit rabbits and other animals? Is the ingestion of rabbit meat hedged by taboos? Do the natives consider it sacrilege to talk to strangers about the most shrouded aspects of their culture, so that what one hears is only part of the truth or even deliberately misleading? All such questions must be taken up and answered.

3. This tight weave of the various strands of an interpretation means that the enterprise cannot be conducted by taking one sentence at a time. We cannot "crack the code" of a foreign language by first conclusively determining the meaning of one sentence and then proceeding to the next. There is a sense in which it is true to say that we can interpret *one* sentence only by interpreting them *all*. Naturally, this does not mean that we have to work with all sentences at once – a patent impossibility. It *does* mean that we have to work at the interpretation of every individual sentence on the understanding that we can have no assurance that our interpretation of it is correct until we know that those of all other sentences also are. This situation is reminiscent of the filling in of a crossword puzzle: for, analogously, the puzzle-solver can only work on one word at a time. And he is continually aware that any answer remains provisional so long as uncertainties persist elsewhere in the grid: he can be forced to change an earlier answer to a clue, whatever its repercussions for the whole puzzle – even for those entries he felt were most secure.

This interconnectedness is particularly well illustrated by the way ascriptions of desires and intentions to the natives depend on what we make out to be their conception of the world, and vice versa. Let us imagine that the anthropologist observes that the natives make rabbit a major staple of their diet. He might be tempted to say that this surely shows quite conclusively that the natives do not consider rabbits sacred or in other respects specially designated animals, for in that case eating them would be sacrilegious. But this is too quick. For it is possible that rabbits are conceived of as venerable ancestors who at death assumed animal form. Were this a belief held by the natives, it would be co-tenable with the belief that in consuming their ancestors they are infused with ancestral wisdom and strength: their partiality for rabbit would thus be fully compatible with the belief that rabbits are their reincarnated ancestors. Further, they need have no cause for anxiety about ultimate ancestral destinies, for they might also be convinced that when a rabbit is consumed, the indwelling ancestor now released from the slough of the humble rabbit comes to inhabit a different, nobler beast. (It is worth bearing in mind that religious practices in our Christian culture also include the consumption of the deity inasmuch as communicants purport to ingest the body and blood of Christ. This ceremony would doubtless pose difficulties for an anthropologist from an island in the Pacific undertaking a radical interpretation of us. They would ask themselves, can it really be that these comparatively civilized people *eat* their god? Have we not gone astray in our hermeneutic enterprise?)

4. The forging of a radical interpretation of foreign-language utterances is tantamount to an interpretation of the language users' entire worldview. Any such interpretation is a *holistic* task, which in turn means that no one part of an interpretation is secure until all parts are; and conclusively secure, never. Given the holistic nature of the task, the criteria of success are likewise holistic: they are properties of the interpretation as a whole, not of parts of it. We have seen that whatever the apparent plausibility of the interpretation of an individual sentence or an individual act, it affords no warrant for its correctness: the anthropologist was certain that his observation of the natives partaking of rabbit showed beyond reasonable doubt that it was not an object of reverence. But we framed a thought experiment in which that conclusion proved to be mistaken: this practice proved compatible with a conception of rabbits as reincarnated ancestral worthies.

A number of principles have been proposed as appropriate constraints on the interpretation process. One single overarching principle termed *the principle of charity* stands out. It exists in several versions, the simplest of which has it that the interpreter should avoid ascribing to the subjects of his interpretation false conceptions of the world. Since this is a holistic principle it does not mean that every attribution of an erroneous conception is in itself suspect. Rather, it means that the interpretation should be so constructed that the number of false conceptions attributed to the interpretees is minimized: in practical terms, given the choice between two equally adequate total interpretations, the one that attributes to the natives the fewest erroneous conceptions is to be preferred.

This principle may be illustrated by an example drawn from anthropology that turns on the question of whether certain Aboriginal tribes are aware of the connection between sexual intercourse and pregnancy. The problem is posed by what the natives say, which, on a literal translation, would suggest that they believe that pregnancy results when a woman receives a fish of a particular kind from a man and cooks it for him. The principle of charity bids us be circumspect in the way we approach this account: it would be uncharitable to attribute this outlandish idea to the natives if there is an alternative candidate. In fact, that would appear to be the case here: the entire sequence may be construed as a ceremony through which the man expresses recognition of the fact that he has made the woman pregnant and accepts paternity. On this interpretation, then, what we are presented with is a public gesture of commitment and not a deficient grasp of reproductive biology.

The principle of charity has been widely debated and subjected to many attempts at refinement and improvement. For instance, it has been argued that it cannot in itself be an argument against an interpretation that it attributes to the natives radically mistaken conceptions if it can be *explained* why they hold them, which is to say, explained in a way that does not impugn their intellectual capacities. If, say, it emerged that the natives held erroneous beliefs about the shapes and sizes of celestial bodies that would hardly be surprising. Accurate knowledge presupposes a developed science that deploys telescopes and other sophisticated instruments of observation that the natives are without. But this deficiency hardly reflects on them as individuals. It is not an indication that they have inferior intellectual powers but is bound up with the stage of technical development that their society has reached. So it does not automatically count against an interpretation that it attributes false beliefs to the interpretees. Their believing that the earth is immoveable at the centre of the universe while all other bodies orbit it is explicable. What *does* count against an interpretation is its assignment to the natives of *inexplicable* false beliefs. That would be the case with the earlier example: it would be very strange if the Aboriginal tribe in question should have missed the relatively obvious connection between sexual intercourse and pregnancy since it has not eluded the generality of so-called "primitive" cultures. No explanation of this phenomenon is offered other than that to the effect that the tribe in question is less well equipped intellectually than other tribal peoples. This is obviously an "uncharitable" interpretation which should be rejected if a charitable rival is available.

Another dominant principle enjoins minimizing the attribution of practical irrationality. If an interpretation of a group of individuals includes the attribution to them of a specific desire and knowledge of how to fulfil it, it tells against this interpretation if, well knowing that they have the means to do so, the interpretees fail to fulfil the desire attributed to them. Let us imagine that an anthropologist from an alien culture has undertaken a radical interpretation of the Germanic languages spoken by the peoples of Northern Europe, and that his tentative interpretation of the utterances of his informants – gathered by means of a questionnaire – leads him to conclude that the inhabitants of these countries are deeply concerned about the welfare of livestock. But he also records the finding that organically produced meat, where the animals enjoy better living conditions, chalks up only a very modest market share. One possible interpretation might be that these people are blindingly irrational: they say they feel very strongly about improving the living conditions of farm animals and yet act in a manner that defeats this aim. Now the principle of practical rationality instructs the visiting anthropologist to reject this hypothesis if another is to be found – for example, that people are not strictly honest when they say how much they care. At any rate, it matters to them more to be able to purchase meat products as cheaply as possible.

In other cases it may not be possible to find a superior alternative hypothesis and the anthropologist has to attribute irrationality to the act. He may, for example, be struck by how many people in these same countries declare their overwhelming interest in a healthy diet and the avoidance of overweight. But, for all their avowals, he observes that the self-same people generally eat too much and tend to be overweight. He considers the self-deception hypothesis but rejects it: their subscription to expensive slimming diets convinces him that their desire is sincere. So he concludes that in this area irrationality is indeed rife, *in casu* weakness of the will: people really do want to lose weight but are unable to resist the temptations posed by junk food.

5. There is a standard term for the dialectical character of the interpretation process. It is called *the hermeneutical circle*. The concept derives originally from the traditional textual hermeneutics alluded to above and was launched by the German nineteenth century theologian and philologist Friedrich Ast. The doctrine of the hermeneutical circle underwent further elaboration at the hands of the theologian and philosopher Friedrich Schleiermacher, with whose name it is traditionally associated. Clearly, this notion is transferable to the context of radical interpretation.

In traditional hermeneutics, the hermeneutical circle refers to the movement, described by every interpretation of an obscure passage, between the various moments in the interpretive process. First, there is the movement between the interpretation of a particular passage in a text and the text as a whole. The result must be free of incoherences: the interpretation of a part must be assessed in the light of the interpretation of the whole to check for possible contradictions. The interpretation of an individual parable in the New Testament must be compared to the exegeses of other parables. The detection of a discrepancy does not mean, however, that the part-interpretation is automatically jettisoned; sometimes it is accepted and the global interpretation modified. The modified interpretation may mean adjustments being made to some of the part-interpretations on which it was based, with these latter in their turn occasioning further adjustments to the global interpretation, and so on until the interpretation has been rendered internally coherent. The process of interpretation, then, traces a circular movement between part-interpretations and the global interpretation, with both being transformed in the process.

Second, there is a movement between the interpretation of a given text and the understanding of the whole culture or period to which the text belongs. As a general rule, no given interpretation should be at odds with the interpreter's understanding of the relevant culture or period. Consideration of the wider context can sometimes force the interpreter to modulate the principle referred to in the previous section. If a text represents a period and genre which privileges the fragmentary and the oxymoronic, the interpreter must be patient of contradictions. An interpretation of modernist poetry, for instance, must accordingly be based on other principles in this respect than that of a legal document. Here too it is the case that the movement between the interpretation of the part and the interpretation of the culture is not unidirectional but, precisely, a circle: the reading of an individual work can sometimes change the reader's understanding of an entire culture. The interpretation of individual works and the formation of an understanding of the culture proceed in tandem. Finally, there is a more general dialectic in play between the interpreter and the object of interpretation sometimes referred to as the *subject-object circle*. We saw above that, on the principle of charity, the interpreter must seek to avoid ascribing to the text patently erroneous conceptions of reality. However, it may happen that the interpreter's view of what constitutes a mistaken conception of reality changes in the course of his reading. A belief that, prior to his encounter with the text, he would have considered absurd, and which, antecedently, he would have been chary of reading into a text emerges, in the course of his reading, as plausible and indeed, persuasive, as an interpretation of the work. By virtue of this complex feedback process, reading has the potential to mediate radical changes in a reader's perception of reality.

The very same circular movements inform radical interpretation, but at a deeper level. Radical interpretation does not start from the assumption that the interpreter already possesses an essentially correct understanding of the subjects – their world picture, desires and aspirations. All this has to emerge from the process of interpretation itself. It evolves through a circular movement which passes through every fresh concrete attribution of an understanding of reality and the sum of previous attributions and, similarly, between the attribution of a fresh desire and the sum of previous attributions. If conflict between later and earlier attributions is identified, one or the other has to go. The same applies if, in the light of the attribution of a belief-plus-desire an interpretee appears to be irrational: he performs an act which, given the conjunction of his beliefs about the world and his desires, is irrational. If, for example, the desire to lose weight and knowledge that chips are high in fat content is attributed to a given individual, that person is going to appear irrational when consistently observed exercising no self-restraint when chips are readily available.

As we saw above, it is always possible to avoid irrationality in the relation between behaviour, desires and beliefs if further elements are introduced into the interpretee's conception of reality. The interpreter might, for example, attribute to the natives the desire to eat rabbit along with the conviction that rabbits are their ancestors in animal form without making them irrational, if this attribution is conjoined with that of the belief that their ancestors, subsequent to consumption, will re-emerge in new and nobler incarnations. This latitude in the process of interpretation means that the principle of charity plays a crucial, controlling role. As we have seen, it bids us minimize the number of false or outlandish beliefs that we attribute to the native subjects. We cannot proceed just as we please; we are constrained not to attribute beliefs to our subjects that will make them appear practically rational without regard to the plausibility of these beliefs. This means that the fate of an interpretation depends to a considerable extent on how well it conforms to the principle of charity.

This creates a new variant of the hermeneutical circle, this time at bedrock level. Every particular interpretation of an utterance or act must be followed up by an investigation into what implications it has for the interpretation of the natives and their world picture as a whole: does it increase the volume of false beliefs ascribed or is the opposite the case? The interpretive endeavour will describe a circular movement between the given part-interpretation and its global counterpart and judge how well the latter fares when measured against the principle of charity.

6. The special nature of the interpretive process is thrown into relief by comparing it with our acquisition of knowledge of the physical world.

The first thing to be noticed is that the interpretation of an individual's language is more like the formulation of a general theory of natural science than a concrete description of nature, such as, say, a geographical description. This is surprising since at first glance the opposite seems to be the case. If an anthropologist and a geographer find themselves in the midst of a remote island community with the remit, respectively, of mapping the natives' language and culture, and the topography of the island, their tasks would appear to be at roughly the same level of abstraction. The geographer describes the island's rivers, woods and mountains just as the anthropologist describes the language. Both descriptions are *idiographic*, which is to say that, as opposed to *nomothetic* representations which give comprehensive accounts of generically similar phenomena, they describe one individual or a limited number of phenomena.

A closer look, however, reveals important differences between the two tasks, to the effect that that of the anthropologist more nearly approaches that of a natural scientist, developing a general (i.e. nomothetic) theory. This explains why, beforehand, we referred to the interpretation of a language precisely as a theory. The fact is that in interpreting even the simplest utterance the anthropologist must draw upon a wide spectrum of data gathered from far beyond the concrete situation of utterance itself and which would invariably include facts about the utterer's worldview, religion, customs and conventions. Interpretation is based on the collation of a vast amount of data, drawn from very different times and situations. This feeds into the elaboration of a general theory that ascribes semantic content not only to the sentences that are part of the material but, again, to a potential infinitude of sentences. Matters are different where the geographer is concerned: his description of a river or a mountain range reproduces data which derive in large part from the object of description itself. Reference to data from distant sources is limited. The geographer's comprehensive description of a river builds as he covers its progress downstream to the point at which it flows into the sea. The description of its spring is not dependent on data drawn from other points along its course, or vice versa. No "hermeneutical circle" is involved, then, in the description of the river. And no matter how full and detailed the description of the river might be it does not contain an infinite store of information as a theory of meaning does.

Given its holistic character, interpretation bears strong analogies to theory formation in natural science. Theories are developed through a holistic process and not through the accumulation of individual data. Consider, for example, one of the most important theories in the history of science, the heliocentric world picture: the theory that places the sun at the centre of our part of the universe, orbited by the planets. This theory was not constructed as a generalization from the accumulation of individual facts but as the best scientific explanation of a vast amount of diverse data. Notably, it was a case of the assignment of these trajectories of the celestial bodies turning out to be the simplest. The theory was chosen because it could account for the facts in a way that best agreed with certain general principles governing theory choice, thus giving it the edge on the rival geocentric theory. This form of scientific reasoning is known as 'inference to the best explanation'.

Moreover, the theories of natural science are often the result of a dynamic dialectic between data and theory which exactly mirrors the hermeneutical circle. Recent studies of natural science have shown that in theory formation data have no automatic priority relative to theory; in cases of conflict between the two it is often the data that are thrown out or explained away. A famous example from science concerns the determination of the unit of electric charge, i.e. the negative charge of the electron, as measured by the American physicist Robert A. Millikan. An examination of Millikan's laboratory notebooks revealed that he systematically discarded measurements that failed to fit with his prior expectations (based on earlier theoretical assumptions) of what the charge was. He consistently dismissed them as the result of measurement errors. "Data" were thus selected and shaped in the light of theory. The fact that neither data nor theory is prior relative to the other often means that there is a gradual mutual adjustment of both in a process strongly reminiscent of the hermeneutical circle: theories are modified to fit the data and vice versa.

7. This leads us on to a question that has often been raised: is the interpretation of human language and human agency akin to theories about inanimate nature, or are they essentially different?

There is a traditional response which maintains that the two processes are fundamentally different. Human reality, inclusive of human language and culture, is apprehended through a process of "identification" or "empathy" with the interpretees. This process is in the nature of an intellectual intuition, i.e. a kind of direct process of cognition, analogous to perception. In the act of cognition we enjoy an immediate experience of the thoughts, desires and feelings of the other. These phenomena become objects for the observer's understanding through his entering into a process of vicarious participation.

This contrasts with our acquisition of knowledge of physical nature, which is scarcely the product of intuition; certainly, it involves neither affinitive sympathy nor empathy. No amount of identification with a celestial body will deliver an explanation of its movement on its orbit; nor does it make any sense to try to imagine what a comet feels as it passes through the solar system. Instead, processes have to be explained from "the outside", i.e. by appeal to causal laws. The latter describe the regularities evinced by the observed phenomenon. Such theories can only be set up through the marshalling of a broad spectrum of data. The method deployed is the so-called hypothetical-deductive method: a hypothesis is framed and a consequence deduced from it. If there is congruence between this consequence and reality the hypothesis is thereby buttressed. If there is a lack of agreement, the hypothesis is modified to accommodate the observations, and testing continues. If such modifications fail to align theory and observations, the theory is ultimately rejected and attempts are made to frame a successor.

It emerged from our previous considerations that this old-established contrast between interpretation and theory formation in natural science is, at the most basic level, false. First, interpretation is not mediated by an intellectual intuition but by a discursive step-by-step approach. This is the process described by the "hermeneutical circle". This circle may aptly be seen as a special case of the self-same hypothetico-deductive method as that used in the natural sciences. A radical interpretation is a theory that takes a very broad spectrum of utterances and actions triggered by the interpretees' confrontation with the external world (perception), and integrates them into a coherent picture capable of explaining those actions and utterances. It is generated through the articulation of a tentative interpretation subsequently to be modified by confrontation with the "data", i.e. the utterances of, and observations of the behaviour of, the interpretees. The alleged difference here between the hermeneutical circle and the hypothetico-deductive method consists solely in the fact that in textual interpretation it is sometimes the "data" that are modified while in the hypothetico-deductive method, on its traditional understanding, it is always the theory that "loses out" in a confrontation with the data.

However, second, when the hypothetico-deductive method is applied in natural science it turns out, as we saw above, not always to be the case that data win out over theory. Sometimes the data are modified to fit the theory; Millikan manipulated his data to that end. A historical account of the use of the hypothetico-deductive method reveals that on this count there is almost nothing to choose between this method and that of the hermeneutical circle.

While there are substantial affinities between interpretation and natural science theory at a fundamental level, clear differences appear when we turn to the detail. The principles governing theory choice in interpretation are very different from what they are in natural science. We saw that the principle of rationality and the principle of charity played pivotal roles in the former. These latter are *normative* principles that, for good reason, play no role in physics. A physical theory is not selected because it presents atoms and molecules as rational, and chemical substances would never have a worldview attributed to them. However, there is a principle in play which has as much clout in natural science as does the principle of charity in interpretation. This is *the principle of simplicity*, which bids us select the explanatory theory which deploys the least number of laws of nature and exhibits maximal parsimony in its postulation of existents. By contrast, this principle plays but a very minor role in interpretation. We are not interested in getting the simplest interpretation of an alien culture: quite the reverse – we want one that gives us as full and fine-grained a picture of the culture as possible. Any such picture will scarcely be simple.

8. There is yet another aspect of the difference between theory in natural science and interpretation that has attracted attention. It concerns the degrees of objectivity exhibited by each.

There is a school of thought in traditional hermeneutics that makes much of the disparities in this area. Its leading protagonist is Hans-Georg Gadamer. Gadamer's thesis is that traditional natural science obeys the canons of classical methodological ideals that enjoin, *inter alia,* the suppression of all prejudices and preconceived ideas. Ideally, then, the senses should be allowed to do their work of delivering generalizable observations undisturbed by abstract ideas. The situation is quite the reverse, Gadamer maintains, in the case of the interpretation of human speech and behaviour. He highlights some of the features we noted above. The interpretation of human speech is never a neutral matter of observation followed by hypotheses but always involves a focused effort to extract meaning from a text or a set of utterances in light of certain prior principles. We examined one of these principles above, the principle of charity (which Gadamer construes slightly differently and calls the anticipation of completeness or perfection (*der Vorgriff der Vollkommenheit*).

It has to be said that Gadamer has a somewhat naïve conception of how the natural scientist works. As demonstrated above, we never approach nature with our minds a complete blank. Were we to do so, we should never get to learn anything, as philosophers such as Karl Popper, Thomas Kuhn and others have persuasively argued. Instead, we seek to interpret our experiences in the light of a theoretical framework; we hazard bold conjectures and then observe how they survive a confrontation with the natural world – as we saw above.

Gadamer also emphasizes the impossibility of explicitating the criteria we use in interpretation; understanding is something that *happens* to us, not something we actively control. But on this head too there is no essential difference between natural science and hermeneutical methods. The trend in the philosophy of natural science over the past 40 years has increasingly been a movement away from the conception of science as a process that can be rendered fully explicit. For it too is an "event", or, in the preferred terminology, a *practice* into which enter thought processes that are essentially tacit; besides, it is influenced by ineliminable social and historical factors.

It might be objected that these reflections overlook the important distinction between the *genesis* and the *justification* of an interpretation, or of a theory in natural science. It is correct that discoveries and fresh insights are produced via processes not fixed by canons of rationality. No rational procedure can be set up for the making of new discoveries; novelty could hardly be produced through a process fixed by what has gone before. Consequently, discoveries and inventions are aptly describable as events in which contingent and psychological elements play a role. What is crucial, however, is that discoveries or inventions come about through processes that are repeatable and assessable in the light of rational principles. This lends support to the idea that reflections about the genesis of interpretation in a dialectical hermeneutical process count for little, and that any possible affinities between this process and scientific discoveries are irrelevant from an epistemological standpoint.

This objection fails to recognize that Gadamer and recent natural science theorists are not merely talking about the genesis of the theory: their thesis extends to the question of the assessment and justification of interpretation and theories. Indeed, discovery and justification are fused in the account that these theorists offer of the interpretation process. Their claim is that justification is not a strict rule-governed process and that acceptance of a textual interpretation or a scientific theory is ultimately something in the nature of a "conversion" (Kuhn) or as we have seen, an "event" (Gadamer). There is scarcely any significant difference between the rigour of the principles used in the assessments of interpretations and natural science theories, respectively.

To repeat, it is not being denied that there are important and relevant differences between natural science methods and interpretive methods. On the contrary, we have just highlighted what they are. They are inherent in the principles used in selecting from among interpretations and candidate theories of natural science. They are not, then, where much traditional debate has located them. For instance, it is alleged that the principles governing interpretation are vague and the process circular, whereas natural science is hallmarked by clear and unambiguous methodical principles which make the acquisition of knowledge a one-way street leading from data to theory.

9. But are these reflections on the anthropologist's situation not, basically, a niche occupation within epistemology, of little import for the philosophy of language? Surely, with the discovery of completely isolated populations and so of radically unknown languages fast becoming a thing of the past, radical interpretation has had its day. However, nothing could be further from the

truth. The objection quite overlooks the fact that the exercise that is nowadays rarely undertaken by anthropologists is engaged in by millions at any one time, since it is that undertaken by all young children at the stage of first language acquisition. The task facing the child here is precisely that of decoding a language of which it has no prior knowledge, simply because it has no language at all. Moreover, it has to solve the large problem that confronted the anthropologist in our account, which is that of developing a total interpretation not just of language but also of behaviour.

Now it might be argued that the tasks of the anthropologist and the child are different: the anthropologist's remit involves his having to divert his focus from one culturally determined conception of reality in order to penetrate another, while the child's is that of constructing a conception of reality from the ground up. And it might be contended that the anthropologist's task is really the more demanding, since he has to jettison cultural ballast in order to progress. But this contention is mistaken. It is based on a naïve epistemology which assumes that knowledge is arrived at not through hypothesis-formation, but by casting aside all prejudices and observing reality with an impartial eye. That too, however, is an illusion.

Naturally, none of this alters the fact that there is indeed one point at which the respective tasks of the child and the anthropologist are fundamentally different. The anthropologist's remit is to formulate an explicit theory about the culture he investigates, while the child only has to achieve an implicit understanding – an understanding-of-use. The anthropologist has to reproduce his insights in a form that is accessible to others so that they can absorb his findings. He must therefore provide explicit formulations of the norms and precepts of the culture, and likewise frame at least a rudimentary grammar and semantics for the language. The child in the process of becoming acquainted with the culture in which it finds itself is happily free of any such obligation; he does not need to learn the rules of good behaviour off by heart so long as he has an implicit knowledge of what those rules are and seeks to comply with them. Nor does the child need to worry about getting the rules of grammar straight so long as he has a non-defective command of the spoken language. But this difference marks no difference in the cognitive process.

Chapter 11
Two critics: Quine and Dummett

1. The earlier chapters have documented the attempts made in contemporary philosophy to develop a theory of linguistic meaning based on the concept of truth conditions in tandem with the notion of language users' intentions. As will have become evident, the resultant theory is somewhat complex.

And yet for all the many refinements that have accrued to it, in the view of some philosophers this theory is naïve. What makes it so, according to these philosophers, is that it takes the concept of meaning for granted. For it is assumed without argument that linguistic expressions possess something that we can call 'meaning' and that this meaning more or less corresponds to our ordinary understanding of the term. According to these critics, both assumptions are questionable. To be sure, they do not deny that there is something identifiable as 'linguistic meaning' but they are concerned to show that meaning is somewhat different from, and in one sense "less" than, we normally imagine it to be. In this chapter we shall be considering the views of two of the most prominent of these critics: Willard Van Orman Quine and Michael Dummett.

2. To understand Willard Van Orman Quine's critique in context we need to begin by outlining his metaphysical position. Quine is a physicalist, which is to say that he espouses the view that an adequate description of reality ultimately has to be couched in the language of physics (*qua* most fundamental science) since, finally, the world contains only those things that are referred to in physics.

This does not mean that Quine would outlaw the use of idioms other than that of physics – so to do would cause us great inconvenience in everyday life. In those contexts it is unquestionably useful to be able to refer to a certain fluid as 'milk' rather than having to reel off the chemical formulae for each of its constituents, just as it is easier to speak of something being 'red' than to start specifying the wavelengths of the light it reflects. All the same, it remains indisputable that the referents in these examples have exact chemical or physical descriptions.

The spheres of reality that are described in an idiom far removed from that of physics but which, according to Quine, are essentially physical in nature, include ourselves as agents and reasoners. We do not describe one another in terms of the language of physics but in intentional terms, namely as desiring, willing, thinking and speaking agents. And Quine readily concedes that our mutual relations and interactions would be limited indeed if we did not make use of intentional concepts. But, again, in the final analysis, their subject matter is a purely physical reality: human beings are essentially physical systems composed of complex organic molecules, and a strictly scientific account of them would not include reference to thoughts, intentions, feelings and the like but would confine itself to describing human behaviour (body movements) and to explanations that appeal to the external stimuli to which they have been exposed. This position goes under the name of *behaviourism*.

In his criticism of intentional descriptions, Quine may be seen as a latter-day representative of a generic position that traces a long lineage in the history of philosophy. It consists, on the one hand, in a very high regard for the remarkable successes of natural science, especially within theoretical physics, and on the other, of scepticism about talk of the mind, consciousness, the "soul", or whatever term one prefers. Physics has achieved spectacular results in its description of reality and it is difficult to see how a case might be made for the accommodation of the mental in any universe so described. These are difficulties that thrust themselves on any theorist attempting to introduce intentionality into the picture. Admit it, and the universe is at once awash with highly mysterious entities – minds or souls – whose relation to physical reality is unclear or even paradoxical.

3. We now turn to Quine's most influential criticism of the concept of meaning. In rough outline, Quine's argument runs as follows. When we describe the semantics of a language and the thoughts, intentions and feelings that its users communicate, we tend to introduce very subtle distinctions into our account. However, these fine-grained meanings do not actually pick out any similarly differentiated reality, there being nothing in the minds of the language users themselves nor in the world around them that answers to those subtle discriminations. The belief that there is, is induced by the syntactic complexity of language. Close critical analysis will reveal that many of the manifold expressions language contains find no non-linguistic counterparts in reality.

Quine's argument exists in two variants, with one applying to the notion of reference and the other to the meanings of sentences. Let us start with the questions Quine raises about reference. Quine's argument proceeds from an analysis of the interpretive or translational situation. His strategy amounts to showing that, given the application of probing interpretive methods, some of the distinctions drawn between the referring expressions of language at the grammatical level show up not to reflect differences at the semantic level. This is his famous thesis of the "inscrutability of reference".

We need briefly to recapitulate certain points made in the preceding chapter in order to set the scene for Quine's critique. The situation Quine has in mind is one of *radical interpretation*, i.e. a situation where our task is the interpretation of a language of which we have no prior knowledge. This would be, say, the situation of the anthropologist confronted with a tribe hitherto completely isolated from the wider world.

Roughly, then, the anthropologist's task is to establish a correlation between the tribal language and the reality that defines the semantics of that language. In the preceding chapter we stressed the point that such correlations need to begin at sentence level. We cannot begin by correlating individual words with items in the world to which they correspond – partly because words only have a meaning in a sentential context, and partly because the sentence is the smallest linguistic unit with which a "move in the language game" may be made. Consequently, the anthropologist has to interpret every instance of linguistic behaviour as the equivalent of the utterance of a sentence – as corresponding to a complete speech act. This applies even when a sentence comprises just one word.

In practice, any such correlation of sentences with the world will inevitably amount to a correlation between sentences, namely between those in the object language and those in the language of the interpreter, since the object language's correlation with reality amounts to its correlation with reality as limned by the language of the interpreter, which, in methodological terms, comes down to a direct correlation between the two languages. And this is indeed the way Quine conceives of the nature of the anthropologist's job.

Quine stresses that to be able to pair off sentences in the foreign language with suitable counterparts in our own language we have to begin with observation sentences. As their name suggests, observation sentences have the advantage that their truth conditions can be read off directly from the situations in which they are uttered. Our task as anthropologists, then, is to correlate the observation sentences in our own language with the observation sentences in that of the natives. We ask ourselves which observation sentence we would utter in English in the situation in which the natives utter S in their language. This pairing may proceed without anthropologists' needing to worry about the internal structure of the observation sentences, or attempting to determine which of the constituents are referring terms. It is simply a matter of correlating each observation sentence in the foreign language with the observation sentence in the object language that is true under the same conditions. Quine expresses this by saying that at this stage the interpreter approaches the foreign sentences *holophrastically*, i.e. as unanalysed wholes.

When speaking of the natives uttering certain sentences in "the same situation" as those in which the interpreters would utter certain other sentences, Quine means a situation where the interpreter is subjected to the same physical stimuli as the natives. This is a consequence of his physicalism, according to which human behaviour, including linguistic behaviour, is ultimately explained by reference to physical causes. Quine labels such sentences uttered in situations in which the subjects are exposed to the same stimuli as 'stimulus-synonymous'. On his view, this is preferable to saying that the two sentences have the same meaning, in that the latter too readily suggests a reification of meaning, a conception of meaning as a determinate well-defined "thing".

With that accomplished, the anthropologists can go on to break down the sentences of the foreign language into the elements that are constituent in the semantic structure of the sentences. As we have already had occasion to note, bringing this off is a condition of our being able to account for how a human language user with a finite memory is able to utter or grasp a sentence he has never previously uttered or heard, and how it comes about that he musters the potential to utter and understand an infinitude of different sentences. This capacity admits of explanation only on the assumption that the speaker commands a recursive theory that enables him, on the basis of a finite number of reference-ascribing axioms and rules of combination, to generate truth conditions for the potential infinitude of sentences constructable in the language in question.

4. Let us illustrate the issue by appeal to an example introduced in the previous chapter. We shall see how Quine exposes the problems inherent in the kind of account offered there. The natives utter the expression 'Gavagai' (or readily assent to it) every time there is a rabbit in their whereabouts and they are aware of its presence. The anthropologists will thus pair 'Gavagai' with the English sentence:

1. There's a rabbit over there

which is true under the same conditions.

We may get a more precise grasp of what is going on here by redescribing it in a way that draws on the Davidsonian approach outlined in chapter 6. A Davidsonian approach provides the meaning of a language by pairing its sentences with specifications of their truth conditions. The anthropologists' method, as described here (and as analyzed by Quine), consists rather in pairing up sentences in the anthropologists' language with ones in the native language, a pairing mediated by the identification of their matching truth conditions. This means that the identification of truth conditions enters into the antropologists' project as well.

Described in Davidsonian terms, then, the anthropologists submit the following T-sentence for the sentence 'Gavagai':

> NN's utterance of 'Gavagai' is true-in-L, if and only if there is a rabbit near NN at the time of utterance.

We saw in the preceding chapter that to reach this point the anthropologist must be able to rule out a host of alternative interpretations, such as 'There goes a reincarnated ancestor'. We have already noted the difficulties inherent in this procedure. Here, however, we are interested in a slightly different problem.

Let us imagine that the anthropologists have been able to frame a string of such candidate T-sentences. Their next step is to uncover the structure of the natives' sentences so as to be able to set up hypotheses concerning the theory's axioms of reference-ascription. Their aim is to formulate axioms capable of generating the tentative T-sentences already formulated. That accomplished, they conjecture that they will be capable of generating further T-sentences to be verified in the ongoing testing of the theory.

Since 'Gavagai' is true under the same conditions as the English sentence 'There's a rabbit over there', it might seem that the task is the relatively simple one of identifying a component of the sentence 'Gavagai' that refers to a rabbit. Unfortunately problems arise at this point. For the sentence 'There's a rabbit over there' is not the only English sentence that is true under the same conditions as the sentence 'Gavagai'. There are countless other possibilities:

2. There is some rabbit over there.
3. There is an undetached rabbit-part over there.
4. A stage in the life history of a rabbit is going on over there.

5. Rabbithood is instantiated over there.
6. Over there is a point that is a mile to the left of a point a mile to the right of a rabbit.

And so on.

All these sentences are true under the same conditions, and not just fortuitously, but are so each time they are uttered: if there is a rabbit present so too are the various parts of the rabbit (organs and limbs) not separately but in their natural configuration. Rabbithood is likewise present, i.e. a concrete manifestation of the features definitive of a rabbit. And every rabbit inevitably finds itself at a point which is one mile to the left of a point one mile to the right of a point at which there is a rabbit. But while these sentences are true under the same conditions, they appear to have utterly different references. (1) refers to rabbits, (2) refers to the "mass" rabbit, (3) refers to rabbit parts, (4) refers to stages, (5) refers to rabbithood, and (6) refers to distances in space.

Which of these should the anthropologists opt for, then, as the translation of the sentence 'Gavagai' and as specifying this sentence's referring expression? It is impossible on the basis of the natives' linguistic and non-linguistic behaviour in connection with the utterance of the sentence 'Gavagai' to determine which of the sentences (1)–(6) the anthropologists ought to prefer, on strict empiricist principles. All the sentences are true and the natives assent to the sentence 'Gavagai' whenever sentences (1)–(6) are true. Consequently, the anthropologists put their trust in the question being decidable from the perspective of the natives' language as a whole. The proposed axioms will generate other T-sentences and the anthropologists will attempt to establish whether these latter are true. They have to hope, then, that reference-conferring axioms constructible on the basis of (2)–(6) will generate further T-sentences which will subsequently be falsified. If, let us say, interpretation (6) were the correct one, the supposition would follow that some part or aspect of the sentence 'Gavagai' would correspond to the word 'mile' in English; and one would then expect this word to occur in contexts where the natives discuss the distances separating things. If the word turned out never to figure in such contexts, that fact would tell against the interpretation. By so proceeding, the interpreter would hope to be able to eliminate all options bar one.

However, this elimination procedure would enjoy only qualified success. For given the holistic character of the semantic theory – i.e. a totality of axioms and compositional rules tested against the empirical data – the anthropologists are not able to say, on the basis of a string of false T-sentences alone, which axioms or rules of composition need to be revised. It will always be possible to construct six different theories that underpin a pairing of 'Gavagai' with each of the individual sentences (1)–(6). Each of the theories will be compatible with the totality of empirical data, i.e. the sum of the observations of the linguistic acts performed by the natives.

5. Quine offers a non-fictitious example to illustrate his point. Japanese contains parts of speech known as 'classifiers', which may be parsed in either of two ways, namely, as a kind of numeral or as a kind of abstract general term. The two construals are equally acceptable or, rather, the two construals yield the same predictions about one and the same utterance by a Japanese speaker. For the words with which the classifiers occur may be parsed in different ways and these joint construals of the classifier along with the co-occurring words cancel each other out, as it were, in respect of their empirical consequences: the two construals of the classifiers along with the interpretations of the other words in the phrasal unit yield the same predictions in respect of the linguistic behaviour of a Japanese speaker.

On the one interpretation, the classifiers are numerals or rather, are associated with ordinary numerals, but with their application restricted to certain determinate categories of entity. One classifier indicates that the numeral is used when counting animals, another that the word is applicable to the counting of slender items such as pencils or chopsticks. On this interpretation the attached substantive has to be construed as a general noun as in the expression 'seven cows'. On the other interpretation, the classifier attaches to what it is that is being counted, now construed as a mass term (cf. chapter 4): in other words, in those contexts it has the same individuating function as the term 'head' in the expression 'seven head of cattle', which makes synecdochical allusion to the animal considered as an individual specimen.

But according to Quine, what is particularly noteworthy is that there is nothing to choose between these two interpretations on the basis of their contexts of use, because whichever concatenation of sentences or context of use presents itself, the interpreter would be justified in aligning it with each of the two interpretations. By interpreting the accompanying term either as a general name or a mass term, the observable difference between the two interpretations is neutralized, as it were; in these identical modes of use, the two construals are equally plausible candidates. This is the case, says Quine, irrespective of the size of the sector of language involved. It is always logically possible to construct the linguistic contexts and the situations in which the expressions occur so that the two interpretations appear equally plausible.

6. Up to now, it looks as though Quine is simply concerned to drive home the point that in the interpretation of foreign languages there resides the indeterminacy and thus the uncertainty that infects all empirical theory. We stressed in chapter 8 that, in the complexity stakes, an anthropological interpretation compares with a theory in natural science. This means that while the anthropologist can never be absolutely sure that his translation is the correct one, he remains confident that there is a fact of the matter as to whether by 'Gavagai' the natives are referring to rabbits or rabbit parts.

However, Quine's position is more radical. For his claim is that there is no correct answer to the question whether the natives mean the one thing or the other. All language use is subject to the publicity principle (viz. chapter 1), the constraint to the effect that the semantic content of language is essentially public or intersubjective and so exhaustively manifested in behaviour. This implies that the meaning attributable to language and language users cannot go beyond that manifested in behaviour and captured by us when we pair our observation sentences with those of the natives: there are no transcendent facts lurking "behind" our observations. This feature has the consequence that the referential relations of a foreign language remain indeterminate. There is no basis beyond the speakers' behaviour by appeal to which one choice among alternative ascriptions of reference is more correct than another.

The culmination of Quine's argumentation is his extrapolation of his findings to the vernacular of the interpreters – *our* language. For naturally, our language use, to be meaningful, is subject to the same constraints governing meaning as those governing the utterances of the natives. No more than the natives can we, the interpreters, be said to refer to rabbits rather than rabbit parts, and so on; our immediate sense of the obviousness of interpretation (1) above and our rejection of interpretations (2) to (6) is an illusion. This brings us to the final and most radical version of Quine's thesis of the indeterminacy (inscrutability) of reference: the grammatical expressiveness of language and its diversity of alternative syntactic structures induces in us the belief in semantic differentiation, a fine-grained spectrum in language's meaning-aspect that finds no counterpart in reality. We draw distinctions in language that pick out no differences in the actualities of which people speak. The realm to which the traditional notion of linguistic meaning purports to refer is in considerable measure one of pure fiction.

7. The indeterminacy thesis examined thus far seems radical enough, but Quine sharpens it further. Up to this point we have demonstrated indeterminacy in respect of the referential apparatus of the language without this

indeterminacy extending to the truth-values of those sentences in which the referring expressions occur. All the alternative translations of the sentence 'Gavagai' are true or false under precisely the same conditions.

But Quine propounds a yet more radical indeterminacy thesis, which concerns the truth conditions of sentences. His claim is that for any sentence in a foreign language, it will be possible to propose two empirically equivalent translations that construe certain sentences in the object language in divergent ways. Indeed, the divergence amounts to the logical incompatibility of the relevant sentences: they cannot possibly both be true. In other words, the two renderings translate one and the same sentence in the object language into sentences that have incompatible truth conditions in the metalanguage.

Let us take one of Quine's own examples and imagine that we are confronted with a foreign culture apparently in possession of a theory of physics: they have certain rules set down in writing that they ostensibly apply in calculating and explaining events in nature and they perform innovative experiments in the hope of expanding their sets of formulae. We embark on the construction of a theory of meaning for their language with the aim of producing a translation of their physical theory.

Let us imagine further that the situation in physics – i.e. *our* physics, the physics that we, the interpreters espouse – is one where virtually all the members of the scientific community subscribe to a standard theory, A. But notwithstanding this near-consensus, a group of researchers have elaborated a bold alternative, B, that contradicts the standard theory at crucial points. These contradictions concern only strictly theoretical issues, i.e. they are expressed in sentences that do not refer directly to observable phenomena. The relevant theoretical sentences in A and B are logically incompatible inasmuch as they cannot both be true. However, physicists have been unable to devise an experiment which would decisively settle the matter in favour of one or other of the two theories. For each time the proponents of A think up an experiment and carry it out the supporters of B are able to show that, given certain assumptions, the experimental evidence is compatible with B; and vice versa when the supporters of B contrive an experiment. The fact of the matter is that no experiment and so no observation sentence is capable of deciding the matter in favour of A or B. But there is no question that there is a truth about the constitution of the world even though it seems incapable of being established by the physicists. We shall assume that reality is in fact as A describes it. A is true, then, and B, which is incompatible with A, is accordingly false.

With this background in place, we shall set ourselves to translate the natives' physics (which translation will only come about as part of a global interpretation of the native language). Let us assume that we have had some initial success in matching their physical observation sentences with our own, so that when a theory of physics is confirmed by one of their observation sentences – i.e. when the natives declare that the available observation data confirm their theory – our preferred theory of physics, A, is confirmed by precisely those observation sentences in our language that we have picked out as the counterparts of theirs.

We then follow this up by translating those sentences in the foreign language which articulate their physical theory. And it is precisely here that the problem of the indeterminacy of translation sets in. Our immediate inclination would naturally be to think that the natives' theory equates with our theory A, and so we will begin by translating its sentences into the equivalent sentences in our theory. But at this point, we recall the fact that there exists an alternative theory, B, which contradicts A while sharing the same observational base as A, and indeed, by the same token, as that adopted by the natives. In consequence, B's credentials for being a good translation of the natives' theory match A's.

As Quine sees it, then, we are constrained to conclude that our translation of the natives' theory of physics will remain indeterminate. For it is indeterminate whether their theory is the equivalent of our A or our B, since both translations are equally plausible. The problem cannot be resolved simply by saying that the translations are ultimately equivalent, with the result that there is nothing to choose between them. The two translations are not equivalent since the theories A and B are incompatible.

Remember: Quine's claim is not that it is merely undecidable whether the natives accept A or B. It is not a variant of the oft-voiced view to the effect that people from different cultures inhabit different conceptual schemes, and that it is impossible for a representative of our cultural world to grasp the concepts of another. Quine's position is that there simply is no answer to the question whether the natives live in the one or the other conceptual universe. Our language induces in us the belief in a possibility which turns out to be vacuous.

8. Now the objection might be raised at this point that there is a difference between the way in which we have treated the physical theories A and B, and the way we interpreted these theories (as part of a global interpretation); let us call the two interpretations I_A and I_B, respectively. Our physical theories were similarly underdetermined by observation sentences, and yet we as-

sumed that there is indeed a truth of the matter concerning the constitution of the physical world, for we made the assumption that theory A expressed it. We assumed, in other words, that there exist features of reality in virtue of which A is true even though this might remain forever unascertainable by us. Might it not similarly be the case that either I_A or I_B is true despite its being beyond our powers to determine which? Is it not possible that the natives subscribe to theory A with the result that the interpretation I_A is true even though we are unable to establish the fact?

Quine's reply is that there is a difference between the underdetermination of physical theories and that of theories of interpretation. The two types of theory are indeed both underdetermined by observation sentences. But theories of interpretation are further underdetermined by the fact that even though we might discount the underdetermination of a physical theory – which we can do as a thought experiment by hypothetically assuming the truth of one particular physical theory – the underdetermination of interpretation persists. We assumed above that theory A is true and B false. We can thus add all the (theoretical) facts that follow from A to the observational truths that we have already established, thereby fixing all the physical facts about the world, including facts about human behaviour. Next we pose the question again as to whether these facts suffice to determine whether the natives subscribe to A or to B. The answer, according to Quine, is that this question remains indeterminate: establishing the ultimate true physical theory of the universe does not suffice to determine whether interpretation I_A or I_B is correct. And there are no further facts beyond the physical ones that could be deployed to fix the truth-value of the interpretation. There is then, according to Quine, no truth of the matter here at all.

It will have been obvious that the publicity principle plays a crucial role in this reasoning. Quine starts out from the premise that the semantic content communicated by means of language must in principle be intersubjectively accessible. According to Quine, it all boils down to what human agents are able to manifest in terms of behaviour. Quine dismisses the idea that there should exist facts concerning communicative intentions to which an individual speaker has privileged access; and even were there such facts, they would be incapable of playing a role in language use and other communication that is essentially public.

The conclusion to be drawn, then, is that while theories of physics are merely underdetermined by the empirical data but ontologically determined in virtue of certain facts that go beyond observation, empirical theories of meaning are not simply underdetermined relative to observation but are also ontologically indeterminate. There is simply no aspect of reality in virtue of which the one of two empirically equivalent but incompatible theories of meaning may be said to be true and the other false. In other words, we cannot profitably ask which of the two physical theories, A or B, the natives endorse and express in their language, for there is no answer to this question. The meaning that the natives attribute to their physical theory is indeterminate as regards A or B.

9. There would appear to be an incoherence in Quine's argumentation as we have traced it to this point: he has arrived at the result that there is no fact of the matter as to whether the natives endorse A or B. But evidently, his reasoning has been predicated on the assumption that there is a fact of the matter as to whether we, the interpreters, accept A or B. This is surely incoherent unless one is prepared to claim that the interpreters are somehow exempt from the constraints governing meaningful communication to which the natives are subject, and such a contention is one Quine would naturally repudiate.

However, there are passages in which Quine hints at a refinement of the theory that circumvents this difficulty. There it is acknowledged that no more than the natives can we, the interpreters, be said to assume A rather than B; our certitude that we are assuming A and rejecting B is an illusion. The further conclusion, then, is that there is no truth of the matter as to whether language users who talk about the physical theories are referring to theory A or theory B. This holds both for the natives and for us. Nonetheless, it can still be maintained that A is incompatible with B for, ex hypothesi, our intuitive feeling is that the two cannot both be true at once. Therefore it remains the case that theory A is distinct from theory B and we can maintain that reality conforms to the one but not the other – and yet be unable to specify the difference! Thus it still holds that physical reality extends beyond what can be established through observation whereas this does not apply to the reality that comes to expression in semantic interpretations and in the language of intentionality.

With this final step, Quine's thesis undergoes generalization from being a claim about the indeterminacy of translation or interpretation to being one about the indeterminacy of meaning as such. It has not merely been shown – on the assumption that Quine's argument holds – that there is no fact of the matter with regard to whether the native subscribes to physical theory A or B, and similarly for other theoretical questions. It has been demonstrated that there is no truth of the matter as to whether *we*, the interpreters, subscribe to A or B. In brief, it has been shown that as language users, in what concerns large sectors of our linguistic use, we "mean less than we think we do"; on the level of the surface grammar of the language we draw distinctions unmatched by any underlying semantic or psychic reality. Linguistic meaning is something other and less than we commonly take it to be.

10. The debate about semantic indeterminacy is still running strongly and our aim here has been merely to present the problem, not to deliver a verdict on it. All the same, a concluding critical comment is in place.

When all is said and done, it remains a striking feature of his account that Quine only argues for the abstract logical possibility of the indeterminacy of translation. He never offers serious examples taken from actual anthropological or linguistic research. The examples with which Quine spices his account are only illustrative. This is true of the patently constructed 'Gavagai' example but also of the reference to the Japanese taxonomies we looked at above. When it comes to the crunch, Quine does not claim that he has incontrovertibly documented that the two stated interpretations would be on a par relative to whatever linguistic or behavioural data might be forthcoming. Moreover, Quine has only given examples of referential indeterminacy. He has not adduced examples of the kind of indeterminacy that leads to translations with incompatible truth conditions.

Indeed Quine declares that actual documentation of indeterminacy is not possible since the 'indeterminacy draws too broadly on a language to admit of factual illustration'. The documentation of indeterminacy requires a comprehensive account of the whole language and the demonstration that no feature or situation yields a basis for a distinction between two interpretations. Quine is naturally right to say that such a detailed linguistic account does not really belong in a philosophical text. On the other hand, he must also concede that such documentation is nonetheless what is required if the philosophical argument is to go through. It is not sufficient to demonstrate the sheer logical possibility of indeterminacy; for the mere logical possibility of a state of affairs is not sufficient to show that we need to take its actuality seriously. Until a more substantial justification of indeterminacy becomes available we have to consign Quine's thesis to the category 'unproven'.

We may conclude, then, that Quine has not demonstrated that the phenomenon of meaning suffers from a form of indeterminacy that makes reflection on semantics in the philosophy of language a delusion. We do not have to discard the findings set out in earlier chapters of this book as based on utter fiction.

11. We have to this point proceeded from the assumption that meaning is to be understood on the basis of truth. We shall now see how Michael Dummett

calls this into question, like Quine, by using the principle of publicity as an adequacy constraint. Dummett asks whether a theory of understanding based on the concept of truth attributes to language users knowledge not publicly manifestable. If so, the status of such purported knowledge is highly dubious. By advancing this contention, Dummett sets the stage for a thorough revision of traditional philosophical semantics.

In agreement with Quine, Dummett warns us against talking about linguistic meaning in abstraction from human thought and action. Quine refuses to talk about meaning in terms of other or more than what a linguistic expression shares with its translation into another language and, by the same token, Dummett argues against speaking of the meaning of an expression as anything over and above its role as a correlate of the knowledge the language user possesses when he understands an expression. Our basic hypothesis to this point, namely that the meaning of a sentence is its truth condition, should be construed as the claim that the language user's understanding of the sentence consists in a knowledge of the truth condition of that sentence. We may note, then, that in line with Frege, Dummett regards meaning as a cognitive concept.

This line of thinking imposes the following well-founded constraints on a semantic theory: a semantic theory for a language is acceptable only if it provides a basis for a plausible theory of the language user's grasp of the relevant language. This is Dummett's thesis to the effect that a theory of meaning is a theory of understanding. (Henceforth we will follow Dummett in talking about a *fragment* of a language rather than of a language as such in order to emphasize that, as against Quine's holism, a speaker can indeed understand parts of a language without necessarily understanding the language as a whole.)

Now we cannot ask a language user to explicitate the knowledge in which his understanding purports to consist. If that lay within his powers, there would be no need to speculate about what a theory of meaning for a given language ought arguably to look like, or indeed to engage in the philosophy of language at all. Above all, understanding and speaking a language consists in the practical ability to use the language in our day-to-day dealings with others and with the things that make up the world's rich inventory.

That this practical character of linguistic knowledge should not be seen as a purely psychological peculiarity is clear from the following. Let us imagine that an African who only understands Swahili learns the contents of an English dictionary and grammar off by heart. What he learns, then, is not how to translate from English to Swahili, but only how English words phonetically and typographically are put together to yield syntactically well-formed sentences. He is also able to cite correct dictionary definitions of English words. Moreover, he can draw syntactically correct inferences between related English sentences and transform such sentences into other English sentences. If he is given the sentence 'There is an armchair next to the table' he can transform it into the sentence 'Next to the table is an upholstered item of furniture that seats one'. But we would not say that this individual understands English. What is it, then, that a language user who understands English can do that the African cannot? Precisely this: the competent language user is able to relate the referential and predicative expressions of the English language to the world. For example, when asked to point out an armchair, say, he can do so correctly. And, most pertinently, he can recognize sentences in English as true when their truth conditions are fulfilled and as false when they are not.

However, the knowledge we possess of our native language is not purely implicit even though it might conceivably have been. Dummett points out that, typically, we know whether we understand a word or not, independently of any actual situation of use, and that we all have a rudimentary knowledge of a part of the theory of meaning for our language. We are thus able to express the meanings of words in different ways and to rephrase our sentences, and we need have had no brush with the philosophy of language to be capable of answering the persistent child's irrepressible stream of questions about the meanings of words.

But while mastery of language is primarily a practical ability, it can, in line with other practical abilities be accounted for in terms of the attribution of theoretical (i.e. explicitly formulated) knowledge. We are able to explain our ability to speak grammatically correct English by appeal to our acting as though we possessed an explicit knowledge of the rules. The alternative way of putting this is to say that we have an implicit knowledge of them.

The practical ability evinced by the language user in speaking and understanding his language is explainable in the same way. First, we seek to frame a theoretical representation of that ability in the form of a theory of meaning for the language in question. The theory of meaning is subject to the constraint that a person with explicit knowledge of the theory would be capable of speaking and understanding the language. Next, we explain the ability of language users to understand the language by advancing the claim that the individual has an implicit knowledge of the relevant theory of meaning, which enables him to speak and understand the language.

In chapter 6, we presented one candidate theory of language, namely Davidson's theory, which builds on Tarski's recursive truth definition. Dummett accepts that such a recursive structure might constitute the kernel of a theory of speakers' linguistic mastery. So cast in terms of Davidson's programme, Dummett's thesis runs as follows: the language user's ability to speak and understand his native tongue consists in an implicit knowledge of a Tarskian theory of truth for the language in question. We attribute to the language user an implicit knowledge of the theory's reference-stipulating axioms and rules of composition so that, for every sentence S formulable in his native tongue, the language user has implicit knowledge of S's truth condition. Dummett supplements Davidson's programme with a theory of force which allows the language user to utter and to understand utterances produced through the deployment of the differential types of illocutionary force operating in tandem with the individual truth conditions of the sentences (cf. the discussion of speech acts in chapter 8.)

12. The thesis that a semantic theory should be capable of serving as the basis for a plausible theory of understanding implies an important adequacy constraint to the effect that it is impermissible to attribute to a language user linguistic knowledge (understanding) that he cannot in principle manifest in language use. For if linguistic knowledge is ultimately implicit practical knowledge, this knowledge must be manifest in agency – or else its ascription is vain.

To illustrate we can draw a parallel to our readiness to attribute to higher mammals knowledge that they patently cannot make explicit. We do not think twice about saying of a dog that it knows that a particular call means that it is going to be fed, or that it shows that it recognizes its owner. It comes when called in a certain way but does not respond to other sounds; it is overjoyed when its owner appears or when it hears his approaching footsteps, but behaves quite differently towards other people, and so on.

By contrast, it is incoherent to attribute to a dog (implicit) knowledge of how many days there are to Christmas, so long as this ascription is not backed by appeal to the skills it possesses, such as an ability to count on its paws, to use a calendar so that it can point to the current date and turn the pages until reaching the one on which Christmas day is marked, and so on. It is only meaningful to attribute such knowledge to the dog if the relevant knowledge can be correlated with its practical abilities, its behaviour.

By the same token, Dummett maintains that a hypothesis to the effect that a language user understands a fragment of the language has to be able to point to some correlation of that understanding with the language user's publicly observable skills: there has to be a publicly identifiable difference between a language user alleged to possess the implicit knowledge in question, and someone who lacks it. This is the so-called *manifestation constraint*.

These skills will include, first, the language user's ability to reproduce the content of a sentence in other words. However, this ability is not one we can invoke globally, for a language user cannot possibly explicitate the truth condition for every sentence by using other words without his account ultimately becoming circular. So the language user's implicit knowledge must therefore, second, and more importantly, be correlated with his ability to recognize sentences as true when he is presented with states of affairs in which their truth conditions are met. Further, Dummett formulates an *acquisition constraint*: it must be possible to point to publicly ascertainable conditions in which the sentence would be appropriately uttered, enabling the language user to acquire implicit knowledge of its truth condition. In other words, the language must be shown to be learnable and scrutable.

These constraints may be seen as particular specifications of the publicity constraint, to which reference has been made earlier. The point is that linguistic meaning must be publicly accessible: as Wittgenstein's dictum tells us, a language user cannot in principle grasp more of the meaning of a sentence or a word than he is capable of conveying to others in his publicly observable use of the expression.

13. Now on Dummett's view of the matter, truth-based theories of meaning of the form that philosophers have traditionally advanced offend against the publicity principle inasmuch as they require that the language user's understanding be explainable by appeal to implicit knowledge that goes beyond what the language user is able to manifest in his linguistic use. Dummett traces the lineage of such theories back to Frege with Davidson's theory, as we have seen, figuring as a contemporary exemplar. The fundamental problem with these theories, according to Dummett, is that they assume what he terms *semantic realism*. A theory of meaning founded on semantic realism is distinguished by the following:

a) First, truth is regarded as the core concept of a theory of meaning. Meaning is explicated in terms of truth. In consequence, we need a semantics of truth conditions for the relevant fragment such as that offered by Frege or Davidson. The sentences in the fragment are linked to those conditions through their being true or false according as the world fulfils the conditions. The sentence 'John's bunch of keys weighs 51 grams' is, accordingly, true provided that John's bunch of keys weighs 51 grams.

b) Second, the so-called principle of bivalence is assumed to apply to the sentences in the relevant fragment. This means that the sentences in the fragment are either true or false; there is no third possibility. The sentence 'John's bunch of keys weighs 51 grams' is accordingly determinately true or false purely in virtue of whether the world fulfils the truth condition or fails to do so.

c) Finally, the claim of semantic realism has bite only if the two above theses are asserted of those sentences (contained in some fragment) of which we have no guarantee that we can either prove or disprove them – i.e. establish whether they are true (verify them) or discover that they are false (falsify them). Only if the two theses (a) and (b) are asserted of sentences of which we do not know whether they are effectively decidable do we have semantic realism. It is thus being claimed not just that sentences are true or false in virtue of certain conditions in the world, but, further, that sentences are determinately true or false in virtue of conditions whose fulfilment or lack of it may transcend our capacities of recognition.

Such sentences are encountered when our compass of reference includes infinite domains, as for example in mathematics (e.g. Goldbach's conjecture to the effect that every even number is the sum of two prime numbers), when we advance claims about the remote past ('Certain dinosaurs became extinct due to an HIV-type viral epidemic') or the future ('Either New Labour will win a new term or they will not'), use subjunctive conditionals ('If the present heir to the throne marries a divorcee, the reigning monarch will insist that he renounce his right to the throne'), or counterfactual conditionals ('Had it not been for Princess Diana's "martyr's" death the British monarchy would have been abolished by the end of the century'). They are also found in third person ascriptions (Greta Garbo harboured a secret sorrow which she shared with no one) and character traits ('Even though he never had a chance to show it, Jones was indeed a thoroughly courageous man') as well as in sentences that involve theoretical entities: e.g. statements about what happened in the first three seconds subsequent to the Big Bang.

Semantic realism is thus the thesis that sentences about which we do not know if they are effectively decidable have, none the less, truth conditions (possibly proof- or verification-transcendent conditions) by virtue of which the sentences are true or false according as the world satisfies those conditions.

14. The manifestation and acquisition constraints and the definition of semantic realism produce the difficulty besetting realism to which Dummett has untiringly drawn attention. Dummett prefers to talk about the *challenge*

to the realist: he does not argue that these problems constitute a refutation of the realist position. The challenge requires that the realist specify wherein the language user's implicit knowledge of the language consists when attributing to him a grasp of sentences for which no effective decision procedure is to be had. For if there is no decision procedure, the language user's knowledge patently does not consist in the performance of any procedure. In what, then, does it consist?

Let us first elaborate on Dummett's challenge with a simple example. Take the sentence '30 is the sum of two prime numbers'. According to the semantic realist the meaning of this sentence is given with its truth condition: the sentence is true if and only if 30 is the sum of two prime numbers. According to Dummett, this semantic theory only meets its remit if it is able to deliver an account of the language user's understanding of the sentence. There must be some substance to our assertion that Peter's understanding of the sentence '30 is the sum of two prime numbers' consists in the implicit knowledge that '30 is the sum of two prime numbers' is true if and only if 30 is the sum of two prime numbers. It is only meaningful to give an account of a language user's understanding of a sentence by attributing to him possession of a particular item of implicit knowledge if the ascription can be correlated with the language user's ability to recognize the sentence as true when it is true. For it is precisely such behaviour that would distinguish Peter from some other language user – Paul, say – who cannot be said to be in possession of the same implicit knowledge. What is it that Peter is capable of that Paul is not?

By way of reply we can point to two things. Either Peter is able to state the truth condition of the sentence using different words, or he is able to declare that the sentence's truth condition is fulfilled when, say, we present him with a mathematical calculation which shows that 13 plus 17 makes 30 and that 13 and 17 are prime numbers. (Instead of a calculation we might show him a list of prime numbers to see whether, with its aid, he is able to work out whether the sentence is true.) The first mode of manifestation explicitates the relevant knowledge. This, as already pointed out, cannot hold globally since an explication of every sentence's truth condition through rephrasing it using other words will inevitably lead into a closed circle. The other feat of which Peter is capable, that of declaring that the sentence's truth condition is fulfilled when presented with an appropriate calculation – is therefore the most important form of behaviour that can be appealed to when the attribution of implicit knowledge is to be grounded.

Let us turn next to a sentence for which there is no guarantee that we can decide its truth-value. One such is 'Goldbach's conjecture' which says that every even number is the sum of two prime numbers. This sentence has proved to hold of all the even numbers so far examined – including astronomical numbers analyzed by computer – but as yet no proof of it has been found. According to the realist, the meaning of the sentence is given with its truth condition: 'Every even number is the sum of two prime numbers' is true if and only if every even number is the sum of two prime numbers.

This semantic account is satisfactory only provided it also yields a theoretical account of our understanding of the relevant sentence. Peter's understanding of Goldbach's conjecture must, then, consist in the implicit knowledge that the sentence 'Every even number is the sum of two prime numbers' is true if and only if every even number is indeed the sum of two prime numbers. This account, however, is only adequate if we can identify something in Peter's behaviour that warrants our attributing to him the relevant implicit knowledge. In particular we must identify something that distinguishes him from a third individual, Percy, from whom we withhold the attribution of such implicit knowledge. Percy is someone who, as the realist would say, still fails to recognize the universal validity of the sentence. He is prepared to assert it only of the sentences he has examined and of which it has been established that they are indeed composed of two prime numbers. Percy denies that this affords him an insight into what it means to say that Goldbach's conjecture holds of all even numbers.

Peter may now try to phrase the truth condition differently, first by showing that every even number up to 100 is the sum of two prime numbers, and then by explaining that the sentence is true if we are able to continue getting consistently analogous results while it is false if we turn up an even number which is not the sum of two prime numbers. But evidently, such an explanation is one Percy too may offer. He agrees that Goldbach's conjecture is true if every even number can be broken down into two prime numbers, while it is false if we turn up an even number which is not the sum of two primes. But Percy repudiates the idea that these forms of words offer any real insight into the truth condition for Goldbach's conjecture. The problem lies in the infinite extension involved: for while Percy readily acknowledges that he understands what it means to carry out a division into two prime numbers of each member of a finite set of whole numbers – even a very large set – he still fails to grasp the meaning of a claim about the resolution of an infinitely large set. He deems it a naïve misconception to believe that we are capable of extrapolating from what is achievable in the case of a finite set – the completion of the series by going through the elements one by one – to an infinite set. We can only mentally grasp the notion of an infinite set if we possess a proof of its properties. But that is precisely what we lack in the present case.

The realist's problem – imputed to him by Dummett's challenge – is that of being able to show a difference between Peter's and Percy's behaviour which justifies the realist in attributing to Peter a knowledge, not just of the truth condition of a sentence involving reference to a finite domain but, further, a knowledge of the appropriate verification-transcendent condition in virtue of which the sentence is true or false of an infinite domain, i.e. the set of all even numbers. However – as is manifestly the case with Goldbach's conjecture – there is nothing in Peter's behaviour that counts as a recognition of the truth condition's being fulfilled, if it is. For so long as an analysis of an infinitely large set of numbers remains beyond his capacities, the truth condition of the sentence clearly transcends Peter's possibilities of determining it. Consequently, there is nothing in his use of the sentence that warrants our ascription of implicit knowledge of a possibly verification-transcendent truth condition for the relevant sentence to Peter (we recall that there exists no general proof of Goldbach's conjecture). In particular, there is nothing in his behaviour that marks Peter off from Percy. The general conclusion, therefore, is that it is not meaningful to apply a realist semantics in an account of the language user's understanding of arithmetical statements.

If the realist fails to meet Dummett's challenge but otherwise accepts the premises of the argument (i.e. the thesis that a theory of meaning is a theory of understanding coupled with the publicity principle as embodied by Dummett's manifestation constraint), the realist must abandon the attempt to explain linguistic understanding by attributing to the language user an implicit knowledge of a realist understanding of the relevant fragments of the language. He must similarly abandon the claim that a realist semantics is the correct account of the semantic content of a natural language. The realist concept of truth can no longer serve as the core concept in a theory of meaning.

15. So far Dummett's challenge to the realist, which might also be called his negative programme. However, he also propounds a positive programme that takes the form of a set of ideas for an anti-realist semantics. If the realist concept of truth is not to serve as the pivotal concept in our theory of meaning, with what, according to Dummett, should we replace it?

The anti-realist proposes that we explain the meanings of sentences by reference to conditions that are related to abilities manifestable by the language user deploying those sentences. (We are again put in mind of Wittgenstein's dictum that meaning is use.) In consequence, truth conditions are applicable insofar as we have a warrant that the language user is in principle able to recognize the sentences as being true or false when their truth conditions are fulfilled or unfulfilled, respectively.

But if such warrants are not available, the meaning of a sentence has to be explained on the basis of the practical procedures that we use when seeking to show that we are justified in making the relevant assertion. For the majority of sentences, there do indeed exist such procedures; not ones that present the actual facts that make the sentences true, but ones which sufficiently ground our assertions. The merit of such procedures is that they are intersubjectively accessible, thus satisfying the publicity principle. When we explain a person's understanding of the language by appeal to them, we are not in the business of issuing semantical blank cheques – as do appeals to implicit knowledge, not manifestable by the utterer, concerning the verification- or proof-transcendent conditions of those sentences whose truth conditions they are.

In the mathematical case, this anti-realist proposal implies that the meanings of sentences are fixed by their proof-conditions. For we say that a person's understanding of, say, Goldbach's conjecture consists in his implicit knowledge of what would constitute a proof or a disproof of the sentence – and this knowledge is capable of immediate correlation with a corresponding ability to recognize a mathematical construction as a proof or a disproof, were the language user confronted with one. That knowledge of a proof is different from knowledge of truth conditions becomes clear from our knowledge of the truth condition of a sentence such as '30 is the sum of two prime numbers': a spot of mental arithmetic tells us that the figure is the sum of 17 and 13. By contrast, we have absolutely no abstract proof of such a division being possible for 30 in virtue of its being an even number. Conversely, one could imagine some future mathematician having the luck to prove Goldbach's conjecture but still without knowing what it was that made it true in its application to a specific (large) number such as 51654438 to the power of ten.

For sentences such as those that ascribe mental events and states to other persons, refer to the distant past and future, express subjunctive conditionals and others, Dummett proposes that we generalize the conclusion drawn in the mathematical case and use analogous concepts such as assertibility conditions, verifiability conditions, or falsifiability conditions to determine their meaning – the conditions, in fact, that practically warrant our assertion of such sentences or which are accounted satisfactory justifications or refutations of them.

In more recent writings Dummett has framed his conclusions differently. We can retain the concept of truth as the core concept of semantics, while construing it as an anti-realistically acceptable concept, defined in terms of proof- or verification-conditions. Such a concept does not endorse the ascription to sentences of proof- or verification-transcendent truth conditions and so neither does it endorse the assertion of the principle of bivalence for sentences about whose effective decidability we have to remain agnostic. The difference between these two variants of Dummett's conclusion is primarily a terminological one.

16. We might wonder whether any consequences whatever follow from our being forced to abandon a realist concept of truth as the core concept in our semantics. For did not the comparison between Peter and Percy clearly show that there is no difference between a person who subscribes to a truth conditional semantics and one who applies a semantics based on assertibility conditions? However, according to Dummett, dropping the realist concept means that the inferential practices of classical logic for the relevant fragment of language cannot be justified, with revision of the logic and ontology of the fragment following as an inevitable consequence.

Classical logic is, *inter alia*, characterized by the universal validity of the law of the excluded middle: A or non-A is always assertible. This principle reposes on a realist semantics, namely the assertion of bivalence or the determinacy of truth, which again is tenable only insofar as sentences are ascribed truth conditions in accordance with a realist concept of truth (i.e. sentences are true or false in virtue of possibly proof- or verification-transcendent states of affairs). When, for every sentence A, it holds that either A or its negation non-A is true, it is so in virtue of the purported fact that (as the realist maintains) there exists an independent reality which makes one or other of the sentences true, irrespective of our ability or the lack of it to recognize which.

If, instead, we replace the realist semantics with one or other of the anti-realist proposals, the result will be a radical break with the principle of bivalence for fragments of the language for which we are in principle precluded from guaranteeing a more or less effective decision procedure. If the truth of a mathematical claim consists in there being an available proof of it, and the truth of its negation consists in there existing a disproof of it, the global assertion of the principle of excluded middle is without warrant: for it may be that at any given time there is no available proof, nor a disproof, and no guarantee that the claim is susceptible of either. (This is precisely the case with Goldbach's conjecture.) This implies that our classical inferential practice cannot seek its justification in any plausible semantic theory for the language. It should be revised and replaced by an alternative inferential practice in which the universal assertion of the excluded middle, either A or non-A, is abandoned.

This has serious revisionary consequences for our classical inferential practices in mathematics where so-called indirect proofs are common. According to classical logic, a sentence S is provable by the demonstration that its negation, non-S, entails a contradiction: if the assumption of non-S entails a contradiction, we can infer non-non-S, and then by the rule of double negation infer S. This inference conserves truth within classical logic: if non-non-S is true, then S too is true by the classical truth table definition of negation (see chapter 5).

Now given the anti-realist's understanding of the concept of truth, truth is linked to the existence of proof. Hence, the truth of S consists in the existence of a proof of S, and the truth of non-S consists in there being a disproof of S. It follows that the rule of double negation is not anti-realistically sound since it does not conserve provability. The truth of non-non-S consists of our knowledge that there is no disproof of S. But obviously, this does not constitute a positive proof of S.

It further follows that if the rule of double negation is not anti-realistically warranted, then neither is the principle of excluded middle, since the classical proof of the principle is an indirect proof essentially involving the rule of double negation.

17. The realist can adopt one of two different postures in the face of Dummett's criticism: he can seek to answer the anti-realist challenge or he can attempt to undermine one or more of the premises on which it builds. In the following we shall take a critical look at one of the premises.

Dummett's two major premises are that a theory of meaning is a theory of understanding and that the manifestation constraint holds. In chapter 3 we touched briefly upon a possible criticism of the first constraint, namely that extractable from Kripke's causal theory of reference, which presupposes that a speaker can use a name without possessing any identifying knowledge about the referent, i.e. without having any ability to pick out the referent of the name. We noted that this thesis is at odds with Dummett's conception of linguistic meaning but hinted that the issue remained undecided. Here we shall further examine the manifestation constraint, which is probably the premise most vulnerable to criticism. Recall again that it is imperative for Dummett to distinguish between sentences known to be effectively decidable and sentences that are not so known, since it is within the latter category that the anti-realist challenge has bite.

Against this, the objection may be raised that it is only in mathematics and logic that it makes sense sharply to distinguish between sentences that we know to be effectively decidable and sentences on which we have no such purchase. For it is only within such areas that the ideal of conclusive proof procedures in the form of algorithms and the like has a hold. We can state precisely what counts as a conclusive proof, and if we neither miscalculate nor commit other errors in the execution of a proof it is logically impossible that a sentence should be false if a proof of its truth is available.

The problem is that nothing corresponding to the conclusive justifications of mathematics and logic exists in other regions of knowledge and language. In consequence no clear line can be drawn between sentences known to be effectively decidable and sentences that fall outside that category.

Take, for example, as mundane a sentence as 'There's milk in the fridge'. What counts as a verification of this sentence? Is there in fact any verificatory procedure guaranteed to eventuate in our knowing either that the sentence is true or that it is false? We can of course go to the fridge, open the door and look. And indeed there on one of the shelves is a blue-coloured carton bearing the legend 'milk'. Is there milk in it? We open and tip the carton and out flows a white fluid. Is it milk? Well, it certainly tastes like milk and milk thus packaged is a standard item in our local supermarket. But could it not be the case that the producers have hoodwinked both customers and supermarket by producing a synthetic product superficially indistinguishable from milk and tasting like the regular article but in terms of its chemical constitution not remotely like milk? In other words, is it not conceivable that it is a synthetic ersatz surreptitiously released into the market to exploit the economic advantages accruing to long-life products? In other words, we need to have a chemical analysis done on the white substance currently before us to decide the matter. But can we trust the laboratory technicians who will be applying the tests? Could they not be in collusion with the manufacturer or have other interests that render them unreliable?

Obviously, we would be able to go on putting such questions; there is no end to them, which is enough to show that nothing like a rationally-grounded conclusive verdict is forthcoming. We have to manage with less: there is every indication that the carton contains milk and we have no reasonable basis for the doubt that it does. Here we must make do with a fallible and defeasible justification, which means that we have to accept an ineradicable epistemological gap between our evidence for the truth of a sentence and the fulfilment of its truth condition. Logically, even the best evidence fails of conclusiveness. Further, the justification of truth conditions on the basis of defeasible evidence bears interesting points of resemblance to the inference to the best explanation – i.e. the scientific form of inference to the effect that theoretical entities exist because the assumption that they do is what most effectively explains immediate sensory experience.

Dummett's anti-realist challenge needs modifying, then, when the manifestation constraint is invoked outside mathematics and logic. Instead, the claim has to be that we can only attribute to a language user implicit knowledge of the truth condition of a sentence insofar as the person is indefeasibly able (possibly by means of reference to criteria or by inference to the best explanation) to recognize a sentence as true, given that its truth condition is fulfilled.

This leaves the anti-realist open to the following objection from the realist: if even a Dummettian anti-realist is forced to accept defeasible justifications in the case of sentences designated 'conclusively verifiable', why not make the same concession in the case of sentences whose conclusive verification, even if possible, is currently beyond our reach (as, for example, those that concern infinite domains or reference to unobservable theoretical entities)? For now there seems to be only a difference of degree between the acceptance of defeasible justifications and the use of inconclusive forms of inference deployed in areas such as inductive generalization or inference to the best explanation. The defeasibility solution would save the realist from the difficulties in which he is mired when seeking to meet the manifestation constraint for sentences of the problematic class.

At this point it becomes clear that Dummett's reflections on philosophy of language are inextricably bound up with certain classical and as yet unsolved problems in epistemology. These concern the nature and reliability of our knowledge within such areas as theoretical natural science, the existence of other minds, and so on. We cannot pursue these questions within the confines of the present context. We must content ourselves with concluding that Dummett's challenge to the realist still stands, regardless of the difficulty Dummett faces in delimiting the areas where this challenge can be met, as against those where it cannot. It remains reasonable to insist that the onus is on the realist to explain to us how a language user is able to manifest the linguistic knowledge that the realist attributes to him and in what it consists.

Chapter 12
Wider philosophical perspectives

1. In our attempt to achieve philosophical insight into the most basic linguistic categories we have repeatedly run up against problems which, although they sprang from very different sources, manifested themselves in the same way, viz. as obstacles to an extensional construal of natural language. In this chapter we shall be training our spotlight on these problems and their interrelations. Our brushes with them in previous chapters have already suggested that they link up with certain traditional philosophical themes that might offhand appear to belong to quite a different part of the philosophical landscape.

Our first encounter with the problem of extensionality coincided with the attempt to determine the meanings of predicates in chapters 1 and 4. We sought to steer clear of a naive referential semantics for predicates, i.e. a theory to the effect that the meaning of a predicate consists in its referring to some mysterious entity over and above the items to which the predicate applies. Quite apart from the fact that it is ill equipped to deliver the hoped-for solution, such a theory faces considerable difficulties. First of all, it is difficult to accommodate such "universals" in our normal world picture. Where are these entities to be sought and how, in cognitive terms, do we latch onto them? The question of their relations to individual items also raises difficult issues. Universals express what is common to a plurality of individual items and so must in one sense be distributed across these. But what then becomes of the unity that the predicate is supposed to possess? This difficulty is one with which already Plato grappled.

These problems would evaporate if we could simply define a predicate by reference to the class of items to which it applies and forget about the mysterious metaphysical entities known as universals. The result would be a purely extensional theory of the meanings of general concepts taking the form of a list of the things that satisfy the predicate. Or rather, as we saw in chapter 4, it would take the form of a list of the entire inventory of the universe combined with the truth-values generated by these objects when characterized by the predicate in question. Predicates would be understood as functions from objects to truth-values. On the face of it, this method would appear to capture the specific contribution predicates make to the semantics of sentences.

This promising-looking proposal, however, proved not to be feasible (cf. chapter 4). The most major difficulty is the fact that all predicates sharing the same extension would have the same meaning. Thus all predicates with an empty extension – i.e. all that have nothing in reality answering to them – would have the same meaning: 'mermaid' would have the same meaning as 'unicorn'. Further, the proposal assigns the same meaning to predicates that have the same non-empty extensions as do, say, the expressions 'blue whale' and 'the largest animal that has ever existed'. But these expressions do not have the same meaning.

2. In our presentation of Donald Davidson's theory of meaning in chapter 6, we came across the extensionality problem again, this time in a slightly different guise. This had to do with sentences reporting the mental goings-on of human beings, such as in the sentence 'Wilfred claims that the blue whale is threatened with extinction'. We can replace the expression 'blue whale' with the coextensional expression 'the largest animal that has ever existed' and so get the sentence 'Wilfred claims that the largest animal that has ever existed is threatened with extinction'. It is clear that the two sentences do not automatically have the same truth-value. For it may be that Wilfred is unaware that the blue whale is the largest animal that has ever existed; he believes, erroneously, that dinosaurs were larger. Consequently, the first report about Wilfred might be true and the latter false.

It will be recalled that Davidson sought to tackle this aspect of the intensionality problem through the introduction of a special way of dealing with indirect contexts. The core of Davidson's proposal was to break down a sentence like that above into a complex expression of the form 'Wilfred asserted that. The blue whale is threatened with extinction'. Here the word 'that' is a demonstrative that refers to the sentence 'the blue whale is threatened with extinction'. This sentence is not a part of what is asserted by a person who says 'Wilfred claims that the blue whale is threatened with extinction'; but the sentence cited above refers to this sentence by means of a demonstrative. It provokes no surprise, then, that the truth-value of the sentence 'Wilfred claims that' varies in accordance with whatever sentences are substituted for 'the blue whale is threatened with extinction'. This corresponds to the situation where saying 'This is a cup' varies in truth-value depending on what 'this' refers to. However, we expressed reservations about Davidson's analysis. There are sentences for which the meaning-fixing analysis would lead to circularity. We considered the sentence 'There exists a planet of which Galileo said that it moved' and established that Davidson's method failed to deliver an adequate analysis.

3. It is not difficult to identify the feature that undermines the extensionality of the sentences above: there is a sense in which they are not about the world in itself, but about thoughts, conceptions, beliefs and utterances concerning it. For sentences about the world itself, their truth-values are unaffected by how we refer to the items the sentences are about. If the blue whale is the largest animal that has ever existed, and if the blue whale is threatened with extinction, we can infer that the largest animal that has ever existed is threatened with extinction. Expressions with the same extension can be substituted one for the other with the truth-value of the sentence remaining unchanged (true or false). But in the case of sentences describing a person's cognitive relationships with the world, there is a difference. Wilfred believes that the blue whale is threatened with extinction. But he does not believe that the largest animal that has ever existed is threatened with extinction despite its being identical with the blue whale. This is due to the fact that Wilfred does not know that the blue whale is the largest animal that has ever existed.

Non-extensionality is a feature of all sentences that express a person's mental or psychological dispositions vis-à-vis the surrounding world. We might, then, formulate sentences about Wilfred in the style of 'Wilfred hopes that ...', 'Wilfred fears that ...', 'Wilfred has decided that ...' and encounter the same non-substitutability. However, non-extensionality does not occur if we describe relations of a purely bodily or physical nature between a person and the world. If we say 'Wilfred ate meat that came from a blue whale' this sentence retains its truth-value if we substitute 'the largest animal that has ever lived' for 'the blue whale'.

Non-extensionality is due, in other words, to the particular mental subject matter figuring in the sentences under scrutiny. In the eyes of many philosophers this circumstance merely casts more suspicion on an area that in their view is suspect already. The difficulties attaching to the articulation of a semantics for a language are generated by descriptions of the mental, which already feature sufficient peculiarities for sceptical doubts about its status to be entertained. Mental items are associated with the existence of mysterious entities, "minds" or "souls", which already seem to block a coherent conception of reality. Minds are mysterious immaterial things in a world that would otherwise appear to be amenable to description in terms of purely material, physical categories. Indeed minds would seem to violate the laws of physics by spontaneously initiating movement in the form of actions. "Mind" ostensibly initiates actions, i.e. physical movement, without containing power in itself and without itself being influenced by any physical power.

Throughout the entire history of Western philosophy the assumption of souls or minds has been under attack by philosophers, some of whom have championed a radically materialist position to the effect that the world contains only material things, things of the kind describable by physics. Those arguing against the notion now receive support from fellow philosophers engaged in developing a recursive theory of meaning for natural languages. These latter note that descriptions of mental items in language result in non-extensional sentences for which, to date, it has proved impossible to devise an adequate semantics. Here, then, is another difficulty that would disappear if we were able to rid our world picture of mental elements.

4. Scepticism in respect of mental entities is only deepened by our subsequently finding that there is yet another area where extensionality does not hold, and where the mental, yet again, is implicated – namely, modal sentences. Modalities are the aspects of events and things expressed by the terms 'possible', 'necessary', 'impossible' and their cognates, and modal sentences are sentences containing such terms.

Let us consider an example to briefly remind ourselves how this non-extensionality manifests itself. Take the true modal sentence, 'It is necessary that 5 is a prime number'. Now five is the number of digits on a human hand; 'five' and 'the number of digits on a human hand' have, in other words, the same extension, i.e. they stand for the same set of things, namely everything that is 5 in number. (This is the set of all the sets that may be correlated one-to-one with the numerals 1 to 5). We next insert this co-extensional expression into our modal sentence and get the result 'It is necessary that the number of digits on a human hand is a prime number'. This sentence is obviously false – for is it not conceivable that evolution might have furnished us with four or six digits? There are animals with four digits per limb that cope admirably. We started with a true sentence, substituted for one of its expressions a different but co-extensional expression and ended up with a false sentence. We have shown that the sentence in question was non-extensional. Similar examples may be construed involving the other modalities.

In the view of some philosophers modalities are dubious entities. Either a thing exists or it does not. There is no mysterious intermediate stage between existence and non-existence, no such thing as possible existence. Moreover, things that exist just do, outright: there are no existent things whose existence is of a specially privileged kind, namely necessary. Many philosophers subscribe to some brand of empiricism, i.e. they recognize only those properties of the physical world which, in some respect, can be manifested in experience. But how might necessity be manifested in experience? Experience shows us only contingent states of affairs: it offers us no intimation of whether a thing is necessary. Similarly with impossibility: experience only tells us that, up to this point, such-and-such has not occurred, but not that it is impossible, i.e. that it cannot occur. Experience shows us only the contingent, not the necessary or the impossible.

In consequence, many philosophers have held that modalities are human constructs, projected onto reality – more an expression of how we relate to reality than of reality itself. The archetype of this kind of projectionism is Hume's account of causality and the way that the necessity felt to pertain to the causal tie is really just a reflection, cast upon external reality, of our subjective habit of expecting the effect to happen once we have observed the occurrence of the cause. Similarly with 'possibility' and 'impossiblity': these modalities are merely reflections of our willingness to entertain certain hypotheses while we reject certain others out of hand. To put it in speech act terms, the modal operators, 'possible', 'impossible' and 'necessary' have no referential function but a purely performative one, viz. to express the speaker's epistemic attitude to the issue under discussion. Modalities thus are not aspects of the external world but features of human thinking. In this manner, modalities and the problems they create for a proper understanding of how language works are related, behind the scenes, to the problems posed by sentences reporting mental states.

Moreover, the philosophers who are sceptical of modalities point out that necessity and impossibility are concepts whose track records in the history of philosophy have done them little credit. Many have been the phenomena proclaimed necessary or impossible as the case may be by one philosopher after another, only to be contradicted outright by other philosophers, or more often, to have their asseverations refuted by the science of a later period. The Greek thinkers and their successors in the Middle Ages accounted it a necessary truth that the earth was at the centre of the universe and the other celestial bodies orbited it in perfect circles. The scientific revolution that began in the Renaissance demonstrated that both 'necessities' were false. Immanuel Kant believed himself able to show that the universe was necessarily describable by means of Euclidean geometry and that the principle of causality was universally valid. The theory of relativity revealed that the first assumption is not necessary and most probably false. And quantum mechanics indicated regions of reality – namely at the subatomic level –

where the principle of causality seems not to find application since the "quantum leaps" encountered here are fundamentally unpredictable. The "necessities" and "impossibilities" of philosophers often prove to be precipitate extrapolations from everyday experience; they show the limitations of our imaginative compass rather than of reality itself.

5. The above reflections would suggest that all the problems for a theory of meaning that we have considered are interlocked. First, when people use a term such as 'the blue whale' or 'the largest animal that has ever existed' they (very often) have not only the actually existent exemplars of these creatures in mind. And even when they make a statement that is not meant to cover more than all the blue whales that have ever existed, exist today or will exist in the future, they have no direct epistemic access to this set of animals. Nobody is acquainted with the extension of such general terms, which comprises a multitude of anonymous individuals scattered across the past, present and future. Hence speakers can only pick them out as animals that answer to a particular abstract definition or abstract concept. Thus the meanings of these terms are not exhausted by their extensions. In a word, the expression 'blue whale' cannot be defined by reference to a list of such creatures.

Second, this means that if Wilfred starts musing on the blue whale – a state of affairs expressible, maybe, in the sentence 'Wilfred believes that the blue whale eats krill' – this situation is not equivalent to that presented by the sentence 'Wilfred believes that the largest animal that has ever existed eats krill'. It is indeed the case that the class of blue whales is identical with the class of the largest animals that have ever existed. But Wilfred's thought has not, as its object, the extension of the expression 'blue whale'; his thought goes beyond extension and concerns itself with the abstract conceptual content (intension) or meaning; and this is different from the meaning of the expression 'the largest animal that has ever existed'. One cannot, therefore, substitute certain expressions for others in sentences that describe people's thoughts (and feelings, hopes, plans, and so on) with any security that truth-values are preserved. And this, as we have seen, creates difficulties for the endeavour to construct an extensional theory of meaning.

Third, this means that human beings can think hypothetically, in brief, in terms of possibilities. They can conjure up ideas of things that find no counterparts in the actual world – i.e. which do no belong to the actual extension of any concept – and introduce these hypothetical entities into hypothetical situations. Such aspects of human thinking are expressed in the modalities of language. Language users can reflect on the abstract conceptual content of the terms 'blue whale' and 'the largest animals that have ever existed' and recognize that, although these two expressions designate the same class of beings in our actual world, things might have been otherwise. This insight can only be expressed in a modal (non-extensional) sentence, of the type 'There might have been dinosaurs that were even larger than the blue whale'. It is non-extensional because it concerns things and situations that go beyond the factual.

6. The connection between the semantic problem and mentalism comes out clearly in the philosophical theory of language that goes by the name of 'conceptualism' (cf. chapter 4). For conceptualism represents an attempt to solve the semantic problems by postulating a special mental mechanism or mental medium to deal with them. In general terms, conceptualism holds that meaning is a mental, psychological entity. We have already (chapter 1) looked at one somewhat naive version of the theory, viz. Locke's ideational theory of meaning. Locke contended, it will be recalled, that the meanings of words consisted in the "ideas" that language users have in their minds when speaking. Locke conceived of these ideas in concrete terms, as images, and so ran into difficulties with general concepts, which involve images of several incompatible things at once. In contrast to this, other, later conceptualists have conceived of them as something more abstract, as "concepts". Concepts are mental tools with which a language user grasps the world. They are thus capacities rather than concrete "things". According to conceptualism, words get their meaning by expressing such concepts.

Conceptualism would appear to offer an elegant solution to Plato's problem, i.e. the problem of how forms can both be individual entities and yet apply to a plurality of things. The answer would seem to be that a concept is one thing qua proficiency, one thing qua mental capacity, but universal in its applicability to a plurality of things. In this sense it is like other capacities or tools: a monkey wrench is a single item but is used to seize and manipulate a diversity of objects. So too with concepts. Conceptualism can also explain how things with empty extensions can have meanings, even different meanings. Expressions such as 'unicorn' and 'mermaid' both lack extensions, i.e. there is nothing that falls under them. But they are none the less meaningful for that since they refer to mental entities, capacities in the mind of the speaker. Referring to discrete capacities, they are invested with different meanings.

However, this variant of mentalism too runs into difficulties. When called on to give an account of the capacity that the possession of a concept consists in, reference to the things conceptualism is supposed to eliminate is unavoidable: the capacity has, among other things, to be describable as the capacity to think of possible things of the given kinds. In the absence of this aspect, the assumption of the existence of the concept would not explain what it is designed to explain. In contrast to a monkey wrench, the concepts manipulate not only actual entities but also possible ones. This is what is involved when we say things like 'Let's imagine that unicorns actually existed ...' But then we are back with possible entities again. Instead of providing a solution to the problems of philosophical semantics conceptualism begins to look more like an additional problem.

7. If these problems all hang together in the manner indicated, it is reasonable to assume that, if they can be solved at all, they can be solved together: a solution to one will be a solution to all.

In chapter 7, we explored one suggested general solution, based upon the notion of a 'possible world'. The strategy was to claim that, among these intertwined problematic notions, the modalities are the ones most amenable to systematic treatment. This notion can then be used to throw light upon all the others. The crucial move is to go beyond the intuitive understanding of such modal notions as 'possible', 'necessary', and so on and to spell them out in terms of the notion of 'possible worlds'.

The solution which this picture offers is of a non-reductive kind: it does not deny that non-extensional phenomena exist, but shows us how we can live with them, i.e. how we can recognize their existence and still enjoy a perspicuous picture of the way our language functions when we report them. The perspicuousness is basically the same as that possessed by extensional theories of meaning. Such theories define the semantics of terms by means of listing the items falling under them. Now possible world semantics adopts the idea that terms are definable by a list of items, only now the lists comprise not only items that exist in the actual world, but in possible worlds too. But from a technical point of view, this is only a minor complication. It only calls for an indexation of the lists of items, to indicate whether they belong to the actual world or to one or another of the numerous possible worlds.

Most philosophers agree that from a technical point of view, possible world semantics represents a major advance. It has allowed logicians to systematize modal inference and to construct well-defined modal logics. The question is whether the same verdict goes when we adopt a broader philosophical perspective which includes metaphysical and epistemological concerns as well. That is, does the admission of possible worlds into our picture of reality create any difficulties for our view of the furniture of the universe, or challenges to our view of how we know this reality? We touched briefly upon these issues in chapter 7, and shall give them a little closer scrutiny here.

How are we to conceive of possible worlds from a metaphysical point of view? That is, how do we fit these items into our picture of the universe? The most sanguine proponent of possible worlds, David Lewis, looks upon possible worlds rather on the model of the "parallel universes" that certain physicists (and science-fiction writers) speculate about. Possible worlds are worlds which are somehow isolated from our own, and from each other, in the sense that there is no causal interaction between them. Nor are there any temporal or spatial relations between them; we cannot ask whether an event in another possible world happened before, after or at the same time as one in our world, nor about the distance between an object in that world and one in ours.

This isolation, however, gives us no reason to doubt the existence of such a world, according to Lewis. For the status of these possible worlds and our actual world is perfectly symmetrical. These worlds may be inaccessible from ours, but then our actual world is inaccessible from theirs. From the point of view of the inhabitants of a possible world *our* world is merely a possible world; the situation is perfectly symmetrical. Lewis assimilates the logic of the expression 'the actual world' with that of indexicals. When we refer to a certain region as 'my country' or to a certain period in time as 'the present epoque', we do not attribute any unique property or any ontological privilege to it: we just single it out by means of a certain kind of demonstrative linguistic device. In the same way, the expression 'the actual world' does not indicate any ontologically privileged mode of existence: it merely points to that region of reality, *sensu largissimo*, in which we live.

Unfortunately, there are deep problems with Lewis's suggestion. One is epistemological: if possible worlds are causally closed off from the actual one, then how can we ever know what goes on in them? We can never dream of travelling to such worlds to explore them, nor even hope to receive signals of any kind from them which could serve as a basis for theorizing about what goes on in them. From an epistemological point of view, nothing in our actual world will ever be different depending upon whether such worlds exist or not.

This is an aspect of a deeper problem, which is that Lewis's theory fails to capture the role which hypothetical reasoning and musings about possibilities play in our lives. Imagine that God were to appear to mankind and reveal to us that in no possible world did any creature exist larger than the blue whale in our actual world. How could this revelation render invalid the claim that such creatures might have existed in our world? What has this divine revelation to do with our notion of possibility and the normal ways we reason about it? Such as, for instance, a demonstration that, given the laws of physics and chemistry, an even larger creature would still have been able to move about and to sustain the basic biological functions necessary for survival? In the normal run of things, we would take this as pertinent and weighty evidence that an animal larger than the blue whale is indeed a biological possibility. But how could that be, if the truth or falsity of the modal statements is indeed determined by states of affairs completely unrelated to this mode of reasoning?

This problem is accentuated by a further oddity of Lewis's proposal. If possible worlds are indeed "parallel universes", no individual entity may be found in more than one such world: no individual entity may exist (in its entirely) in two different places, let alone in two different worlds. But this means that if we ask, of any individual thing, person or animal, whether that item could have had other properties in another, possible world than it actually has, the answer must be 'no' since the contrary answer would presuppose that this item might also have existed in another world. But such multiple location is impossible. Hence it seems that all modal statements about particulars will lack a truth value, given Lewis's semantics.

Lewis handles this problem by invoking what he calls the *counterpart relation*. It is indeed true that no individual thing found in this world may simultaneously inhabit another, possible world. However, other worlds might be home to counterparts of individual denizens of our world, that is, individual items that closely resemble items in our world, and in particular resemble them more than do any other items in the other world. They are, so to speak, the *doppelganger* of the inhabitants of this world. The counterpart relation provides the semantics for modal statements about individuals: a statement to the effect that Tony Blair could have been a Tory prime minister means that, in a given possible world, the Tony Blair *doppelganger* – his closest counterpart – is indeed the prime minister, representing the Conservative Party.

Again we may feel that this semantics is at odds with the role of modal discourse in our lives. What relevance does it have for the career options of Tony Blair that a person different from him could have held a certian job? And how does this relate to the way that we would actually try to establish the possibilities open to Blair? Ontology and epistemology seem to be strangely out of joint here.

It might be thought that the standard argumentative moves invoked when discussing possibilities are relevant after all, since they raise the likelihood that a possible world conforming to them might exist. But this would be a mistake. It presupposes a premise to the effect that modal reasoning in our world has repercussions for alternative, possible worlds, construed in a Lewisian fashion. This is a premise for which there is not a shred of evidence, nor could there be any, in the nature of the case.

It is fair to say that, despite the skill and verve with which he has defended his metaphysical proposal, Lewis has made very few converts. Nor does any other theory about the semantics of modal sentences command general assent; the field remains one of great controversy, once we move beyond the cosy discussion of technical details in order to face the metaphysical implications. This conclusion may be extended to cover the other non-extensional linguistic contexts as well. There is no received view with respect to the construction of a truth-conditional semantics for contexts dealing with propositional attitudes (mental states), counterfactual conditionals, and the rest.

Thus, this is the situation with respect to the programme of developing a semantics for natural language, based upon the notion of truth conditions: the chief virtue of such a theory is the perspicuousness of its account of the semantic workings of the various parts of language. Unfortunately, this virtue is to be enjoyed only under a purely extensional interpretation of language. Such an interpretation faces serious challenges in the form of the numerous apparently non-extensional contexts of natural languages. The attempt to extend the simple model to such contexts are typically seen to carry the cost of an excessive ontological load: it has led philosophers to embrace metaphysical positions which seem to be at odds with the way we conceive the word when we adopt other cognitive stances, such as those of common sense, or of empirical science. Overcoming these metaphysical obstacles remains the most fundamental challenge to a truth-conditional semantics.

8. We shall end our book by offering a sketch of the metaphysical picture that has been dominant in European philosophy for two and a half millennia, in order to make it clear what is at stake in this entanglement of philosophy of language and metaphysics. In offering this picture, we shall in part be going over ground that is already largely familiar from the preceding pages. This should cause no surprise, since reflection on the nature of linguistic meaning has been a crucial factor in the formation of the classical metaphysical account of reality in European philosophy. Evidently, this account has other sources too, epistemological and religious ones among others, but it is impossible to understand its fine details if its roots in reflections on language are overlooked.

According to the classical picture, reality is made up out of three basic spheres. First, there is the concrete sensory world of material things. Second, there is a world of forms, concepts, principles, abstract entities such as those that enter into mathematics, and so on. This is basically the extra-sensory realm whose existence was asserted by Plato – one cognized when we move beyond the sensory realm of the body and the material world, which only tells us about concrete things, in order to place greater reliance on abstract thought. Thought, along with other mental entities, comprises the third domain of reality; collectively these constitute "soul", "mind", "the mental". Now this picture of reality postulates a dimension inaccessible to sense perception, and attributes to human subjects the powers that enable us to cognize this reality. These two features are regarded as special spheres of reality alongside the material world.

The metaphysical picture generated by such reflections about linguistic meaning has in recent times been vividly argued for by Karl Popper, who calls it the doctrine of the Three Worlds. For historical accuracy, it should be noted that Popper's perspective has been that of philosophy of science rather than the philosophy of language, with which he has little patience. Still the intellectual concerns and the reasonings involved have been the very same, viz. the need to find an objective correlate of meaningful language, besides reference. World One is physical reality, ultimately consisting of particles or forces distributed in empty space. World Two is the psychological or mental world, consisting of minds and their contents of thought processes, feelings, intentions, and so on. World Three consists of objective claims and thought contents. Here, for example, we find the objects of mathematics, but also the thought contents of scientific theories, books and indeed every meaningful sentence. According to Popper the content of this world is the creation of human agents; in this he marks himself off from Plato who ascribed to such entities independent existence. But Popper agrees with Plato in contending that these entities (once created) are, so far as their properties go, independent of human beings. Their independence is manifest, *inter alia*, in our not being simply able to postulate properties belonging to them, although we can discover such properties, through proofs, should we be sharp enough to hit upon them. We cannot, for example, postulate that the square root of 2 is a rational number, or for that matter, an irrational number. But by means of a proof we can demonstrate its irrationality, i.e. its inexpressibility in terms of a finite decimal expansion.

According to Popper, interactions between World Three and World One can only take place via World Two: abstract entities such as proofs, arguments and the like cannot in themselves affect the physical world, or vice versa. The physical world can, however, be affected through the mental world. Ideas from World Three affect World Two, as illustrated, say, in the case of an engineer mastering a mathematical theory. This theory subsequently finds application in his work of bridge construction, with the result that bridges are built using methods that would not otherwise have been attempted. This, according to Popper, is an instance of World Three affecting World One through World Two and the result is the creation of a bridge. Conversely, World Three can be affected by World One only by means of World Two. Legend has it that Newton was struck on the head by an apple, a physical event which inspired him to formulate the law of gravity, which is an entity in World Three (as against gravity itself, which operates in World One). It is only in virtue of Newton's possession of consciousness and the powers of thought and so belonging to World Two that the fall of the apple could mediate an expansion of World Three. If, instead, the apple had hit a stone at the foot of the tree, unnoticed by Newton, no comparable effects would have been triggered.

9. This metaphysical picture has by no means gone unchallenged over the history of European thought. Indeed, it has been the target of criticism from the beginning. The critics may be divided into two groups. The first oppose World Two, the realm of the mental. Against this they urge an out-and-out *materialism* (or *physicalism*): in the empirical world there exist only physical things – not necessarily those recognized by contemporary physics but entities, rather, that will figure in a more developed, future physics. In any case, they would not be items that could be characterized as thoughts, feelings, intentions or other things that require non-extensional linguistic tools for their description. The other group of critics are *nominalists*. Their criticism is levelled at World Three particularly, which is to say that they protest the postulation of abstract entities such as numbers, universal concepts, and so on; mental entities, qua intrinsically individual items, do not offend the nominalist.

Critics have often combined materialist and nominalist criticisms. One reason for this is the recognition that there is a close link between mentalism (which is the opposite of materialism) and Platonism (which is the opposite of nominalism). The mental, World Two is, as we have seen, an intermediary between Worlds One and Three. This means that acceptance of Worlds Two and Three are closely linked. A good reason for believing in the first is that we believe in the second, and vice versa. Further, a criticism of one of these worlds is by the same token an objection to the other.

Now it is no part of our brief to summarize two and a half thousand years of philosophical grappling with these problems or to pass judgement on the outcome. But it is worth drawing attention to a couple of difficulties that materialists and nominalists face. We can readily agree that the realm of the mental is something we are best rid of if it is viewed in terms of a home to mysterious ghostly items, "souls" that are thought to exist independently of the body. But this is hardly the sort of conception entertained by any mentalist today. Rather, the mental is conceived of as a property of the body, in particular of the brain. Further, many mentalists would maintain that the ascription of these properties to the body ties in with the fact that in describing human beings we use a particular idiom with distinctive non-physical predicates. In describing human subjects and their behaviour it is impossible to dispense with intentional terms. As we have seen, intentional terms characterize human subjects as directed towards some object or other. This object may be concrete, such as a table or chair, or abstract such as the content of a sentence. Intentionality is attributable to us when we say such things as 'Wilfred thinks that ...', 'Wilfred hopes that ...', 'Wilfred intends that ...'. Intentionalists are concerned to emphasize that these propositions do not imply that the mental consists of some special 'stuff', and so are not vulnerable to the materialist's criticism that the mentalist conjures up occult entities. Contrariwise, the language of intentionality is clearly not descriptive of the physical realm. This appears not least from the fact that it is a non-extensional language.

Furthermore, contemporary mentalists point out that intentional descriptions of persons contain a vast amount of information that defies substitution with information about the physical states of individual bodies. Suppose that we know of Harry that he believes skating to be dangerous when the ice is thin, and that the ice gets thinner if the temperature rises to the point at which it melts, and finally, that the temperature is above melting-point if the snow is easily compactible. (We might know these things about Harry simply on the basis of what he has told us; in other words, we use his linguistic output as a source of knowledge about him. Note that this involves an intentional interpretation of what he says.) There are sets of conditions, then, in which we are able to infer that Harry will desist from skating, especially if we observe him testing the consistency of the snow and noting how easy it is to form a snowball. It would be indescribably difficult to discover physical information about Harry that would enable us to predict with comparable certainty that he would 'drop the idea of going skating' – i.e. to discover determinants expressible in physical terms to the effect that his body will predictably turn 180 degrees and gravitate away from the skating rink. The latter could scarcely be achieved without a comprehensive dissection of Harry that exposed the current state of his brain and central nervous system. He would hardly be able to survive such an invasive intervention, which would certainly put an end to his skating. In brief, the information articulated in intentional sentences, acquired simply by talking to a human agent, cannot be replaced by detailed information about his physical state.

Modalities likewise, also the target of the nominalist's criticism, are difficult to dispense with in a description of reality that goes beyond its most superficial features. In particular it might be asked whether the nominalist is not contradicting himself in his critique of modalities. For does he not want to persuade us to remove modal expressions from our language by arguing that modalities are in some sense incoherent and so cannot possibly be a part of reality? In other words, does he not avail himself of a modal expression, namely impossibility, in his argumentation, or at least implicitly presuppose it? The nominalist is not just someone who reports that up to now in his progress through the world he has not come across modalities: he seeks to have us acknowledge that modalities will never be found. And he does it by means of arguments that show that modalities cannot exist: that they are impossible.

Fortunately, it is not our task here to arrive at answers to these fundamental and immensely complex metaphysical questions. Our aim has been limited to showing their connections with the philosophical enquiry into language. We have sought to show that the particular problems we have encountered in our attempt to formulate a theory of meaning for natural languages are interwoven with, and further fuel, classic and fundamental problems in metaphysical thinking. The difficulty of giving a definition of meaning in purely extensional terms is interconnected with the problems surrounding the concepts of modality and the problems attaching to the description of people as minded, intentional beings. These problems form a tight-knit cluster and in any attempt to solve them the philosopher finds himself juggling with the entire panoply of concepts.

References and suggestions for further reading

The following list comprises our chief sources for the presentation in each chapter. In addition, we cite works in which the reader may further explore the topics in question. References are to the Bibliography, where full data are provided.

Introduction
Crystal (1987) offers a good introduction to the various aspects and levels of linguistic description, while Morris (1938) contains a classical account of the divisions in the theory of language. Among introductory texts in the philosophy of language, Martin (1987), Devitt & Sterelny (1987) and Lycan (2000) deserve mention. Blackburn (1984) is an excellent but somewhat more demanding treatise in philosophy of language, while Miller (1998) and Taylor (1998) presupposes some familiarity with logic. Martinich (1985) is a very useful antology of classical articles in Anglo-American philosophy of language, as is Harnish (1994).

Chapter 1
Locke's philosophy of language is laid out in Locke (1690 (1961)), while Berkeley's critique is found in Berkeley (1710). Frege's arguments against the referential theory of meaning were presented in Frege (1892 (1952)). The most systematic presentation of Plato's theory of ideas is found in the dialogue *The Republic*, while Plato himself exposes its inherent weaknesses in the dialogue *Parmenides*. Both are found in the complete dialogues of Plato, Plato (1997). Meinong's theory of linguistic reference is found in Meinong (1914 (1960)). Martin (1987) provides good accounts of the classical theories of meaning and the equally classical objections to them.

Chapter 2
The title of this chapter is inspired by Hegel's *Phenomenology of Spirit*. While Hegel seeks to trace the development of consciousness in its historical guises, stretching from its origins in immediate sensory consciousness to its con-

summation in Absolute Spirit, we employ a historical myth to suggest a parallel story about the development of language from inchoate communicative actions to full-dress compositional and conventional languages. Among the sources for this chapter is Dennett (1987), chapter 7, which discusses the signaling systems of certain monkeys; the distinction between language as an activity (speech) and as a system originates in Ferdinand de Saussure (Saussure 1916 (1959)); the concept of language games was introduced by Wittgenstein (1953 and 1958); the theories of communicative intentions and speech acts derive from Grice (1957), Austin (1962), and Searle (1970); the analysis of convention is owed to Lewis (1969 and 1975); and finally, the reflections on the functions of the various parts of language in section are based upon Strawson (1959). The fundamental idea that truth constitutes the key concept in a theory of meaning is due to Frege (1892) and has been thoroughly examined by Dummett (Dummett 1976 and 1990).

Hypotheses about the actual origins of language, representing concerns rather different from ours, are put forth in Bickerton (1990) and Deacon (1997). For a very radical and ambitious attempt to derive the basic semantic categories from a use-based (pragmatic) account of language, see Brandom (1994)

Chapter 3
The label theory is presented in Mill (1843), while Russell's famous exposé of its weaknesses is found in Russell (1905) and in Russell (1918). Frege first introduced the distinction between sense and reference in Frege (1892 (1952)), while the cluster theory was suggested in Wittgenstein (1953) and more explicitly proposed in Searle (1958) and in Strawson (1959). The causal theory of reference was introduced, in slightly different versions, in Kripke (1971) and in Putnam (1975). Dummett's criticism of Kripke is found in Dummett (1973b) and in Dummett (1981). Evans develops his compromise position in Evans (1982).

A good account of Russell's philosophy of language is found in Sainsbury (1979), while an introduction to Frege's semantical ideas is given in Kenny (1995). However, the most penetrating and thorough studies of Frege's philosophy of language are found in the writings of Dummett (Dummett 1973b and 1981). The causal theory of reference is treated in Salmon (1982). Finally, McCulloch (1989) deserves a mention as a fine general introduction to the semantics of names.

Chapter 4
Strawson (1959) and Strawson (1974) offer illuminating accounts of predication. The analysis of predication as a logical function was introduced by Frege in Frege (1891 (1962)). The analyticity objection to extensional definitions of predicates was raised by Popper (1963), chapter 11. Putnam discusses the semantics of "natural kind" terms in Putnam (1975). Jubien (1997) contains a critical discussion of nominalism, while mass terms and their relationship to a language of subject-predicate form is discussed in Strawson (1959).

Chapter 5
Kirkham (1992) offers an excellent overview of the various theories of truth. In a famous debate, Strawson attacked the correspondence theory of truth while Austin defended it (Strawson 1950; Austin 1950). Trope theory is expounded in Campbell (1990). An influential defence of the coherency theory of truth was given by Bradley (Bradley 1914). Peirce's theory of truth is developed in a number of articles collected in Peirce (1879), vol. 2, while Habermas's version of the consensus is presented in Habermas (1974) which has not yet been translated into English. James's pragmatism was put forth in James (1907 (1975)) and James (1909 (1975)). Tarski's theory of truth is found in Tarski (1943–44), a somewhat more accessible version is offered in Tarski (1956). Horwich (1990) offers a version of the redundancy theory of truth. The problems inherent in defining such fundamental concepts as that of truth are discussed in Davidson (1990) and Davidson (1996).

Chapter 6
Davidson's reflections on the proper form of a theory of meaning were first laid out in Davidson (1967b), another important source is Davidson (1970). The Davidsonian analysis of adverbial modification is given in Davidson (1967a) and that of indirect speech in Davidson (1968–69). In the foreword to Davidson and Harman (1975), Davidson points to the problem for the latter analysis discussed in this chapter. Davidson's latest formulation of the relationship between truth and meaning is found in Davidson (1990).

Competent accounts of Davidson's philosophy of language are provided in Platts (1979), in Ramberg (1989) and in Evine's introductory text (Evine 1991). Important criticisms of Davidson's programme are raised in Foster (1976) and in Dummett (1975), Dummett (1976) and Dummett (1991). A précis of the Davidson-Dummett debate is given in Kirkham (1992), chapter 8.

Larson and Segal (1995) contains further extensions of the Davidsonian programme. In Schiffer (1987) fundamental reservations are made concerning the possibility of a systematic, compositional theory of meaning in general.

Chapter 7
Frege's thoughts about substitution in extensional and non-intensional contexts are presented in Frege (1892 (1952)). The purely functional reinterpretation of Frege's concept of sense was suggested by Hintikka in "Carnap's Heritage in Logical Semantics", in Hintikka (1975). We took a brush up course in the history of the Cuba crisis from David Detzer's book *The Brink* (Detzer 1980). The intensional semantics for our toy languages is inspired by Dowty et al. (1981), by Thomasson's introduction to Montague (1974) and by Cresswell (1973). Possible world semantics has its origin in Kripke (1963) and the term 'rigid designator' was introduced in Kripke (1980). Our remarks on propositional attitudes borrow from Mark Richard's article on 'Propositional attitudes' in Hale and Wright (1997). The distinction between non-extensional and hyper-intensional contexts is from Cresswell (1985). The source for our presentation of a Stalnaker-inspired way of handling propositional attitude ascriptions is Stalnaker (1984), chapter 4. A good introduction to indexicals and demonstratives is Taylor (1998), while Recanati (1993) is a more advanced text. The distinction between character and content is developed in Kaplan (1989), while the 'dthat'-operator is introduced in Kaplan (1978). We end our presentation of intensional semantics with some reflections from Lewis (1972).

Gamut (1991), vol. 2, and Dowty et al. (1981) are good first introductions to intensional semantics. An elementary introduction to modal logic is given in Girle (2000); slightly more advanced accounts are found in the classical text by Hughes and Cresswell (1996), in Chagrov and Zakharyaschev (1997), and in Blackburn et al. (2001). A useful supplement to these titles is Fitting and Mendelsohn (1998), especially with respect to first-order modal logic. For a comprehesive study of the metaphysics of possible worlds, the reader may consult Divers (2002).

Chapter 8
Seminal contributions to speech act theory are Grice (1957) and (1969), Austin (1962) and Searle (1970). Searle (1979) is an anthology of articles recording Searle's later work on speech acts. Schiffer (1972) presents astute criticisms of the original, naïve speech act theory as well as suggestions for its improvement. Searle's classification of speech acts is found in Searle (1975), while Grice's theory of conversational implicature was put forth in Grice (1975). Lewis presented his theory of convention in Lewis (1969), and

demonstrated how speech act theory and truth-based formal semantics can be theoretically integrated in Lewis (1975).

Recanati (1987) offers a careful analysis of some fundamental issues in speech acts theory and its relation to semantics. Some of the same themes are treated in Alston (2000). See also the references in relation to "truth conditional pragmatics" for chapter 9.

Chapter 9
The main source for "truth conditional pragmatics" is Sperber and Wilson (1986). Bach and Harnish's chief contribution to the topic are found in Bach and Harnish (1979), while the main source for Kamp and Reyle's theory is Kamp and Reyle (1993). There are ideas pertinent to the topic in Kaplan (1978) and in Kaplan (1989). *Synthese*, vol. 128, nos 1–2 (2001) is a special issue dedicated to topics within truth-conditional pragmatics with contributions from Bach, Recanati and others.

The sources for Lakoff's campaign against truth-conditional semantics are Lakoff (1987), Lakoff and Johnson (1980), and Lakoff and Johnson (1999). Rosch gives an account of prototype theory in Rosch (1981), while Fillmore presents his 'bachelor' example in Fillmore (1982).

Chapter 10
Within Anglo-American philosophy of language, the most important original sources for the discussion of radical interpretation are Quine (1960), Davidson (1973) and Lewis (1974). In Continental philosophy, the main contribution to hermeneutics is Gadamer (1960 (1994)). Palmer (1969) tells the history of hermeneutics in the context of theology and law.

A discussion of the obstacles to radical interpretation of foreign cultures is found in Hollis (1967a), Hollis (1967b) and in Lukes (1982). Føllesdal (1979) compares the methodologies of hermeneutics and natural science.

Chapter 11
Quine's indeterminacy thesis was first formulated in Quine (1960) and has since been further developed in Quine (1969) and Quine (1970). Other relevant texts are Quine (1951), a celebrated article containing the first presentation of Quine's semancical holism, Quine (1992) and Quine (1995). The literature on Quine is vast, but we limit our references to a couple of introductory texts, Hookway (1988), Romanos (1983) and Orenstein (2002). Kirk (1986) is dedicated to the issue of determinacy of meaning.

Dummett's reflections on realism and anti-realism are distributed across his entire philosophical oeuvre, but the most important presentation is arguably in Dummett (1973a), reprinted in Dummett (1978); the latter also contains Dummett's previous articles on the subject. Later developments are found in Dummett (1977), Dummett (1991) and Dummett (1993). The literature on Dummett is extensive and in part quite technical. Here, we shall only mention two texts, Weiss (2002) and Green (2001).

Chapter 12
Popper's theory of the Three Worlds is found in Popper (1972). Jubien (1997) gives an introductory account of modalities, possible worlds, Platonism and nominalism, while Loux (1998) contains an elementary discussion of the pros and cons of possible worlds. Divers (2002) gives a more advanced account of the same topic. A good selection of papers on the ontology of possible worlds can be found in Loux (1979). Dennett (1987) discusses the epistemological role and metaphysical status of intentional states. For Lewis on counterparts, see Lewis (1968) and Lewis (1971).

Bibliography

Alston, W. (2000): *Illocutionary Acts and Sentence Meaning*, Cornell U.P., Ithaca.
Austin, J.L. (1950): 'Truth', *Proceedings of the Aristotelian Society*, Suppl. vol. 24.
— (1961): 'The Meaning of a Word'. In J.L. Austin, *Philosophical Papers*, Oxford U.P., Oxford.
— (1962): *How to do Things with Words*, Oxford U.P., Oxford.
Bach, K. & Harnish, R. (1979): *Linguistic Communication and Speech Acts*, MIT Press, Cambridge, Mass.
Berkeley, G. (1710): *A Treatise Concerning the Principles of Human Knowledge*, Dublin.
Bickerton, D. (1990): *Language and Species*, University of Chicago Press, Chicago.
Blackburn, P., de Rijke, M. & Venema, Y. (2001): *Modal Logic*, Cambridge U.P., Cambridge.
Blackburn, S. (1984): *Spreading the Word*, Clarendon Press, Oxford.
— (1987): 'Morals and Modals', in C. Wright & G. Macdonald (eds): *Fact, Science and Value, Essays in Honour of A. J. Ayer's Language, Truth and Logic*, Basil Blackwell, Oxford.
Bradley, F.H. (1914): *Essays on Truth and Reality*, Oxford U.P., Oxford.
Brandom, R. (1994): *Making It Explicit*, Harvard U.P., Cambridge, Mass.
Campbell, K. (1990): *Abstract Particulars*, Blackwell, Oxford.
Carnap, R. (1947 (1956)): *Meaning and Necessity*, 2nd edn, University of Chicago Press, Chicago.
Chagrov, A. & Zakharyaschev, M. (1997): *Modal logic*, Clarendon Press, Oxford.
Cresswell, M.J. (1973): *Logics and Languages*, Methuen, London.
— (1985): *Structured Meanings: The Semantics of Propositional Attitudes*, MIT Press, Cambridge, Mass.
Crystal, D. (1987): *The Cambridge Encyclopedia of Language*, Cambridge U.P., Cambridge.
Davidson, D. (1967a): 'The Logical Form of Action Sentences', in N. Rescher (ed.): *The Logic of Decision and Action*, University of Pittsburgh Press, Pittsburgh, reprinted in Davidson (1980).
— (1967b): 'Truth and Meaning', *Synthese*, vol. 17, reprinted in Davidson (1984).
— (1968–69): 'On Saying That', *Synthese*, vol. 19.
— (1970): 'Semantics for Natural Language', in *Linguaggi nelle Società e nella Technica*, Milano, reprinted in Davidson (1984).
— (1973): 'Radical Interpretation', *Dialectica*, vol. 27, reprinted in Davidson (1984).
— (1980): *Essays on Actions and Events*, Oxford U.P., Oxford.

— (1984): *Inquiries into Truth and Interpretation*, Oxford U.P., Oxford.
— (1990): 'The Structure and Content of Truth', *Journal of Philosophy*, vol. 87.
— (1996): 'The Folly of Trying to Define Truth', *Journal of Philosophy*, vol. 93.
Davidson, D. & Harman, G. (eds) (1972): *Semantics for Natural Language*, D. Reidel Publishing Company, Dordrecht.
— (1975): *The Logic of Grammar*, Dickinson Publishing Comp., Encino, CA.
Deacon, T. W. (1997): *The Symbolic Species*, W.W. Norton, New York.
Dennett, D.C. (1987): *The Intentional Stance*. Cambridge, Mass, MIT Press.
Detzer, D. (1980): *The Brink. The Cuban Missile Crisis, 1962*, Dent, London.
Devitt, M. & Sterelny, K. (1987): *Language and Reality*, Basil Blackwell, Oxford.
Divers, J. (2002): *Possible Worlds*, Routledge, London/New York.
Dowty, D.R., Wall, R.E. and Peters, S. (1981): *Introduction to Montague Semantics*, D. Reidel Publishing Company, Dordrecht.
Dummett, M. (1973a): 'The Philosophical Basis of Intuitionistic Logic', in H.E. Rose & J.C. Shepherdson (eds): *Logic Colloquium '73*, Amsterdam, reprinted in Dummett (1978).
— (1973b): *Frege: Philosophy of Language*, Duckworth, London.
— (1975): 'What is a Theory of Meaning?', in S. Guttenplan (ed.), *Mind and Language*, Oxford U.P., Oxford.
— (1976): 'What is a Theory of Meaning (II)?', in G. Evans & J. McDowell (eds), *Truth and Meaning*, Clarendon Press, Oxford.
— (1977): *Elements of Intuitionism*, Oxford U.P., Oxford.
— (1978): *Truth and Other Enigmas*, Duckworth, London.
— (1981): *The Interpretation of Frege's Philosophy*, Duckworth, London.
— (1990): 'The Source of the Concept of Truth', in Boolos, G., *Meaning and Method: Essays in the Honor of Hilary Putnam*, Cambridge.
— (1991): *The Logical Basis of Metaphysics*, Duckworth, London.
— (1993): *The Seas of Language*, Oxford U.P., Oxford.
Evans, G. (1982): *The Varieties of Reference*, Oxford U.P., Oxford.
Evine, S. (1991): *Donald Davidson*, Polity Press, Oxford.
Fillmore, C. (1982): 'Towards a Descriptive Framework for Spatial Deixsis', in R.J. Jarvella & W Klein (eds), *Speech, Place, and Action*, John Wiley, London.
Fitting, M. and Mendelsohn, R. L. (1998): *First-Order Modal Logic*, Kluwer Academic Publishers, Dordrecht.
Foster, J. (1976): 'Meaning and Truth Theory', in G. Evans & J. McDowell (eds), *Truth and Meaning*, Oxford U.P., Oxford.
Frege, G. (1891 (1962)): 'Funktion und Begriff', in G. Patzig (ed.), *Funktion, Begriff, Bedeutung*, Vandenhoeck & Ruprecht, Göttingen.
— (1892): 'Über Sinn und Bedeutung', *Zeitschrift für Philosophie und philosophische Kritik*, N.F. 100, reprinted in G. Patzig (ed.): *Funktion, Begriff, Bedeutung*, Göttingen 1962.
— (1892 (1952)): 'Sense and Meaning', in Geach, P. & Black, M., *Translations from the Philosophical Writings of Gottlob Frege*, Basil Blackwell, Oxford.

Føllesdal, D. (1979): 'Hermeneutics and the Hypothetico-deductive Method', *Dialectica*, 33.
Gadamer, H.-G. (1960 (1994)): *Truth and Method*, 2nd edn., Continuum, New York.
Gamut, L. T. F. (1991): *Logic, Language, and Meaning vol. 1 and 2*, University of Chicago Press, Chicago/London.
Girle, R. (2000): *Modal Logics and Philosophy*, Teddington, Acumen.
Green, K. (2001): *Dummett. Philosophy of Language*, Polity, Cambridge.
Grice, H.P. (1957): 'Meaning', *Philosophical Review*, vol. 66.
— (1969): 'Utterer's Meaning and Intentions', *Philosophical Review*, vol. 78.
— (1975): 'Logic and Conversation', in Davidson, D. & Harman, G. (eds.),*The Logic of Grammar*, Dickinson Publishing Comp., Encino, CA.
Habermas, J. (1974): 'Wahrheitstheorien', in Fahrenbach, H. (ed.), *Wirklichkeit und Reflexion: Walter Schultz zum 60. Geburtstag*, Neske, Pfullingen.
Hale, B. & Wright, C. (1997): *A Companion to the Philosophy of Language*, Blackwell, Oxford.
Harnish, R.M. (1994, ed.): *Basic Topics in the Philosophy of Language*, Harvester Wheatsheaf, New York.
Hintikka, J. (1975): *The Intentions of Intentionality and Other New Models for Modalities*, D. Reidel Publishing Company, Dordrecht.
Hollis, M. (1967a): 'The Limits of Irrationality', in *Archives Européennes de Sociologie*, vol. 7, 1967, reprinted in M. Hollis & S. Lukes (eds): *Rationality and Relativism*, Basil Blackwell, Oxford 1982.
— (1967b): 'Reason and Ritual', *Philosophy* vol. 43, 1967, reprinted in M. Hollis & S. Lukes (eds): *Rationality and Relativism*, Basil Blackwell, Oxford 1982.
Hookway, C. (1988): *Quine*, Polity Press, Cambridge.
Horwich, P. (1990): *Truth*, Blackwell, Oxford.
Hughes, G. E. and Cresswell, M. J. (1996): *A New Introduction to Modal Logic*, Routledge, London.
James, W. (1907 (1975)): *Pragmatism*, Harvard U.P., Cambridge, Mass.
— (1909 (1975)): *The Meaning of Truth*, Harvard U.P., Cambridge, Mass.
Jubien, M. (1997): *Contemporary Metaphysics*, Blackwell, Oxford.
Kamp, H. & Reyle, U. (1993): *From Discourse to Logic*, Dordrecht, Kluwer Academic Publishers, 1993.
Kaplan, D. (1978): 'Dthat', in Cole, P. (ed.), *Pragmatics, Syntax and Semantics*, vol. 9, New York, Academic Press, New York.
Kaplan, D. (1989): 'Demonstratives' , in Almog, J., Perry, J. & Weinstein, H. (eds), *Themes from Kaplan*, Oxford U.P., Oxford.
Kenny, A. (1995): *Frege*, Penguin, Harmondsworth.
Kirk, R. (1986): *Translation Determined*, Oxford U.P., Oxford.
Kirkham, R.L. (1992): *Theories of Truth*, MIT Press, Cambridge, Mass.
Kripke, S.A. (1963): 'Semantical Considerations on Modal Logic' from *Acta Philosophica Fennica*, vol. 16, reprinted in Linsky. L. (ed.) (1971).

— (1971): 'Identity and Necessity', in Munitz, M.K. (ed.): *Identity and Individuation*, New York U.P., New York.
— (1980): *Naming and Necessity*, Basil Blackwell, Oxford.
Lakoff, G. (1987): *Women, Fire and Dangerous Things*, University of Chicago Press, Chicago.
Lakoff, G. & Johnson, M. (1980): *Metaphors We Live By*, University of Chicago Press, Chicago.
— (1999): *Philosophy in the Flesh*, Basic Books, New York.
Larson, R. & Segal, G. (1995): *Knowledge of Meaning*, MIT Press, Cambridge, Mass.
Lewis, D. (1968): 'Counterpart Theory and Quantified Modal Logic', *Journal of Philosophy* vol. 63.
— (1969): *Convention*, Harvard U.P., Cambridge, Mass.
— (1972): 'General Semantics,' in Davidson & Harman (1972).
— (1971): 'Counterparts of Persons and their Bodies', *Journal of Philosophy* vol. 68.
— (1973): *Counterfactuals*, Basil Blackwell., Oxford.
— (1974): 'Radical Interpretation', *Synthese*, vol. 23.
— (1975): 'Languages and Language', in K. Gunderson (ed.), *Language, Mind and Knowledge, Minnesota Studies in the Philosophy of Science*, vol. 7, University of Minnesota Press, Minneapolis.
Linsky, L. (ed.) (1971): *Reference and Modality*, Oxford U.P., Oxford.
Locke, J. (1690 (1961)): *An Essay Concerning Human Understanding*, Dent, London.
Loux, M.J. (1979): *The Possible and the Actual, Readings in the Metaphysics of Modality*. Ithaca/London, Cornell University Press.
Loux, M.J. (1998): *Metaphysics: A Contemporary Introduction*, London, Routledge.
Lukes, S. (1982): 'Relativism in its Place' in Hollis, M. & Lukes, S. (eds), *Rationality and Relativism*, Basil Blackwell, Oxford.
Lycan, W.G. (2000): *Philosophy of Language, A Contemporary Introduction*, Routledge, London/New York.
Martin, R.M. (1987):*The Meaning of Language*, MIT Press, Cambridge, Mass.
Martinich, A.P. (1985, ed.): *The Philosophy of Language*, Oxford U.P., Oxford.
McCulloch, G. (1989): *The Game of the Name*, Oxford U.P., Oxford.
Meinong, A. (1914 (1960)): 'The Theory of Objects', in Chisholm, R.M., *Realism and the Background of Phenomenology*, Glencoe, Ill.
Mill, J.S. (1843): *A System of Logic*, Longmans, Green, London.
Miller, A. (1998): *Philosophy of Language*, University College London, London.
Montague, R. (1974): *Formal Philosophy*, Yale University Press, New Haven, CT.
Morris, C. (1938): *Foundations of the Theory of Signs*, University of Chicago Press, Chicago.
Orenstein, A. (2002): *W.V. Quine*, Acumen, Chesham.
Palmer, R. (1969): *Hermeneutics*, Northwestern U.P., Evanston.
Peirce, C.S. (1931–58 (1879)): *Collected Papers*, vol. 2, Harvard U.P., Cambridge, Mass.
Plato (1997): *Complete Works*, J.M. Cooper (ed.), Hackett, Indianapolis, IN.
Platts, M. (1979):*Ways of Meaning*, London.

Popper, K.R., (1963): *Conjectures and Refutations*, Routledge & Kegan Paul, London.
— (1972): 'On the Theory of the Objective Mind', in *Objective Knowledge. An Evolutionary Approach*, Oxford U.P., Oxford.
Putnam, H. (1975): 'The Meaning of 'Meaning'', in K. Gunderson (ed.), *Language, Mind and Knowledge, Minnesota Studies in the Philosophy of Science*, vol. 7, University of Minnesota Press, Minneapolis.
Quine, W.V.O. (1951): 'Two Dogmas of Empiricism', *Philosophical Review*, vol. 60, reprinted in Quine, *From a Logical Point of View* (2nd ed.), Harvard U.P., Cambridge, Mass. 1961.
— (1960): *Word and Object*, MIT Press, Cambridge, Mass.
— (1969): 'Ontological Relativity', in *Ontological Relativity and Other Essays*, Columbia U.P., New York.
— (1970): 'On the Reasons for Indeterminacy of Translation', *Journal of Philosophy*, vol. 67.
— (1992): *Pursuit of Truth* (2nd ed.), Harvard U.P., Cambridge, Mass.
— (1995): *From Stimulus to Science*, Harvard U.P., Cambridge, Mass.
Ramberg, B. (1989): *Donald Davidson's Philosophy of Language*, Basil Blackwell, Oxford.
Recanati, F. (1987): *Meaning and Force. The Pragmatics of Performative Utterances*, Cambridge U.P., Cambridge.
— (1993): *Direct Reference*, Blackwell, Oxford.
Richard, M. (1997): 'Propositional Attitudes', in Hale and Wright (1997).
Romanos, G.D. (1983): *Quine and Analytical Philosophy*, MIT Press, Cambridge, Mass.
Rosch, E. (1981) 'Prototype Classification and Logical Classification: The Two Systems'. In E. Scholnik (ed.), *New Trends in Cognitive Representation*, Lawrence Erlbaum Associates, Hillsdale, N.J. 1983.
Russell, B. (1905): 'On Denoting', *Mind*, bd. 14, reprinted in R. Marsh (ed.) *Logic and Knowledge*, Allen & Unwin, London 1956.
— (1918): 'The Philosophy of Logical Atomism', *The Monist*, vol. 28, reprinted in R. Marsh (ed.): *Logic and Knowledge*, Allen & Unwin, London 1956.
Sainsbury, M. (1979): *Russell*, Routledge & Kegan Paul, London.
Salmon, W. (1982): *Reference and Essence*, Basil Blackwell, Oxford/Princeton.
Saussure, F. de (1916 (1959)): *Course in General Linguistics*, McGraw-Hill, New York.
Schiffer, S.R. (1972): *Meaning*, Oxford U.P., Oxford.
— (1987): *Remnants of Meaning*, MIT Press, Cambridge, Mass.
Searle, J.R. (1958): 'Proper Names', *Mind*, vol. 67.
— (1970): *Speech Acts*, Cambridge U.P., Cambridge.
— (1974–75): 'The Logical Status of Fictional Discourse', *New Literary History*, vol. 6, reprinted in Searle (1979).
— (1975): 'A Taxonomy of Illocutionary Acts', in Gunderson, K. (ed.), *Language, Mind and Knowledge, Minnesota Studies in the Philosophy of Science*, vol. 7, University of Minnesota Press, Minneapolis, reprinted in Searle (1979).
— (1979): Expression and Meaning, Cambridge U.P., Cambridge.

Sperber, D. & Wilson, D. (1986): *Relevance. Communication and Cognition*, Basil Blackwell, Oxford.
Stalnaker, R. (1984): *Inquiry*, MIT Press, Cambridge, Mass.
Strawson, P.F. (1950): 'Truth' *Proceedings of the Aristotelian Society*, Suppl. vol. 24.
— (1952): *Introduction to Logical Theory*, Methuen, London.
— (1959): *Individuals*, Methuen, London.
— (1974): *Subject and Predicate in Logic and Grammar*, Methuen, London.
Synthese (2001), vol. 128, nos 1–2.
Tarski, A. (1943–44): 'The Semantic Conception of Truth', *Philosophy and Phenomenological Research*, vol. 4, reprinted in Feigl, H. & Sellars, W. *Readings in Philosophical Analysis*, Appleton-Century-Crofts, New York 1949.
— (1956): 'The Concept of Truth in Formalized Languages', in *Logic, Semantics, Metamathematics*, Oxford U.P., Oxford.
Taylor, K. (1998): *Truth and Meaning, An Introduction to the Philosophy of Language*, Blackwell, Oxford.
Weiss, B. (2002): *Michael Dummett*, Acumen, Chesham.
Wittgenstein, L. (1953): *Philosophical Investigations*, Basil Blackwell, Oxford.
— (1958): *The Blue and Brown Books*, Basil Blackwell, Oxford.
— (1966): *Lectures and Conversations on Aesthetics, Psychology and Religious Belief*, ed. C. Barret, Blackwell, Oxford.

Index

abstractive theory of meaning   39, 81
accessibility relation   154–55, 157–58, 161
adjective   9, 11, 15, 18, 38, 65, 67, 83, 130
adverbial constructions   129–30, 139
analytic sentences   54–55, 69, 164
anti-realist semantics   263–66, 268
Aristocles   57
Aristotle   3, 55, 68, 172, 219, 225
assertibility conditions   264–65
assertion   23, 30–35, 41–42, 44, 96, 175–79, 182–83, 185–92, 194–97, 202–3, 209
   speech act analysis of –   189–91
assertives   176–77, 194
Ast, F.   234
Atlantis   44, 47, 54
Austin, J.L.   21, 177–78, 188–89, 205, 225

Bach, K.   207
basic level categories   219–23
basic meaning   213, 217
Bedeutung   49, 51, 53, 74, 141
behaviourism   244
Berkeley, G.   10, 11

Carnap, R.   154, 166–67
causal theory of proper names and reference   62–63, 80, 96, 114
character (in Kaplan)   169–71
Chomsky, N.   176, 215

circularity of definitions   68, 78, 90, 100, 116, 118, 121, 146, 185, 208, 223, 258, 271
circumstances of evaluation   169–71
classical logic   265–66
classification   38, 73, 76–77, 219, 222, 225
classifiers in Japanese   249
cluster theory of names   54–55, 57
code   206, 208, 231
co-extensional   74–75, 77, 121, 131, 134, 140, 143–45, 156–57, 162, 164, 272
cognitive science   207, 210, 214
coherence theory of truth   90, 98–101
   critique of –   99–100
command   23, 29–31, 33, 35, 42, 181, 193–94
   speech act analysis of –   193
common nouns   9, 38, 65, 67, 83–86
communication   182–83, 189–93, 196–203, 210–14
compositional theory of semantics   39, 161–62
compositionality principle   139–45
conceptualism   76–77, 223–24, 275–76
connectives   36, 71, 97, 110–11, 141, 150–51, 153, 158
consensus theory of truth   90, 101–3
constructivist concept of truth   223
content (in Kaplan)   169
context   42ff, 73, 169–72, 196–99, 206–17
convention   27–29, 199, 201–3
Convention T   123

conventionalization 28–30, 182, 198–200
conversational implicature 196–98, 206–7, 212
copula 66
correspondence theory of truth 90–93, 95, 97–98, 100, 113, 116, 223
  critique of – 92
Creswell, M.J. 164
Cuba crisis 97, 149ff

Davidson, D. 117–32, 133–37, 139–40, 145–46, 175–76, 203, 206, 208–9, 214–17, 227, 247, 257–59, 270–71
Davidsonian programme 117ff, 139, 175–76
declarations 194
declarative sentences 32, 41
decoding 206–7, 212–13, 216
definite descriptions 37, 38, 41, 44–45, 47, 49, 51, 57–58, 68, 70, 157, 159
demonstratives 37, 41, 168, 171–72, 217
Dewey, J. 103
directives 194–95
Discourse Representation Theory 214f
dthat-operator 171–72
Dummett, M. 5, 63, 243, 255–68
Dummett's challenge to realism 260ff
Dummett's theory of meaning 263ff
  critique of – 266f

empiricism 8, 273
empty names 14, 47, 68, 172, 190, 204
equivalence thesis 90–91
essential condition 190–91, 193
expressives 194–95
extension 16–18, 67–69, 73–75, 77–78, 93, 96, 107, 131, 139–140, 142–43, 146–48, 152–53, 158–160, 163, 171–72, 270–72, 274–75
extensional context 140, 143, 145

extensional definition 69, 106–8, 124, 126
  critique of – 266f
extensional semantics 75, 139, 141–46, 148, 152, 161, 172

facts 92, 95
Fauconnier, G. 220
fiction 2, 99, 227
Fillmore, C. 220
force 30–31, 33–35, 178–79, 188, 258
Frege, G. 15, 49–55, 57–58, 60–61, 72, 74, 139, 141–46, 148, 168, 172, 217, 256, 259
function, logical 71–74
function of language 22, 23, 29, 36
functional analysis of language 73–78, 81, 86, 96

Gadamer, H.-G. 240–41
Galileo Galilei 131–37
generativity 2, 5, 36, 119, 137, 176, 206
Goldbach's conjecture 260–65
Grice, H.P. 177, 183–85, 196–97, 205–7, 212

Habermas, J. 102–3
Harnish, R. 207
Heim, I. 214, 216
hermeneutical circle 234, 236–39
hermeneutics 227f, 232, 234, 236–40
holism 256
hyper-intensional contexts 164, 167–68

idea theory of meaning 7
identity sentences 15, 49–51, 53, 61, 74, 141, 172

idiographic 236
illocutionary 178–81, 184–85, 188, 195, 197, 205, 217
implicit convention 201
  knowledge 242, 257–64, 268
  messages 212
indeterminacy
  of meaning 249–50, 252–55
  of reference 245, 250
  of translation 252, 254–55
indexicals 41, 48, 61, 124, 168–71, 217, 277
indirect contexts 129–30, 132–34, 136–37, 139, 164, 270
indirect reference 53, 57, 140, 145
indirect speech acts 197–98, 213
inference to best explanation 237, 267–68
intension 17, 147–48, 157, 159–60, 163, 166–67, 169–71, 274
intensional semantics 139–74
intention and communication 24–30, 121, 125–27, 180, 183–93, 200
intentional states 161, 244, 282–83
interpretation 2, 118, 126, 158, 173, 208, 210, 214–16, 227ff, 245ff
irrationality 233–34, 236

James, W. 103–5
Johnson, M. 218, 220–26

Kamp, H. 214–16
Kant, I. 273
Kaplan, D. 168–69, 172, 217
King of France 44–46
Kripke, S. 58, 79, 154, 157
Kuhn, T. 240–41

label theory of names 43–44, 48–50, 53, 58, 60–61

  Frege's critique of – 49–50, 53
  Russell's critique of – 47–48
Lakoff, G. 218, 220–26
Langacker, R.W. 220
language game 21, 23, 29, 33–35
Leibniz, G.W. 153
Lewis, D. 166–68, 172–73, 201, 203, 227, 277–79
linguistic community 30, 55–58, 61, 63, 96, 126, 203
linguistic division of labour 56, 61, 114
linguistics 2–4, 177, 217, 218
Locke, J. 7–13, 16, 19, 22, 38, 76–77, 218, 225, 275
locutionary 178, 180, 184, 189, 205
logical form 94, 115, 120, 129, 141, 161–62, 213–15
logically proper name 48

mass terms 83–86, 94–95, 228–29, 248–49
materialism 281
Meinong, A. von 17–18, 47
mentalism 275, 281–82
metalanguage 112–13, 120–22, 124, 126
metaphor 220–25
Millikan, R.A. 235, 239
modal
  contexts 142, 144, 156–57, 161, 163
  logic 173–74
  operators 150–51, 155, 158, 160–61, 273
  statements 97–98, 272, 275, 278–79, 283
modalities 272–74, 276, 283
mode of presentation 51–53, 58, 148, 168
money 40, 198
Morris, C. 4

name 2–3, 8–9, 11, 14–15, 17–18, 35–38, 41–44, 46–63, 68–70, 80–83, 110–12, 139–42, 150–52, 157–60, 219–20
natural kinds 79–83, 172
natural language 2, 4, 23, 36–37, 55, 109, 113, 115, 117–19, 124, 128–31, 137, 139–46, 204, 214–16, 263, 269, 272, 279
necessity 154–55, 160, 273–74
negation 70, 97, 160, 265–66
negative existence sentences 44, 47
negative sentences 96–97
nominalism 77–78, 281–83
nomothetic 236–37
non-extensional contexts 124, 129, 134, 136–37, 139, 141, 143–46, 157, 161, 163–64, 271–72, 275–76, 279, 281–82

object language 109, 113, 119–22, 126, 140, 245–46, 251
objectivity 19, 224–26, 240, 280
objectivity of interpretation 240
open sentence 111–12, 213
order 195

paradox 108–9, 114
parole 204
Peirce, C.S. 101–3
performatives 179–81, 184–85
perlocutionary 180–81, 185, 188, 195, 205, 229
physicalism 243, 281
Plato 15, 19, 55–57, 59, 68, 74, 269, 275, 280
Popper, K.R. 240, 280–281
Popper's Three Worlds 280–81
possibility 154–55, 160, 273–74, 278
possible worlds 148, 154, 157–66, 168–70, 172–75, 276–79

pragmatic theory of meaning 213, 216
pragmatic theory of truth 90–91, 103–6
  critique of – 104–5
pragmatics 4, 195, 198, 205–10, 212–13, 216–17, 222
predicate logic 109, 124, 128–30, 214–15
predicates 15–17, 35, 38–39, 41, 59–60, 65–78, 81–83, 85–87, 92–96, 108, 110–15, 123, 127, 129, 135, 139–41, 143–44, 146, 148, 151–53, 156–60, 162–63, 172, 175, 178, 218, 225, 228, 269–70, 287
predication 76, 78, 86–87, 95, 116
predicative form 66
preparatory condition 190, 192–93, 197
principle of bivalence 259, 264–65
principle of charity 126, 133–34, 136, 232–33, 235–36, 239–40
principle of extensionality 130
projectionism 224, 273
promise 30, 33–35, 179–80, 191–93, 195, 197
  speech act analysis of – 191–93
proof 164, 261–67, 296
proof conditions 260, 264
proper name 8–9, 11, 14, 17–18, 41, 47–49, 51–52, 54, 57–58, 60, 62–63, 68, 70, 80–81, 83
property 19, 66, 69–70, 79–80, 82–86, 90, 93–94
propositional attitude 143–45, 161–68, 279
prototype effect 219–20
publicity principle 12–13, 250, 253, 259, 263–64
Putnam, H. 55–56, 61, 79, 172

quantifier 110–12, 123, 140–41, 160
question 23, 32–33, 189, 194

Index

Quine, W.V.O. 82, 146, 227, 229, 243–47, 249–56

radical interpretation 126, 227–35, 239, 241, 245
rationality principle 233–236, 239, 241
realism
 embodied 226
 semantic 259–60
recursive 107, 109, 114–15, 123–24, 158–59, 176, 206, 213–15, 246, 257, 272
reference 2, 16–18, 37, 42–45, 48–54, 57, 60–64, 73, 80–82, 86, 95, 108–16, 123–27, 130–31, 139–51, 157–58, 169, 172, 207–10, 245–50, 280
referential theory of meaning 14–18, 35, 38, 74, 269
relativism 105
Reyle, U. 214–16
rigid designator 157, 159, 167, 172
Rosch, E. 219–20
Russell, B. 53–54, 57–58, 60–61, 68

satisfaction 108–15, 123–24, 127–35
Saussure, F. de 203–4
Schiffer, S. 184
Schleiermacher, F. 234
Searle, J. 54, 177, 185, 189–91, 194–95, 205
semantic representation 213–16
semantic theory of truth 106ff, 116
semantic value 139–40, 148, 157, 159, 168
semantics vs. pragmatics 4, 195,198, 204–7, 210–212, 216–17, 222
sincerity condition 190–94
singular terms 9, 38–39, 41–45, 47–49, 51–55, 57, 59, 61–67, 70, 72–73, 76, 81–83, 86, 92–93, 95–96, 113–14, 116, 140–41, 143, 175, 218, 228
Sinn 49–53, 58, 74, 141
speaker meaning 185–86, 212, 217
speech 1, 7–8, 21–27, 30–39, 42, 65, 126–28, 175–84, 188–94, 197–98, 202–5, 211, 213, 229, 240
speech act 24–26, 30–39, 42, 65, 95, 175–84, 188–94, 197–98, 202–5, 213, 229, 245
Sperber, D. 207–16
Stalnaker, R. 164, 166
Strawson, P.F. 37, 42, 54, 83
subject-object circle 235
subject-predicate structure 19, 38, 45, 86, 94–96, 228
subsistence 18
substitutability principle 139–45, 163–64
success condition 25, 32–35
syntactic form 141, 176, 198

T-sentence 107, 135, 206, 208, 247
Tarski, A. 106–10, 113–15, 122–24, 128–29, 136
theory of interpretation 207, 214–16, 245ff
theory of meaning 3, 5, 8, 11–15, 18, 23–24, 34–35, 39, 74, 89, 92, 117–18, 122–24, 126, 130, 133–40, 145–46, 162, 174–77, 198, 205–9, 218, 222–23, 256–59, 263, 266, 274–75
translation 229–32, 245, 248, 250–56
truth 99–116, 121–29
truth conditional meaning 172, 206, 217–19, 223–26, 279
truth conditional pragmatics 217
truth conditions 32–35, 38, 41, 65, 81, 86, 93–95, 97, 106–7, 112–17, 122–26, 134, 157, 161–62, 164–67, 172–76, 186, 196, 203–9, 213–19, 222–

29, 243, 245–47, 250–51, 255–68, 279
truth function 72, 123
truth predicate 91, 107, 121

underdetermination 253
universals 15–19, 21, 74–78, 87, 269, 281
use 21ff

verification conditions 260, 263–65

Wilson, D. 207–16
Wittgenstein, L. 23, 31, 35, 54, 205, 259, 263

Zork 24–26, 28–30, 32, 34–37, 42, 48, 182–83, 186–87, 199

www.ingramcontent.com/pod-product-compliance
Lightning Source LLC
Chambersburg PA
CBHW032001220426
43664CB00005B/103